THE JEWS OF THE SOVIET UNION

SOVIET AND EAST EUROPEAN STUDIES

SOVIET AND EAST EUROPEAN STUDIES

Rudolf Bićanić *Economic policy in Socialist Yugoslavia*

Galia Golan *Yom Kippur and After: The Soviet Union and the Middle East Crisis*

Maureen Perrie *The Agrarian Policy of the Russian Socialist-Revolutionary Party from its Origins through the Revolutions of 1905–1907*

Paul Vyšný *Neo-Slavism and the Czechs 1898–1914*

Gabriel Gorodetsky *The Precarious Truce: Anglo-Soviet Relations 1924–1927*

James Riordan *Sport in Soviet Society: Development of Sport and Physical Education in Russia and the USSR*

Gregory Walker *Soviet Book Publishing Policy*

Felicity Ann O'Dell *Socialisation through Children's Literature: The Soviet Example*

T. H. Rigby *Lenin's Government: Sovnarkom 1917–1922*

Stella Alexander *Church and State in Yugoslavia since 1945*

M. Cave *Computers and Economic Planning: The Soviet Experience*

Jozef M. Van Brabant *Socialist Economic Integration: Aspects of Contemporary Economic Problems in Eastern Europe*

R. F. Leslie, ed., *The History of Poland since 1863*

M. R. Myant *Socialism and Democracy in Czechoslovakia 1945–1948*

Blair A. Ruble *Soviet Trade Unions: Their Development in the 1970s*

Angela Stent *From Embargo to Ostpolitik: The Political Economy of West German–Soviet Relations 1955–190*

William J. Conyngham *The Modernisation of Soviet Industrial Management*

Jean Woodall *The Socialist Corporation and Technocratic Power*

Israel Getzler *Kronstadt 1917–1921: The Fate of a Soviet Democracy*

David A. Dyker *The Process of Investment in the Soviet Union*

S. A. Smith *Red Petrograd: Revolution in the Factories 1917–1918*

Saul Estrin *Self-Management: Economic Theories and Yugoslav Practice*

Ray Taras *Ideology in a Socialist State*

Silvana Malle *The Economic Organisation of War Communism 1918–1921*

S. G. Wheatcroft and R. W. Davies *Materials for a Balance of the Soviet National Economy 1928–1930*

Mark Harrison *Soviet Planning in Peace and War 1938–1945*

James McAdams *East Germany and Détente: Building Authority after the Wall*

J. Arch Getty *Origins of the Great Purges: The Soviet Communist Party Reconsidered 1933–1938*

Tadeusz Swietochowski *Russian Azerbaijan 1905–1920: The Shaping of National Identity*

David S. Mason *Public Opinion and Political Change in Poland 1980–1982*

Nigel Swain *Collective Farms Which Work?*

Stephen White *The Origins of Détente: The Genoa Conference and Soviet–Western Relations 1921–1922*

Ellen Jones and Fred W. Grupp *Modernization, Value Change and Fertility in the Soviet Union*

Catherine Andreyev *Vlasov and the Russian Liberation Movement: Soviet Reality and Emigré Theories*

Anita J. Prazmowska *Britain, Poland and the Eastern Front, 1939*

Allen Lynch *The Soviet Study of International Relations*

David Granick *Job Rights in the Soviet Union: Their Consequences*

Jozef M. Van Brabant *Adjustment, Structural Change and Economic Efficiency: Aspects of Monetary Cooperation in Eastern Europe*

Susan Bridger *Women in the Soviet Countryside: Women's Roles in Rural Development in the USSR*

Benjamin Pinkus *The Jews of the Soviet Union: The History of a National Minority*

THE JEWS OF THE
SOVIET UNION

The History of a National Minority

BENJAMIN PINKUS

*Professor of History, Ben-Gurion University of the Negev,
Beer–Sheva, Israel*

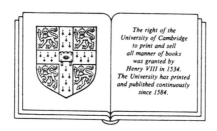

The right of the
University of Cambridge
to print and sell
all manner of books
was granted by
Henry VIII in 1534.
The University has printed
and published continuously
since 1584.

CAMBRIDGE UNIVERSITY PRESS

CAMBRIDGE

NEW YORK   NEW ROCHELLE   MELBOURNE   SYDNEY

Published by the Press Syndicate of the University of Cambridge
The Pitt Building, Trumpington Street, Cambridge CB2 1RP
32 East 57th Street, New York NY 10022, USA
10 Stamford Road, Oakleigh, Melbourne 3166, Australia

© Cambridge University Press 1988

First published 1988
Reprinted 1989

British Library cataloguing in publication data

Pinkus, Benjamin
The Jews of the Soviet Union: the history
of a national minority. – (Soviet and
East European Studies).
1. Jews in Russia – History
I. Title   II. Series
947′.004924   DS135.R92

Library of Congress cataloguing in publication data

Pinkus, Benjamin, 1933–
The Jews of the Soviet Union.
(Soviet and East European studies)
Bibliography.
Includes index.
1. Jews–Soviet Union–History–1917
2. Soviet Union–Ethnic relations. I. Title.
II. Series.
DS135.R92P55   1988   947′.004924   87-11609

ISBN 0 521 34078 0 Hardcover
ISBN 0 521 38926 7 Paperback

Transferred to digital printing 2003

CS

Contents

politanism'   145

4   THE POST-STALIN PERIOD, 1953–1983
    The Soviet creed regarding nationalities and its conse-
    quences for the Jews   210
    Anti-Semitism   216
    The Jewish share in government   235
    Jewish 'autonomy' in eclipse?   241
    The fight against Zionism and Israel   245
    Demographic and socio-economic processes   261
    Education and culture   271
    Religion   283
    National identity: the national movement and connec-
    tions abroad   299

    Notes   322
    Select bibliography   368
    Index   380

Acknowledgements

During the long period that this book has been in the making, I have been fortunate to receive help and encouragement from both individuals and institutions.

First, and above all, I should like to express my sincere thanks to my friends and colleagues Jonathan Frankel, Nissan Oren, Ezra Mendelsohn, Mordechai Altshuler and Israel Getzler of the Hebrew University. Israel Oppenheim of the Ben-Gurion University of the Negev carefully read the manuscript and made many suggestions which proved to be of great value and for which I am very much in his debt.

The Ben-Gurion Research Center of the Ben-Gurion University, under the auspices of which this project went forward, gave it throughout both moral and material support, and its successive directors during this period – Meir Avizohar and Ilan Troen – together ensured that it would be seen through to completion.

Financial help was also given by the Research Center for Russia, East Europe and their Jewish Communities of the Ben-Gurion University.

Abroad, I received help and encouragement from friends and colleagues: Karl-Heinz Ruffmann of the Erlangen University, Heinrich Vogel of the Bundesinstitut für ostwissenschaftliche und internationale Studien (Cologne) and Alain Besançon of the University of Paris – I cannot find words to thank all of them enough.

And, finally, I should like to take this opportunity to thank Mrs Jean Field of Cambridge University Press, who has been responsible for the final copy-editing and displayed quite remarkable professionalism going over this exacting text.

vii

Introduction

The study of the history of the Jews of the Soviet Union has made considerable progress in the last thirty years. The subject has been treated from new angles, using new methods of research, and central issues have been tackled that were previously almost completely ignored. Nevertheless, the results have been patchy and we still lack even the raw materials for a definitive history of the Soviet Jewry.

The aim of the present book is modest: to present the successive stages in the annals of Soviet Jews since the outbreak of the October Revolution. There will be little descriptive writing, only essential quotations, and a pre-defined set of central themes.

As early as 1891, Shimon Dubnov, the most influential historian of East European Jewry, asked, 'Is there a historiography of the Jews of Russia?' and replied without qualification, 'No such historiography exists in the true sense of the word.'[1] He may have been right, and the general and specialized works on Russian Jewry that began appearing early in the nineteenth century were of little help in the historiography of Russian Jews towards the end of the century. This writing reached its peak, in quantity and quality, between 1900 and 1917.

Interest in the history of Russian Jewry was first aroused in the 1870s by the publication of a two-volume collection of articles by a young Jewish jurist, I. Orshansky.[2] Orshansky did not have much historical material at his disposal[3] but he strove to apply methods of comparative historical research in 'placing' the legal and economic status of Russian Jews as regards that of Jews in other countries. Orshansky rejected the apologetics common to most Jewish publicistic writing in Russian at that time. He concentrated on research into the whole body of legislation on Jewish matters, basing his work on facts and striving for objectivity.[4]

A key figure in the legal school of history-writing in the 1880s was Sergei Bershadsky, a pupil of Leontovich and Gradovsky.[5] Bershadsky worked on numerous documents concerning Lithuanian Jewry in the state archives of Poland and Russia. His publications on the history of the Jews of Lithuania and Russia were the basis of the historiography of Russian Jewry at the beginning of the twentieth century. Since the legal material collected by Bershadsky mainly concerned the relations of the Jews with the outside world and the attitude of the administration towards them, the unique internal community life of the Jews was ignored.

The second historical school, which could be termed archaeological in its search for origins, is represented by the pioneer studies on the Khazar Empire by A. Harkavy and his original approach to the earlier language of the Russian Jews.[6] His 1865 study gave rise to academic disputes, but stimulated research in this difficult field.[7]

The first historian to attempt to provide a complete history of the Russian Jews was Gessen. His publications – seventy-five between 1900 and 1917[8] – on a wide range of subjects covered virtually all aspects of the life of Russian Jewry from the first settlement in the Princedom of Kiev to the 1890s.[9] His work on the publication of the *Jewish Encyclopaedia* in Russia (between 1908 and 1913) and his help in establishing the Ethnographic–Historical Society made Gessen the central link in the chain connecting early research into 'external' legal–political history with later more comprehensive social, economic and cultural research.

Gessen came under heavy fire when Dubnov reviewed his book[10] and has remained so. He is still being criticized for his one-sidedness, for his apologetics and for his ignorance of the internal community life of the Russian Jews.[11] These criticisms are only partly justified. It is not accurate to say that Gessen used only official Russian sources, since his source material included extensive literature that cannot be considered official, both in Russian and in other languages. The main deficiency in his sources lay in his failure to use archive material in Hebrew and Yiddish. While there are mistakes in Gessen's writing, it is going too far to speak of 'superficiality' and 'distortions'.

The central criticism of Gessen's one-sidedness and 'external' approach, voiced by Dubnov and others, is that his books constitute 'a chapter of Russian history concerned with the Jews', and not Jewish history. Was Gessen really no more than 'an expert on the history of the Jewish question in Russia'? A more just evaluation would be that although Gessen's writings need supplementing and updating they remain among the best basic books on the history of Russian Jews from 1772 to 1882.

We come now to Dubnov himself, the greatest Russian-Jewish and 'general-Jewish' historian since Graetz.[12] The development of Russian-Jewish historiography is unthinkable without Dubnov's work. His contribution is not confined to 'pure' research, to the publication of many articles and the creation of a school of Jewish historiography based on the history of Jewish autonomy; nor even to his new methodology in Jewish historical study. It also encompasses years of collecting and publishing extensive source-material, establishing the Ethnographical–Historical Society and founding the historical periodical, *Evreiskaya starina*. Around Dubnov were gathered the finest Jewish historians of Eastern Europe.

One aspect of Dubnov's work that requires elucidation is the contrast between the considerable attention given to the Jews of Poland and Russia in his *History of the Jewish People*, and the much briefer mention of them by Jost and Graetz, the two 'general–Jewish' historians who preceded him. Concerning Jost, writing in the 1820s, the 'lack of sources' argument is perhaps applicable; but it is less convincing in the case of Graetz, writing thirty to fifty years later. Dubnov himself dealt with this question in his article, 'Graetz: Historian of the Jewish People',[13] noting that Graetz was considered suspect in Russia, both because he allotted little space to that country's Jews and because he ignored the Jewish 'Enlightenment' in Russia. Dubnov contended that Graetz did all the research he could on Polish Jewry, but less than he might have done on Russian Jewry. Dubnov thus appears to agree with the prevailing opinion that Graetz's attitude towards Russian Jewry was prejudiced, possibly even contemptuous.[14]

How far was Dubnov's writing on Russian Jewry affected by his views on autonomy and the historic Jewish centres, his sociological method and his desire to free himself from the metaphysics and mystique of Jewish history? He sought to free himself from all the main conceptions and preconceptions of his predecessors. He rejected the view of Jewish history as the history of the Jewish religion only, to the exclusion of the secular, national element. He turned away from the formless eclecticism of *Wissenschaft des Judentums* ('Science of Judaism'), which dealt with Jewish cultural and intellectual life on the one hand and on the other dwelt on the millenary annals of Jewish martyrology, suffering and affliction. He found the legal–external approach formalistic and inadequate. He sought a historical theme that would bind the data together and explain Jewish historical developments satisfactorily, but he only partially succeeded.

Dubnov's central theme was the Jewish community, with Jewish self-rule as the dominant factor in the life of the Jews in the Diaspora. Around this he constructed his historiosophy of autonomy, which he sought to impose on historical reality. The artificiality of this system was sometimes apparent; for example, it led him virtually to sever the Russian Jews from other Jewish centres throughout the world! He gave only superficial treatment to the complex connections and reciprocal relationships of the various Diasporas, as well as to their influence on governments, and vice versa. His idealization of the community as such resulted in inadequate social analysis of the community's internal regime.

The synthesis Dubnov aimed at, which he wrote about at length,[15] calling it 'the unfolding of the general historic development latent in the mass of facts', his attempt to fuse 'external–political with internal–social and intellectual–literary manifestations', was also only partially successful. Because of his reaction against the 'external' legal–political approach – and certainly also because of the difficulty obtaining the material he needed from the Russian State Archives – Dubnov's work contributed little to an understanding of the legal-political status of the Russian Jews. More seriously, the desired fusion of 'external' and 'internal' spheres, essential to his system, was handled mechanically. He failed to achieve a blend of the complex reciprocal relationships and of the dynamic and static elements which exist both in the life of every people and in that of an extra-territorial, national minority.

Dubnov's sociological conception is not convincing, either. He apparently thought that his conception was sociological because he made 'the people' a decisive factor in the way he saw history; but this was too facile. 'It can be said', comments Rotenstreich,[16] 'that the question of sociological understanding begins where Dubnov leaves off.'

These are criticisms of central issues, and much could be said about details; but criticism cannot detract from the importance of Dubnov's work. His greatest contribution to historiography was the impetus he gave to his many pupils and followers to pursue the study of the Jews of Russia and of Eastern Europe. They then studied two spheres – the economic and the demographic – which their master had neglected. To name them – Yitshak Shiffer, Meir Balaban, Mark Wischnitzer, Dov Weinryb, and Yaakov Leshchinsky – is sufficient to attest to the scope and value of their contribution; without them, the historiography of the later period would not have been born. Other scholars studied religion, education, folklore, literature and art – S. Ginzburg, P. Marek, I. Tsinberg, L. Bramson, S. Pozner, V. Pereferkovich, and others.[17]

Only three general histories of Russian Jewry have appeared in the last sixty years: those of J. Meisl in the early 1920s, in German;[18] of L. Greenberg in the years 1944 to 1951, in English;[19] of S. Baron, part of which is devoted to the Jews of the USSR, in the 1960s, in English.[20] None of these historians has used new primary sources; they have not made any methodological breakthrough, nor was their work based on original studies. Compared with their predecessors, their importance lies in having supplemented and brought up to date a number of themes which had previously received little attention. Since the 1940s, there has been a great increase in the preparation and publication of important monographs.

Although seventy years have passed since the Russian Revolution, the historiography of Soviet Jews is still in its infancy. The explanation is mainly objective. From the 1920s to the 1940s, the necessary historical perspective was lacking. Sharp ideological confrontation and political controversy, together with the solutions which the new regime proposed and sought to implement *vis-à-vis* the Jews, deterred some students from engaging in this field and led to distortions in the work of others. In addition, the task of the historian of the Soviet Jews is hampered by the continuing difficulty of access to archives, a problem overcome by research methods worked out over the last thirty years by general historians of the USSR.

A turning point, both in methods of research and in objective reassessment of the role of the Evsektsia, came with the doctoral dissertation of Ch. Shmeruk, presented to the Hebrew University of Jerusalem in 1961.[21] In addition an interesting attempt to apply the research methods of the social sciences to the study of Soviet Jewry was made by Z. Gitelman in his doctoral dissertation for Columbia University (later published in book form)[22], and in M. Altshuler's doctoral dissertation – an important supplement to the study of the Evsektsia and of Soviet Jewry in the 1920s.[23] The 1930s, so important for the understanding of extensive changes in the life of the Soviet

Jews and in government policy towards them, have for some reason
not been studied seriously.

The many obstacles to research on Russian and Soviet Jewry come
under three main headings: (1) finding and utilizing the sources; (2)
working out methods of research, (3) periodization.

SOURCES

Despite the denial of access to Soviet archives in the 1920s, the sources
for the history of pre-Soviet Jewry are satisfactory, although many of
them have not yet been used for research. As classified by Dubnov and
Ginzburg, the sources are both internal and external; the *internal sources*
are the registers of Jewish communities and societies of various kinds;
rabbinical literature (meditations and *responsa*); memoirs; travel
literature; folklore; letters; wills; marriage contracts; business papers,
and so on; and the *external sources* are laws, decrees, decisions concerning
Jews; archives of various ministries, the Senate, the State Council, the
Holy Synod, and of Jewish committees; the Jewish and the general press.

Access to sources for the Soviet period is more difficult. The Soviet
archives have never been open for independent research. The only
archives at our disposal are those of the Smolensk District, and the
private files of individuals and institutions active in the USSR,
mainly in the 1920s and the first half of the 1930s. Special mention
must be made of the files of Yosef Rosen, Lucien Wolf and Elias
Cherikover and the letters of Soviet writers and officials, located in
the Yiddish Scientific Institute in New York. The New York archives
of the *Bund* also contain some relevant material. In Israel there is
important material on the Zionist Movement in the USSR in the
1920s and 1930s in the General Zionist Archives in Jerusalem and in
the Labor Movement's archives in Tel-Aviv. Some additional material is also to be found in the National and University Library, the
Central Archives for the History of the Jewish People, and in the
Centre for Research and Documentation on East European Jewry;
all three are in Jerusalem.

As far as printed material is concerned, the Soviet periodical and
daily *press*, both Jewish and general, is particularly important. A
partial comparison of the Smolensk archive material (some of it classified 'top secret') and reports on the same subject in the local press
show no significant divergences between the two sources. The press,
therefore, at least as regards the 1920s and perhaps the 1930s and

even later, could be a crucial source for the study of Soviet Jewry. Then there are important *collections of documents* which have been published throughout the period since 1917; a number of *surveys, memoirs and studies published in the USSR* on the history of the Jews there; and the *Samizdat* materials. Finally, there are the *personal memoirs and oral history* of people who lived in the USSR and were involved in public activity relating to the Jews.

METHODS

We must try to fuse 'internal' and 'external' aspects, common features and divergencies. The history of the Soviet Jews cannot be adequately described in any one dimension. The 'external' dimension is the history of the Soviet Union and its people – among whom live the Jews – and it includes that country's complex relations with the rest of the world. For each period, there has to be an examination of the legal–political status fixed by the government for the Jews as a minority – national, religious, or other. In spite of the difficulties, it is important to tackle the question of whether this status is the same as that of other minorities, or different, or perhaps unique. Then there is the reciprocal relationship between the majority population and the minority; this is the essence of the story, ranging from brotherhood and cooperation to hostility and repulsion. The relationship was expressed in scientific and publicistic thinking, in *belles-lettres*, and in daily acts, which are, however, difficult to verify, because of the lack of data.

This method of approach does not endorse any foregone conclusion about congruence between the 'external' history of the ruling majority and the 'internal' history of the national minority; but there is no doubt that the connection between them is close and the influence reciprocal. The 'internal' dimension is made up of demographic, economic and social processes, simultaneously affecting, and affected by, national life within the frames of reference of religion, education and culture.

Finally, criss-crossing these two dimensions is another complex network of ties, between the national minority in the country and its own mother-country, and between this same minority and its sister-minorities in the other Diasporas.

Historiographic methods were coloured in the past by ideology and by the temptation to try to make the facts fit rigid systems. As against this, a research instrument, the model, limits the effects of ideology and permits the analysis of complex processes involving a large number of variables. Models help the historian to sort out from the mass of available facts those elements that recur most often in given combinations, without pigeon-holing them in a pre-fabricated framework. The criterion in choosing a model must be its effectiveness in enabling the researcher to carry his investigation to the requisite depth. The most relevant model for analysis of the 'external' dimension seems to be authoritarian–totalitarian, emphasising the political elements; for the second and third dimensions, I suggest a modernization model, emphasising the economic and social elements. The models focus on different elements, thereby complementing each other.

PERIODIZATION

Historians differ as to when Jewish history in Russia actually begins, and this raises another, more important, question: is the history of the Russian Jews separate from that of the Polish Jews, or do they form an organic unity, which split up in one historical period and re-united in another?

How have these questions been treated by the historians of Russian Jewry? The history of European Jews is generally divided into two periods – the Middle Ages and the modern era; but division into periods is little help when applied to the history of Russian Jewry, because of the differences between the various Diasporas. Virtually all historians of Russian Jewry, even if they accept the basic assumption that 'The Jewish nation constitutes a particular national entity, whose parts are connected and inter-connected by life-processes unique to them alone',[24] adopt an 'external' division into historical periods, based on Russian history, regardless of the differences between the historians about the importance of 'internal' factors in determining the development of Russian Jewry.[25]

On the second question, the interconnection between the Jews of Poland and those of Russia, Dubnov maintains that their common past precludes any separate treatment.[26] His view is reflected not only in the title of his *History of the Jews in Russia and Poland*, but also in the space he devotes to Polish Jews.[27] Gessen, on the other hand, does differentiate between the histories of Polish and of Russian Jewry, as the title of his book makes clear, yet he too spends a lot of time on the

Polish Jews;[28] indeed, the first volume of his collected work, *History of the Jews of Russia*, which appeared in 1914, is devoted to Polish Jews.[29] In contrast, the later historians Greenberg and Baron totally ignore them. This approach was supported by Dinur in his article, 'On the Historical Nature of Russian Jewry and Problems in its Study':

The name 'Russian Jewry' is usually given to the Jewish community which was concentrated within the Russian Empire from 1772... it does not include the Jewish settlements in the lands of the Empire prior to 1772, in the lands of the Caucasus, the Khazar Empire, Kievan Russia or the Russian districts that were linked to Lithuania and Poland in the Middle Ages and at the beginning of the modern era.[30]

In this book, the division into the periods listed below aims at both 'internal' and 'external' factors. It does not accept Dubnov's approach on the inseparable link between the Jews of Poland and of Russia; but it rejects Dinur's ruling that the history of Russian Jews begins in 1772. To ignore the situation of the Russian Jews before that date would mean neglecting to trace the causes that affected the determination of the legal–political status of Russian Jewry after 1772.

Historical periods

(1) *The ancient period and the Middle Ages* – from the earliest Jewish settlement on Russian soil to the first partition of Poland.
(2) *The early modern period* – from the first partition of Poland to the pogroms of the early 1880s (1772–1881).
(3) *Into the modern era* – from the pogroms of the early 1880s and the formation of the major political movements to the October Revolution.

The October Revolution began a new chapter in the history of the Russian Jews. As far as Jewish national survival was concerned, it marked profound changes and radical reforms that shattered the foundations of the former structure of Jewish life, where modernizing processes had only just begun. Amidst the bloodshed, new ways of life came into being, and new patterns of thought.

It is not easy to draw up a satisfactory list of periods from 1917 to

the present day, because the revolutionary changes themselves suffered more than one reversal and there was continuity in many
spheres – all this taking place simultaneously, without clear dividing
lines. Nevertheless, three sufficiently different periods can be discerned, each with distinguishing features peculiar to itself:

> *The years of construction* – from the October Revolution to the out-
> break of the Second World War.
>
> *The years of destruction* – from the beginning of the war until the
> death of Stalin.
>
> *After Stalin* – from 1953 to the present day.

Each period can be divided into sub-periods, which I will indicate at
the appropriate time.

I shall, therefore, examine first the external factors, by analysing
the official approach to the Jewish national question expressed in the
Soviet theory of nationalities, which settled the juridical–political
status of the Jewish national minority as one of the extra-territorial
nationalities. The degree of autonomy or 'statehood' granted was
based on an amalgam of this theory with a pragmatic solution arising
from the changing historical conjuncture. I shall then try to estimate
how far the Soviet Jews fitted into the new regime. I shall close this
section with an analysis of the phenomenon of anti-Semitism in its
new form, as part of the relationship between Soviet society and its
Jews.

I shall consider next the overall ideological, political and economic
changes which profoundly affected every nationality; in particular,
religion, education and culture reflected the degree of the Jews' sense of
their national identity.

In the third section, I shall consider the network of relations between Soviet Jews and world Jewry, and observe the results of all the
processes operating simultaneously in everything concerned with the
Jews' national survival.

I

The Jews of Russia: historical background

FROM THE EARLIEST JEWISH SETTLEMENT TO THE FIRST
PARTITION OF POLAND

The remote past of the Russian Jews, like that of the Russians themselves and of other people of that land, is uncertain.[1] Because of the
scarcity of historical material, serious researchers as well as publicists
echo old legends and traditions and lose themselves in conjecture.[2]
The main issues are: when did the Jews first arrive in Russia, whence
and how did they come, where did they settle, and how were they
received by the rulers and the local population? There is also the issue
of whether Russian Jewry can be treated as a historical continuity.

This first period can be sub-divided as follows: the Crimea and
the Caucasus; the Khazars; Kiev; Tatars, Genoese, Turks; and the
Moscow period.

The Crimea and the Caucasus

In the legends of the Georgian Jews, the Mountain Jews of Caucasus
and the Bukharan Jews, the arrival of Jews on Russian soil in the
Caucasus and Central Asia is linked with the exile of the 'Ten Tribes'
(720 BCE) or with the Destruction of the First Temple (586 BCE).[3]
According to the 'Scythian' theory, the Jews arrived in Scythia as
prisoners straight from the Land of Israel and from there they
reached Russia and settled in the region between the Black Sea and
the Caspian Sea in the years 635 to 610 BCE.[4] The 'Caucasian'
theory also links the arrival of Jews in Russia with the defeat of the
Kingdom of Israel and the exile of its population.[5] The 'Bosphorus'
theory, however, appears to be on firmer ground: according to this
view, Jewish communities began growing up in the Greek colonies

along the north shore of the Black Sea from the fourth to the first centuries BCE, arriving there from the various Diasporas that already existed in Asia Minor in this period.[6]

The Jews lived under three successive political regimes: Greek (fourth to first centuries BCE); Roman (first to fourth centuries CE); and Byzantine (fourth to seventh centuries CE). However, from the point of view of the legal–political status of the Jews and the attitude of the rulers and the local population towards them, an equally important division is that between the pagan period, which was conducive to economic consolidation, and the Christian period, which saw intensifying pressures. Yet it appears that precisely at this time there was an increase in the Jewish settlements in the Black Sea region, as a result of persecution of the Jews in Byzantium and the flight from there, especially at the beginning of the fifth century. Such emigration led, over a long period of time, to an intermingling of people of diverse geographical and cultural origins.[7]

The few fragments of evidence that we have – mainly a small number of inscriptions on tombstones – indicate that in this period the Crimean Jews were steeped in Hellenistic culture, speaking and reading Greek and even praying in Greek in the synagogue. Their childrem bore Greek names. All the same, the Jews conserved the framework of their community life, which had attained a degree of autonomy, and were in contact with the two main Jewish spiritual centres of the time, Babylon and the Land of Israel. The widespread activity of the Jews in international trade, together with the development of relations with the local population, seems to have given rise to conversions and the birth of Jewish–Christian sects, a state of affairs which aroused the wrath of the Church authorities and of the militant zealot administration in Byzantium.[8]

In the fifth to seventh centuries CE, Jewish population centres in the Caucasus were strengthened by emigration from Asia, via Persia. The data we have from inscriptions and from Armenian–Georgian chronicles do not permit us to speak with any certainty about the numbers, livelihood, way of life, or community structure of the Caucasian Jews.[9]

The Khazars

From the days of the great Khazar Empire to our own time, the empire itself and its connection with Judaism have aroused curiosity, sparked innumerable controversies and produced numerous commentaries, some of them by scholars of archaeology, history and linguistics, others by publicists and writers with well-developed imaginations and a variety of apologetic aims.[10]

This empire of semi-nomadic Finno-Turkish tribes flourished over extensive regions of southern Russia in the seventh to tenth centuries CE – from the lower Volga to the Crimea and the Dnieper area.[11] In 740, King Bulan selected the Jewish religion for his empire from the three monotheistic faiths that competed for hegemony at his court. This was obviously very important for the older Jewish communities in the region and for those soon to be established, but the Khazars had been well-disposed towards the Jews even before this. During the period of the rise of the Khazars, the major Jewish communities appear to have been: Feodosia, Khersonos, Taman, Sarkl and Choput-Kaleh. These communities offered a refuge for persecuted Jews and were also a magnet to Jews seeking to improve their social and economic situation.[12] Most waves of immigrants came from Byzantium and the Muslim Empire in the eighth to tenth centuries CE, and apparently from the countries of the West as well, but in smaller numbers. Commerce developed greatly in the Khazar Empire because of its central geographical location, while agriculture and the arts lagged behind, and the Jews became the international traders of Europe in that period. Among other things, the Jewish merchants engaged in the slave trade; virtually all the slaves were pagans from Slavic tribes, who were captured by Christians and sold to Jews, who in turn sold them to the lands of Islam. It may well be that the cooperation which grew up between the Jewish merchants and the Khazar military and economic leaders was the basis for the latter's adoption of Judaism when they sought a monotheistic religion.[13]

Arabic and Hebrew sources indicate that the legal–political status of the Jews was secure and that they were able to maintain their religion and culture without interference.[14] In disputes that sometimes occurred between the local Muslim or Christian populations and the Jews, the latter would be protected by the king and the ruling stratum that had adopted Judaism. Influence was brought to bear not only by the local Jewish population but also by rabbis and scholars invited from Babylon. The converts probably had some knowledge of Hebrew; the Jews certainly did.

The expansion of the Princedom of Kiev into the Khazar regions in the years 966 to 969 reduced the Empire to no more than half the

Crimean Peninsula, and Jews from other regions of Russia began to concentrate there. This was the genesis of 'mixed' Jewish–Crimean communities.

Kiev

It is reasonable to assume that Jews from the Khazar Empire were brought to Kiev by Sviatopolk, though a few Jews may have been there even earlier. We do not know how much truth there is in the popular legend, recorded in an ancient Russian chronicle, concerning the debate arranged in the year 986 by Vladimir, Prince of Kiev, between representatives of the three great religions, as a result of which Vladimir decided to adopt Christianity. What is clear is that the introduction of Byzantine Christianity had far-reaching consequences for the Jews: it strengthened the ties between the Jews of Byzantium and those of Kiev, while it exacerbated relations between the Jews on the one hand and the Church and the local population on the other.

The first clear, historically documented report of a Jewish settlement in Kiev dates only from 1018, when Jewish homes were raided by soldiers. In the early period, apparently, Khazari Jews did not live together in one quarter with Byzantine and Western Jews. The local population gave the different quarters separate names: 'Khazaria' and 'Zhidovia'. We hear later of 'the fortress of the Jews'.

As far as can be ascertained from the scanty material at our disposal, the legal–political status of the Jews of Kiev was different from what was customary in Western Europe at that time. They were not the property, protégés or vassals of the prince, but free men. They belonged to the urban commercial stratum, though they were apparently at the same time in the prince's service. Thus they were protected from oppression by hostile groups (mainly the Church) but were also bound to suffer during disorders, disturbances and changes of rulers, as in the period of Vladimir Monomakh.

From the outset the new Church, with its anti-Jewish heritage, gave a central place to polemics and accusations directed against the Jews. This was not necessarily part of a sustained indoctrination, but may have originated in an actual Jewish–Christian disputation conducted in Kiev at that time. The Jews may also have attempted to proselytize. There was, at all events, Jewish influence behind the formation of the Judaizing sects, something which would later affect the attitude of Moscow towards the Jews. What is clear is that anti-Jewish preaching and writings by Church leaders troubled the atmosphere and disturbed relations between the Jews and the local population.

The Jews were important to the economic life of Kiev and in the trade relations of the princedom with Central and Western Europe. The main 'trade route' led from Regensburg or Prague across Poland to Kiev. The Jewish merchants, the Radhanites, were known in the Hebrew sources as 'those who go about in Russia'. They took industrial goods from Regensburg to Russia, and brought back slaves, furs, wax and honey. These visits established social and cultural relations. First, scholars from 'Ashkenaz' (Germany) would sometimes arrive in the princedom with the traders' caravans, while pupils from Russia would travel to Central or Western Europe to study at rabbinical seminaries (*yeshivot*) there. Second, the Jews of Kiev also maintained relations with those in Babylon; for example, in the twelfth century, Rabbi Moshe of Kiev was in contact with both sages of 'Ashkenaz' and with Rabbi Shmuel ben Ali, head of the Babylonian *yeshivah*, on matters of *halakhah* (practical applications of Jewish law). Third, despite the generally low level of Jewish culture in that period in Kiev, the Jews there succeeded in producing several publications, including a commentary on the Torah (Pentateuch) composed in 1124, in which the influence of the German Jews is evident, and a translation into Russian of passages from the Hebrew-language *Book of Yossipon*, which meant that at least some of them were fluent in Slavic. Finally, an organized, close-knit Jewish community life was maintained.[15]

Tatars, Genoese, Turks

The Jewish settlement in the Crimea did not, apparently, cease to exist. The conquest of the Crimea by the Tatar Khans and the extension of their rule over the Russian princedoms led to renewed links between the Jews of the Crimea and of Kiev.[16]

A change came, however, with the establishment by charter of an autonomous Genoese colony in the Kaffa region (Feodosia) of the Crimea, which extended its influence to neighbouring regions during the years 1260 to 1475.[17] Thus, an important commercial centre arose, which fitted itself into the international trade of the period. The Genoese authorities wanted to see the region prosper and instructed their official representatives in the colony to exercise caution *vis-à-vis* the heterogeneous local population and to observe religious tolerance.

According to Schiltberger, who toured the Crimea between 1396 and 1427, there were in Kaffa two sorts of Jews with two synagogues (apparently Jews and Karaites), residing in 4,000 houses.[18] Even if this figure is exaggerated, there was clearly a large Jewish community at Kaffa. However, the situation seems to have deteriorated when the Genoese colony declined in the fifteenth century, and many Jews left, most of them going to Lithuania.

In the three centuries from 1475 to 1783, when the Turks ruled the Crimea, there was constant commerce between that region and the Principality of Moscow. The Crimean Jews played a part in developing this trade. One of them, Khoza Kokos, even became a representative of Ivan III, Prince of Moscow, in the negotiations with the Tatars between 1471 and 1475. It is not certain whether Zekharia Guizolfi ('Prince of Taman'), who also played an important role in diplomatic relations between the two states between 1484 and 1500, was Jewish.[19]

In the fifteenth and sixteenth centuries, a new Jewish sect appeared in the Crimea, the Krimchaks. Their separation was apparently a matter of religious observance and a new 'Kaffa ritual' began to be customary among some Crimean Jews. However, there could not have been any considerable differences initially between the Krimchaks and other local Jews, since the rabbi of the Kaffa community, Moshe Hagoleh, put out a common prayer book for his congregation and for the Krimchaks and the Babylonian and Ashkenazi Jews as well. The Krimchak language has not yet been properly studied but it appears to belong to the Igtaic dialect of the Tatar tongue, with many pre-Tatar archaisms. The Krimchaks knew very little Hebrew and the prayers had to be translated into their language, though they used the Aramaic–Hebrew alphabet.[20]

In the seventeenth and eighteenth centuries, the situation of the Krimchaks, the Mountain Jews and the Georgian Jews, worsened, because of the incessant wars in which they were involved, together with the other local peoples, against the Persians, the Turks and the Russians.

The Moscow period

During the two centuries that the Principality of Moscow was under Mongol rule, from the thirteenth to the fifteenth, only individual

Jews seem to have arrived there. They are first mentioned in 1445, at the time of the connection between Ivan III and the Crimean Jews.[21]

In the last quarter of the fifteenth century, the affair of 'the heresy of the Judaizers' took place, which was to have major repercussions for Russian Jews for many years.[22] At this time, Russia was swept by a powerful religio-political movement, which influenced much of the nobility. The agitation against the Jews originated in Novgorod in the 1470s, triggered by serious rivalry between the camps of supporters of Poland and of Moscow. Some say that a Jew named Zekharia, who had arrived from Kiev in the entourage of the Polish Prince Mikhail Olalkovich, had a share in provoking religious unrest in the city of Novgorod. The spread of the Judaizing movement to Moscow after 1479, where prominent personalities of the Royal Court – Helena, daughter-in-law of the duke, and Feodor Kuritsyn, one of the duke's chief advisers – joined it, led the heads of the Church to embark on energetic counter measures. Political and economic issues were no less important than the supposed danger of the heresy itself: there was a battle over the succession: there was the question of foreign-policy orientation; and there was the issue of monastic estates. In 1504, the leaders of the sect were executed and their followers went 'underground'.

These events had a traumatic impact and the memory of them remained alive for a long time. Where the Jewish question in Russia was concerned – and the general attitude to foreigners in the Principality of Moscow – the 'Judaizing heresy' produced intensified religious zeal, introverted social conservatism, patriarchalism, and the adoption of the aim of economic autarchy.

Ivan III's successors, Vassilii Ivanovich (1505–33) and more particularly Ivan IV – Ivan the Terrible – (1533–84) bore down harder still on the Jews. Thus, in 1550 when a Polish diplomatic mission to Moscow requested Ivan the Terrible to give permission for Polish Jews to visit Russia to trade there, he replied: 'We have more than once written and noted the evil deeds of the Jews, who have led our people astray from Christianity, who have brought poisonous weeds into our land and also wrought much wickedness among our people'.[23] Hatred became murder during the taking of the city of Polotsk in 1563, when Ivan ordered every Jew who refused to adopt Christianity to be thrown into the river and drowned, together with his whole family. This apparently also took place in other conquered places; it was not just an example of the tsar's cruelty: it was also the expression of an agreed attitude on the part of the rulers in Moscow.

In the struggles for the succession to the throne after the death of Ivan the Terrible, the fact that Jewish merchants had accompanied the army of Dimitrii the Pretender (1605–6) was held against the Jews as a whole; during negotiations between the Polish King Sigismund III, and the nobles of Moscow in 1610, concerning the election of the Polish king's son, Wladislaw, to the Russian throne, one Moscow noble demanded that Jews be forbidden to enter Moscow.

Though the accession of Feodor Mikhailovich of the House of Romanov in 1613 brought an easing of the traditional xenophobia in Moscow ruling circles, this was not perceptible to the Jews. When the Tsar issued a decree (October 1634) permitting prisoners-of-war to return to their homeland, he did not forget to include the customary anti-Jewish clause forbidding Jews to enter Russia.

The first encounter with Jews *en masse* following the Khmelnitsky rising – when Jews organized themselves in communities and lived according to their own lights, oddly dressed and speaking a foreign language – came as a surprise to the Russians. That uprising, and the Russian–Polish war which followed, were accompanied by massacres which virtually annihilated the Ukrainian Jewish community. Enmity towards the Jews was vented when Tsar Aleksei Mikhailovich and his military commanders would not allow Jews to leave besieged Polish cities together with the Polish nobles and clergy; instead, the Jews were plundered, their villages sacked, and their children exiled into the interior of Russia, the aim being to convert them to Christianity.

In 1644, a clause was introduced into the codex of laws which fixed the death penalty for any attempt to seduce Russians from their faith and circumcise them. Theoretically, this could apply to all non-Christian faiths, but its target was, of course, the Jews.

This anti-Jewish outlook, based on religious fanaticism and deep-rooted prejudice, continued to prevail in the reign of Peter the Great (1682–1725), who refused to include Jews among the experts whom he invited to settle in Russia. Nonetheless, it is clear that there were changes for the better, *vis-à-vis* not only converted or apostate Jews, but also certain Jews who had not given up their faith. Peter the Great's ambition to modernize his country led to attempts to utilize Jewish capital to develop commerce – as a result, Jewish bankers were granted permits to settle in Moscow, and the settlement of Jews in the border regions was permitted.[24] However, the difficulty of the border Jews' position is evident from the blood-libel charge against two Jews living on the Chernigov estate in Gorodniya.[25]

This easing of restrictions was short-lived and ceased after the death of Peter the Great, when Catherine I issued a decree banishing Jews (1727), despite opposition from nobles residing in regions where a Jewish population existed. The objections of these nobles were not humanitarian, but were based on their evaluation of the damage to the economy if the expulsions should be carried out.[26]

A new expulsion decree was issued on 11 July 1740, almost immediately after the signing of the Russo-Turkish peace pact, but it is not clear how far it was put into operation. The policy of exclusion and expulsion reached its peak during the reign of Elizabeth (1741–62), who was a religious fanatic. Another expulsion decree, in 1742, asserted that 'they [the Jews] shall henceforth not be admitted to Our Empire for any purpose'.[27] An exception was made for those Jews agreeing to adopt the Russian Orthodox faith: such persons would be allowed to live in the empire, but not to leave it. All protests from various groups, and efforts made by members of the Senate to amend the decree on grounds of 'the good of the state', were of no avail; Elizabeth noted on the margin of the Senate memorandum: 'From the enemies of Christ, I desire no profit'.[28] Anti-Jewish policy had become so firmly entrenched that the new queen, Catherine the Great, whose views were more liberal, was obliged to persist in it until the partition of Poland and the subsequent incorporation of Jews into Russia.

To determine the legal–political status of Russian Jews, it is necessary to distinguish more fully between two categories referred to above, of Jews residing in Russia in the century preceding the partition of Poland: those Jews (or, more precisely, former Jews) who had been forced to convert, or were apostates; and true Jews. The former increased slightly during this period (though the number of Jews baptized in the years 1744 and 1745 was only twenty-five), and were mainly in Moscow and St Petersburg; they were recognized as full Russian citizens and could occupy any position, as long as their social and personal status permitted it. Many of them made careers in commerce, medicine and the army, or in the service of the tsar and the nobility. Several former Jews – Haden, Shafirov, Veselovsky, and Devier, for example – rose to high rank, mainly in the foreign service, but at times their Jewish past was used against them in political struggles at court, and they remained suspect; one man, Antonio Sanchez, a well-known doctor and a member of the Academy of Science, was even expelled from Russia in 1749.

Jews who did not convert were in a very different position. The few who managed to reach Moscow or other cities in the interior, and others in outlying districts (such as Riga, Smolensk, Chernigov, Poltava, and Kiev) who managed to hold on to their places of residence between one expulsion and the next, were never recognized as citizens or permanent residents. They were considered foreigners and even with that status, which afforded certain rights, they were discriminated against. According to a contemporary Russian historian, 35,000 Jews were expelled from Russia in 1753, but this figure appears to be much exaggerated.

The poor economic situation of Russian Jews was aggravated by frequent wars, the attacks of the Haidamaks, and repeated expulsions. The Jews were engaged principally in petty trading, as middlemen, or holding various rights leased to them by the landowners, such as milling, fish ponds, and orchards; most of them, however, earned their livelihood by the sale of liquor. Much of the Jews' social and economic life centred around various fairs, but these were not always open to them.

Jewish religious observance and study of the Torah and rabbinic lore were difficult in Russia during this period. We have already seen that the Jews were widely dispersed, that the environment was hostile, and that the rulers feared Jewish religious influence. An example of this is the death of Baruch Leibov, who tried to establish a synagogue in the village of Sverovich, near Smolensk. He was accused of converting a retired Russian naval officer, Aleksander Voznitsyn; the two were condemned to death by burning and the sentence was carried out on 15 July 1738.

To sum up, this period was marked by deep hostility towards the Jews, originating not only in the general xenophobia prevailing in ruling circles in Moscow, but also in fear and hatred of the Jews, because they were judged 'enemies body and soul of Christianity'.

TOWARDS EMANCIPATION, 1772 TO 1881

The years 1772 to 1881 are important in the history of Russian Jewry. In these 110 years, the characteristic traits of Jewish life, both 'external' and 'internal', were formed. Externally, government policy towards the large Jewish minority was determined after many contradictions. This policy was both influenced and was influenced by the relationships that developed between the Jews and the surrounding population. Internally, complex forces were at work sculpting the character of Russian Jewry. On yet another level, partly internal, partly external, a system of mutual relations developed between what was then the largest Jewish population in the world, that of Russia, and the other major Diasporas.

Traditional policy towards the Jews, summed up in the well-known expression, 'Jews excepted', was maintained under Catherine the Great immediately after she came to the throne, from 1762 to 1771; she was reluctant to clash with the powerful Russian Orthodox Church or with the nobility, the merchants or high-ranking officials, all of whom were hostile to the Jews. A shift became unavoidable with the decisive changes between 1772 and 1795, which brought with them the annexation of a large and widely distributed Jewish population. An official policy evolved which affected the entire lives of Russian Jews, laid down in an extensive collection of complex and often conflicting laws, enacted in successive periods.[29]

Catherine the Great

The attitude of the empress towards the Jews was not straightforward. It played an important part in dictating policy and, like that policy, it was the product of a variety of often contradictory influences on the Russian ruling class.[30] She was unable to free herself from the traditional Christian attitudes embodied in the Russian Church, but she was also affected by the rationalistic doctrines of the Age of Enlightenment and of Mercantilism. These doctrines generally included some appreciation of the Jews' economic role and of Jewish abilities which could both be of use to the rulers and at the same time turn the Jews into useful citizens. The empress had before her the example of political and practical legislation passed in Austria and Prussia at this time in an attempt to work out a policy of enlightened absolutism regarding the Jews.[31]

The anti-Jewish tradition in Moscow was now reinforced by Polish hatred of Jews, particularly that of the Catholic Church in Poland. An expression of this hatred among officials can be seen in the Memorandum (1773) by the Governor of the District of Mohilev, Mikhail Kakhovsky: 'The Jews, though not drunkards ... are lazy, deceitful, superstitious, unclean and inferior householders.... They live by deceit and on the fruit of the labour of those who work the land'.[32]

A contrary tendency was shown by Prince Chernyshev, ruler of

Belorussia. He drew up a decree on the instructions of Catherine the Great, which was promulgated on the 16 August 1772, formally proclaiming 'freedom of religious worship and the sanctity and integrity of the property of each and all.... The Jewish communities will preserve and maintain all the freedoms that are theirs in matters of religion and of property'.[33] Although it was only a formal proclamation, whose practical operation depended on the passing of extensive legislation and proper interpretation, this constituted the first official recognition of Jews as citizens with equal rights. Moreover, the Jewish autonomy it granted, local and district, and including judicial authority, was fuller than that conceded to other national and religious minorities within Belorussia. It is also noteworthy that, from this time, a new formula, 'without regard to national origin and religion', begins to appear in important edicts.[34]

Legislation concerning the Jews, both general and specific, began in 1775 and continued for about twenty years. The basis for determining the status of the Jews was the division of the urban population into merchants on the one hand, and town residents (townsmen) on the other. Those who owned property worth more than 500 roubles could register with the merchant class, according to the following scale: the first guild, at least 10,000 roubles; the second guild, between 1,000 and 10,000; the third guild, between 500 and 1,000; those owning less than 500-roubles-worth of property were registered as townsmen. Jewish merchants applied to be admitted to the class of merchants and they were granted this privilege in 1780. In 1783 all the rest were registered as townsmen. The significant effect this was to have on the general status and rights of the Jewish community will be seen later.[35] Another landmark – one of the most progressive legislative decisions of the day with respect to Jews – was the grant of the right to participate, both as voters and as candidates, in local government councils, the sole criterion for eligibility being social status.

There are two distinct phases in the Jews' situation: first, from 1772 to 1790, the cause of the discrimination against them was the way in which the Senate and the local governments applied the 'Jewish policy' of Catherine the Great, and their narrow interpretation of the legislation; in the next phase, from 1791 to 1794, liberal policy was in retreat, due to external influences, fear of the French Revolution and the demographic and national upheaval following two more partitions of Poland. This was also due to the internal pressures of the Church, of the Polish urban population, and of the merchants of

Moscow, together with the inability of the central government to withstand them.

In the first phase, the main restrictions were: in the *economic sphere*, (1) the Jews (about 800,000 in 1795) were made permanently dependent on the landowners on whose property they lived; (2) the right to brew and sell spirits was revoked, and although the law of 1783 was not explicitly directed against the Jews, circumstances were such that they were its principal victims; and (3) there was a general expulsion from the villages following legislation forbidding townsmen to reside in the rural areas. In the *political sphere* of civil rights, Jews were denied the privilege of serving in the royal administration; and in the cities where they were actually a majority, their voting rights were cut down so that they could not exceed half the total number of voters. Because of this, the Jews secured only twenty-five official posts in the district of Mohilev in the elections of 1784, and only four places in eleven towns in the district of Polotsk.[36] Similarly, the qualifications needed for office holders in the towns resulted in restricting Jewish representation, for example, the proviso that they must wear Russian or German dress, and be able to read and write Russian, German and Polish – and this when the majority of those elected were illiterate. There were also various attempts to restrict *internal autonomy* as far as possible, contradicting earlier proclamations, as well as damaging government interests.

Harsher, explicitly restrictive legislation was passed in the next phase. Many historians think that the Edict of Catherine, sent to the Senate on the 23 December 1791, marks the establishment of the Pale of Settlement.[37] It stated: 'We hereby rule that Jews have no right whatsoever to register as merchants in the towns and in the internal harbors of Russia, and only by our express command have they been permitted to enjoy civil and urban rights in White Russia.'[38] Even this does not provide for the establishment of a Pale of Settlement for the Jews and it is possible to show that the edict derives from the corporative–feudal structure of the Russian regime. Nevertheless, it constitutes the beginning of discriminatory legislation directed against the Jews as a religious and/or national minority. Three years later came Catherine's Edict to the Senate (June 1794) requiring Jews to pay twice the amount of tax fixed for townsmen and merchants of the Christian churches.[39] Granted that the object of this was fiscal and/or sprang from the government's desire to direct the Jews to the new districts of Ekaterinoslav and Taurida, it does not change the fact that there was anti-Jewish discrimination in the sensitive matter of taxation.

Paul I and Alexander I

During the short reign of Paul I (1796 to 1800) there was no change in the legal–political status of the Jews, apart from a severer application of the existing laws. Ominously, this was linked with food shortages amounting to famine in the district of Minsk. Because of reports received from the representatives of the nobility of the district about the reasons for the spread of famine conditions, Paul I sent an order to the Senate on 8 July 1797, calling for restrictions on the rights of the Jews, the 'exploiters of the peasantry'. In 1800, any Jews whose payments to the government were more than three years in arrears were ordered to be sent to government undertakings extracting minerals from the mines.

This period was nevertheless important for Jewish policy, since it saw the birth of proposals for 'reform', one by Governor Ivan Friesel, and the other by Senator Gabriel Derzhavin, which later had a considerable effect. The reform proposed by Friesel was appended to a statement by representatives of the nobility in April 1800. For the first time, a far-reaching and relatively liberal-minded project was drawn up, advocating changes in the life of Russian Jews.[40] Friesel wanted to abolish the customary Jewish ways of earning a livelihood, such as innkeeping and liquor distilling. He suggested putting the Jewish population on a new footing in three areas: (1) merchants with rights equal to those of all other merchants in the country; (2) artisans in their several trade guilds; (3) workers on the soil. Regarding religion, Friesel proposed first to reform the system of religious instruction and then to extend the reforms to general education. He even proposed that religious affairs be conducted in Polish. On the question of internal autonomy, Friesel's ideas were extreme: the communities should be abolished, being the cause of all the trouble, and the Jews should be satisfied with one religious tribunal in each district.

The reform proposed by Minister of Justice Derzhavin was very different, being anti-Jewish and thoroughly reactionary.[41] It was more detailed, and based on a wider range of occasionally inconsistent sources. In both sets of proposals, however, it was admitted that government compulsion would be needed to impose the new system.[42]

Derzhavin apparently had no previous knowledge of Jewish problems, and drew inspiration from a variety of sources.[43] He defined the Jews as parasites, having no conception of love for their fellow men or hatred of avarice. He said that in their places of worship, they learned to hate Christianity; they used their community organization (the 'Kahal'), violence, and boycott to secure monopolies for themselves; their tenancies and inns were means of exploitation. Since Derzhavin thought it impossible to rid Russian soil of 'this dangerous nation', he made a series of 'constructive' proposals, to which he annexed a long list of prohibitions. To turn the Jews into useful members of society, he suggested putting them into the following four categories: (1) merchants in the three existing guilds; (2) townsmen, half of them artisans and the rest small shopkeepers and pedlars; (3) townsmen residing in villages, occupied mainly in manufacture and workshops; (4) villagers, who would not be permitted to live by tenancy or the sale of liquor. Regarding religion, all Jews would have to join one united official organization. There would be one synagogue in every district, and government supervisors would officiate as well as Jewish religious judges. Over them would be a 'Sanderin' ('Sanhedrin') in the capital, a sort of high court, whose members would be a Christian 'protector', and four 'educated' or 'enlightened' German or local Jews, who spoke Russian and European languages, headed by a chief rabbi or 'patriarch'. Derzhavin also wanted to abolish the communities and place the Jews under the direct supervision of the authorities. Finally came the numerous prohibitions, aimed at limiting 'the harmful influence' of the Jews as far as possible. Jews should not be allowed to: employ Christian servants; entice Christians into becoming Jews; enter inner Russia; send money to the Land of Israel, or maintain unauthorized contact with heads of the Jews there. They should no longer participate in elections to town and city councils.

Practical deliberations on these proposals for 'reform' were entrusted to a public committee set up by Alexander I in November 1802. Among its members were General Zubov, Minister of the Interior Kochubei, Minister of Justice Derzhavin, Senator Potocki, and Foreign Under-Secretary Czartoryski. It was the first time representatives of the Jewish community had appeared before a public body of this kind, and Minister Kochubei and two representatives of Polish origin, all of whom held liberal views, exerted a decisive influence.[44] Sessions were held for two years; then, on 9 December 1804, the committee adopted the 'Regulations Regarding the Jews',[45] which provided for something like a 'Jewish Constitution', the first in Russia. As we shall see, these Regulations represented a compromise between Friesel's liberal views and the anti-Jewish attitude of Derzhavin.

Economically and socially, the regulations divided the Jews into four categories: (1) free farmers; (2) manufacturers and artisans; (3) merchants; (4) townsmen. The positive side of these regulations was that they encouraged Jews to change over voluntarily to agriculture, manufacture, and labouring, and gave relief from 1809, by abolishing the double tax; on the other hand, they prescribed a more immediate fate for the 200,000 to 300,000 Jews, mostly poor, who were to be expelled from the villages before 1 January 1807.[46]

Politically, the area of the Pale of Settlement was extended to the districts of Astrakhan and the Caucasus. Manufacturers and artisans, with their families, were given the possibility of leaving the Pale for limited periods, to pursue their occupations. On the other hand, local government rights were curtailed: it was laid down that not more than one-third of the members of local councils were to be Jews, even in towns where they formed the majority of the inhabitants.

Regarding internal autonomy and religion, the regulations did provide for official recognition of 'congregations', but their powers, and those of the rabbis, were reduced. The synagogue authorities were forbidden to exercise any pressure, except reprimand and warning. Rabbis and heads of the congregation were to be elected every three years, and the elections would have to be ratified by the district administration.

The most progressive feature of the regulations was their educational provisions. All Jewish children were to be admitted to elementary schools, high schools (*gymnasia*) and universities. Jewish clothing was to be permitted. Jews were not to be made to change their religion. Jewish schools were granted official recognition, and it was laid down that they should be maintained out of public funds provided and earmarked for this purpose. One negative aspect, though, was that in the future all educational certificates would have to be in a language of the country – that is to say, not in Hebrew or Yiddish.

The implementation of the main provisions of the regulations – resettlement in southern Russia, and expulsion from villages – began in 1807; however, the measures had to be suspended for a variety of reasons, partly internal, such as opposition on the part of estate owners, and partly political, such as the new situation prevailing in Europe as a result of Napoleon's conquests. At the end of 1808 a new edict ordered the expulsions to stop.

Napoleon's eastern campaigns changed the situation again. Under the French conquest, the Jewish population gave full proof of its loyalty to Russia, and even made a slight contribution to the fighting,[47] unlike the Polish population, for example, which openly supported the armies of Napoleon. In spite of this, the programme of expulsions of Jews was made harsher still, and they were forbidden to reside in the fortified towns on the western frontier and in ports serving as bases for the Russian navy. In 1824, the last year of Alexander's reign, orders were given to expel all Jews, except those communities in small towns and villages, from a strip of territory fifty versts wide along the whole western frontier; this was part of the tsar's mystic–Messianic policy.

Nicholas I

Legislation concerning the Jews reached a peak in the reign of Nicholas I. Over six hundred edicts, regulations and ordinances were enacted during these thirty years, that is to say, half of all the legislation on the Jews in the 232 years from 1649 to 1881. The tsar's enthusiasm for regulation played a part in the flow of new laws, but the decisive factor was the importance of the Jewish question itself in the eyes of the tsar and his entourage, and their efforts to solve it in the light of their religious beliefs and political views.

The first important law affecting the Jews in this period was the enactment of 'Regulations for Conscription of Jews and their Service in the Army', which were adopted on 26 August 1827.[48] On the face of it, the law aimed at promoting Jewish emancipation. The money payment which had been levied on the Jews since the days of Catherine the Great in lieu of military service,[49] had in fact constituted discrimination in their favour compared with the Christians, among whom only the nobility and the merchants enjoyed this privilege. But its real aim was to encourage assimilation, in line with the laws passed by Alexander I in the last year of his life, but using harsher methods.

Under the terms of this law, the Jews had a quota of conscripts fixed for them, which was meant to be higher than that of the Christian population. Jews were called up for service every year, while for the general population it was every two years. The general draft age was from twenty to thirty-five, but for the Jews it was twelve to thirty-five, in order to enable the young Jews to be put into cantonments where they would be given special pre-military training. Such institutions had been set up as early as 1721 for the education of sons of serving soldiers from the age of fourteen.[50] Since the period of military service was twenty-five years, it followed that the Jews had to serve an additional six to eight years, because of their early call-up. Worst of all was the regime of fear in the cantonments; the brutal treatment dealt out there, particularly to the Jews, was the cause of innumerable tragedies.[51]

Exemption from conscription was granted to merchants of all guilds, artisans connected with the guilds of their trades, rabbis, school-teachers, apprentices who had been apprenticed to Christian artisans for at least three years, and agricultural settlers. Under the government plan, Jewish conscripts were supposed to number about 3% of the total. An increasing number of young Jews fled the country, or maimed themselves, or paid bribes; thus, for example, the number evading the draft in 1833 was 255, but in 1837 it reached 2,074.[52] It seems that the total percentage of Jews called up was about the same as for the general population.[53] The authorities made only negligible progress towards their aim of promoting rapid assimilation: a tiny percentage of apostates was for the most part swallowed up in the new surroundings without producing any wave of mass conversions to Christianity.

The 'Jewish Regulations' of 31 May 1835 form the 'Jewish Constitution', on which all legislation up to the time of the Revolution was based.[54] The first clause of the regulations affirmed the special status of the Jews, deriving from their religion, way of life, and places of residence.[55]

Special importance attached to the precise delineation of the *Pale of Settlement*, which was now reduced in size. Jews leaving Russia without permission would forfeit their nationality and not be permitted to return. There was, however, no explicit provision for general expulsion of the Jews from the villages. Jews were now obliged to register under fixed family names. Marriages were forbidden under the age of eighteen for men and sixteen for women. Jews were not permitted to employ Christian servants. No synagogue could be built next to a church.

Censorship had been in force in Russia since 1826, but Nicholas I felt that the Jews needed extra censorship. On 27 October 1836, a ministerial committee decided to close all existing Hebrew printing presses, except two – one in Kiev and the other in Vilna, where two censors were entrusted with the task of examining all printed books.

At the end of 1840 a committee, proposed by Kisilev, Minister of State Property, was set up, 'to determine ways and means for the reform of Jews in Russia'.[56] The lengthy series of laws enacted from 1844 to 1855 emerged from its deliberations. The committee addressed itself to the need for 'moral instruction' of the younger generation. On 20 April 1843, an ordinance was issued which arranged for all Jewish teaching institutions to be supervised by the Ministry of Popular Education and specified which institutions should be Jewish and what methods should be used in them. The final details of the establishment of special schools for the instruction of Jewish youth were laid down in the ordinance of 13 November 1844.[57]

The 1840 committee had studied the question of abolishing Jewish communal institutions, and the purpose of the ordinance issued on 9 December 1844 was to transfer the Jews to the authority of the local administration – the police and the municipal councils.

The urge to 'Europeanize' the Jews led to the government to prohibit the wearing of traditional Jewish dress, because it 'draws a sharp line of distinction between the Jews and the main body of the population'. Similar decisions were taken in 1848, 1850 and 1853, illustrating the difficulty of carrying out the policy, and finally a limited interpretation of the ban was handed down, restricting it to the 'capote' (long-skirted coat or gaberdine) and to special Jewish headgear, such as skullcaps and fur-edged hats.

One of the guide-lines of the 1840 committee had been the need to classify the Jews according to their 'usefulness' and this was a more serious matter than capotes. Merchants, artisans, agriculturalists and clerics were said to be 'useful' in their varying degrees, and were granted permanent residence. They were a small part of the Jewish population and the rest – small traders, shopkeepers, carters, goldsmiths, and others – were adjudged 'exploiters and parasites', against whom special measures had to be taken, such as setting the army conscription quota three times higher than for other categories of the population. This proposal caused the Jews acute concern and might have been catastrophic, had it not been opposed by some members of the senior administration, who succeeded in postponing its implementation and finally, after the death of Nicholas I, in getting it annulled.

Alexander II

On his accession to the throne, Alexander II continued his father's policies, sharing the view that the Jews were both foreign and of dubious honesty. In this, as in other matters, the tsar was influenced by his counsellors and ministers; but the latter did not always agree with each other, resulting in a lack of consistency in Alexander II's 'Jewish policy'. Kiselev, head of the 'Jewish Committee', submitted a report to the tsar of 14 March 1856, which amounted to a confession that the efforts of the committee to weaken the religious outlook of the Jews and turn them into useful, hard-working citizens had been in vain. He proposed 'a reexamination of all the existing Regulations concerning the Jews in order to adapt them to the general aim of absorbing the Jews into the main population, insofar as their moral condition makes it possible to do so'. This proposal was accepted and, for the next seven years, from 1856 to 1863, senior officials of the various administrations and the 'Jewish Committee' itself proceeded to 'reexamine' the legal–political status of the Jews. The Jews themselves did what they could to influence the tsar and his ministers, in order to secure a real reform of the existing laws and regulations. Besides books and newspaper articles, the main Jewish effort was made through intercession by individuals – Brainin, a Riga merchant; Levin, secretary to Baron Ginzburg,[58] and in 1862, the baron himself[59] – and by groups such as the merchants of St Petersburg and some Jewish medical students. The effect of these intercessions seems to have been limited. More important, but equally ineffective, were the efforts made by liberal-minded ministers and high-ranking officials – Interior Minister Lanskoi, Education Minister Kovalsky, Governor-General of New Russia Stroganov – to weight the scales in favour of equal rights for the Jews. They were opposed by the conservative majority, which included the new head of the 'Jewish Committee', Bludov, who argued that equal rights could only come with the spread of enlightenment among the Jews and a change in their way of life in the direction of 'useful' vocations. This was the policy adopted by Alexander II in minor reforms which affected some of the Jewish population.

There was, however, one important improvement, affecting the whole Jewish population: the abolition (on 26 August 1856) of the cantonments, the special schools for sons of soldiers, and the reduction of conscription of the Jews to the same level as that for the rest of the population. That year also saw the repeal of the 1844 regulation barring all Jews, even those with academic qualifications, from government employment. After two years of deliberations, another ordinance was issued on 6 March 1859, enabling Jewish merchants of the First Guild to register in all the cities of Russia. This right was extended on 27 November 1861 to persons with the qualification of 'doctor of medicine, doctor of surgery, doctor, master and bachelor of the other faculties', who could henceforth reside anywhere and could hold office without any restriction as to their place of residence.[60] The right to settle outside the Pale was only extended to Jewish artisans – mechanics, distillers of wines and spirits[61] – on 28 June 1865, after eight more years of deliberation. Soldiers who had served during the reigns of Nicholas and his descendants were added to the list on 25 June 1867.

Jews residing in the former realm of Poland also saw their legal–political status considerably improved in 1862, when they were granted the legal right to settle in all cities and towns: they had previously been barred from 107 out of 453.[62] In 1868, residential permission for Polish Jews was extended to the Ukraine and Belorussia.

Important as these reforms were, it must be remembered that they only affected a small part of the Jewish population. Furthermore, the rights accorded even to this group were not equal to those enjoyed by other classes of 'privileged' citizen in Russia. The Jews lived in a permanent state of dependence on the administration and on the Senate's interpretation of often arbitrary regulations.

In 1864, the first two important reforms of the Zemstvo and the judiciary brought about an extension of Jewish rights, in that they did not include explicit restrictions applying to Jews. In this way, individual Jews succeeded in obtaining posts in the Zemstvo and the judicial service, mainly as advocates or in charge of investigations. However, the municipal regulations of 1870 did not lift the old restrictions banning Jews from the office of mayor, or limiting the number elected to municipal councils to a third of the total (a restriction applying to all non-Christians).[63]

The general reform of the army, enacted in 1874,[64] was important for the Jews, as it made them liable for military service under the same conditions as all other citizens. The only remaining military discrimination against the Jews was in exemptions for the clergy, military exemptions being granted only to Christian clergy. This discrimination arose because the authorities did not officially recognize rabbis, ritual slaughterers, cantors, or those performing the circumcision rite, classifying them simply as 'townsmen'. Despite these reforms, however, the provisions regarding exemption from conscription were interpreted to the disadvantage of the Jews during the 1870s, when the official attitude towards Jews worsened.

Thus in the 100 years from 1772 to 1881, in spite of the reforms and the partial improvement in conditions resulting from the relative 'liberalism' of Catherine the Great, Alexander I and Alexander II – a liberalism usually seen in the first half of each reign, with a retreat in the second – the Jews were not yet 'emancipated' in the sense of being formally accorded equal rights. Their peculiar legal status of '*inorodtsi*' – people within the gates, somewhere between foreigners and Russian nationals – with all its restrictions and qualifications, was maintained throughout the period.

INTO THE MODERN ERA, 1881 TO 1917

The short period between the first anti-Semitic outbreaks in 1881 and the 1917 October Revolution witnessed the most far-reaching changes in the history of Russian Jewry up to that time. A complex amalgam of influences, both internal and external, accelerated the processes that had first become visible in the preceding period, processes marking Russian Jewry's emergence into the modern era.

The administration's Jewish policy

The 1877–8 Russo-Turkish War, with its encouragement of nationalist extremism, growing revolutionary ferment and rising tide of terrorism, together with the weakness of the regime, culminated in the assassination of Alexander II on 1 March 1881 by the members of the 'Narodnaya volya', in whose ranks the ethnic minorities were well represented, with Poles and Jews in the first places.

Alexander III, coming to the throne after these events, soon became the leader of the conservatives and reactionaries, who were determined to block the move towards revolution. Some were inclined to do this by authoritarian methods, while others were ready to try newer methods borrowed from the revolutionary movement itself. Both groups shared a common objective, but the opposing methods employed by the ruling circles could be seen in their policy on the

Jewish question. The conservatives wanted to reach a point where the government had the situation in hand; but they hesitated to risk using 'revolutionary' means, which might produce unforeseeable results. Thus, men like Dmitri Tolstoy, Minister of the Interior fom 1882 to 1889, who had no sympathy for the Jews, opposed using pogroms or forced emigration as a means of strengthening tsarist rule. He even believed that methods like these endangered the regime itself. His watchword, which embodied his whole political creed, was 'Order, first and foremost.'[65]

The second, essentially Slavophile, approach, was typified by Nicholas Ignatyev, Minister of the Interior from 1881 to 1882, a leader of the 'Sacred Society' (an organization of noblemen and high-ranking officials, which, at the date of its dissolution, 26 November 1882, numbered 729 full members and 14,676 volunteer supporters, apparently from among the forces concerned with organizing pogroms).

The attitude of Alexander III and his adviser, Pobedonostsev, was more complicated. On the one hand, Pobedonostsev's name was connected with the notorious declaration on solving the Jewish problem in Russia: 'A third of the Jews will be wiped out, a third will be converted, and a third will emigrate.'[66] On the other hand, he is known to have advocated a limited anti-Jewish policy and to have opposed instigating pogroms, and it was this policy that led to Ignatyev's dismissal from the post of Minister of the Interior in May 1882. Alongside this relative restraint, however, the Tsar Alexander III – and even more so his son, Nicholas II – were imbued with the ancient Russian religious heritage of anti-Semitism. This was now reinforced by modern anti-Semitic ideas from France and Germany, which were exerting an increasing influence on the court and on official circles in the 1880s.[67]

RESTRICTIONS AND DISCRIMINATION THROUGH LEGISLATION

Extreme anti-Jewish policy in the twenty-five years from 1881 to 1905 was manifested in the legislation, just as it was when anti-Jewish feeling recurred during the First World War. In the reign of Alexander III (1881–94), sixty-five anti-Jewish laws were promulgated; under Nicholas II, fifty laws; and in the month of June 1914 alone, fifty laws, ordinances, projects of law, and orders were brought out against the Jews.[68]

This legislation was initiated by Ignatyev as soon as he was appointed Minister of the Interior on 2 May 1881. The statement appended to the ordinance establishing 'District Commissions on the Jewish Question' was a clear reflection of Ignatyev's aims. The commissions were directed to answer the following questions: What activities of the Jews are harmful to the local population? What are the main obstacles hindering the implementation of existing laws affecting the Jews as regards purchase and lease of land, trading in liquor, and money-lending at interest? What changes is it desirable to make in the existing regulations, either annulling them or supplementing them, in order to prevent the Jews from circumventing them?[69] Most of the members of the Commissions, drawn from the local senior officials, were overt or secret anti-Semites, opposed to any policy of emancipating the Jews.

At the same time, Ignatyev set up a 'Commission for Jewish Affairs' under the Ministry of the Interior, presided over by his deputy, Gutovtsev, which drew up the 'Temporary Regulations' of 2 May 1882; these remained in force, with minor amendments in 1893 and 1903, until the outbreak of the Revolution in February 1917. These regulations were clearly a compromise between the extremist approach, personified by Ignatyev himself, with its demand for far-reaching restrictions on the Jews, and the more moderate approach of a number of ministers who were more sensitive to international public opinion and who feared the cessation of foreign investments in Russia. The 'Temporary Regulations' forbade Jews: (1) to settle outside the cities and towns; (2) to build or purchase houses for themselves outside the cities and towns; (3) to own or use land by purchase, lease, or mortgage or economic stewardship outside cities and towns; and (4) to trade in liquor in the villages.[70] These harsh regulations affected about half a million Jews – the whole Jewish population in the villages except for those working in agriculture – and indirectly affected the entire Jewish population in the Pale of Settlement by increasing the internal competition there, which could only worsen the economic situation. The ruling of the Gutovtsev Commission, that the Jews were 'aliens', also had harsh implications, tightening the control exercised over them by the local authorities, especially the police. This state of affairs was confirmed in the Orders of the Council of State of 29 December 1887.[71]

The politico-legal situation of the Jews living outside the Pale of Settlement was also seriously affected. First, there was a definite tendency to reduce the Pale by excluding certain cities from its limits.

Secondly, regulations were issued from time to time restricting the right of residence in the District of Moscow of different categories of Jews: regulations of 28 March 1891 regarding artisans; of 15 October 1892 regarding Jewish soldiers demobilized from the ranks (not officers); of 13 November 1897 regarding male nurses and midwives; and finally of 22 January 1899 regarding merchants of the First Guild.[72] So far, all these were prohibitions and restrictions applying in one area only, that of the fundamental right of free choice of residence and freedom of movement. However, as we shall see, the policy of discrimination was soon extended to apply to almost every aspect of the Jews' existence.

Restricted admission of Jews to the state service. Under the law of 1889, all non-Christians (Jews, Moslems, Karaites, etc.) were barred from practising law; in fact this law applied almost solely to Jews, who had been 'assistant attorneys' for years, though this status had never been formally fixed by the Ministry of Justice. On 25 June 1912, a law was passed forbidding Jews to hold the post of Justice of the Peace or District Court Judge.[73] Other restrictions affected positions in medicine, for example, the limit on the number of Jewish military doctors to five per cent of the total number.

Restricted civil rights. The Municipalities Law of 1892 limited the rights of the Jews still more than the law of 1870 had done, so that they were now excluded from participation in the local authorities. Limitations on the right of Jews to vote were introduced before the elections to the fourth Duma in 1912, to reduce the number of Jewish representatives and therefore the influence of Jewish voters on the election of non-Jewish representatives.

Restrictions regarding military service. The first discriminatory measures regarding Jews in military service dated from 1876 and these were now considerably widened.[74] First came the ban on posting Jews serving in the artillery to fortresses, the navy or the frontier guard. Next, Jews were no longer permitted to take entrance examinations to the officer corps. Then came the veto on appointing Jews as conductors of military bands; further, the number of Jews in these bands was restricted to one-third of its members. Then, it was laid down that the family of a Jewish deserter had to pay a fine of 300 roubles – a heavy penalty. There were many families whose sons had emigrated from Russia without their names being removed from the lists of those liable for service and consequently the families had a heavy financial burden laid upon them. Finally, Jewish soldiers were forbidden to spend their leave outside the Pale of Settlement, not even in places where their units were stationed. Thus, Jewish soldiers had to fulfil all the duties and obligations of military service but had their rights severely restricted. Despite all these restrictions, and the discrimination they were subjected to, 425,000 Jews served in the Russian army in the years 1880 to 1909; in 1897 they constituted 5.2% of the army, as against 4.13% of the population as a whole. During the First World War, the number of Jewish soldiers serving was estimated to be between 400,000 and 500,000.[75]

Restrictions in education.   The operation of the *numerus clausus* marks the turning point in the connection of the authorities with the solution of the Jewish problem. In 1883, the number of Jews who might be admitted as students in the School of Mines was limited to 5%. In 1885, an official instruction was issued setting a quota of 10% of Jews in the new Technical Institute in Kharkov, and in 1886 all admission of Jews to the Kharkov Veterinary Institute was stopped.

The instructions issued in 1886–7 were particularly important: they set a quota of 10% of Jews in any institution of higher learning in the Pale of Settlement, 5% outside the Pale, and 3% in the cities of Petrograd and Moscow;[76] in 1901–2, these quotas were further reduced to 7%, 5% and 2% respectively. For secondary education the following quotas were set: 15% in the Pale of Settlement, 10% outside the Pale, and 5% in the two capital cities. A number of institutes were also closed to Jews.

Senate rulings, given the obsolescence of a great deal of legislation, became the sole law in many instances, and these rulings or interpretations also limited the rights of the Jews. However, a few fruitless attempts were made by high-ranking officials in Russia during this period to alter the laws discriminating against the Jews, laws which the local authorities exploited shamefully by taking revenge or by extorting bribes. The first and most important attempt to change the course of legislation was that of the 'High Commission to examine existing legislation regarding the Jews' or, as it was called after its chairman, the 'Pahlen Commission', which did important work during the five years of its existence, from 1883 to 1888. The Commission comprised representatives of various ministries and the Senate. Most of its members concluded that it was necessary to extend the rights of the Jews gradually, with the aim of making them equal with all the other inhabitants of the country in the eyes of the law, but the Commission's recommendations were rejected by Alexander III. A second attempt was made by Count Witte, against the background of the abortive revolution of 1905; he submitted a memorandum to the tsar on 8 October 1905, in which he proposed 'granting equality to all citizens without distinction of nationality or origin'.[77] But once appointed Head of Government, Count Witte dropped the matter, deciding to leave it to the State Duma which was about to be established. Witte thought that the Jews ought to be given equal rights but only gradually, to prevent a backlash among the Russian people, who were hostile to the Jews, which could even lead to bloodshed.

The last attempt of the authorities to solve the Jewish question, by means of emancipation and abolishing the Pale of Settlement, was made during the First World War. It was not until August 1915 that the conflict between those who favoured maintaining the Pale by means of anti-Jewish decrees and those demanding a more liberal attitude was debated in the Council of Ministers. The result was a compromise. It was decided to open the gates of the interior of Russia to Jews, except for the capital cities and places under the control and supervision of the Ministry for Imperial Court Affairs and of the army.[78] The frequent expulsions of the Jewish population had in any case brought about the transfer of Jews to regions outside the Pale of Settlement. The *de jure* abolition of the Pale had to await the February Revolution and the establishment of the new regime.

Pogroms and blood-libel cases

The first wave of disturbances began on 15 April 1881 in Elizavetgrad and spread rapidly to other towns in the region; it reached Kiev and Zhmerinka between 26 and 28 April, Aleksandrovsk on 1 May, Odessa between 3 and 7 May, and Warsaw on 13 December 1881.[79] The riots in the city of Balta on 29 March 1882 were particularly violent, marking the beginning of a new phase, which continued intermittently until 1884, when the riots reached a new peak of cruelty at Nizhnii-Novgorod.

One outstanding characteristic of the pogroms in the years 1881 to 1884 was that they were mainly concentrated in a number of districts of the Ukraine and New Russia, apart from isolated instances, such as that of Warsaw, where the authorities and the instigators of the pogroms were anxious to show that anti-Semitism was a general phenomenon and not specifically a Russian one. There were also isolated spontaneous outbreaks in other places outside the Pale, against the background of blood libels and the general anti-Semitic atmosphere in Russia. The pogroms were concentrated along both banks of the Dnieper, in regions which had a tradition of rebellion favourable to outbreaks of all kinds and were easily diverted in the direction desired by the authorities. These regions also had a strong anti-Jewish tradition. Finally, as a consequence of the freeing of the serfs, there was an economic situation that bred friction between the local population and the Jews.

The second outstanding characteristic of the pogroms was their lack of spontaneity. The regions where they were carried out, and the fact that they were so widespread – in 1881 alone there were pogroms in 215 places[80] – constituted proof that there was a directing hand. Besides this circumstantial evidence, a body of reliable evidence exists testifying to the presence of emissaries from Moscow who spread rumours and incited riots in the pogrom towns, and also to the existence of bands of rioters who went openly from town to town to take part in the pogroms. Who had an interest in the eruption of the pogroms and who was behind their organizers? The central authorities, headed by the tsar himself, were apparently not against 'clean' pogroms of the 'accepted' kind: it was hinted authoritatively both by word of mouth and in writing that, in the event of a pogrom, the reaction should be permissive and tolerant, and use should not be made of fire-arms. The difference of opinion between those openly advocating pogroms and their opponents sprang mainly from the fear that it would be difficult to control the pogroms if they got out of hand and went beyond the 'accepted' bounds; furthermore, they were liable to make a bad impression abroad, with all that this entailed economically and politically. Against the background of this confused policy of the central authorities, the local authorities could do a great deal either to encourage the rioters or else to suppress them firmly. A semi-official body that had a considerable role in organizing pogroms was the 'Sacred Society', founded on 12 March 1882, which numbered among its leaders the Minister of Interior, Ignatyev, and his deputy, in charge of internal security affairs, General Chervonin.[81]

The official explanations for the pogroms were full of contradictions, the two main ones being that 'This is the judgement of the people on their Jewish exploiters' and 'The pogroms are the work of nihilists, anarchists and revolutionaries aimed at undermining the regime.' In fact, there was no way of masking the direct responsibility of the authorities for the atrocities that were committed.

The third characteristic of these pogroms was that this time not only were the peasants and *lumpenproletariat* incited to take part, but also factory and railway workers. Moreover, revolutionary circles viewed the violent outbursts against the Jews as a people's movement, to be harnessed and directed until it turned into a general rebellion against the autocratic regime. One result of the first pogroms of the 1880s was that they administered a shock to the Jewish population, and in particular to the Jewish intelligentsia.

In the twenty years from 1884 to 1903 pogroms took place on 18 and 19 February 1897 in the town of Spola, at Passover 1899 in Nikolaev, and on 19 August 1900 in Chęstochowa. A second wave of pogroms of unprecedented cruelty occurred in Kishinev on 6 and 7 April 1903, as a result of organized anti-Semitic incitement in the local paper *Bessarabets* (owned by an anti-Semite, P. Krushevan), which exploited the blood-libel cases in Dubasari and Kishinev. In two days of rioting, 45 persons were murdered, 86 seriously wounded and 500 less seriously hurt, while some 1,500 houses and shops were sacked and pillaged.[82] On 1 September a pogrom broke out in the town of Homel, but on this occasion there was organized Jewish defence.[83] In 1904 and 1905, at the time of Russia's ill-fated war with Japan, pogroms were carried out by soldiers and by the mob in the towns of Smila, Rovno (22 August), Aleksandria, Mohilev-on-the-Dnieper (6 and 7 September) and in many other places where there was incitement to riot. The most serious pogroms occurred at the time of the attempted revolution of October 1905, and the wave of rioting spread to all the most important Jewish centres: Odessa (18 to 21 October) where over 300 persons were killed and thousands injured,[84] Kiev, Kishinev, Romi, Kremenchug, Kamenets-Podolsky, Elizavetgrad, Chernigov, Simferopol, Nikolaev and Ekaterinoslav. In a relatively short time, there were 64 outbreaks in the cities and 626 in the towns and villages, in which 800 Jews lost their lives and thousands were wounded.[85] The last offshoots of these pogroms were in 1906 (in June in Bialystok, with eighty dead, and in August in Sedlets), with the active participation of the police and military. The final cost of these four years was not only hundreds dead, thousands wounded and enormous material damage, but also, and above all, the deep shock experienced and the feeling of hopelessness and lack of expectation of any change in the policy of the autocratic tsarist regime.

There was a resemblance between the 1903 to 1906 wave of pogroms and those of the preceding period; both were the result of systematic incitement against the Jewish population, whether on anti-Semitic lines, or for considerations deemed sufficient by the authorities, or both.[86] The non-intervention by government in the initial stages was still more apparent in the later pogroms, as was the failure to impose serious punishment on rioters brought to trial, and the active participation in the pogroms of police and soldiers. It was also obvious in the 1903 to 1906 pogroms that the decisive role in initiating and organizing the rioting was taken by the anti-Semitic organizations, in collusion with the local authorities, which enjoyed political and financial support from the central power.

I have already indicated the close tie between the pogroms and the blood-libel cases. Interestingly, there were no blood-libel cases during the reign of Alexander III, despite his anti-Jewish policies. This situation changed with the accession of Nicholas II and the increase in the influence of anti-Semitic elements in the administration during his reign. In this period, blood-libel cases began to play an important part in the new Russian anti-Semitic ideology, which reached its peak with the forging of the *Protocols of the Elders of Zion.* The most notorious blood-libel cases, which received wide publicity, were the Blondes affair in Vilna in 1900; the Dubasari and Kishinev affairs in 1902 and 1903; and especially the Beiliss affair in Kiev, which lasted for two years, from 1911 to 1913, and was comparable to the Dreyfus affair in France at the same time.[87] The Beiliss trial proved more conclusively than ever that anti-Semitism had been elevated into a political system in Russia and was being used by the administration and the reactionary forces to bind the nationalist forces together in their fight against oposition to the regime.

During the First World War, while the tsarist regime still existed, a third and final wave of pogroms occurred in a number of places, with both the local population and the retreating armies taking part. However, the greatest suffering was caused by the mass expulsions of the Jewish population.

The policy of expulsions and emigration

As we have seen; the expulsion from places where they were forbidden to reside was a recurring phenomenon in the lives of the Russian Jews. The expulsions in the period dealt with in this chapter, however, surpassed everything that had preceded them.

The complicated body of legislation concerning the right of residence outside the Pale of Settlement, patched with amendments, served as a basis for night-time raids and round-ups of Jewish residents who had become 'illegal' or 'semi-legal' because of changes in their legal status following, for example, a change of occupation. It also served as a convenient instrument for the extortion of bribes, maltreatment, and arbitrary decisions by officials. On 29 March 1891, under a decree of Alexander III, some 30,000 Jews living in Moscow, who had been registered as artisans under regulations dating from Alexander II or had succeeded in infiltrating the city in various ways, were rounded up and expelled, in the biggest and cruellest operation of the kind so far;[88] they had constituted 86% of the Jews in Moscow.[89] This new policy of expulsions was initiated by the new governors of Moscow, the Grand Duke Sergei Alexandrovich, Pobedonostsev, and Istomin, all three known to hate the Jews. Even though the reasons for this measure were not made public, the aim was clear: 'to purge the capital city of Jews'. It was also planned to expel the Jews from Petrograd, but the angry reaction in European countries and in the USA caused the plan to be delayed and in the end it was never implemented.

The harshest expulsions were carried out during the First World War, when the Jews were accused of spying and collaboration with the enemy, and many of them were executed. The ground was prepared for expelling all Jews from the frontier regions by means of an anti-Semitic campaign in the press, with false accusations against whole Jewish communities, in spite of severe military censorship. With the retreat of the Russian army, the expulsions were constantly extended and accelerated until they included the greater part of the Jewish settlement in the Pale.

Even if the expulsions were not directed exclusively against the Jewish population, and were carried out against the background of the war being waged in the region, the trend was clear. The expulsions began on 15 March 1915 and reached their peak on 3 May, when 200,000 Jews of Kovno and Kurland were ordered to leave their homes within forty-eight hours.[90] An estimated total of over 600,000 were expelled, only 5% of whom succeeded in taking their movable possessions with them, 22% being forced to abandon everything, and the remainder saving some of their goods and chattels. The property losses of the Jews who were expelled or who fled of their own accord was estimated at between 350 and 400 million dollars, an enormous sum at that time.[91] Some ministers cautiously opposed the expulsions for the usual reasons: the harm liable to be done to Russia's national interests, and the criticism to be faced from progressive political forces in the Duma, but these calculations carried no weight with the army, led by Grand Duke Nicholas Nikolaievich, who decided to continue the expulsions.

The policy-makers in the administration who framed 'Jewish policy' may have considered the forced movement of Jews from one region to another a temporary and partial solution to the Jewish problem. Their policy on emigration, however, was self-contradictory. On the one hand, the administration was interested in reducing the size of the Jewish population, but on the other, because of the nature of the regime, emigration was a felony under the criminal laws enacted from 1835 to 1857.[92] This duplicity was reflected in the declarations of the heads of state in the early 1880s: Minister of the Interior Ignatyev[93] and State Prosecutor Strelnikov[94] declared that the western frontier was open and the Jews could leave; on the other hand there were reports that the Tsar Alexander III had had meetings with the Jewish bankers H. Ginzburg and A. Zak, suggesting that they use their influence to stop Jewish emigration[95], and S. Polyakov told the meeting of heads of the Jewish *Kehillot* in St Petersburg in 1882 that Ignatyev had demanded an end to attempts to promote Jewish emigration. For Russian citizens, the idea of emigration did not exist.[96]

It was not until 1891 that a change in the attitude of the authorities to Jewish emigration took place, following the criticism of the expulsions from Moscow, and Baron Hirsch's appeal to the Russian authorities to permit the new Jewish Settlement Association (ICA) to organize Jewish emigration to the Argentine. The constantly swelling stream of emigrants after 1904, which included Poles, Finns, Germans, Lithuanians and Latvians as well as Jews, called for legislative and administrative measures. However, differences of opinion between the various ministries resulted in repeated postponements; it was not until 1914 that an Emigration Law was drafted but, because of the war, it was never brought before the State Duma for debate. Without benefit of legislation and despite the administrative obstacles and the large sums levied for passports, the stream of emigration continued uninterrupted. If the average number of Jewish emigrants from 1881 to 1886 was 12,856 annually, in the following five years the figure reached 28,509, and from 1891 to 1910, 44,829 annually. The peak years were 1906 to 1910, with 75,114 emigrants annually. The total of Jewish emigrants from Russia between 1881 and 1914 was about two million,[97] and the size of this Jewish emigration would have been higher if emigrants had been granted facilities by the authorities, and if greater financial assistance had been available from Jewish philanthropic bodies.

Religion, education and culture

Religion, education and culture form the core of Russian Jewish life, and changes in these fields had a significant effect on the existence and evolution of intellectual currents and on reactions to the surrounding society.

RELIGION

The process of secularization was a characteristic of the modernization of the life of Jewish society in Russia. At the end of the nineteenth century the process was still a slow one, in spite of strong forces, both internal and external, which were weakening the traditional framework and threatening its breakdown. The process was accelerated, however, by historical factors operating before the First World War, and in particular the rapid development of Jewish socialist parties, practically all of them anti-religious.

The duplicate structure of the rabbinate continued to exist throughout the historical period covered in this chapter, and it was one of the factors that weakened the influence of religion. A fundamental change took place in the character of the office bearers of the 'official rabbinate' as early as the mid 1880s, because of the application of the 1855 law which provided that the position of 'official rabbi' could be held by high-school graduates, doctors, veterinary surgeons, chemists, lawyers and engineers.[98] This provision created an opening for a large number of persons in the free professions who had failed to make good their chosen callings and found a way out of their difficulties by taking posts in the rabbinate. A situation arose whereby people were chosen for the rabbinate who were completely ignorant of things Jewish and had insufficient knowledge of the Hebrew language.

On the other hand, the political and intellectual changes resulting from the 'storms in the south' (an expression as it were in code for the pogroms in southern Russia) and the crystallization of the Zionist movement produced a new type of 'official rabbi' with a national –Zionist outlook. These new men were to be found among rabbis trained in the old-style *batei midrash*, as well as among younger people who had completed their studies at the universities. Consequently, the tendency among community leaders was to unite to two posts into one, in the person of a rabbi with a broad education, both Jewish and general.[99] For this purpose it was necessary to set up new rabbinical *batei midrash* similar to those in the Jewish Diasporas in the West, or to change the structure of the existing *yeshivot*, so that the new type of rabbi could be trained within their walls. But all attempts made by the heads of an educational society to set up a rabbinical seminary, attempts that began as early as 1888, were defeated by the determined opposition of traditionally observant circles; and the second solution only began to be carried out at the beginning of the twentieth century by Rabbis Reines and Chernovits (the 'Young rabbi').

EDUCATION

Between 1881 and 1917, significant social and economic changes took place in the system of education of Russian Jews, which was being subjected to the influence of Jewish political parties and organizations. Traditional Jewish education was still a central force, but different from what it had been in the previous period. An illustration of this can be obtained from the numbers of pupils in the *heders* (in spite of differences in statistical data). In 1894, the number of pupils in *heders* was 201,964, and that of teachers 13,689; over half (53.8%) of all Russian Jewish children were taught in *heders*.[100] In 1910, there were, according to H. Pialkov,[101] 325,000 *heder* pupils. Even if this is an over-estimation, it seems that the number of pupils learning in *heders* had not declined; this can be explained not only by the strong conservatism of Russian Jewry but also by its political situation and the hostility of the non-Jewish (Russian, Ukrainian and Polish) society, which deterred many from sending their children to general schools. The partial re-organization of the *heders* at the end of the nineteenth century improved the level of the institution, but in general the situation remained as difficult as it had been before.

The most important change in Jewish education came with the creation of the *ḥeder metukan* ('improved' or 'reformed' *ḥeder*) in the latter half of the 1890s. Doubtless the new name contributed to its success, for reform was needed: externally, it was necessary to overcome the administrative difficulties deliberately created by an official policy that aimed at suppressing all nationalist education but was prepared to agree to religious teaching; internally, it was important to weaken resistance among the religious and traditionalist parents to sending their children to Jewish secular schools. The language taught in the *ḥeder metukan* was Hebrew and the method of teaching the 'natural' one – 'Hebrew through Hebrew'. The subjects taught were: Hebrew language and literature, history of the Jewish people, the Bible, and the geography of Erez Yisrael. General subjects like mathematics, general history and the language of the country were taught, but in outline only. As a result, the *ḥeders* were not always able to prepare their pupils adequately for the transition to general studies in government secondary schools; but they were of the utmost national and Zionist importance, for not only did they teach Hebrew subjects in the Hebrew language, but most of the teachers were Zionists, who instilled into their pupils the longing for Erez Yisrael. Another important aspect of the *ḥeder metukan* was that it provided education for girls, for whom separate schools were set up. We lack data on the number of schools of this type and the teaching provided there, but they certainly flourished in the first decade of the twentieth century and existed in most Russian cities and towns despite opposition from both ultra-Orthodox and Yiddishist circles. In 1917 and 1918, a new Hebrew educational institution grew out of the *ḥeder metukan* called 'Tarbut' (culture), secular in character and national in spirit.

There was also a different type of traditional Jewish school, the *Talmud Torah* run by the *Kehillot* under the close surveillance of the authorities, which served mainly the poorer Jews; in spite of their name, these schools also taught a certain number of secular subjects. In 1912 there were 147 of them,[102] with about 100 pupils each,[103] and even before the First World War, the authorities granted these schools permission to teach a number of subjects in Yiddish.

The Chernovits conference of August 1908 declared Yiddish to be the national language of the Jewish people, and Yiddishist circles increased their efforts to set up a network of secular Yiddish-language schools; but they had little success, despite the fact that, according to the 1897 census, more than 97% of all Jews in Russia gave Yiddish as their mother tongue. Although there was an official prohibition on creating new Yiddish-language schools, which remained in force until 1914, the main reason for the failure to set up these schools was strong opposition from the ultra-Orthodox, the Hebraists and Jewish assimilationists. A change took place during the war, when official restrictions were lifted and there was mass Jewish migration to the Districts of Inner Russia, and by 1916 there were 42 Yiddish-language schools outside the Pale of Settlement, having about 6,000 pupils and 130 teachers.[104]

Finally, there were private Jewish schools using Russian-language teaching, which mainly served the wealthy Jews. The number of pupils learning in these schools before the outbreak of the war was 30,000 – that is to say, 7.5% of all Jewish pupils of school age.[105]

The *yeshivot* continued to play a central role in Jewsih secondary and higher education. Other institutions were founded between 1907 and 1917. In 1907, members of the Society for the Propagation of *Haskalah* in Grodno, headed by Aron Kahanshtam and Dr Y. Charna, opened 'pedagogical courses' to train Jewish teachers. in 1917, *batei midrash* for teachers and kindergarten teachers were functioning in Odessa, Kharkov and Moscow. Attempts were made to create a sort of Jewish University for Jewish Studies (*Jüdische Wissenschaft*) with the support of Baron Ginzburg, to follow up courses in 'Orientalism' that were begun in 1907.

During this period, the rate of entry of young Jews into general Russian high schools was the result of two contradictory influences: on the one hand, the process of modernization that was sweeping over Russian Jewry, and on the other, the official government policy of reducing the number of Jews in the general educational system, a policy effected by means of the *numerous clausus* and by official harassment. In 1901, the number of Jewish pupils in state schools was estimated to be 49,000, mainly from well-to-do families.[106] To this must be added a large number of external students.

In 1881 there were 783 Jewish students in higher educational institutions in Russia, comprising 8.8% of all the students in the country, and the Jewish student population reached its highest point in 1886, the 1,856 Jewish students being 14.5% of all students.[107] The policy of quotas introduced in 1887 reduced the percentage, in spite of the great efforts made by the Jews to circumvent it, by petitions, pressures, influence, and bribery. There were still 1,853 Jewish students in 1894 (13.3% of all students) but by 1902 the number was down to 1,250 (7% of all students). The general improvement in admitting Jewish students to higher educational institutions, which had begun between 1905 and 1907, now raised their number to 4,266 (12% of all students). But renewed reaction was also expressed regarding Jewish admission to the universities, and in 1913 the figure of Jewish students in all institutions of higher learning was again down to only 2,505 (7.3% of all students in the country). It is important to remember that this policy led to a constant increase in the number of Jewish students from Russia entering universities in Europe, mainly in Switzerland, Germany, Austria, and France. It is estimated that in 1902 and 1903 between 1,895 and 2,405 Jewish students were studying at universities outside Russia, that is to say, more than twice as many as those studying in Russia itself in those years.[108] This phenomenon had important social and political consequences: some of these students became politically active and contributed greatly to the formation of Russian political parties, both Jewish and general.

CULTURE

There was an unprecedented blossoming of Jewish culture in Russia between 1881 and 1917, as a result of expanded general Jewish education, economic and social changes and the extraordinary growth and extension of the Jewish press in three languages (Yiddish, Hebrew and Russian) to serve the needs of the newly developing political parties and organizations.

Most Jews had at least a passive comand of Hebrew and the language enjoyed a renaissance at the end of the nineteenth century. Periodicals appeared in Hebrew on a level comparable to Russian publications of the day: *Ha-shiloah*, edited by Ahad Ha'am; *Ha-tsfirah*, edited by Nahum Sokolow; the daily paper *Ha-yom*, edited by Kantor. The Warsaw publishing firms Ahiassaf and Tushiyah enabled Jewish authors who wrote in Hebrew to have their works published in Yiddish as well, and facilitated the appearance of a wide range of party-political publications. Special importance attached to the publication of the *Yiddisher folks-bibliotek* of Shalom Aleikhem and the *Yidisher bibliotek* of Y.L. Perets. In the Russian language, the periodical *Voshkod* 'Sunrise' secured a central place for itself in political and cultural life from 1881 to 1906; the outstanding scientific–historical publications *Perezhitoe* and *Evreiskaya starina* appeared in

1908 – the former ceasing publications in 1917, but the latter continuing to exist in the USSR until 1930. Before the First World War there were thirteen daily papers appearing in Yiddish and two in Hebrew, but during the war government policy led to their being closed down, and it was not until after the February Revolution that an enormous increase in the number of Jewish newspapers took place. Between 1917 and 1918, 171 newspapers and periodicals appeared, 81 of them in Yiddish, 80 in Russian and 10 in Hebrew.[109]

The most striking cultural advance was the flowering of Jewish literature in all three languages, many of the writers being bilingual or even trilingual: Bialik, Perets and Shneur all wrote in Hebrew and Yiddish, Shimon Frug in Russian and Yiddish, and the historian Shimon Dubnov in all three languages. Secular Jewish literature came into being very largely under the impact of the *Haskalah* movement. It met the needs of the increasing number of Jews who could no longer identify themselves whole-heartedly and unconditionally with Jewish religious culture. The numerous social and political divisions among Russian Jews at the end of the nineteenth century also gave a powerful impetus to the creation of this trilingual Jewish literature, rich both in form and content, and modern; for example, the poetry of Bialik with its national inspiration, its combination of lyric power and the spirit of the ancient prophets of Israel; or the nature poetry of Shaul Chernihovsky, overflowing with romantic vitality.

In spite of the veto of 1883 on the establishment of a Jewish theatre, the emigration from Russia of some of the best actors, and the prolonged opposition by both the ultra-Orthodox and the assimilationists, a professional Jewish theatre began to develop.[110] There was a steadily growing audience interested in having a Jewish theatre and seeing Jewish plays at a satisfactory literary and professional level. The transition from the popular historical operettas of Goldfaden can be traced through adaptations by Y. Gordon of European plays, to the production of original stage plays by Shalom Aleikhem, Asch, Pinsky, Perets, Hirshbein, Nomberg, Vaiter and others.

There was also rapid development in historical research in this period. Historical, ethnographic and demographic research was given impetus with the establishment of the Ethnographic–Historical Society in 1908 by eminent researchers in these fields – Dubnov, Tsinberg, Leshchinsky, Rappoport-Ansky, Kulischer, Pozner, Shterenberg, and many others. Apart from scientific periodicals, the two biggest research undertakings were the publication of the *Jewish Encyclopaedia* in Russian, in sixteen volumes between 1908 and 1913, and the preparation of a series on Jewish history by the Mir publishers, only two volumes of which appeared, in 1914 and in 1915, when the enterprise had to be stopped because of the war.

All in all, the growth of Jewish national culture in this period was astonishing. Under conditions of oppression and discrimination, pogroms and poverty, with sharp internal contradictions producing deep fissures in the social structure, the national culture grew and flourished and, became the basis of modern Jewish culture throughout the world.

Intellectual currents and political organizations

The variety of intellectual and political opinions among Russian Jews and the resultant speedy growth of party organizations, were the product of many complex forces operating simultaneously. The most important was the shock administered by the serious riots and pogroms of the 1880s, with its catalytic effect – the deepest shock being the indifference of the Russian intelligentsia, whom the Jewish *maskilim* had regarded as their allies. Second, the Jewish intelligentsia were influenced by the national and revolutionary movements in Europe and in Russia itself. Third, the revolutionary political changes of the years 1905 to 1907 and from 1917 onwards at last opened the way for broad political, social and cultural activity. Fourth, the sharpening internal conflict within the Jewish population weakened the Jewish social structure still further and called for an attempt to organize Jewish society in the new way. Finally, there was an urgent inner need to find some radical solution to the problems of the Russian Jews and the Jewish intelligentsia was impelled to propose lines of action based on new doctrines.

Because of their variety, it is difficult to classify political and intellectual trends in Russia; but it is possible to speak of four main currents which assumed well-defined party-political forms in Russian Jewry from 1881 to 1917: Zionism, socialism, liberalism and Orthodoxy.

ZIONISM

The rudiments of Zionist thinking appeared in Russia before the 1880s, in the writings of David Gordon, Perez Smolenskin and

Eliezer Ben Yehudah. But for these to develop into a fully-fledged Zionist movement, a specific stimulus was needed, and it came early in the 1880s when the 'storms in the south' (the pogroms in southern Russia) led to a national awakening.[111] Since the 1890s, and mainly in the first decade of the twentieth century, three main ideological schools have formed within Russian Zionism: liberal-centre; socialist; and Orthodox.

Zionism and the liberal centre.   This 'centre' or 'general' Zionism was represented by Leon Pinsker and Aḥad Ha'am (Asher Ginzberg). Pinsker, a doctor by profession, decorated for his military services in the Crimean War, and a leader of the *maskilim* in Odessa, had been an enthusiastic supporter of the assimilationist solution; but for him too the pogroms of 1871 in Odessa began a process of awakening which reached its peak with the pogroms of the 1880s, and resulted in his anonymous essay, written in German, 'Auto-emancipation', published in 1882.[112] Most of the ideas in this essay were not new but they had never been put together as clearly and systematically. His analysis of the phenomenon of anti-Semitism led Pinsker to conclude that it was a hereditary disease which could only be cured by removing its cause. The solution had to be both radical and implemented by the Jews themselves. Just as the peoples among whom the Jews were living had secured their own national emancipation, so the Jews' national crystallization and concentration within a state of their own had to be an act of self-liberation. At this stage, Pinsker was not yet a territorialist, but became a Zionist under the influence of Lilienblum and Mandelshtam. When a large number of small local clubs or 'unions' came together, at a first 'Lovers of Zion' conference at Kattowitz in 1884, he headed the new movement.

   In contrast to the 'practical Zionists' – Pinsker, Lilienblum and Ussishkin – Aḥad Ha'am founded a 'spiritual Zionism' which criticized not only the Zionism of 'day-to-day action' but also Herzl's 'political Zionism'. According to Aḥad Ha'am, Erez Yisrael could not offer a solution for the material problems of the Jewish people, nor was there any practical prospect of gathering all the Jews there; but Erez Yisrael could become an asylum and even a 'model', and as such, a centre of redemption for the Diaspora. Convinced of the importance of forming a new generation, Aḥad Ha'am founded the 'Sons of Moses' League in 1889 on the pattern of an élitist order, moulding its members for spiritual leadership of the people. In fact, although short-lived (lasting only until 1896) and having less than 200 members, his League made a real contribution to the progress of Hebrew culture.

Aḥad Ha'am's criticisms of the Zionist movement led to the convening in Warsaw in 1898 of the first over-all Zionist conference in Russia, which was attended by representatives of 373 clubs or unions. The heated discussions between secular and Orthodox Zionists over cultural activity at this conference, and at a second one in Minsk in 1902, helped to bring about the creation of the socialist and Orthodox Zionist movements.

Zionist-socialism. This movement first took shape among the various clubs or unions of 'Lovers of Zion'. Naḥman Syrkin was its outstanding theoretician; in 1892 he published *The Jewish Question and the Socialist Jewish State*, written in German, in which he sought a synthesis of Zionist–national elements and socialist elements. Influence by socialist circles and using Marxist dialectics, Syrkin analysed the situation of the Jewish people: he concluded that a socialist Jewish State would be capable *a priori* of solving the Jewish problem and should be established in Ereẓ-Yisrael. Syrkin published an appeal to Jewish youth in 1901, calling for the immediate creation of a mass Jewish social-democratic organization to work for the establishment of this state.[113]

Zionist-socialist organizations named 'Workers of Zion' (*Poalei-Ẓion*) already existed in Russia at the end of the nineteenth century. The Minsk branch laid the main stress on Zionism; in southern Russia the stress on the socialist component was stronger. These two branches united at Poltava in 1906 and set up the Workers' Social-Democratic Party (*Poalei-Ẓion*) under the leadership of Ber Borochov, an original political thinker. His views were a synthesis of Marxist–Bogdanovist socialism and Zionism. He affirmed that Jewish migration would flow to Israel by a spontaneous process of natural attraction. The Zionist revolution would be carried out by the Jewish proletariat through class struggle.

Orthodox (religious) Zionism. Rabbi Mohilever, a religious leader among the 'Lovers of Zion', proclaimed an Orthodox religious Zionism fairly early on, but an independent, organized, religious Zionist movement did not take shape till 1902, when a religious–national federation was established, calling itself 'Mizrahi' – an acronym of the Hebrew words for 'spiritual centre' – (*Merkaz ruḥani*). Its leaders were Rabbis Reines and Yaveẓ, who wrote the programme of the new movement, describing Zionism as a triple bond of Torah, Israel and Zion.

Before the October 1917 Revolution, the Zionist movement as a whole had around 300,000 members, distributed in 1,200 towns. In that year, the Zionist won an outstanding victory in the various elections to the Jewish *Kehillot*, becoming the majority of representatives of the organized Jewish public.

SOCIALISM

The Jewish intelligentsia was inclined to support the socialist movement. The number of adherents might decline for short periods but increased again under the influence of the pogroms. The actual number of Jews who joined socialist parties, either directly or through Jewish socialist movements, was not great and came mainly from among the students; but individual Jews played an important and sometimes decisive part in the leadership of the three main socialist parties – the SR (Socialist Revolutionaries), the Mensheviks, and the Bolsheviks – and were to be found in other movements as well.[114] The most important phenomenon, however, was the birth and swift growth of the Jewish socialist nationally minded parties.

There were four main Jewish socialist movements: *Am olam* ('The World People'); the *Bund*; the Zionist–Socialist Workers' Party (SS); and the Socialist Workers' Party ('Seimists').

'*Am Olam*'.   This movement came into being, just as 'Lovers of Zion' did, in the wake of the pogroms of 1881 and the resultant controversies over emigration. Still weak in organization and with an undefined ideological platform resembling that of the Russian Narodniks, the movement comprised students and young workers.[115] The theoretical foundations were mainly anarchist or Tolstoyan: national and spiritual rebirth, and healing and normalization of the economic structure of the Jewish masses, with particular emphasis on work on the land, in communal settlements to be established in the USA. The membership of the movement seems to have been less than a thousand and its influence was felt in Russia for a short time only. Its main achievement was the creation of the Jewish labour movement in the USA.

The 'Bund'. This was the most important Jewish workers' socialist party, and was established in 1897 by the unification of workers' and intellectual groups in Vilna, Minsk and other towns.[116] Formally, the *Bund* was a section of the general Russian Social-Democrats and accepted that party's line on the national question. From its inception, the *Bund* affirmed that the Jewish people as a whole and the Jewish proletariat in particular had their own specific interests and therefore needed a special organization of their own, However, it was not until the fourth congress of the *Bund* in Bialystok in May 1901 that the party formulated its programme for national cultural autonomy, founded on the 'extra-territorial' principle, and became a component of the Russian Social-democratic Party *qua* federation of national parties. However, the demand for 'extra-territorial' national autonomy soon produced a schism and the *Bund* left the Social-democratic Party in 1903. Membership was 5,600 in 1900 and reached a peak of 30,000 in the years 1903 to 1905.[117]

The *Bund* was not only a political party but also a trade union, school, militant fighting organization, and spiritual home for the Russian Jewish worker; this was the reason for its success. It also had to face some difficulties: first, its position between social-democracy and Zionism, constantly criticized by each; second, the need to decide between struggle within Russia and emigration; and finally, the urgent need to find an immediate solution to the miserable condition of Jewish workers in Russia.

In the reactionary years from 1907 to 1916, the *Bund* declined in size and strength and its activities were reduced.[118] With the 1917 Revolution, it recovered rapidly – by December of the same year, its membership had jumped to 33,700, organized in 302 branches.[119] The political line of the *Bund* at this time was Menshevik in general policy and *Bundist* in the national sphere, that is, for Yiddish culture, and against Jewish religion and Zionism.

The Zionist–socialist Workers' Party (SS). Though influenced by the ideas of Syrkin, and despite the addition of the word 'Zionist' to its name, this was a territorialist socialist party and not a Zionist one. It was formed in 1904 under the leadership of Yaakov Leshchinsky, V. Latski-Bartoldi, Sh. Niger, and V. Chernikhov, all of whom wanted to create a Jewish socialist party on orthodox Marxist principles.[120] This party fought the *Bund* with fierce determination, differing from it on all the basic assumptions regarding the solution of the Jewish question. According to this party, there was no possibility of normal economic development of the Jewish people in Russia, since the changes taking place in its social structure were not in the direction of proletarianization but of pauperization of the *petit-bourgeois*. Nor would emigration be a cure for the economic ills of the Jews, because Jewish emigrants in the countries of immigration were taken into marginal occupations. The only solution remaining, therefore, was to find a suitable territory where it would be possible to construct a new economic and social structure. Thus, in spite of its strictly orthodox socialism, this party joined the Territorialist Organization (ITO) when the Jewish writer Zangwill founded it in England in 1907.

In the early revolutionary period, this party had enjoyed considerable influence in workers' circles through its trade-union activity. In April 1917, at the party's sixth congress, the view was expressed that a territorial solution would come about after the achievement of national autonomy in the places where Jews lived, and, when the time was ripe, there would also be a territorial concentration which would constitute a cultural centre (similar, perhaps, to the spiritual centre advocated by Aḥad Ha'am). This change in policy enabled the party to join the Jewish Socialist Workers' Party in May 1917 and form the United Jewish Socialist Workers (UJSW). This new party received about 8% of all Jewish votes in the various elections that took place at the time, for both Jewish and non-Jewish bodies.

The Jewish Socialist Workers' Party ('Seimists'). This movement developed from the 'Re-birth' circles of the years 1904 to 1906, its spiritual progenitor being Ḥaim Zhitlowsky. The leaders were A. Rozin (Ben-Adir), Dr M. Zilberfarb, N. Shits and M. Ratner. Ideologically, this party was very close to the SR and was not convinced by a Marxist solution to the Jewish question in Russia. It saw future progress in two stages: first, a struggle for national autonomy on a federative basis, with an elected representative institution with wide powers (like the Seim) at the head of each nationality; later, they argued, it would be possible to work for a territorial concentration of the Jewish people.[121]

LIBERALISM
The Russian autocratic regime, flawed by anti-Semitism – both official and popular – presented fertile soil for the growth of liberalism among those of the Jewish population who wanted to fit into the

society around them without losing their national identity. The Jewish intelligentsia was more attracted to the radical groups seeking immediate solutions for the material distress of the Jews, and Jewish national survival. A number of liberal groups and parties took form in the years 1905 to 1917, and were loosely connected with each other in the 'League for full and equal rights for Jews' established in 1905.

The 'Volkspartei' (Jewish People's Party).   This party was founded by the Jewish historian Shimon Dubnov, who drafted the party's political manifesto.[122] In the general part of the programme, Dubnov based his ideas on those of the 'Cadets' (Constitutional Democratic Party), while his national programme was based on the 'autonomist' doctrine formulated in his *Letters on the old and new Jewry.* The basic unit of national autonomy was to be the Jewish Kehillah, of which every Jew would automatically be a member as long as he did not declare that he wished to leave it. The Kehillah would be headed by the Kehillah Council, and a League of Kehillot would coordinate activities in all the countries. This League would be governed by a congress to be convened at set intervals. From its inception, this party was little more than a small group of public personalities drawn from the intelligentsia, with limited influence on the general Jewish public. Thus, in the election to 193 Kehillot in the Ukraine in the summer of 1917, this party succeeded in winning only 3% of the Kehillot.

The 'Volksgruppe'.   Founded in 1906, this was an even smaller group of liberal personalities within the 'Cadets'. It was headed by Vinaver, Gruzenberg and Sliozberg, the most eminent Jewish jurists in Russia. Their demands in the national sphere were limited: equal civil rights, independence of religious institutions, and the right to learn Jewish languages (Yiddish and Hebrew) in the schools, but did not include what was the central demand of most of the Jewish parties at this time – national autonomy. In the elections, this group received only one percent of the votes.

RELIGIOUS PARTIES

The religiously minded groups were less organized than other intellectual–political movements, but the general politicization of Jewish life, the weakening of the Kehillot structure and of the traditional religiousness, and the sharpening of internal social struggles led them to become party-political organizations.

The rudiments of political organization can be seen in the establishment of a clandestine league aiming mainly at arousing a protest movement abroad, against the anti-Jewish policy of the Russian government. This movement called itself 'Two-edged Sword' (presumably a reference to Psalm 149, verses 6–7, 'with a two-edged sword ... to wreak vengeance on the *goi-im*').[123] This was a group of ultra-observant Jews, who also organized the 'Black Office' in Kovno to combat reformist ideas in Jewish life, general (i.e. not traditional) education, and the 'Love of Zion' movement.

A different kind of organization was produced by two sectarian movements among religious Jews: 'Biblical Spiritual Fraternity' and 'New Israel'.[124] The former, established in Elizavetgrad on 2 January 1881, sought a common ground between religion, intellect, and science. Led by Yaakov Gordon, it received some government recognition and existed until 1891. The sect inclined towards a *rapprochement* with Christianity. It spoke of 'spiritual participation' but also of actual cooperative living in agriculture. The other sect, 'New Israel', was founded in Odessa in the same year, 1881, by Yaakov Prilutsker, a teacher, and Joseph Rabinowich, who wanted to reform the Jewish religion. In the end, most of its members went over to Russian Evangelism. The political influence of these two sects was negligible and the number of members, including their families, does not seem to have exceeded a thousand.

'Religious Zionism' has been described above. Jewish religious organization in the proper sense of the term began later, during the First World War. The religious party, 'Masoret Veḥerut' ('Tradition and Freedom') was founded in April 1917, its centre being Moscow. The political programme demanded the 'grant of national autonomy, the Sabbath as a day of rest, government assistance for the Kehillot'. Similar groups were created in other cities, mostly having Hebrew names with Biblical associations: 'Neẓaḥ yisrael' in Petrograd; 'Knesset yisrael', 'Shomrei torah', 'Edat yisrael', 'Jerusalem', 'Agudat yisrael'. Fifty of these groups, representing religious Jewry, held their first congress in July 1917. Their demands included an eight-hour working day,, the right to strike, freedom of conscience, agrarian reform, and support for religious education – on the whole, demands resembling those of the Jewish socialist parties.

The contradiction between the Zionist religious groups and the non-Zionist ones soon came to the fore. Ultra-orthodox circles viewed Zionists as dangerous and heretical, as if they were 'an attempt to force the hand of God' – all non-practising Jews were in effect 'heretics'. These circles therefore decided to appear independently in the various political elections that took place at the time and this produced a split in the religious camp. The split gradually disappeared, however, under Soviet rule, which made little distinction between religious parties, Zionist or non-Zionist.

Relations with other Jewish Diasporas in the world

The tendency already perceived in the previous period to extend relations between the Jews of Russia and Jews in the rest of the world was strangest in the years 1881 to 1917. The reciprocal relations referred to in the preceding sections of this chapter were constantly expanded. What concerns us here is the assistance extended by the Jews in the 'outside' world to the Jews of Russia in their ordeals. The pogroms of the 1880s had strong repercussions, producing widespread, energetic protests against the oppression of Russian Jewry. A mass protest meeting was held in London on 1 February 1882, called by Jewish and Christian personalities and organizations and attended by great numbers of people.[125] This meeting made a profound impression and led to the establishment of a 'Russo-Jewish Committee' in England, to assist Russian Jewry. In 1891, Lucien Wolf began publishing a special periodical devoted entirely to this cause, called *Darkest Russia*, and he had a meeting with von Pleve, Minister of the Interior and the real power in the Russian government, on 23 October 1903.[126]

The difficult economic situation and the pogroms of the 1900s led to great activity on the part of German and Austrian Jews. A Jewish Aid Society, 'Ezra', brought together representatives of the Jewish organizations in different countries for action on behalf of Russian Jewry. After the pogroms of October 1905, two large meetings were held, one in Brussels, and the other in Frankfurt, both in January 1906.[127] Attempts were also made to influence the Russian royal family through the kings and princes of Western countries, especially those related to the House of Romanov; but these efforts, unlike those of the 1880s, had no real effect.

It was the American Jewish organizations, and particularly the American Jewish Committee, that initiated most of the activities on behalf of Russian Jews during this period. Exploiting the discrimination by the Russian authorities against Jews who were American citizens, the committee succeeded in influencing President Taft, so that in 1911 he threatened not to renew the 1832 American–Russian trade treaty if discrimination did not cease. This threat could have had great influence, but the war and the Revolution pushed it into the background. If we recall the plight of the Jewish emigrants from Russia, who left their homes and all their possessions in search of a new life, we shall understand how important was the help afforded them by worldwide Jewish organizations.

2

The Jews of the Soviet Union: the years of construction, 1917–1939

The heading 'years of construction' should not be taken to imply that this period was entirely constructive for Soviet Jews. In fact, much damage was done to autonomous Jewish communities, to the Jewish religion, to Hebrew culture and to the Zionist and Socialist Parties; but when the achievements of this period are compared with the two later ones, which were unparalleled in their destruction of the Jewish nation, the choice of heading will be vindicated.

Soviet historiography, followed to some extent by the West, divides this period into three sub-periods: war communism, 1918 to 1921; the New Economic Policy, 1921 to 1927; and the period of industrialization and collectivization, 1928 to 1939. From the Jewish point of view, a different periodization is needed based on an analysis of official policy on nationalities and on internal Jewish national processes, as follows:

(1) 1917 to 1922: the search for solutions of the nationalities question;

(2) 1923 to 1932: the period of *korenization* (implanting, entrenching) in the new policy on nationalities;

(3) 1933 to 1939: the campaign against 'nationalist deviations', and the eclipse of autonomy for extra-territorial national minorities.

SOVIET NATIONALITY THEORY AND THE JEWS

For a state like the Soviet Union, based *par excellence* on ideology in the first period of its existence, a scrutiny of its nationality theory is necessary if we are to understand its official policy towards nationalities in general and the extra-territorial national minorities in particular.

The main issues to be considered in studying the Soviet doctrine on nationalities and the attitude taken, directly and indirectly, to the Jewish question are as follows: did the Soviet Jews constitute a nationality similar to other nationalities in the multi-national Soviet state? Was the Soviet Jews' juridical–political status determined according to the Marxist–Leninist theory of nationalities, or solely in line with pragmatic political calculations? And lastly, was there in fact any fixed Soviet policy on this question?

There is no doubt that Marxist theoreticians were engrossed in the Jewish question, starting with Marx himself, who devoted one of his earliest essays to the subject. A complicated question, whose anomalies made containing it within a rigid, theoretical framework difficult, it offered a serious challenge and became a permanent stumbling-block. Marx treated the Jewish question on the plane of religious emancipation, in the general category of alienation (of which religion, according to him, is an extreme form)[1]; but Lenin and Stalin used ethnic patterns and terminology. Both Lenin and Stalin were, however, consistent followers of the line denying the existence of a Jewish nationality. Faithful to his mentor, Marx, Lenin made an early declaration that the Jews did not constitute a people, but were a historical survival perpetuated by anti-Semitism; he fiercely attacked not only Zionism but also the *Bund*, because in his opinion it had fallen victim to the reactionary Zionist idea of a 'Jewish nationality'.[2] Lenin based his ideas on those of Kautsky, affirming that the Jews no longer existed as a people, since it was inconceivable that a people should exist without either a territory of its own or a common language.[3] So nothing remained for the *Bund*, Lenin argued, except to propound a special nationality for the Russian Jews, their language 'jargon' and their history – the Pale of Settlement.[4] It followed that the idea of a Jewish people would not withstand scientific criticism and was politically reactionary.[5] The Jews, Lenin concluded were nothing but a sect.[6]

Stalin repeated Lenin's assertions more briefly and in grosser terms in his pamphlet, 'Marxism and the Nationality Question'. According to him, the Jews were a nationality only on paper, Zionism was a reactionary bourgeois movement and the Yiddish language a mere jargon. Given this state of affairs, Stalin argued, 'the demand for national autonomy for Russian Jews is something of a curiosity – proposing autonomy for a people without a future and whose very existence still remains to be proved'.[7]

Lenin, Stalin and all the other Bolshevik leaders were, therefore, firmly opposed both to the Zionist solution of the Jewish question and also to the solution that the *Bund* proposed, according to the formula accepted by the Austrian Social-Democratic Party – cultural national autonomy. Under this programme, all the citizens of the state who had different nationalities would be organized – without reference to their place of residence – in national units, responsible for conducting their own educational and cultural affairs, while subserving the political and economic unity of the state. Lenin called this solution, propounded by the socialist leaders, 'bourgeois culture', invented to dazzle the eyes of the proletariat; it would mean intensified nationalism and separatism and would exacerbate the differences already existing between nationalities living together in one state. The only solution that Lenin would accept at this date was self-determination, and even that in theory rather than practice, so nothing remained for extra-territorial peoples but assimilation. The generally held belief that socialism would be a panacea for the nationalist contradictions inherent in the capitalist system and would solve all the problems connected with the nationality question was still alive after the October Revolution. In the new circumstances, however, it was impossible to remain content with this abstract approach; a pragmatic response had to be found to the rising demands of the different nationalities within the new socialist state. The solution found for the extra-territorial minorities was a mostly unsuccessful copy of the *Bund* doctrine. An attempt was made to combine two contradictory doctrines: one, national cultural autonomy on the extra-territorial principle, and the other, the Leninist–Stalinist theory of regional autonomy on the territorial principle. This attempt was pragmatic and bore within it the confusions and inconsistencies that were to beset Soviet policy on the nationalities question.

The Evsektsia leaders, particularly those who came from the ranks of the *Bund*, knew that when the convenient conjuncture provided by the twelfth Communist Party congress's decision to pursue *korenization* ('implantation' of the national minorities) came to an end, as it was bound to do, this would also end Jewish national 'statehood', which lacked a solid territorial basis. They knew the Leninist–Marxist ideology on nationalities too well not to have grasped that only the grant of a territory to the Soviet Jews, and their concentration in this territory, would make it possible to transfer them from the 'morbid' and 'dribbling away' category (to use Stalin's graphic phrases in 1921) to the more honourable category of real nationalities; hence the Evsektsia leaders' increasing exertions for a 'Jewish republic in the Soviet Union'.[8] Efforts to have a Jewish republic established in the Crimea were nullified by the opposition of the local population, and the authorities' obvious unwillingness to hand over this region for Jewish settlement. The Birobidzhan experiment was destined to failure from the outset.[9]

In the 1920s, there were two opposing theories among the Soviet rulers as to the solution of the Jewish question: most of the leaders of the Communist Party, including Stalin, favoured of assimilationism; the main representative of the anti-assimilationists was Kalinin. Anti-assimilationism vanished in the late 1930s after the changes in the party and the state, and Stalin's 1913 definition of nationality was restored: 'A nationality is a fixed human community existing historically on the basis of a common language, common territory, common economic structure, and a psychic structure expressed in a common culture.'[10] This definition, refusing the title of nationality to all ethnic groups lacking even one of the four features automatically excluded the Jews from the category of nationality.

THE JURIDICAL–POLITICAL STATUS OF THE JEWS

The problematic nature of the Jewish question was exemplified not only in the Soviet theory of nationalities developed in the years 1903 to 1929, but also in the great number of constitutional documents adopted in the 1920s, based on this theory, with necessary adjustments. These documents fall into three main groups: Communist Party resolutions; constitutions and declarations of Independence; laws, regulations, decrees and government resolutions.

Communist Party Resolutions

Resolutions of the Communist Party of the Soviet Union and of the various republics laid the foundations of Soviet nationalities policy: under the Soviet regime, party resolutions were not only politically important but were recognized as legislative acts.

Four of the six party congresses held from 1917 to 1923 dealt fully with the nationalities problem. The first two (the seventh and eighth congresses) dealt with it theoretically when preparing the new party platform; while the other two (the tenth congress in 1921 and the twelfth in 1923) tried to solve the problem practically: one resolution of the tenth congress was concerned with extra-territorial minorities, the examples cited being the Latvians, the Esthonians, the Poles and the Jews. Clause 4 laid down that these nationalities must be helped to develop their free nationality.[11]

A resolution adopted at the twelfth congress was more important; for the first time, a definite plan was adopted to solve the problem of national minorities.[12] Members of the Evsektsia Central Bureau were very active when the resolution of the twelfth congress was drawn up, and even helped to draft one of its main clauses.[13] The other party congresses held between 1924 and 1939 (the thirteenth to the eighteenth) added nothing to the rights of national minorities. From the sixteenth congress, in 1930, onwards, however, all the resolutions dealing with the nationalities question were increasingly unfavourable to the nationalities' rights, since they were concerned with the need to fight 'local nationalism', that is, to cut back the rights granted to the minorities in the 1920s.

These were party resolutions on the all-Soviet level. The way they were transferred to the level of the republics and the local level is important. We have chosen the Republic of the Ukraine, where the majority of Soviet Jews lived, for this purpose, since the solution of the nationalities problem was most comprehensive there.

The first major resolution on the nationalities question was passed by the Central Committee of the Communist Party of the Ukraine on 6 February 1922, dealing mainly with the majority nationality, the Ukrainians. Regarding the national minorities, the most important resolution was that adopted at the seventh congress, calling for an energetic fight against the *petit-bourgeois* parties which had gained strength among the Jews and the Germans in the republic.[14] A resolution adopted by the Central Committee in 1925 stated that the nationalities policy must be applied to national minorities in the Ukraine in the following spheres: distribution of national administrative units; establishment of law-courts in the national minorities' mother-tongues; provisions of textbooks for nationalities' schools and extension of the party network of mother-tongue schools.[15] A resolution adopted in 1927 regarding work among the national minorities called for an increase in the number of party and Komsomol members in the minorities' areas.[16]

Constitutions and declarations of independence

The first policy resolution of the Soviet government on the nationalities problem was adopted in November 1917, only a few days after the Revolution broke out. It was proclaimed as a 'Declaration of Rights of the Peoples of Russia', and laid down the four principles on which future Soviet policy was to be based. It is the fourth principle that particularly concerns us, a declaration on 'free development for the national minorities and ethnic groups among the population residing on Russian territory'.[17]

The Constitution of the Russian Soviet Republic of July 1918 (Clause 22), the Constitution of Belorussia of February 1919 (Clause 15) and the Constitution of the Ukraine of March 1919 (Clause 32) all promised equal rights for all citizens, irrespective of racial and national affiliation. They laid down that the grant of any privileges on the basis of such affiliation, any repression of national minorities or limitation of equal rights was opposed to the basic Constitution of the Republic.[18]

The Declaration of Independence of Belorussia on 1 August 1920 is important in this context; it stated *inter alia*: 'Full equality of rights is secured for all the languages (Belorussian, Russian, Polish and Yiddish) in relations with government institutions and with the organizations and institutions of nationality education and socialist education.'[19] Great importance attached to this Declaration, which was signed by representatives of the Communist Parties and organizations of Belorussia (among them A. Veinshtein, representing the *Bund*) and was intended to provide a basis for the solution of the nationalities problem in this Republic. In the second Constitution of Belorussia, adopted on 14 April 1927, detailed provisions were laid down (Clauses 20, 21, 23) affirming the rights of national minorities; these included the right to establish nationality soviets in places where the national minority constituted a majority of the local population, and the right to free use of the mother-tongue at meetings, in the law courts, in government institutions and in public life. Belorussia was also the only republic where the Constitution guaranteed not only equality for the national minorities but also equal rights for all the languages – Belorussian, Yiddish, Russian and Polish.[20]

Laws, regulations, decrees and government resolutions

Constitutions are usually brief documents covering only the most general matters of administration. The constitutions of the republics did not lay down detailed provisions to ensure the rights of national minorities; this was done through laws and other measures implemented by the authorized institutions of different republics; their measures in defence of the national minorities also varied. The three that concern us are the Russian, Ukrainian and Belorussian Republics, where, according to the 1926 census, 97.9% of the Soviet Jews were living. The Resolutions concerning national minorities were mostly adopted only in the Republics of the Ukraine and Belorussia (with 76.1% of the Soviet Jews), while in the Russian Republic the laws and regulations on the use of the national language in schools, law-courts and local administrative bodies were directed to protecting the nationalities that constituted a majority in the republic or in a given autonomous district (and not the minority).[21] The reasons for this will be explained later; here I shall briefly list the documents that laid the foundation for equal rights for all the languages and also led to the establishment of special administrative institutions for the nationalities.

The first Code of Criminal Law Procedure (13 September 1922) decreed that a trial had to be conducted in one of the two languages of the State – Ukrainian and Russian – or in the language of the majority local population.[22] The Decrees of the All-Ukraine Central Executive Committee and the Council of People's Commissars of the Ukraine of 27 July 1923 laid down in detail the status of the different languages in the Republics, confirming equal rights for all the languages of the nationalities in the Ukraine and the right of every citizen to use his mother-tongue in his dealings with the administrative institutions and public organizations. What was new was the affirmation with regard to the Ukrainian language. Ukrainian had had a status equal to Russian from 1919 to 1922, but now under the new Decree (of 1 August 1923), Ukrainian was given preference. Even so, Russian became the most widely spoken language, because of its cultural and political importance. As regards the languages of the minority nationalities, the Decree stated that the language of the national minority would be used in all the administrative territorial units (provinces, districts, village soviets) where this minority constituted the majority of the local population. In places where no one minority had an absolute majority, the authorities would use the language of the nationality which had a relative majority.[23] These clear and detailed resolutions and decrees might be thought sufficient to implement the nationalities policy of the Ukraine, but this was not so. The Russificatory trends were so strong and the execution of the policy of Ukrainization so slow that the highest institutions of the republic had frequently to revert to the problem.

On 10 April and 16 July 1925 the Central Executive Committee and the Council of People's Commissars of the Ukraine adopted two Resolutions on implementing Ukrainization. They contained nothing new, and were only intended to enforce the carrying out of earlier decisions. Regulations issued on 22 July 1927 were the most detailed ever to be adopted in the Soviet Union on equality of languages – there were seventy-two clauses. They can also be seen as the culmination of the new nationalities' policy inaugurated at the twelfth Communist Party congress. The more important clauses were 1 to 8, which affirmed the equality of the languages and provided effective guarantees for their use in public life.[24]

In Belorussia the enactment of legislation on national minorities was undertaken later than in the Ukraine; probably the first step was the Decree of the Central Committee of 15 July 1924, which reaffirmed the equality of the four official languages: Belorussian, Yiddish, Polish and Russian. The Executive Committee called on the Belorussian government to take appropriate steps for the practical implementation of the policy. There were some surprising provisions in this decree; for example, clause 2 stated that because the Belorussian population was the largest, the Belorussian language was designated as the principal language of the State trade union and social institutions. Clause 10 stated that all the basic laws of the Republic would be published in all four languages, but other legislative documents only in Belorussian and Russian.[25]

The most important document of all for the entire Soviet Federation, was the Resolution of the third Soviet Congress of 20 May 1925, which had a whole section devoted to national minorities. This Resolution provided *inter alia* that the Central Executive Committee of the Soviet Union was to take appropriate measures in the following areas; co-option of representatives of the national minorities on to all Soviet elective institutions and creation of a special soviet for large national-minority populations, using the mother-tongue and special schools and law-courts.[26]

The juridical–political status of Soviet Jews was determined by a temporary compromise between the Marxist–Leninist doctrine, denying them the status of a nation, and the pragmatic–conjunctural approach of the 1920s. Like all compromises, this created a paradoxical situation. On the one hand, the Jews were recognized as a territorial national unit with an appropriate juridical status that gave them certain rights; but on the other hand, owing to the proportionately low concentration of Jews in the Birobidzhan Autonomy, the authorities continued to catalogue them as an *extra-territorial national minority* (mainly in the 1930s) or as an *ethnic group* on the brink of assimilation (mainly from the end of the 1930s). This situation was further complicated by the fact that the Jews were also recognized as a *religious community*; since nationality and religion were largely identical among the Jews, the Soviet anti-religious policy when directed against the Jewish faith became a fight against Jewish national existence.

Significant both for the authorities and for the Jews was a Decree of the Central Executive Committee of the Soviet of People's Commissars of 27 December 1932, which laid down that the passports of urban residents aged sixteen and over must register the *nationality* of the bearer.[27] The passport has always played an important role in the Soviet Union, in obtaining employment or an apartment, and in the frequent contacts the Soviet citizen has to have with governmental authorities; and it now became a powerful instrument for the authorities, to be used for discrimination on grounds of national background. The citizen could not choose his own nationality (except when the parents were of different nationalities, in which case either nationality could be chosen, or if there was a forgery), and this juridical category, which is the most stable element in Soviet nationalities policy, is crucial to the survival of the Jews as a nationality in the Soviet Union.

JEWISH AUTONOMY AND 'STATEHOOD'

In spite of their stubborn opposition to the 'federative' idea, the communist leaders realized, even before the October Revolution, the need for compromise over the demands of the national minorities, which were beginning to make their weight felt in the party. Understandably, they did not object when national Sections were formed within the party in the months from July to October 1917. The many Bolshevik leaders of Jewish origin did not, however, exploit this situation. They did not consider themselves to be representatives of the Jewish people, a people which did not exist in their conception of the world, and they wanted to harmonize with Russian society, hoping that a socialist regime would not only settle social problems but would solve their national problem as well.

Three sets of organizations of the new Jewish autonomy and 'statehood' were created after the October Revolution: the Jewish Commissariat (Ministry), the party's Jewish Section (Evsektsia), voluntary and state institutions and organizations; the 'nationality' administrative institutions; and a 'federative unit' of the Jewish nationality.

The Jewish Commissariat, Jewish Section and Jewish organizations

After the October Revolution, an immediate solution was needed, not only to the problem of territorial nationalities but also to the problem of the national minorities dispersed throughout the country.

The first step was the creation of the Commissariat for Nationalities Affairs (Narkomnats) on 8 November 1917, headed by Stalin and his aide, S. Pestowski.[28] The Jewish Commissariat ('Evkom') within the Narkomnats, under Shimon Dimanshtein – one of the few Bolsheviks with strong Jewish ties – was set up on 1 February 1918, whereas the Polish National Commissariat had been set up on 28 November 1917. The reason for the delay was not only the lesser importance of the Jewish question compared with the Polish one at that stage, but also the difficulties encountered by the Bolsheviks in finding Jewish communists able and willing to act in the 'Jewish street'. It was, therefore, inevitable that the Jewish Commissariat would be made up mainly of representatives of the left socialist parties like *Poalei-Zion*, the Left Revolutionary Socialists and non-party people.[29]

Like the other national commissariats (there were eighteen in October 1918), the Jewish Commissariat was an administrative body, comprising six departments with limited functions. It was supposed to act through representatives in the provincial towns, but Jewish national Commissariat offices were set up in just thirteen towns, of which only two had any considerable Jewish population. The reasons for this were the civil-war conditions, the scarcity of Jewish communists willing to function in the Jewish population, and the opposition of well-established Jewish communities to Soviet rule.

The main tasks of the Jewish Commissariat, in its brief existence from 1918 to 1923, were:

to fight the Zionist and Jewish–Socialist Parties (which we shall discuss later) with their decisive influence on the Jewish population, in order to bring about their complete liquidation;

to conduct propaganda in Yiddish in order to attract the Jewish masses, who were indifferent to the new regime (certainly unenthusiastic and at times openly hostile);

to advise the central and local institutions on all questions connected with the Jews, and to seek solutions;

to set up Jewish institutions to carry out the Soviet government's
policy;

to help Jewish refugees return to their previous homes and to give
them economic assistance.

With the establishment of the Soviet Federation in 1924, the Narkomnats was disbanded and its main function transferred to the new
institutions of the administration: the Council of Nationalities, the
Nationalities Department of the Central Executive Committee of the
USSR, the Presidium of the Central Executive Committee in each
republic, and the Commissariats for Nationalities Affairs in the Ministries of the Interior of the republics.[30] This change was disastrous
for the national minorities, which thereby lost their sole representation in the central government. Under the new system, they were
represented only at local level, by paid functionaries empowered to
act in their name but dependent on the local government authorities
that employed them.

The Jewish Commissariat cooperated closely with the Jewish Section (Evsektsia) in the Communist Party, and there was frequently
an intermingling of the activities of these two institutions. The national Commissariats were open in the early years of the Federation
to members of other parties and to non-party people; but the national
sections inside the party were open to members of the Bolshevik Party
only. These sections were therefore more important than the commissariats and lasted longer.

There is no doubt that of all the Jewish bodies established in the
Soviet period, the Jewish Section (Evsektsia) was the most important
and representative, despite the generally inferior status of the national sections in the party. This was because, first, they were a party
institution and an integral part of the ruling party in the state; second, the Section succeeded not only in liquidating the independent
Jewish parties and organizations but also in bringing over leaders
from the other Jewish parties, for example, the *Bund*, the 'United',
and the Left *Poalei-Zion*, thereby raising the standing of the Section
among the Jewish public; lastly, the Section became practically the
only organization to turn to in dealing with Jewish affairs.

The Jewish Section was set up on 20 October 1918 at a meeting of
sixty-four representatives, thirty-three of whom were not Bolsheviks.
The leaders of the Jewish Section (and of the other national Sections

as well) made numerous attempts to secure an autonomous status for themselves, but throughout their existence, from 1920 until January 1930, they remained sub-sections of the Central Committee Department of Information and Propaganda.[31] The national Sections were thus no more than a technical apparatus of the party for carrying out narrowly defined tasks assigned to them by the leadership. These tasks were similar to those of the Jewish Commissariat (listed above) but wider in scope. The Jewish Section can be thought of as a sort of 'head' without a 'body', as regards its organizational structure, with a large number of operatives and very few Jewish communists. Of the 49,627 Communist Party members of Jewish origin in the Soviet Union in 1927,[32] Jewish Section operatives numbered between 2,000 and 3,500, that is to say, about 5%.[33] This is a valuable indicator of the real weakness of the Jewish Section (which also held good for the other national Sections).

The Jewish Section was constructed in three layers, each having a given rating in the hierarchy:

(1) *The leadership*: bureaux like the Central Bureau in Moscow, which was at the head of the Section for the whole country; and the bureaux in the Republics of the Ukraine and Belorussia, which were increasingly at odds with the Moscow Bureau in the last years of the Sections existence. Altogether, between thirty and fifty people constituted the Section's leadership, drawn mostly from the *Bund* and the 'United', parties all of whom were destined to be liquidated in the purges of 1936 to 1938.

(2) *The middle ranks*: representatives of the Jewish sections in communist institutions and government and public organizations, totalling, in the second half of the 1920s, 1,500 to 2,000 persons, who constituted the mainstay of the Jewish Section and directed its work in places with large Jewish populations; most of these representatives were also arrested, either in the purges or later, in the 1930s.

(3) *The bottom rank*: composed of the Section representatives on State bodies – party, public and local – numbering about 1,000 to 1,500 persons and constituting an important link in the activity of the Section.

The work of the Jewish Section revolved round its conferences. The second conference (the first was the conference at which it was founded, in October 1918) took place on 2 June 1919, during the Civil War. Three main views were expressed: the first, and most extreme, held by M. Hefets and his followers, was that there was no need for any Jewish communist bodies and that they should all be disbanded immediately. Delegates holding the second view, from the Komferband in the Ukraine and Belorussia, wanted autonomy within the general Communist Party. The third view was the official one propounded at that time by Sh. Dimanshtein and A. Elsky: there was a place for a Jewish Communist organization, but it could not have autonomous status. The third conference, from 4 to 10 July 1920, reverted to the question of the status of the Evsektsia itself in the party, and again three groups emerged. The majority of the delegates (59%), led by Yehudah Novakovsky, criticized the official policy and demanded a permanent Jewish communist organization (instead of the Jewish Section, which was seen as provisional); a Left faction, headed by A. Merezhin, with 13% of the delegates, called for the dissolution of the section and the establishment in its place of a Department for Propaganda among the Jewish population. The third faction, led by M. Rafes (with about 28% of the delegates), opposed breaking up the Section, which, they thought, still had an important task to perform in the 'Jewish street'. In fact, the section was re-organized and joined forces with the *Bund* and the fourth conference took place on 12 August 1921 with 144 delegates – sixteen from the *Bund*, thirty from the 'United' Party and five from *Poalei-Zion*. The Conference elected a Central Bureau, with the following members: Chemerisky, Merezhin, Esther Frumkin, Veinshtein and Litvakov. The two main subjects debated at the conference were strengthening communist propaganda among the Jews and intensifying educational and cultural activities. The fifth country-wide conference took place on 4 April 1924, after the adoption of the new nationalities policy at the twelfth Communist Party congress; it was attended by the section heads and 34 delegates from 25 population centres. The conference adopted a 'central' position, against both 'deviations' – of Russification and of Yiddish organization. It was also decided to intensify activity within the party and the trade unions. The sixth conference, which signalled the culminating point of the Section, took place on 28 December 1926, with 102 delegates from all over the Soviet Union. After the address of the Bureau Secretary, Aleksander Chemerisky, in which he analysed the economic situation of the Jews and referred to the party campaign against nationalistic 'deviations', the conference discussed Kalinin's address to the Soviet Jewish Settlement Society on the proposal to concentrate the Jews in one region in preparation for the creation of a

Jewish Republic, thus changing from an extra-territorial solution to a territorial one.

The main objective of the Jewish Section had been to use the favourable conditions created in 1923 to construct a sounder basis for the survival of the Jewish nationality. This aim was made increasingly difficult by the changes in the Soviet nationalities policy in the second half of the 1920s, exemplified by the statement in Stalin's letter to Kaganovich and other members of the Ukrainian Politburo that Ukrainization was proceeding too fast.[34] Pressures from outside were supplemented by disputes within the Jewish Section itself (especially between the Central Bureau in Moscow and the Bureau in Belorussia), which reached the point of accusations bordering on defamation. The result was that the internally weakened Sections were abolished on 13 January 1930, on the pretext of an organizational reform within the party.[35] The dissolution of the national Sections stemmed from the strengthening of Stalin's rule by the liquidation of the right-wing opposition and the belief that there was no longer any need to make concessions to the national minorities, either from an internal or external point of view. Stalin's declaration on 'Socialism in one country' led to an about-turn regarding the need to consider the image of the Soviet Union in the eyes of the outside world. With the dissolution of the sections, the national minorities lost their leadership, and all their activities, socio-economic, educational and cultural, were immeasurably weakened.

The Evsektsia had fought hard against the Zionist–Socialist Parties, against democratic Jewish communities, against the Jewish faith and against Hebrew culture. It had, however, succeeded in shaping a secular life pattern based on Yiddish as the recognized national language of the Jewish nationality; in fighting for Jewish national survival in the 1920s; and in working in the 1930s to slow down the assimilatory process of the Sovietization of Jewish language and culture.

As well as all the government and party institutions, the Soviet government established various public organizations to deal with Jewish affairs, which were under government supervision and acted on government orders. Among the more important Jewish public organizations were the Committee to assist Victims of the Pogroms, and OZET ('Company for settling Jewish toilers in agriculture').[36]

In the years of war, revolution and civil war from 1914 to 1921, half a million Jews were expelled, or fled from their homes; 150,000 to

200,000 were killed or wounded, and 300,000 children were orphaned. Those Jews who had lost homes, property and livelihood were in an even worse situation after the Revolution, both because of the Civil War and because of the government policy of 'War Communism'. The 'Jewish Public Committee to assist Victims of the Pogroms' (*Yidgezkom*) was set up in June 1920 with the help of the 'Joint' ('Joint Distribution Committee', founded in the USA in 1914). The Soviet government wanted aid from world Jewry, while the Jewish philanthropic bodies, who wished to provide it would not agree to transfer funds directly to the Soviet government. The Jewish Public Committee was set up to reconcile these differences. It was composed of two representatives from each of sixteen organizations and parties, seven of which were communist. The main organizer of the Committee was David Rabinowich, Doctor of Laws, who had had experience in administering aid to Jewish victims, and was politically close to the communists and loyal to them. The Evsektsia questioned the establishment of the committee, but had to agree to its activity on grounds of Soviet foreign policy at that time, which aimed at breaking the political and economic blockade enforced against it by most other countries. Other Western humanitarian organizations were also active in the Soviet Union from 1918 to 1924 – the German Red Cross, the American 'Relief', Mennonite and Protestant organizations – all of which helped the victims of the early 1920s famine. An appeal for help for the Soviet Union was made by Lenin himself, by Foreign Minister Chicherin, one of the Heads of the Communist International (Comintern), by Kamenev, and by the writer Gorky. In the short time that it was active, the Jewish Public Committee went through several crises, stemming from the distrust prevailing between its members and from differences of opinion within and between the different Soviet bodies it dealt with.

The committee provided assistance to the needy, setting up special institutions to help children and supporting the children's institutions run by the Soviet authorities: in 1921 50,000 Jewish children received food and clothing with the assistance of the committee. Medical services were also provided, and considerable economic assistance was given to Jewish agricultural settlements which suffered in the famine of 1921 to 1922.

At the end of January 1922, the Evsektsia Central Bureau altered the regulations governing the committee's work, to make them conform to those for public organizations established under the Soviet Constitution; this meant the exclusion of Soviet Jews belonging to the category 'deprived of civic rights' (*lishentsi*), owing to their bourgeois origin.

Besides helping children's institutions – it supported 1,440 institutions that cared for about 132,000 children – the committee gave assistance in 1922, in the form of credits, to Jewish artisans. Another important activity was aid to emigrants. There are no precise data on the money transferred to the Jewish Public Committee from abroad, but it was certainly millions of dollars.[37]

Soviet policy on cooperation with external organizations changed, because of what was seen as their interference in Soviet internal affairs, and the Public Committee to assist Victims of Pogroms was disbanded at the end of April 1924.

The second official public organization mentioned above, which was in a sense a successor to *Yidgezkom*, was OZET. Established on 22 December 1924 by the Council of People's Commissars, it began its operations on 17 January 1925. It was meant to assist the state body called *Komzet* (Committee of the Presidium of the Councils of Nationalities of the Central Executive Committee of the Soviet Union for settling Jewish toilers in agriculture) and was charged with planning, managing and supervising Jewish settlement. In its early years, it accepted into its ranks every citizen aged eighteen and over who had no decision against him by a law-court or other legal public body – that is to say, even those 'deprived of civic rights' (*lishentsi*). On the other hand, Zionist organizations were barred (*He-ḥaluz* and the communist *Poalei-Zion*), and Jewish religious congregations and their members could not belong to OZET as legal persons, although their members could join as individuals. This liberal policy came to an end on 24 May 1928 when an amendment was adopted, according to which persons 'deprived of civic rights' under the Soviet Constitution could no longer be in OZET. (In 1926 18% of all OZET members were traders, or in unclassified occupations.)

The number of OZET members increased steadily from about 50,000 when it was founded to 95,000 in November 1927, 300,000 in 1930 and about half a million at the peak of its development, in 1933. As the number of members increased, the proportion of Jews decreased, so that in 1930 there were only fifty-five per cent of Jewish members, and this percentage subsequently decreased.

The forum for the organization was the 'conference', which was supposed to take place every two years. In fact, however, the conference was only convened twice in the thirteen years of the organization's existence. The first time was from 15 to 20 November 1926, with the ceremonious participation of the President of the State (and one of the party leaders), Mikhail Kalinin, who made a speech supporting 'Jewish nationalism'. He proclaimed the need to establish an independent Jewish nationality through agricultural settlements and the concentration of Jews in one region.

At this conference there were two main opinions about a solution for the Jewish national problem in the Soviet Union – that of the non-party people, led by Avraham Bragin and Yuri Larin, and that of the Evsektsia heads, voiced at the conference by the Section secretary, Aleksander Chemerisky, who supported the creation of a Jewish territorial autonomy in principle but only in 'the perspective of history' and not as a task to be undertaken immediately. The second conference, which was also the last, met from 10 to 15 December 1930 and discussed the need to decide between two regions for possible agricultural settlement, the Crimea and Birobidzhan. A compromise resolution was adopted confirming both regions as areas suitable for Jewish settlement. This compromise was not significant, since the government had in 1928 decided in favour of Birobidzhan. One of the main tasks of OZET was to disseminate information both among Jews and among the non-Jewish population. The years 1927 to 1929 saw an energetic campaign against anti-Semitism, which had revived in the Soviet Union. OZET took part in propaganda, issued a large amount of publicistic literature and published a Russian-language periodical, *Tribuna*, which appeared from 1927 to 1937.[38]

OZET also conducted propaganda work abroad, through groups called 'the Friends of OZET', set up by Soviet institutions in Berlin and London, with the help of friendly organizations such as IKOR in the USA, PREKOR in the Argentine, the Jewish Settlement Fund in South Africa, the United Committee in support of Jewish Settlement in the Soviet Union in England, the Company to support Jewish Settlement in Latvia and AGRO in Palestine.

OZET's activities declined in the 1930s because of changes in the Soviet nationalities policy and among the Soviet Jews themselves. The purges affected both settlement activities and OZET, and in the middle of 1938 the organization was disbanded.

The Jewish-nationality administrative institutions

The Jewish-nationality administrative institutions were urban and village soviets, national districts, national law-courts and police stations, established in the whole of the Soviet Union in accordance with the new nationalities policy, which was meant to solve not only the problem of the territorial nationalities but that of the extra-territorial ones as well.

The first attempts to set up Yiddish-language Jewish soviets and law-courts failed,[39] and it was not until the twelfth Communist Party Congress (April 1923) adopted the new nationalities policy of granting extensive rights to all the nationalities, including extra-territorial ones, that the Jews were given proper conditions for establishing their nationality administrative institutions.

The nationality soviets, village and urban, were the same as all other soviets in their structure, functions and workings. Differences did exist, however, affecting two important matters; the Jewish-National Soviet was generally headed by a Jewish communist; and although the work of the soviet was supposed to be conducted in the mother-tongue, this objective was only partly attained. At least a thousand people had to be living in an area for a national soviet to be set up there. Because of difficulties in meeting this quota, it was decided in 1927 to reduce the number to 500 in the Ukraine. The main tasks of the Soviet were: promoting public health, developing culture, and maintaining ties with other public and cultural bodies and local administration. There were generally three departments in a soviet: community, finance, and social–cultural.

Nationality soviets, including Jewish ones, developed fastest in the Ukraine and slowest in the Russian Republic, where there were far fewer of them. Three distinct periods can be indicated: 1925 to 1927, the first impetus; 1928 to 1932, the peak period; and 1933 to 1939, the decline, which accelerated after 1935 until most of these soviets had disappeared by 1939. The Jewish soviets developed relatively slowly compared with those of other national minorities, because the Jews were not living in the principal areas that were being divided up into administrative districts for settled groups. The Evsektsia put forward a demand which was not accepted, that there should be two nationality soviets in places with mixed populations (for example, a small town could be divided in two, so that the area where most of the Jews were concentrated, the market and its immediate neighbourhood, could be represented separately from the periphery where the non-Jews lived, occupied mostly in agriculture) – the idea was even deemed 'nationalistic'.

In 1925 there were 38 Jewish soviets in the Ukraine; in 1927, 125; in 1930, 160 (out of a total of 1,139); in 1932, the peak year, 168; and in 1933, 154. No data were published for the years 1934 to 1939, indicating that there must have been a fall in numbers. The decline stemmed from two main causes: a change in the nationalities policy, signs of which had already been visible in 1929 and 1930, but which was put into effect after 1932 and 1933; and a policy of merging soviets, that is to say creating a mixed soviet of two or more nationalities. The latter was of course a by-product of the former. The Jewish soviets in the Ukraine served less than 15% of the Jewish population, whilst among the Germans, for example, they served 73% and among the Poles, about 40%.

The situation was worse in Belorussia because there, as already stated, the equality of rights laid down in the Constitutions for the languages of the main nationalities and the creation of nationality soviets were enacted slowly. The creation of Jewish soviets was also affected by the different nature of Jewish settlement in the two Republics, Belorussia and the Ukraine. In 1925 there were only 11 Jewish soviets in Belorussia; in 1927, 28; and in 1931, the peak year, 27 (23 of them in towns and 4 in villages). These soviets served only 35,000 Jews, that is to say, less than 10% of the Jews of Belorussia.

In the Russian Republic, Jewish soviets were set up in only two areas: in the western district, 11 soviets in the peak year, 1931, and in the Crimea, 32 in the same year.[40]

For the reasons indicated, the Jewish National Districts were founded later than those for other national minorities. A national district constituted an administrative entity (in contrast to the provinces, regions and republics, which were 'federative' entities) embracing a number of nationality soviets. In the Ukraine, in the first phase 20,000 inhabitants were needed to establish a national district and from 1927 on, 10,000. The functions of the district were similar to those of the soviets. The first Jewish national district was set up in the Ukraine in 1927 while there were five German ones by 1925. In 1930 there were twenty-five districts in the Ukraine, three of them Jewish. Two more Jewish Districts were established in the Crimea, while in Belorussia there was not even a single Jewish District. Five Jewish national districts (Kalinindorf, Novo-Zlatopole, Stalindorf, Freidorf and Larindorf) existed officially until the outbreak of war with Germany, but in fact by 1938 they had already ceased to function as nationality districts.

The district and nationality soviets encountered various difficulties when they were set up and fulfilled only a few of the hopes placed in them. First, on account of the lack of suitable administrative personnel speaking the mother-language, Yiddish, or because of technical difficulties, or simply from negligence, the transition was not made to administration in the mother-tongue and most of the work and deliberations were in Russian. Second, the budgets were limited and did not always permit the proper conduct of affairs. Third, there were frequent differences of opinion with the local authority at the highest level, in the Ukraine and in Belorussia. And last, there was friction in the district soviets, where the national minorities were not identified with 'the rule of the majority'.

The third institution established in the sphere of national autonomy at this time was the nationality law-court, and the police station attached to it, which were set up in a few towns in the Ukraine. The first attempt to set up a Yiddish court was made in Vitebsk from 1922 to 1923. The aim was to use the court in the war on religion, but it did not succeed. The first law-court was established on 5 July 1924 in the town of Berdichev. The number of Jewish law-courts in the Ukraine rose to 15 in 1925, 36 in 1927 and 46 in the peak year, 1931. In 1934 there were 40 Yiddish law-courts in the Ukraine, but their number decreased steadily in the second half of the 1930s, following the policy that had been applied to the soviets: of uniting them and then closing them according to 'the wish of the citizens', because they had already stopped functioning.

In Belorussia the first law-court was established in 1925. From 1926 to 1930 there were six Yiddish law-courts. As in the Ukraine, the peak year was 1931, with ten law-courts; no more data were published after 1931.

In the Russian Republic the first Jewish law-court was established in 1928; and in 1931 there were only eleven, all in the western districts of the republic.

As we have seen, the number of Yiddish-language law-courts in the Soviet Union grew quickly immediately after their establishment from 1925 to 1926; it slowed down from 1927 to 1929, with a renewed spurt from 1929 to 1931. The law-courts then marked time until their decline after 1933. As well as the ordinary law-courts, an attempt was made early in the 1930s to set up Yiddish-language 'comrades' law-courts', which were supposed to train the population in preparation for a communist society where there would be a general, overall judicial system and general legal norms; they were also meant to be turned into auxiliary instruments of the ordinary law-courts. This institution did not function at all when it was established and only appeared in the news on and after 1927. The experiment was a failure, and by the beginning of the 1930s these courts had disappeared.

The initiative to set up mother-language law-courts came from local Evsektsia activists, who put out propaganda to convince the Jewish population that it would be in their interest to have an institution of this kind. Notices, articles and letters appeared from time to time in the Yiddish press, and even in the general press, affirming that a certain town needed a Yiddish-language law-court. After preparing the ground, the request would be put to the local executive committee, pointing out that the population was interested in having a law-court using its mother-tongue. After all this, came the decisive stage, the bodies with carrying out the nationalities policy in the republics being given extensive powers in this matter.

The principle accepted in Belorussia for setting up a nationality law-court was an extra-territorial one: it laid down that regardless of whether or not there was a law-court in the district capital, a nationality law-court would serve the national minority in the whole territory of the district or province. The adoption of this principle immediately increased the number of law-courts in the republic. In the Ukraine, on the other hand, the territorial principle was adopted. The condition that had to be fulfilled in order to open a nationality law-court there was that the national minority must number 10,000, and this caused many difficulties. In time, the extra-territorial principle began to be preferred in the Ukraine as well, but this also had drawbacks. First, it went against the legal foundations on which the establishment of People's Law-courts was based. Second, it created many practical difficulties: witnesses had to be brought from far away to the place of the trial; the investigation processes, execution of sentence and so on were also affected.

As regards structure, the Yiddish-language law-court was modelled on the general People's Court. There was a permanent presiding judge and usually two temporary judges. The permanent judges were elected for one year by the Province Executive Committee, on the recommendation of the Province Law-Court, while the temporary judges were chosen from a select list of 200 persons living within the area of the court's jurisdiction. The judges were generally expected to be party members or at least trade union members, with intact civic rights, political experience, and theoretical and practical training.

The primary problem in the establishment of nationality law-courts was that they were only courts of first instance. Demands to have a higher jurisdiction established were fruitless. The next, equally serious, problem was the absence of Yiddish-language legal codes and legal terminology, and the lack of suitable personnel for law-courts work. The establishment of these courts was opposed by people of Jewish origin, who were assimilated and knew no Yiddish. Finally, there were many obstacles connected with the police and the bodies concerned in investigations – these institutions had no interest in assisting the nationality law-courts' lawyers and judges, who were obliged to go in person and search for the files in the general law-courts and police-stations.

The attitude of the Jews to the Yiddish-language law-courts depended on the stratum of society to which they belonged, its world-outlook and socio-economic situation, and the benefit they thought might be gained from the institution. The judges themselves tried to 'explain' to the Jews that this was not a real Jewish court but a 'Soviet court in the Yiddish language'; but in fact only Jews who had no other choice came to these law-courts, either because they did not know Russian or Ukrainian, or because the police transferred their file to the Yiddish court.

The difficulties besetting the Yiddish-language law-courts were not the cause of their breakdown, however. Partial solutions were found for some of the problems and others could have been overcome. The reasons went deeper, rooted both in the changes that took place in the 1930s to hasten the process of Jewish assimilation and in the new official policy on nationalities, which restricted and even cancelled the rights granted in the 1920s.

Thus when the abolition of the extensive network of Jewish institutions began, early in 1938, the problem of the law-courts no longer existed: most of them had already disappeared as a result of internal breakdown and pressure from the local authorities, and the few courts that still existed served as a kind of 'native reservation' or museum for a few visitors. So the law-courts, soviets and nationality districts set up with ceremony silently disappeared at the end of the 1930s.

Towards a Jewish Republic in the Soviet Union

We have seen that the Evsektsia and part of the Jewish intelligentsia sympathized with Jewish nationality aspirations and understood, early in the 1920s, that only a territorial base would solve the complex Jewish problem under the new regime. The Evsektsia, however, with characteristic caution, refrained from making any clear declaration of long-term national aims. It contented itself with affirming that it was occupied with the practical work of promoting Jewish culture through the Yiddish language and solving the Jewish public's economic problems. All the same, the deliberations held from 1923 to 1927 on subjects which at first seem neutral – such as employment for the Jews in the small towns, the need for 'productivization' of the Jewish population and the question of agricultural settlement – elicited suggestions for long-term solutions from the Evsektsia leaders. Abraham Bragin was one of the first people to suggest creating a Jewish 'federative unit' in the new 'soviet Federation' established in 1924. Bragin was a former member of *Zeirei-Zion* and was 'non-party' in the 1920s; he wrote for the central Communist Party organ, *Pravda*, and was among the organizers of the 1923 agricultural exhibition, in which a *Histadrut* delegation from Palestine took part, headed by David Ben-Gurion. Bragin spoke of a Jewish Republic on the shores of the Black Sea, which would stretch from Bessarabia to the Autonomous Abkhaz Republic, taking in the northern part of the Crimean Peninsula; his idea was that the majority of the Soviet Jews should live in this region.[41] Bragin's project aroused opposition both among the Tatar population in the Autonomous Republic of the Crimea and among the Ukrainian leaders, since large areas would be taken from the Republic of the Ukraine. Evsektsia leaders hastened to express their reservations over Bragin's plan,[42] but did not reject the idea of setting up a Jewish Republic in the future. The Secretary of the Evsektsia Central Bureau, Aleksander Chemerisky, wrote in 1924: 'All the peoples in the Soviet Union – except the Jews and the Moldavians – have set up Republics, Autonomous Regions and administrative entities; the problem of the Moldavians is also on its way to a similar solution and the affairs of the Jews will be settled in the same way.'[43] In 1926 he was more explicit:

'Not only from the political point of view but from the practical one
too, a Jewish Autonomy can be created here. Will this be desirable?
Yes, it will, since a Jewish territorial Autonomy in the Soviet Union –
a possibility both politically and practically – is desirable and necessary, and so we can consider it as a perspective, as a possible-practical
objective of our work, an objective we really want to reach.'[44]

The year 1926 was decisive for the Soviet and for the Evsektsia
leaders in their discussions on the settlement project. Two opposite
attitudes crystallized in the Evsektsia: the demand for the immediate
establishment of a Jewish Republic in the Soviet Union, voiced by
Yuri Larin and Avraham Bragin,[45] and the more cautious attitude of
those who were content to remain silent until a decision was taken on
the issue in the 'supreme institutions' – the view held by Aleksander
Chemerisky, Avraham Merezhin and Avraham Veinshtein.

It is not clear whether the establishment of a Jewish Republic was
ever discussed 'at the top' – that is to say, in the Communist Party
Politburo and the Soviet government – as the Evsektsia leaders expected it to be, but a response to the Soviet Jews' expectations was
given by Mikhail Kalinin in his speech to the OZET conference in
November 1926, later referred to (on the model of the 'Balfour Declaration') as the 'Kalinin Declaration': 'The Jewish people faces a great
task – to preserve its nationality – and for this end a large part of the
Jewish population, hundreds of thousands at least, must be turned
into agricultural peasants settled in a continuous area. Only in these
conditions can the Jewish masses hope to preserve the continued
existence of the Jewish nationality.'[46] Although the phrase 'Jewish
Republic' was not used, it was clear that this was the intention. So at
the end of 1926 the idea of a Jewish national 'federative entity' began
to be realistic, given official authorization by Mikhail Kalinin himself, Politburo member and President of the Soviet Union. It seems
that already the Soviet leadership was thinking not of areas of Jewish
settlement in the Ukraine, the Crimea or Belorussia, but in the Far
East.[47] The programme to earmark the region of Birobidzhan for
Jewish settlement with the aim of turning it eventually into a Jewish
national unit was put forward formally by the heads of the People's
Commissariat for Agriculture of the Russian Republic, with the support of the Commissariat for Defence, and of course of Kalinin.[48] The
Evsektsia leaders were not enthusiastic, and there was no reaction
from them until January 1928 when Chemerisky dealt with the possi-

bility of founding a Jewish autonomous unit in the Far East in an article entitled, 'To the promised land'.[49] Opposition from the OZET leaders was more determined as soon as the official project for Birobidzhan became known, and Evsektsia leaders in Belorussia showed their 'constructive opposition' by calling for increased Jewish settlement in that Republic.[50] The Soviet decision on Birobidzhan was finally taken on both State and Jewish grounds.

GENERAL GROUNDS OF STATE POLICY

First, the Soviet government was trying to solve problems of state security and thought it necessary to populate the frontiers with Japan and China as quickly as possible; second, the young State wanted to exploit the natural riches of those regions and looked for migrants of a relatively high technical and cultural level; third, the government was interested in reducing the population of the European sector of the Soviet Union by transferring people to undeveloped lands; and finally it saw the possibility of mobilizing foreign capital to develop the region.

JEWISH GROUNDS

First, from 1926 to 1928 the Soviet leadership genuinely wanted to find a solution to the Jewish question in their country. Second, popular anti-Semitism, which was especially intense in areas with large Jewish populations, irked the leadership and led them to seek a speedy solution that would not harm other state interests. Third, there was a reluctance to expand Jewish settlement further in the Crimea and the Ukraine, because of opposition from the local leadership and population which saw this as a 'Jewish invasion' and Jewish 'pillage' of their lands, opposition that would lead to further hatred of the Jews. Fourth, the Birobidzhan programme was supposed to be a counter-move against the Zionist solution of Palestine and to divert the Soviet Jews' attention from Palestine.[51] Finally, there were the accumulating difficulties in solving the economic problems of the Jewish populations (as we shall see) and the supposed possibility of finding a speedy and relatively cheap way out of them by mass Jewish migration to Birobidzhan.

In March 1928 the Presidium of the Central Executive Committee of the Soviet Union, at the request of 'Komzet' and the 'Migration Committee of the Soviet Union', passed a Resolution on the possibility of creating a Jewish national unit in Birobidzhan.[52] On 30

September 1931, a decision was taken by the same body on 'Means for implementing the 1928 Resolution on establishing a Jewish Federative national unit in the Birobidzhan Region of the Far Eastern Provinces'. Even if internal policy played a part, it was no accident that this date was ten days after the Japanese crossed into Manchuria (19 September 1931), and it can be assumed that Kalinin and Kaganovich, the 'fathers' of the 'future Jewish State', gave full support to extending Jewish settlement in Birobidzhan. Migration thither was small, however, and many who went there later left. It was not until 7 May 1934 that the Central Executive Committee decided to turn the province (the lowest level in the hierarchy of Soviet federative units) into an Autonomous Jewish Region. (The two levels higher than a region were autonomous republic and republic of the Soviet Union). This decision was not connected with affairs in Birobidzhan, since the Jewish population did not exceed 15% (7,500 out of 51,000 people), but was a political move aimed at resurrecting the faltering project. Events in Germany since 1933 may also have influenced the decision. The establishment of the Jewish Region and the possibility that it might even become an autonomous republic in the future did revive interest among Jewish settlement bodies and in centres of Jewish population. There were repercussions in worldwide Jewish centres and the old debate was rekindled – Birobidzhan or Palestine? Kalinin took advantage of the formal celebration on 28 May 1934 to give a theoretical–political interpretation of the event: the main reason for the creation of the region was that the 3,000,000 Jews living in the Soviet Union were the only nationality without a state of its own. The creation of the Region, Kalinin affirmed, endowed the Jews with the distinctive traits of a nationality. (He was referring to Stalin's definition of a nation, already cited, one of the distinctive marks being a territory and – according to a later interpretation – statehood.) Kalinin also proclaimed that the existence of the region would make possible better development of Jewish culture – national in form and socialist in content (Stalin's 1925 definition again). In closing his remarks to the delegation of workers and journalists, Kalinin hoped that in the next ten years Birobidzhan would become the main, perhaps the sole fortress of Jewish socialist national culture in the Soviet Union.[53]

The last resolution adopted by Soviet State institutions on Birobidzhan in this period was that of 29 August 1936, 'regarding the economic and cultural upbuilding of the Jewish Autonomous Region', which stated that the decision of 1934 had fully justified itself. The document quoted Kalinin's latest declaration: 'For the first time in the history of the Jewish people, its strong aspiration has now been realized for a homeland of its own and national Statehood.' The resolution also affirmed, apparently as a reaction to anti-Semitism in the Soviet Union, that Jews excelled in agriculture and were thus disproving the claim that they were not capable of working in agriculture. The resolution ended by praising the transformation of the region into a centre of Soviet Jewish national culture.

The remoteness of the Birobidzhan Region from the European centres of Jewish population, the harsh climate, the insufficient preparations for Jewish migration to the Region, the opposition by the heads of Jewish settlement bodies and also by some Evsektsia leaders, the budget limitations and, finally, the lack of enthusiasm in the Jewish population all hampered expansion in the region even in its peak periods – the first years of its establishment and the period 1933 to 1934. In 1928, the year the Jewish Province was established, only 950 people moved there; in 1929, 1,875; in 1931, 3,250; and from 1932 to 1933 about 1,100 in all. In the six years the province existed, fewer than 20,000 Jews migrated there, and of these 11,500 left in the same period, that is to say, about 60%.[54] In 1934, the year the Province was promoted to a Region (*oblast*), 5,267 Jews moved there. In 1935, 8,344 immigrants came (1,000 of them non-Jews). In 1936 about 8,000 immigrants came, 6,758 of them Jews, and the number of Jewish inhabitants reached 18,000 out of the 76,000 people living there – 23%. From 1937 to 1939 there was a fall in the number of Jewish immigrants arriving and a rise in the number of those leaving, and in 1937 there were only 3,000 Jews immigrating into the Region.[55] Data are lacking for 1938, but with the liquidation of all the organizations, institutions and agencies like Komzet dealing with Jewish settlement, all effective organization of Jewish migration to Birobidzhan stopped. It should be noted that Jews from abroad were also among the immigrants to Birobidzhan; they came as a result of extensive propaganda by various Jewish pro-Soviet organizations, and numbered 1,374 between 1931 and 1936; 516 from Lithuania, 163 from the Argentine and Uruguay, 89 from France, 76 from Germany, 74 from Palestine, and the rest from a number of countries in Europe and America.[56]

The reasons for the failure of Jewish settlement in Birobidzhan, which was apparent by the end of the 1930s, were therefore both Jewish and general-Soviet:

(1) The choice of a remote region for Jewish settlement, far from Jewish centres, problematic as regards security, with a harsh climate and all the difficulties of an undeveloped area. Possibly there would have been greater success in an easier area, such as the Crimea, but it would still have depended on internal developments in the Jewish population in the Soviet Union and on consistency in Soviet policy towards the Jewish national minority.

(2) The concentration of the Jewish population in the west of the Soviet Union, with increasing possibilities in the 1930s of earning a satisfactory economic and social livelihood delaying voluntary Jewish migration to Birobidzhan.

(3) The lack of consistency in official Soviet policy regarding the Birobidzhan project: the scarcity of resources; the frequent vacillations of the authorities, and their dwindling interest in solving the Jewish question on the territorial principle – an interest that had ceased to exist by the end of the 1930s.

(4) The purges that swept the Soviet Union in the years 1936 to 1938, reaching the Jewish Autonomous Region and paralysing it. Two leaders of the Region, Havkin and Liberberg, were accused of Trotskyism, nationalism and belonging to 'hostile' parties and organizations (*Poalei-Zion*, the *Bund*, etc.),[57] many other founders of the region were removed from their posts; Jewish immigrants from abroad were accused of spying for Japan. It was at this time, in 1937, that the first mass deportations of 'unreliable nationalities' – on this occasion the Koreans – took place. This was a serious setback in the development of Birobidzhan.

(5) The absence of any emotional, historical and national bond between the Jews and Birobidzhan.

THE JEWS' SHARE IN SOVIET GOVERNMENT

The term 'Soviet government' is used here in its widest sense, to refer to the supreme institutions of the Communist Party – Central Committee, Politburo, Organization Bureau, and Secretariat; the state representative institutions (e.g. the soviets); the administrations, the government in all its branches, the senior bureaucracy at the centre and in the republics; and the army heads. I shall consider in a separate chapter the Jews' share in the educational network, information services and institutions of arts and sciences, that is to say, the cultural élite.

The share of the Jews in Soviet government, that is to say, the extent of their 'Sovietization' in the sense of their being firmly established and accepting the State ideology, is complex. The data available are limited, and it is difficult to discern the considerations behind the decisions of the new regime.

Jews in the Communist Party

The party, the sole source of power in the Soviet Union, carries out its functions either directly, by laying down a general policy and by means of resolutions of its supreme institutions, which have the force of law; or indirectly, through party members in influential positions at all levels of government. (A constantly up-dated list known as *Nomenklatura* gives details of the functions open to party members only.) In theory, then, a Communist Party member can influence the leaders; but in practice this influence is limited and it decreases as the level of authority rises and the distance in time from the 1920s increases.

The number of Jews in the Bolshevik faction that existed after 1903 was limited, not only in comparison with the independent Jewish socialist Parties like the *Bund*, the *Poalei-Zion*, the Zionist–Socialist Workers' Party (SS) and the Jewish Socialist Workers' Party (Seimist), but also in comparison with the other socialist parties, such as the Mensheviks.

There is no data about the number of members of the Bolshevik Party before 1917 and nothing about the ratio of Jews within it. If we go by the 1922 census of party members, it appears that out of the total number of Jewish members in 1922, 964 joined before 1917 and 2,182 in 1917. If there were something like 23,000 members in the Bolshevik Party at the beginning of 1917 and roughly 1,000 Jews, this means that they constituted less than five per cent of the membership at a time when the Lithuanians, with a smaller population, formed seven per cent of all members of the Communist Party.[58] For the sake of comparison, it is worth recalling that in 1917 there were about 33,000 members of the *Bund* alone.[59]

From 1903 to 1907 there were Jews among the leaders of the Bolshevik Party, which was run by Lenin as a clandestine organization. In each of the *troikas* ('threes') that headed the party, at least until 1917, there was always one Jew, if not two, except for the years 1903 to 1905: from 1905 to 1907 Viktor Taratuta; from 1907 to 1911,

Grigori Zinovyev; from 1911 to 1914, Lev Kamenev and Grigori Zinovyev; and in the war years Zinovyev was still there.

Among the Jewish leaders at the middle level – the connecting link between the leadership in exile and the head of the branches in Russia – were: Rozalya Zemlyachka, Maxim Litvinov (Valakh), Viktor Taratuta (already mentioned) and Emelian Yaroslavsky (Gubelman). Three of the fifteen members of the Bolshevik Central Committee of 1907 were Jews: Zinovyev, Goldenberg, Taratuta. At the Prague Conference two of the six members of the centre were Jews: Zinovyev and Shvartsman.[60]

In the period between the February and October Revolutions in 1917, the percentage of Jews in the Bolshevik Party leadership rose, mainly as a result of the adhesion of the 'inter-regional' group led by Lev Trotsky. In April 1917, three of the nine members of the Central Committee were Jews: Kamenev, Zinovyev and Sverdlov. In August of that year, six of the twenty-one members of the Central Committee were Jews: Kamenev, Sokolnikov, Sverdlov, Zinovyev, Trotsky and Uritsky.

It follows that despite the relatively small number of Jews in the Bolshevik Party, they held important posts in the leadership and were close associates of Lenin. The geographical and social background of these Jews is interesting: they came from Jewish families that had taken the path of assimilation, coming from the Ukraine ('new' Russia) and inner Russia; they had been educated in Russian schools; their parents had been agriculturists or settlers (Zinovyev, Trotsky, Yaroslavsky) or 'workers by brain' (Litvinov, Zemliachka, Kamenev); the exception was Lazar Kaganovich, who came from a working-class family (his father was a shoemaker). What drew them to the Bolshevik Party was its centralizing and dictatorial character, which offered them an outlet for their revolutionary drive and at the same time promised a solution to their national problem by allowing them to become part of the society surrounding them and of its Russian culture.

In 1918, 2,712 Jews joined the Bolshevik Party, and 11,471 in 1919 and 1920, the years of pogroms and of the strengthening of Soviet rule; this was a period when only 14,120 Ukrainians joined, out of a population ten times greater than the Jews.

In 1922, the year of the membership census, there were 19,564 Jews in the Party – 5.21% of all Communist Party members, while only 2,217 Germans were members, out of a population of 1,400,000.

In 1927, the last year in this period for which there are complete data, there were 49,627 Jewish members, 4.34% of all Party members (as compared with 0.49% Germans, and 1.66% Poles). As regards their social structure, the Jewish members of the party were classified as follows: workers – 67.5% in the Ukraine, 47.8% in the Russian Republic, and 7.22% in Belorussia; clerical workers – 28.8% in the Ukraine, 48% in the Russian Republic, and 19% in Belorussia.[61] The last available data on the Jews' share in the party is from the Ukraine in 1940, where Jews formed 13.4% of party membership in the Republic, but represented only 4.9% of the Jewish population. Since the Jews in the Ukraine in 1939 comprised more than half the Jews in the Soviet Union, and since the ratio of Jews in the Communist Party in the Russian Republic and in Belorussia was not very different from that in the Ukraine, some researchers have concluded that the Jews constituted 4.9% of the Communist Party in the whole of the Soviet Union.[62] However, an analysis of the 1940 development of party membership among other nationalities, which were beginning to take a more important place than they had done in the 1920s, makes it seem more likely that the percentage of Jews in the Party in 1939 was nearer its 1927 level of 4.3%, or even less.

The swift growth of the number of Jewish members in the Communist Party after 1917 had several causes. First, the new regime urgently needed to find loyal cadres to fill posts in the apparatus of the party and the state, people with a social and educational background suited to the party's needs. Second, there were many veteran Jewish socialists with battle experience, who were prepared, willingly or because they had no choice, to enter the service of the new regime. Third, the ranks were opened offering the possibility of getting a well-paid job – one solution to the difficult economic situation in which most Jews found themselves. Last, the Jews, who had been discriminated against under the tsarist regime, now saw ways in which they could realize their ambitions.

The question posed from time to time, whether the Bolshevik regime was 'the handiwork of the Jews' is misconceived – it has no historical basis and has generally been raised by those who hate the Jews. Notwithstanding the important part played by Jews, the October Revolution was the outcome of propitious circumstances and was the handiwork of many peoples: the Russians themselves first and foremost, the Jews, and the Latvians and the Poles all played a decisive role in the critical hours after the installation of the new regime after the October Revolution.

Jews held important posts in the Communist Party leadership in the 1920s and still had considerable power in the 1930s. In 1918, four of the fourteen members of the Central Committee were Jews (Sverdlov, Trotsky, Zinovyev and Sokolnikov); in 1919, again four of the nineteen Central Committee members were Jews (Kamenev, Radek, Trotsky and Zinovyev), while in 1921 five of the twenty-five members (20%) were Jews. The ratio was not as high among the candidate members. In 1939 there were eleven Jewish full members and three candidate members, in all 10.1% of the ruling body, at a time when the Jews formed just over 4% of the Party membership. In the Politburo in the first half of the 1920s the Jews comprised from 23% to 37% (Trotsky, Kamenev and Zinovyev), but after the 'United opposition' had been ousted from the party leadership in 1926 not one Jew remained in the Politburo. In the 1930s, however, there was one Jew in this important organization, Lazar Kaganovich, who also held a central position in the Communist Party in the Ukraine.

In the 1920s and 1930s, Jews held important posts in other party organizations, such as the Organizational Bureau and the Secretariat; among them were Lazar Kaganovich, M. Kaganovich (younger brother of Lazar), Lev Mekhlis, M. Rukhimovich, A. Yakovlev (Epshtein) and Ian Gamarnik. Most of them were liquidated in the 1930s purges, although not necessarily because they were Jews.

No research has been done on the part played by Jews in the leadership of the Communist Party in the various republics, not even in the three republics with the great majority of the Jewish population – the Ukrainian, the Russian and the Belorussian Republics. In the Ukraine in 1927 there were over 20,000 Jewish party members, about twelve per cent of all party members, while in 1940, as noted above, their proportion of the party rose to 13%. In Belorussia, with its large urban Jewish population, there were 6,012 Jews in the party in 1927, about 24% of the total party membership. In the Ukraine and Belorussia, the Jews' share in the party leadership was not as high. Although Lazar Kaganovich was one of the most powerful figures in the Ukraine in the late 1920s, the Jews were not adequately represented in the higher levels of the institutions, given their proportionate strength in the party. The reason for this was the policy of accelerating Ukrainization and Belorussification in these republics, which took an extreme nationalist form and not only ousted the Russians from the leadership but also representatives of their national minorities – mainly the Jews, because of their influence in central government and tendencies towards Russification.

In the Communist Youth Movement (Komsomol) in October 1929, the number of Jews reached 98,823, just over 4% of the total membership. As the Jews were an educated urban population, this was not a high proportion.[63]

Jews in the parliamentary representative institutions

The Soviet parliamentary institutions have no actual authority, but because of their representative status they have had a respected place in the congresses and the Central Executive Committee and, since 1937, in the Supreme Soviet. It seems that, on account of the representative character of the soviets, the Communist leadership sought to have the various nationalities represented according to their relative size and importance. Hence, too, there were fewer possibilities of over-representation than in the party.

On the Central Executive Committee of the Soviet Union (parallel to the Central Committee of the Communist Party) there were 60 Jews in 1927, 42 Latvians (from a relatively small population), 9 Germans and 7 Poles.[64] That is to say, Jewish representation was low in comparison with the Latvians, but high in comparison with the other two nationalities, which were permanently under-represented in relation to their socio-economic weight. In 1929 the number of Jews on this body was 55, Russians 402, Ukrainians 95, Latvians 26, Poles 13, and Germans 12;[65] so Jewish representation declined slightly in comparison with the fourth Congress of the soviets in 1927.

In the 1937 elections, the first elections to be held after the ratification of the new Constitution of December 1936, 47 Jews were elected to the Supreme Soviet out of 1,143 delegates – that is, 4.1% of the delegates of both Houses – while their percentage of the whole population of the Soviet Union was less than 2%. So there was still Jewish over-representation in the highest representative institution of the Soviet Union.

In Belorussia, the share of the Jews on the Central Executive Committee was very high from 1924 to 1925, reaching 22.6% of all the delegates.[66] In the 1938 elections, the percentage of Jews on the Supreme Soviet of this republic was still 7.7%, while in the Ukraine it was less than one per cent – which points to a substantial difference in the 'Jewish' policy of these two republics at the time.

As regards the Central Soviet Executive it is important to note that the two first Chairmen of this body were Jews: Lev Kamenev from 7 November 1917 to 17 January 1918, and Yakov Sverdlov from 18 January 1918 until his death on 16 March 1919. The Jews held important posts on the Presidium in the 1920s and 1930s as well.

Jews had a prominent place in the lower levels of the Soviets (local authorities), mainly in the cities and small towns in the Ukrainian and the Belorussian Republics and a smaller representation in the Russian Republic. For example, in 1924, on the regional level in Belorussia, the Jews comprised 19.5%; in the city of Kiev in 1925, 30.4%[67] and in Moscow in 1927, 6.7%[68] This was not in fact over-representation, as the Jewish population was outstandingly urban compared with the enormous number of peasants in the majority population in the Ukraine and Belorussia.

Jews in the administration

Though policy-making was in the hands of the party institutions, there is no doubt that the administration and senior officials had influence in every sphere of life, especially as those at the head of the party and those at the head of the government were usually the same people.

The 'Administration' is the central government, the governments of the republics and the senior officials at the level of directors, deputy directors, heads of departments and committees, and the senior ranks in the army. Since there has been no research in this area, I can only give examples of the proportion of Jews in the central administration alone.

In the highest position, that of Head of Government of the Soviet Union, up to the 1980s only a limited number of party leaders have served – Lenin, Stalin, Rykov, Molotov, Bulganin, Khrushchev, Kosygin and Tikhonov; there have been no Jews, but the Jewess Rozalia Zemlyachka served as Vice-Premier from 1939 to 1943. It is not, however, the official post in the government that is decisive but its function and the standing in the party of the man filling it. From this angle, a number of senior Ministers were of Jewish origin: Lev Trotsky, Minister of Defence until he was ousted in 1925; Lazar Kaganovich, the Minister of Transport and Building; Yagoda; Litvinov (Foreign Minister from 1930 to 1939); Sokolnikov; Rozengolts; Dreitser; M. Kaganovich; Lifshits, and others.

In 1936 (before the purges), there were six Jews among the twenty members of the Soviet government: Yagoda (Minister of the Interior and the Security Services), L. Kaganovich (Communications), M. Litvinov (Foreign Affairs), Rozengolts (Foreign Trade), Y. Dreitser (Internal Trade), A. Kalmanovich (Agricultural Units).[69]

By 1939, the following Jewish Ministers and Deputy-Ministers were still in the government: L. Kaganovich, M. Kaganovich, B. Antselovich, M. Berman, L. Ginzburg, L. Vannikov and P. Zhemchuzhina-Molotov. Thus, throughout the whole period, Jewish representation in the central administration was well above any proportional relation to the national ratio of the Jews in the Soviet Union, and very high in comparison with all the other national minorities. We can say that the Jews in the Soviet Union took over the privileged position, previously held by the Germans in tsarist Russia. In the senior ranks of the bureaucracy, the Jews held important posts in many ministries, but were particularly numerous in the Ministries of the Interior, Foreign Affairs and Foreign Trade.

If we take all three sectors of the administration, it emerges that of the 417 people who constituted the ruling élite of the Soviet Union in the mid 1920s (the members of the Central Executive Committee, the Party Central Committee, the Presidium of the Executive of the Soviets of the USSR and the Russian Republic, the governments of the Soviet Union and the Russian Republic, the Ministers, and the Chairman of the Executive Committee), twenty-seven (that is 6%) were Jews.[70] The proportion of Jews decreased in the 1930s during the course of a natural process whereby a national élite came into being and found a place in the central administration; but it was still true that the Jews held a share in government more than double their proportion in the population. In the economic élite in the Soviet Union in the 1920s, the share of the Jews was even more impressive, reaching as high as ten per cent.[71]

Finally, we must consider the share of the Jews in the Red Army.[72] As we saw in chapter 1, under the tsars the Jews had no entry into the Army Command at any level, and the Jews conscripted into the army were discriminated against in all respects.

In 1920 about 50,000 Jews were serving in the Red Army – 1.4% of all serving soldiers. Because of the poor economic situation, the Sovietization of the Jewish population and the possibility of personal advancement, the number of Jews serving in the army rose to 1.6% in 1922 and to 2.2% in 1923 – its highest percentage. The proportion dropped slightly to 2.1% in 1926. Jewish representation in the Army was 24% higher than the Jewish share of the male population of the whole country.

In the Red Army High Command in 1926 Jews constituted 4.57%, while the Belorussians for example, with a far larger population, comprised only 4.37%. In the 1930s, many Jews held high rank in the Red Army High Command; prominent among them were Generals Yona Yakir, Ian Gamarnik, Yakov Smushkevich (Commander of the Air Force) and Grigori Shtern (Commander-in-Chief in the war against Japan and Commander at the front in the war with Finland from 1938–39).

ANTI-SEMITISM IN THE SOVIET UNION

The hatred of the Jews endemic in tsarist Russia and the persecutions they were subjected to were intensified during the first World War. The government and nationalist and army circles disseminated propaganda accusing the Jews of sympathizing with Germany and spying on her behalf, to divert public attention from their own responsibility for the disasters at the front. This propaganda succeeded in instilling distrust of the Jews even in circles that had been considered well disposed towards them, and hundreds of thousands of Jews were expelled from the regions where the war was being fought, and were left destitute.

After the establishment of the new regime after the February Revolution in 1917, the various restrictions connected with affiliation to a given class, religion or nationality were removed. On 22 March 1917 the Provisional Government issued a decree annulling all legal restrictions on Jews. Cancellation of official anti-Semitic discrimination did not, however, eradicate the prejudice against the Jews felt by the Russians and by people of other nationalities.

The continuance of the war, the weakening and final collapse of democratic rule and the difficult economic situation provided fertile soil for the resurgence of anti-Semitism. The October Revolution and in its wake the Civil War, with its attendant bloodshed, unleashed the worst instincts bringing the consequences already described[73] – pogroms, loss of life, destruction of property, ruin of family life – in fact, the holocaust that befell the Jews, mainly in the Ukraine. The pogroms, which continued for months, were perpetuated not only by the Ukrainian Army, the nationalist Russian Armies, the Polish forces, anarchist groups led by Nestor Makhno and innumerable lawless bands, but also by some units of the Red Army – this was, however, exceptional and efforts were made to stamp it out. Russia's centuries-old anti-Semitism found expression in the outrages of the Civil War period.

Even before the October Revolution, Lenin and the Bolshevik Party were hostile to anti-Semitism.[74] Lenin castigated it in the strongest terms on a number of occasions.[75] On gaining power, the Bolsheviks took a firm line against the pogroms. The Council of People's Commissars issued a special Decree on 27 July 1918 condemning all anti-Semitic manifestations; it stated, *inter alia*, that 'The Council of People's Commissars declares that the anti-Semitic movement and the anti-Jewish pogroms are a deadly menace to the Revolution of the workers and peasants and calls upon the workers in Socialist Russia to fight this plague with all possible means.'[76] In the same year Lenin recorded a speech specifically directed against anti-Semitism, to be used as propaganda among the people.[77] An information campaign was also conducted in the ranks of the Army and in work-places, and large-scale informative literature on anti-Semitism, both scientific and popular, was published.[78]

It should be noted, however, that in the Codes of Criminal Law adopted after 1922 in all the Soviet republics, there was no explicit ban on anti-Semitism nor a specific clause penalizing manifestations of anti-Semitism. The administration contented itself with a provision forbidding propaganda directed towards arousing hatred between the nationalities living in the Soviet Union. This shortcoming of the law apparently stemmed from a desire not to overstress the Jewish issue, but it actually encouraged anti-Semitism and hindered any effective opposition to it.

As the Civil War came to an end and the 'New Economic Policy' (NEP) was instituted, the propaganda war against anti-Semitism, together with the penalties imposed on rioters, produced temporary relief and a substantial decrease in its more serious manifestations; but in the mid 1920s, mass anti-Semitism once more swept through the whole population, including the industrial workers and the new Soviet intelligentsia. Moreover, as Kalinin noted in 1926, Communist Party and Komsomol members and the new social élite were more anti-Semitic than their predecessors under the tsars.[79] Stalin was engrossed in his war on the 'United opposition', whose leaders were all, or nearly all, of Jewish origin – Trotsky, Kamenev, Zinovyev, Radek, Sokolnokov, Iofé and many more – and he had no scruples about using the anti-Semitism weapon: he himself and his closest associates identified his opponents as Jews and went so far as to declare that the fight within the party had nothing to do with two schools of thought or with opposing political attitudes, but was a clash between patriotic national socialism and 'foreign elements' indifferent to what was good for Russia.[80] At this time, however, Stalin was not yet the omnipotent ruler of the Soviet Union and the period was not propitious for this dangerous anti-Semitic game. The party leaders understood the dangers involved for the Soviet regime in stimulating or even permitting a resurgence of mass anti-Semitism and it seems that in 1927 a decision was reached to take drastic steps to repress anti-Semitism.

What were the reasons for anti-Semitism under the Soviet regime and what form did it take in the 1920s? In those years the country was undergoing far-reaching economic and social changes at dizzying speed. It is sufficient to contrast the policy of 'War Communism' – extreme centralization and collectivization – followed by the NEP, with the contrary line of support for private initiative, partial decentralization and an extensive private economy, and then, in the second half of the 1920s, with the return of enforced collectivization, to realize that such profound changes in a relatively short space of time administered successive shocks to society, and produced extreme reactions in the relations between social strata and nationalities. Of course, Jewish elements were at work in the economy, where specifically Jewish economic development was occurring during the transition from the old to the new regime. The influx of Jews into heavy industry and their move from small towns to the industrialized regions of Russia led to confrontation with a population that hardly knew them and now suddenly encountered them. The prominent place of the Jews in the Soviet government and in economic and educational institutions enabled anti-Semitic circles to spread the idea that 'The Jews have taken over Russia.'

Hatred of the Jews, already strong, was intensified by the presence of Jews in the secret police and in the militia, which was confiscating Church property in this period. At the time of Jewish settlement in the Crimea, there was an outcry that the best land was being handed over to the Jews and that they were getting the best-paid posts. The old envy of 'the successful Jews' now assumed the form, 'They're being given everything at the expense of the Russian people.' Deep-rooted anti-Semitic tradition and the need to find an outlet for resentment against the regime were the main factors that led to a new wave of anti-Semitism, which reached its peak in the years 1928 and 1929.

We can gauge the seriousness of the problem by consulting three main sources: the Smolensk Region records, the Soviet national and local press, and extensive literary and publicistic works.[81] Anti-Semitism during this period was characterized by the use of terms of contempt for Jews (such as 'Yid', 'dirty Jew', 'cursed Jews', etc.) at their places of work, in schools, and on occasions when people meet in public. There were physical attacks on Jews in the factories and in schools, universities, colleges, etc.; rumours were spread of the intention to impose restrictions on Jews and even *numerus clausus* in the colleges; Jews were beaten up, and at times murders were committed openly, with more than one attacker; finally, there were organized pogroms and blood-libel accusations, as in Dagestan in 1926.

A large-scale official campaign against anti-Semitism was conducted in the years 1927 to 1930, in a variety of ways. First, propaganda was disseminated in the press and other media, to the effect that anti-Semitic expressions were the antithesis of socialism and were spread by enemies of the Soviet regime. Books and pamphlets analysed the harm done by anti-Semitism and urged the need to combat it. Public meetings condemning anti-Semitism were held, mostly in the work-places. Plays and films dealt with the subject and there were exemplary public trials. Stalin even thought it necessary to add the word 'anti-Semitism' to the Resolution condemning nationalism at the sixteenth party congress in 1930, calling it a plague to be fought against.[82] In reply to a question from the Jewish Telegraphic Agency (JTA) in the USA on 12 January 1931, Stalin said, 'Anti-Semitism, as an extreme form of racial chauvinism, is the most dangerous vestige of cannibalism.'[83] These words would have fitted in well with the anti-anti-Semitic propaganda campaign, if they had been reported not only abroad but also in the Soviet Union with the usual publicity for such pronouncements, but they were only made public by chance in 1936, showing the about-turn that apparently took place in Stalin's 'Jewish policy' in 1931.[84]

The structural changes in Soviet society early in the 1930s led to a decline in anti-Semitism; but it would be a mistake to think that it had disappeared simply because the media stopped dealing with the subject from 1932 on. Occasional reports of anti-Semitic outbreaks in one place or another appeared in the Yiddish press of this period, but the new political line was stressed, according to which anti-Semitism could be said to exist in the capitalist countries, and especially in Nazi Germany, but not in the Soviet Union itself. An example of this kind of condemnation came from Stalin's senior aide, Molotov, in a speech at the eighth Soviet congress, on the theme of the new constitution: 'Whatever the cannibals in the Fascist anti-Semitic ranks may say, our friendly feelings for the Jewish people stem from the fact that it gave the world the creative genius of the ideas of Communism – Karl Marx.'[85]

It seems clear that it was not by chance that the Jews had such a conspicuous place in the series of trials that shook the Soviet Union from 1936 to 1938, and especially in the political show trials. The Jewish aspect surfaced briefly in the address by Vyshinsky, Prosecutor-General at the show trials, when he ridiculed the accused Rozengolts, in whose pocket when he was arrested the police allegedly found a piece of paper with verses from the Psalms, put there by his wife as an amulet.[86] First to call attention to this aspect was Trotsky, who warned against the exploitation of anti-Semitism in the show trials, but there was no echo of his words in the West, nor in the Jewish press.[87] Stalin appears to have intended to use the purges to curtail the number of Jews in the upper echelons of government institutions,[88] but, as we shall see, this was not achieved until the 1940s. At this stage, the greatest damage to Jewish organizations and institutions and Jewish culture was done as part of the systematic liquidation of the national institutions of most of the extra-territorial national minorities in the years 1937 and 1938, which was actually a blatantly anti-Jewish move.

The Molotov–Ribbentrop Agreements of August–September 1939 meant a worsening of the situation of the Jews in the Soviet Union: first, some Jewish refugees who had escaped to the Soviet Union from areas of the Nazi occupation, including many communists, were handed over to the Gestapo; second, a 'black-out' was imposed on news of the fate of the Jews in the Nazi-occupied areas; third, there was silence about anti-Semitic acts committed in the areas annexed to the Soviet Union under the Molotov–Ribbentrop Agreements; fourth, in these areas a policy was pursued of discrimination against the Jewish minority as regards political representation, education and culture; and finally, less and less statistical and other material was published concerning the Jewish national minority.

DEMOGRAPHIC AND SOCIO-ECONOMIC PROCESSES

So far we have discussed the theoretical, constitutional and especially the political changes that were becoming manifest in the 1930s. These were to affect the entire 'internal' Jewish sphere, from demography, through the complex socio-economic processes of modernization, to the cultural and religious life which is the heart of Jewish national existence.

Demographic processes

Five population censuses were held in the Soviet Union between 1917 and 1939; in 1920, 1923, 1926, 1937 and 1939. The first two were only partial. The 1937 census was cancelled and those who carried it out arrested, tried and condemned as spies and saboteurs. The last census was published only in part, on political grounds.[89] In all the censuses, the questionnaire included a question on the nationality of the individual concerned; but since the answer of the person questioned was purely declaratory, the person conducting the census was forbidden to request verification; but it can be assumed that a certain percentage of the Jews, as of other nationalities preferred for a variety of reasons to hide their real nationality. Additions must therefore be made to the figure given by the census.[90]

The 1897 census had given the number of Jews in Russia as 5,189,401, as against an estimated 800,000 in 1795. By 1917 there were about six million Jews in the Russia of the 1914 borders. In 1923, after the new borders had been drawn and Poland, the Baltic States and Bessarabia had been cut off from the Soviet Union, there were 2,431,000 Jews,[91] and in 1926, 2,680,823 Jews in the Soviet Union. The Soviet Jewish economist Yuri Larin, however, thinks that about 300,000 Jews (approximately 11%) declared that they belonged to other nationalities,[92] and that there were actually about three million Jews in the Soviet Union in 1926. In the 1939 census, 3,020,000 declared themselves to be Jews; but according to the demographer Yaakov Leshchinsky, between 250,000 and 300,000 (8 to 10%) hid the fact that they were Jewish.[93]

The rate of natural increase of Russian Jews was declining slowly at the end of the nineteenth century and more quickly in the first third of the twentieth century. At the beginning of the century, the average annual rate of natural increase among Russian Jews was

1.6% but from 1926 to 1939 it was only about 1%. The reasons for this decline over a relatively short period, were accelerated processes of modernization (which we shall analyse later); the increase in mixed marriages, and the new structure of the Jewish population after World War I and the Civil War. The percentage of Jews in the whole population in this period changed only slightly, from 1.82% (of 147 millions) in 1926 to 1.78% (of 170,467,000) in 1939.

Distribution by sex was fairly equal from 1926 to 1939, but in 1939 there were 1,102 Jewesses to every 1,000 Jewish males, while in the general population there were 1,087 women to every 1,000 men.

The age structure of the Jewish population was as follows: ages 0–14, 29.1%; ages 15–49, 55.3%; over 50, 15.6%. In comparison with the general population, the age composition of the Jewish population was higher in the over-50 group – in the general population it was 13.4% – which marked the beginning of the ageing of the Jewish population in this period.

From 1926 to 1939, the Jews were concentrated in three republics, the Ukrainian, the Russian and the Belorussian. In the Ukraine in 1926 there were 1,574,000 Jews – 59% of the Soviet Jews and 5.4% of the population of the Ukrainian Republic; by 1939, their number had gone down to 1,533,000 – 50.8% of the Soviet Jewish population and 4.9% of the population of the republic. In the Russian Republic in 1926 (with all its autonomous republics) there were 624,800 Jews – 22.6% of the Soviet Jews and 0.5% of the population of the republic; by 1939 their number had risen to 948,000 – 32.1% of the Soviet Jews and 0.8% of the population of the republic. In Belorussia in 1926 there were 407,000 Jews, 15.2% of the Soviet Jews and 8.2% of the population of the republic; in 1939 there were 375,000 Jews there, 12.4% of the Soviet Jews and 6.7% of the population of the Republic.

If we compare the situation in these three republics for the years 1926 to 1939, we see that large-scale migrations took place among the Jewish population. The most striking was from the Ukraine and Belorussia – the areas of the Pale of Settlement under the tsars – to the Russian Republic. If we take into account the natural increase in the Ukraine and Belorussia in these twelve years, we find that these two republics lost more than 300,000 Jews, who chose to migrate to the Russian Republic for economic and other reasons.

In 1926, 3.5% of the Soviet Jews were in the republics in the Caucasus and in Asia and in 1939 4.7%, the result mainly of the higher natural rate of increase among the non-Ashkenazi Jews, but partly also of migration from Belorussia and the Ukraine. The non-Ashkenazi Jews comprised 2.5% of the Soviet Jews. In the 1939 census, no separate data were published on the non-Ashkenazi Jews, but presumably they represented about 3% of the Soviet Jews. This rise in the relative number of non-Ashkenazi Jews is explained by their higher rate of natural increase, which had not yet been affected by modernization and mixed marriages.

The Jewish community in Georgia in 1926 numbered 21,471 and in 1939 24,000 (an average annual rate of increase of about 2%). The next-largest community was that of the 'Mountain Jews' from the Caucasus, mainly in the Autonomous Republic of Dagestan and the Republic of Azerbaidzhan (in the towns of Makhachkala, Buinansk, Derbent and Baku). According to the data of the 1926 census, the 'Mountain Jews' then numbered 26,000, but by 1939 apparently 30,000. The third-largest community was that of the Jews of Bukhara, living mainly in the Uzbek Republic, in the districts of Tashkent, Samarkand, Fergana and Bukhara. According to the 1926 census, Bukharan Jews then numbered about 19,000; in 1939 there were about 21,000. The smallest non-Ashkenazi community was that of the Jews of the Crimea – the 'Krimchaks' as they were called; they numbered 6,383 in 1926 and 7,000 in 1939.

The process of urbanization of the Jewish population had begun before the Revolution, and accelerated in the late 1920s with the growing industrialization of the Soviet Union. In 1926, 2,144,000 Jews lived in the towns, 87% of all Soviet Jews. The large Jewish concentrations centred in villages were in the Ukraine, comprising 14.6% of the Ukrainian Jews. In 1939 in the Russian Republic there were 97,768 Jews in the villages, constituting 10.4% of the Jews in the Republic, while in Belorussia 12.1% were in the villages. In the Georgian Republic, 18.6% of the Georgian Jews lived in villages. As against this, only 2.1% of Bukharan Jews did so. In addition, however, to the accelerated urbanization of Russian Jews in the later nineteenth century, the Jewish population was moving from the villages to the towns and cities. According to some estimates, in 1939 about 40% of the Jews were living in six large towns. In that year there were already about 400,000 Jews in Moscow and 275,000 in Leningrad.[94] The other towns with a large Jewish population were: Odessa, 180,000; Kiev, 175,000; Kharkov, 150,000; and Dnepropetrovsk, about 100,000 Jews.

Socio-economic processes

Russian Jews suffered great economic difficulties, both because of their social structure and because of discrimination against them, and their situation became worse in the years of war, revolution and civil war; the main battle lines went through regions in the Ukraine and Belorussia which had large Jewish populations, and there were the mass deportations, pogroms and pillage. It is difficult to estimate the damage inflicted. According to one source, 62.3% of the houses of the deportees were burnt down, and only 3.2% of their housing property and 16.4% of their work-tools remained to them.[95]

The policy called 'War Communism', implemented from July 1918 to March 1921, was based on the nationalization of all private enterprises (a workshop with five or more workers was considered an 'enterprise'), strict government control, commandeering and confiscation, all of which were damaging to the Jews,[96] for the following reasons:

(1) Because of their importance in trade and commerce, the Jews were severely affected by the destruction of private trading.

(2) Because of their social structure, many of them being classed as 'bourgeois', the Jews were severely affected by the confiscations.

(3) While the Russians and the Ukrainian population had contacts in the villages and could find supplies in times of shortage, no such possibility existed for the Jews.

(4) 70 to 80% of Jews in the small towns (*shtetlekh*) had no steady livelihood, and only a fraction of them found work in Soviet offices; the others were forced to turn to illegal trading, the penalties for which were very severe.

(5) Nothing came of the deliberations in the Evsektsia about 'economic restoration [healing]' and the economic distress of the Jewish population deepened daily.

The New Economic Policy introduced by Lenin at the tenth Party Congress in March 1921 produced a change in the Jewish population's economic situation. The end of expropriations, the encouragement of private initiative, the legalization of private trading, the possibility of hiring workers and starting to cultivate private farms in the villages all allowed the Jews to earn a livelihood. Those who had traded illegally during the period of 'War Communism' started trading openly; artisans reverted to their previous crafts; refugees from the pogroms, who had fled to the large towns, began to return to the small towns and villages.

The economic difficulties did not disappear entirely, however, but changed their nature. First, the Jews, like the rest of the population, were hit by the policy of taxation, and the preference given to cooperatives harmed the independent Jewish craftsman working for a village customer. Jews who had earlier been taken into government offices were now discharged in the name of NEP efficiency and found no alternative employment. Bukharin's adjuration to the peasants, 'Get rich!' led to a gap between the prices of agricultural produce and the prices paid for urban manufactures in the years 1923 to 1925, and this policy acted against the Jews, nearly all of whom were tied to the urban sector. The return to their homes of townspeople who had gone to the villages during the famine also sharpened the competition the Jews had to face. A serious problem was presented by Jews who belonged to the category 'deprived of civic rights' (*lishentsi*). Those who had exploited the labour of others, or who held political opinions judged hostile to the regime, or were occupied in non-productive work, and the clergy of all faiths were not only deprived of the right to vote but could not register at the Labour Exchanges and were thereby deprived of the right to work and so to earn their living. In 1926, of the Jews in the Ukraine, 68.8% were traders 'deprived of civic rights'; 20.8% did not earn a living by working; 4.4% were contractors: and 1.6% were religious personnel.[97]

From 1926 to 1928 a retreat began from Lenin's NEP, with renewed restrictions on private trading; rejection of the previous position on 'development of the peasant and artisan within socialism'; administrative pressures on the cooperatives (which had been joined by many Jewish artisans); and restrictions on credits to the private sector. The economy of the small towns in the Ukraine and Belorussia which had large Jewish populations immediately deteriorated – in Belorussia, 72.2% of Jewish youth in the small towns were without work.[98]

In the last period I shall deal with in this chapter, from 1929 to 1939, the Soviet Union went through a 'Third Revolution' no less harsh than the two of 1917, which shook the foundations of the new state. The planned economy of the Five-Year Plans, with its accelerated industrialization and forced collectivization of agriculture, had an impact on the economic and social situation of the Jews. So the social and economic changes amongst the Jews must be seen against the background of the official economic policies of the 1920s and 1930s, which changed course under the pressures of internal and external constraints but led in the end to the modernization of the Soviet national economy.

In 1897, 38.65% of the Russian Jews were occupied in trade and commerce. From its inception, however, the Soviet regime undermined private trade. The temporary revival under the NEP resulted in 8.8% of Jewish breadwinners' being occupied in trading in 1926; at least another 10% of 'unemployed' Jews made their living from trading that was not declared (in order to avoid paying taxes), so that in that year at least 18% of the Jews were still traders.[99] In the Ukraine in 1926, 20% of Jewish breadwinners stated that they were occupied in trading and in Belorussia 15.8%, to which must be added 15% or more undeclared traders. By 1929 the number of Jewish traders had fallen to 2.3% and at the beginning of the 1930s private trading disappeared completely.

In 1897, 18.4% of the Jews in Russia were craftsmen and artisans. In 1926 the proportion was 22.6%, a rise due both to the encouragement provided by the NEP and to the obstacles to trading, which made some of the shopkeepers undertake different crafts. In 1939, unorganized Jewish craftsmen were 4% and those organized in co-operatives 16.1%, while in the whole Soviet population only 2.3% were craftsmen. The Soviet attitude to artisans in general, and Jewish ones in particular, was ambivalent. On one hand, they were always seen by the communists as individualistic, uncontrolled elements, unreliable as regards class-consciousness; but on the other hand people working with their hands to earn their living were said to contribute to the development of the Soviet economy. Because so many Jews in the 1920s were craftsmen, with a precarious, economic position, a solution was sought, by organizing cooperatives, securing credits, providing raw materials, and so on. The worst-off were the craftsmen in the small towns in the Ukraine and Belorussia, who competed with each other in a limited market.

The attitude to industrial workers, who in theory at least had become the ruling class in the Soviet Union, was different. In 1897 the proportion of Jewish industrial workers was 17.9% and in 1926 15.3%. The decrease can be attributed to the poor economic situation and the possibilities of changing to other occupational categories. With the policy of accelerated industrialization at the end of the 1920s and Jewish migration from the small towns to the bigger towns and cities, the percentage of Jewish industrial workers rose substantially. In 1930 it was 16.3% and in 1939 reached 30%, nearly the same as the percentage of workers in the general population (32.6% in that year). It should be noted that the percentage of Jewish workers was particularly high in the Russian Republic, while in the Ukraine it was only 9.4% in 1926 and in Belorussia only 8.9%.[100]

The occupational distribution among the Jewish workers is interesting, especially when compared with the preceding period. We can take as an The percentage of metal-workers among the Jewish workers was 6.9% in 1926 and reached 11.1% in 1931; the percentage of workers in the mines – nil before the Revolution – was 0.5% in 1926 and 1.4% in 1931; in the chemical industry there was a drop from 14.1% to 11%.[101] There was also a drop in the number of workers in the 'classic' Jewish occupations, but the percentage still remained very high; thus among needleworkers the percentage fell from 73.4% to 60.9% in the years 1926 to 1931; in the food industries, from 28.6% to 25%; in printing from 36% to 34.3%; and remained practically static in leather-working – 48.6% in 1926 and 48.2% in 1931.[102] We have no data for the other republics, but it can be assumed that the distribution was much the same in Belorussia, but apparently different in the Russian Republic, where the percentage of Jews in the less 'typical' Jewish occupations was higher than in the other two republics of the former Pale of Settlement.

In 1897, 3.5% of Russian Jews worked in agriculture, and their number dropped even lower by 1914, because of the anti-Jewish trend in the tsarist governments at that time. It fell to about 2% in the Civil War period, when the pogroms devastated Jewish settlements and Jewish farmers fled to the towns. A change in the opposite direction took place in 1923 and 1924, when the NEP failed to provide a solution for Jewish economic distress.

The hope of finding a solution, including the possibility of changing their civil status, drew many Jews to the villages. The Evsektsia was seeking ways to 'productivize' the Jewish population and at the same time devise a 'national solution' for the Jews by securing territorial continuity as a basis for normalization of the Jewish social structure. The Soviet government supported this programme by establishing organizations for settling Jews on the land, like OZET and Komzet, allocating land, mainly in Belorussia, the Ukraine and the Crimea, granting special budgets and giving management backing. Jewish organizations abroad – the 'Joint', ICA and ORT – gave financial and expert support to the programme of Jewish agricultural settlement. In the years 1924 to 1926, Jewish settlement forged ahead. According to the 1926 census, 8.3% of Jewish breadwinners were involved in agriculture in the Soviet Union as a whole, while in the Ukraine the percentage was 9.8% and in Belorussia 13.1%.[103]

From 1929 to 1930 the number of Jewish breadwinners in agriculture reached its highest percentage, 11.1% of all Soviet Jews. The settlement bodies, however, aimed at transferring half-a-million Jews to the land over a number of years and this was not achieved in the 1930s. On the contrary, with the forced collectivization of the early 1930s the situation became static, and a decline began in the second half of the 1930s, which stemmed not only from the difficult situation of government cooperative agriculture but also from the possibility of earning a better livelihood in the towns.[104] By 1939 the percentage of Jews in agriculture was even lower than in 1926 – down to 5.8%, consisting mainly of Jewish agricultural workers organized in *Kolkhozes*, and a considerable Jewish population in Belorussia, the Ukraine, the Crimea and Birobidzhan. Among the reasons for this decline was the change that occurred in the Soviet nationalities policy in the late 1930s, which in agriculture took the form of pressure on the Jewish *Kolkhozes* to unite with those of other nationalities in the same region and led to quarrels between those of different nationalities.

There were few Jewish clerical workers and officials at the end of the nineteenth century, for internal Jewish reasons and because of the administration's discrimination against them. Working as functionaries now became the main Jewish economic occupation, replacing trade and commerce, which had disappeared under the Soviet regime. In 1897 10% of the Jews were employed as clerical workers, mostly in commerce and industry, but also in public institutions and Jewish religious bodies; in 1926 they formed 24.7% of functionaries in the Soviet Union (in the Ukraine – 20.6%, in Belorussia 17%).[105] It was natural that in a planned socialist economy practically all clerical workers should be functionaries in the government apparatus, and this intensified the process of Sovietization of the Jewish population. Accelerated industrialization and increased concentration of all sources and resources in the hands of government in the 1930s created many jobs in clerical work and the Jews used the opportunities to the full. In 1939, 40% of Jewish breadwinners in the Soviet Union were occupied as functionaries,[106] as compared with only 17.2% in the population as a whole. The internal distribution of Jewish functionaries in 1937 was as follows: senior civil servants: in the Ukraine 20.7%, in Belorussia 24.5%; experts: in the Ukraine 35%, in Belorussia 31.7%; others: in the Ukraine 38.6% and in Belorussia, 32.2%; auxiliary clerical workers: in the Ukraine 5.7%, in Belorussia 11.1%.[107]

It is interesting to assess the place of the free professions in the Jewish population, since their expansion is one of the signs of accelerated modernization. This is not easy, however, because of the blurred boundaries between the notion on the one hand, of 'free professions' and 'the intelligentsia', and on the other the idea of 'functionaries' or 'bureaucrats', to use the statistical terminology of the Soviet records. In 1897, 5.22% of the Jews in Russia were occupied in the free professions, as compared with 2.04% of the whole population. In the first half of the 1920s, there was a decline in this category caused by migration and by the overall economic situation. In 1926, the number of Jews in the free professions was 1.6%, but a percentage has to be added from those classed as 'functionaries', and Yuri Larin estimates the size of the free professions in 1928 at 10%.

In 1939, of 364,000 Jewish breadwinners defined as 'intelligentsia' 125,000 (34.3%) were managers and accountants; 60,000 (16.5%) technicians (of intermediate technical rank); 46,000 (12.6%) teachers; 31,000 (8.5%) medical personnel (nursing sisters and medical auxiliaries); 21,000 (5.9%) doctors; 47,000 (13%) cultural and artistic directors; 7,000 (1.9%) professors and researchers; 2,000 agronomists and 25,000 engineers and architects (taken together, 6.8%).[108]

The accelerated modernization of the Jewish population that began in the last half of the 1920s is exemplified by the influx of Jewish young people into the universities and scientific institutions. In 1927, there were 23,405 Jewish students (compared with 994 Germans and 1,034 Poles) out of a total student body of 162,928, that is to say, 14.37%. In 1929, the percentage of Jewish students was down to 13.5%, in 1933 to 12.2%, and in 1935 up slightly to 13.3%.[109] Among 18,321 persons classified as scientists at the end of the 1920s the Jews constituted 13.6%,[110] and this percentage rose in the 1930s. Among the 'aspirants' (candidates for university posts), the Jews' share in 1934–5 was about 18%. In the Ukraine in 1923, Jewish students in higher education comprised 47.4% of all students, while the Ukrainians were only 24.7% of the total. In 1929, the percentage of the Jewish students in the Ukraine was still 23.3%.[111] If we take into account those Jews who could not be admitted to the universities, being 'deprived of civil rights', the Jewish influx into the institutions of higher learning was extraordinary, and laid the ground for the later changes in the Jewish social structure.

To sum up, the economic situation of the Jews at the end of the 1930s was considerably better than in the 1920s. They occupied influential positions both in the economy and in the institutions of higher learning, research, art and culture, that is to say, in the socio-economic élite of the Soviet Union. The level of education among the Jews, with 72% literacy, already the highest among the Soviet nationalities in 1929 (apart from the Latvians, who constituted a small minority in the Soviet Union), had risen still higher by 1939. The proportion of the working population, which included many women – a sign of modernization – rose among the Jews from about 40% in 1926 to 47% in 1939. The social structure we have outlined, with a stratum of 40% of functionaries and 'intelligentsia', and a high percentage of Jewish students, is proof that by the end of the 1930s the Jewish population had become an advanced, modern society.

RELIGION

Marx's antagonism to religion in general and to the Jewish religion in particular was shared by Lenin and the Bolshevik leadership, but as in many other spheres the Bolsheviks had, after their victory, to take into account the different nationalities and faiths within Russia. They decided to alter the constitution and separate religion both from the State and from education. Religion was therefore declared to be a citizen's private affair and all religions were considered equal before the law.

The legal–political status of the religions

The first resolution of the Communist Party on religious affairs was passed in December 1917, but the first law to be passed on religious activity under the new regime, which served as the basis for later legislation, was the decree of 23 January 1918.[112] The first constitution of the Russian Republic (10 July 1918) laid down (Clause 13): 'Religion is separate from the State, and the school is separate from religion, and all citizens are entitled to freedom of religious and anti-religious propaganda'.[113] The Instruction issued by the Commissariat of Religions on 24 August 1918 and the Instructions of the Com-

missariat for Internal Affairs of 22 January 1919 and 17 February
1925 are important for the application of the laws and decrees.[114]
The criminal codes of the Russian Republic and the other republics
include many sections dealing with religious matters and in particular with implementing the separation of State and religion.

The second and decisive stage in legislation on religion began on 8
April 1929,[115] with a law, which was in force up to 1975, restricting
all religious activities. Among party decisions on religious affairs, the
party platform of 1919 and various Resolutions passed by the Central
Committee constituted the basis for the legislation on religion and for
the consequent activity of party organizations and institutions in the
matter.[116] The adoption of the modern principle of the separation of
State and religion was important for the status of religion under the
new regime, but analysis shows that Soviet legislation was hostile to
religion.

The main provisions laid down in Soviet religious legislation were:
(1) The Churches were forbidden to own property.
(2) They were forbidden to levy taxes or collect any money apart
    from voluntary contributions handed over in places of worship.
(3) Religious companies could no longer constitute corporate legal
    personalities.
(4) All religious institutions concerned with health and welfare were
    closed down.
(5) Religious education was forbidden in all public state and private
    institutions of learning, except for special theological seminaries
    (which were in fact wiped out by the administrative measures).
(6) Action regarding the personal status of the individual was com-
    pletely banned.
(7) Detailed provisions were laid down regarding the rights of the
    Churches to arrange religious activities such as ceremonies, pro-
    cessions and conventions.
(8) Houses of worship could be closed down by an authorized gov-
    ernment body, as a result of the arrest of members of the religious
    organization or of a decision by its members.
(9) All members of the clergy had the status 'deprived of civic rights'
    (up to 1936).

According to the new legislation the basic religious unit was the
'group of twenty' (*dvatsatka*), but the law also recognized groups of
less than twenty and groups of fifty. From 1917 to 1939, direct surveillance of religious affairs was in the hands of the Soviets' Religious

Affairs Commissions, attached to the Supreme Committee of the Central Executive Committee of the Soviet Union. Other administrative institutions, and especially the secret police, also dealt with religious affairs and waged war on the religions with all the means at the disposal of a totalitarian state.

The fight against religion

What can only be described as a fight to the death was waged by the administration against religion in general and against a number of religions in particular including the Jewish religion. Four sub-periods can be distinguished: 1917 to 1920; 1921 to 1923; 1924 to 1928; and 1929 to 1939.

1917 TO 1920

From the beginning of the new regime, the Communist ideology was both anti-clerical and atheistic, but the intensity of the anti-religious fight varied. Despite the anti-religious legislation enacted during these years, the attack on the religions during this period was mild. The Civil War, the efforts to extend the power of the new regime and the need to combat hostile political forces precluded the beginning of a new attack on religion.[117] The government concentrated on breaking up the older Jewish political movements and the democratic Jewish communities that had been established in 1917 as institutions of the new Jewish autonomy. It was not until 1920 that the leadership of the Evsektsia and the Jewish Commissariat began to organize its campaign against the Jewish religious judicial system and religious office-holders.

1921 TO 1923

When victory over the main anti-Communist forces had been achieved religion remained the strongest obstacle to the extension of communist influence. The Soviet government, party activists in the central apparatus and each of the national sections launched an onslaught on the various religions. The national sections were part of the Information and Propaganda Department (Agitprop), which was charged with carrying out the anti-religious campaign in accordance with the Central Committee Resolution of 21 July 1921.[118]

The Communist Party wanted the fight against the Jewish faith to be waged by the Jews themselves, to avoid the accusation of anti-Semitism. The Evsektsia, some of whose leaders were former *Bund* members had its own reasons for waging war on Judaism, which remained almost the only obstacle to its gaining control of the 'Jewish street'.

The anti-religious campaign took the following forms in this period:

(1) Propaganda blasts against religion in all the mass communications media. As well as articles against the Jewish faith in the Yiddish press, special lectures devoted to the campaign, conferences and meetings were held for non-party Jewish workers.

(2) The fight against the ultra-Orthodox and the *Yeshivot*, based on the legal ban on religious education, ended with the closing down of the *Yeshivot* and the pursuit of the ultra-Orthodox, who continued their illegal activity.

(3) The campaign against the religious primary schools, the *heder*, led to the holding of 'public' trials, mainly in towns the large Jewish populations, such as Kiev, Vitebsk and Kharkov, or of symbolic importance, like Rostov. A 'public' trial was staged against the *heder* in January 1921 in Vitebsk; in spite of being 'public', it had all the marks of an official Soviet trial, and the sentence, affirming that the *heders* must be closed as quickly as possible, was carried out by official government agencies.[119]

(4) The expropriation and closing of the synagogues 'in response to the demands of the masses', in order to convert the premises into 'cultural centres'. The Evsektsia members not only initiated these expropriations but actually used force to overcome the resistance of the congregations. The Evsektsia succeeded in closing the central synagogues, while the smaller ones remained in use.

(5) A fierce fight was waged against Jewish holidays, principally through regulations that fixed Sunday as the general day of rest. Anyone refusing to work on the Sabbath was accused of 'clericalism', 'reaction' and anti-Soviet struggle, accusations that could lead to arrest and trial. Evsektsia activists would arrange meetings and even parties at the fixed hours for prayers, and organize marches round the synagogues, sometimes ending in serious clashes.

(6) Harassment and even first-time arrests of rabbis and other religious office-holders increased towards the end of the 1920s.

(7) Thirteen books against the Jewish religion were published in Russian and seven in Yiddish.[120]

1924 TO 1928

The religious campaign slowed down during this period, for both internal and external reasons. First, as we have seen, in 1923 there was a change in the Soviet nationalities policy, a change which also benefited the various religions. Second, at this stage the Soviet Union wanted to widen its economic and diplomatic contacts with the rest of the world. Third, this was the period of the NEP, a policy aimed at helping the rural population, which was particularly religious. Finally, the Evsektsia was beginning its large-scale action to speed up Jewish agricultural settlement and to find ways of helping the small craftsmen, who were firmly rooted in the traditional Jewish way of life; it did not want to create friction with these craftsmen by fighting the Jewish religion at this stage.

In 1925 intense anti-religious activity was begun by a new public body called 'The League of Unbelievers' (later 'The League of Fighting Unbelievers') headed by Emelian Yaroslavsky, a prominent member of the Communist Party leadership. Membership of the League grew from 87,033 in 1926 to 183,402 in 1927. Only six nationalities joined the League when it was formed, but by 1931 there were ninety-seven nationalities in the League.[121] In 1929 there were just 500 Poles, 2,000 Germans and 200,000 Jews.[122] The relatively large number of Jews in anti-religious activity stemmed from the high level of secularization among the Jewish population, from its special demographic and socio-economic structure, not from any supposed anti-religious inclination of the Jewish people. At various times the League put out a news-sheet in Yiddish called 'The Unbeliever' (*Epikoyres*). In these years the number of anti-religious books published rose to twenty-two in Russian and fifteen in Yiddish.

One of the most sophisticated ways of combating religion was the establishment of a new church or synagogue. The 'Living Synagogue', for example, was run by rabbis appointed by the government and ready to cooperate with it to the point of caricaturing the prayers and religious customs. The idea was to provoke quarrels between the two types of synagogues, and those officiating in them, in order to weaken the influence of religion. The 'Living Synagogue' had only limited success with the Jewish public in comparison with this sort of church among other religions, because of the structure of Jewish religion, which has no central body controlling synagogue affairs. With government authorization, a meeting was proposed, for 21 to 25 October 1929, with 179 delegates from 110 Jewish religious congregations, in order to establish a central body which would unite all the synagogues in the Soviet Union. The 'Lubavicher' rabbi at first supported the meeting but in the end abstained, fearing that the Evsektsia would put forward a proposal to establish a 'Living Synagogue'. The authorities also gave up the idea of the meeting, fearing that it would be 'captured' by the Zionist organizations, and the authorization was cancelled.[123]

The first signs of the acceleration of the anti-religious campaign were visible in 1927, and it became more vigorous still in 1928; the changes stemmed both from the alteration of the Soviet nationalities policy and from the retreat from the NEP. There was no longer any need to consider the feelings of the large village population.

1929 TO 1939

This was the hardest period for the survival of religion in the Soviet Union. The League of Unbelievers reached its peak membership in 1932, with 5.5 million members. A decline in the membership began between 1933 to 1936, but there was a recovery in 1938, when the members numbered 1,949,722.[124]

The number of published anti-religious works directed against Judaism reached twenty-six in Russian and fifty-two in Yiddish, and these writings became increasingly extreme. At this time there was also significant pressure for *anti*-religious education in the schools, whereas in the earlier years what had been discussed was *non*-religious education.

In what was to be the last year of its existence, the Evsektsia was attacked both from outside and from within, and tried to show its loyalty to the new party line in a propaganda campaign. Serious accusations were launched against religious office-holders, of spying for foreign powers or being in the service of imperialism and reaction.

From 1930 to 1933, the secret police, who had been under a cloud in the preceding period, progressively took over the anti-religious campaign assisting the 'Unbelievers' League' and other executive organizations. Once more houses of worship were systematically closed down and office-holders arrested *en masse*.[125] From 1934 to 1937, the anti-religious campaign was restored to its earlier fervour and in 1938 the situation became even worse. The most serious accusations were made against Rabbi Medaliah, one of the senior rabbis in the Soviet Union, and against a number of other rabbis. A press announcement stated that 'hiding under the cloak of religion' they had assisted the Fascist security services by despatching agents to ruin socialist construction in Birobidzhan.[126] The purpose of the propaganda campaign and of the arrests was to root out all religious manifestations among Soviet Jews.

Jewish religious activity

The grant of a limited legal status to religions, and their subjection to persecution by a totalitarian State determined to destroy religious faith, placed all religions, including Judaism, in an intolerable situation, calling for skilful manoeuvres and great constancy if religion were to be preserved. Very few data have been published on the number of synagogues that remained open, but in 1925 in the Russian Republic there were 418 officially registered religious groups, while another source gives only 282 religious groups in 230 synagogues. Therefore not every registered group (i.e. of at least twenty worshippers) had a synagogue as its place of worship. In the Ukraine, there were 1,034 synagogues with 830 rabbis in 1927, while an Evsektsia statement of 1 September 1926 speaks of 1,003 religious groups with 137,437 congregants, that is to say, 13% of the adult Jewish population in this republic.[127] By the end of the 1930s, there were fewer synagogues, because many had been closed down, and rabbis and religious office-holders arrested.

The religious group elected a three-member executive body from among its members, to be responsible to the appropriate authorities for the management of the synagogue. We have seen that the authorities used every possible means to force the observant Jew to work on the Sabbath and on Jewish holidays. Despite these pressures, many religious Jews, mainly in the small towns of the Ukraine and Belorussia, tried to observe religious holidays and to be free from their work-places on these days. This was arranged in the Jewish craft-guilds, of which most of the Jewish artisans were members, and in the small Jewish towns, but it became increasingly difficult in the 1930s, and the number of Sabbath and holiday observers diminished.

The struggle to bake unleavened bread for Passover had begun early in the 1920s; the structure of the Soviet economy in this period, and the policy of rural collectivization in the 1930s, made it impossible to obtain large quantities of flour for this purpose. By 1929, however, the Soviet Government permitted Jewish organizations abroad to send in large quantities of flour for *maẓot*, on condition that the costs of transport and the customs duties were paid in foreign currency.

The observance of *Kasher* slaughtering according to ritual prescriptions constituted a special problem. Soviet law did not forbid ritual slaughter but put many obstacles in its way; circumcision was treated similarly. Officiants of circumcision and of ritual slaughter were persecuted as consistently as rabbis and in the 1930s some of them were banished to remote places.

Ritual baths for women, destroyed during the Civil War, had been rebuilt during the 1920s and were now closed down by the authorities on various pretexts. Religious marriage ceremonies, which now became private ceremonies, were still performed in the small towns in the 1920s but became infrequent in the 1930s.

Under the Soviet regime, and more particularly with the intensification of the Evsektsia's anti-religious campaign, it became increasingly difficult to publish prayer-books. In the NEP years of relative liberalization, religious circles published Hebrew calendars, prayer-books, Passover *Haggadot*, the Book of Psalms, etc. In the towns of Poltava, Leningrad, Berdichev, Zhitomir, Bobruisk and Minsk, in the year 1927 to 1928 alone, according to one Soviet paper, the publisher Ginsburg printed 100,000 copies of religious books. The Lubavicher Hassidic group, *Ḥabad*, was particularly active in publishing prayer-books. Sixteen Hebrew calendars were also published between 1922 and 1930, but from the beginning of the 1930s all Jewish religious publication was stopped.[128]

In the 1920s and 1930s the custom of burying Jews only in Jewish cemeteries was observed even by the most fanatically anti-religious Evsektsia members.

Despite these legal restrictions and administrative harassment, Jewish religious faith stood fast and continued to influence a considerable part of the Jewish population in the Soviet Union, especially the non-Ashkenazi Jews. In Georgia at the end of the 1930s there were about sixty synagogues functioning and a number of *Ḥakhams* (rabbis). For local reasons, the anti-religious policy of this republic was less strict than in the European republics; the same was true of the Bukharan and 'Mountain' Jews. At the end of the 1920s, there were thirty-two synagogues in the town of Samarkand alone, but their number decreased steadily in the 1930s.

EDUCATION AND CULTURE

In a multi-national country, government policy on the culture of the national minorities is all-important. As we shall see, the Soviet regime in its early years destroyed the Hebrew branch of the Jewish triple-language culture, condemning it as 'clerical'. The Russian branch was recognized in the late 1920s and in the 1930s, until the independent Jewish research institutions were closed down and the publication of Jewish research papers, literature in Russian and the OZET organ, *Tribuna* was stopped. In the late 1930s extinction also awaited the third branch, Yiddish, a fate suspended only by the change in the general policy on the nationalities and by the war.

The Soviet government planned to cut the Jews off from their past, in order to 'de-nationalize' them completely, and the means of doing this was to be a process of stifling Jewish culture.

Jewish education

At the turn of the nineteenth and twentieth centuries, there were three types of Jewish school: *ḥeders* and 'improved' ('reformed') *ḥeders*, with 325,000 pupils in 1910; secular Russian-language schools, with over 50,000 pupils: and *Talmud–Torah* schools where secular subjects were also taught. Yiddish-language schools were not legitimized until 1914.

In 1917 all types of Jewish school – Hebrew, Yiddish and Russian – flourished. At the end of January in that year, a teachers' seminary was opened in Odessa by the 'Lovers of the Hebrew Language', to train teachers to teach all school subjects in Hebrew. Evening classes in Hebrew literature, history and Talmud were organized in a number of towns.[129] In April 1917, the 'Lovers of the Hebrew Language' arranged a conference, which founded the 'Tarbut' (culture) Association for Hebrew language and culture. In June, the first General Convention of Jewish Teachers was convened in Petrograd, with 139 delegates representing 1,784 teachers, who taught in Yiddish, Hebrew and Russian. At this convention, two factions formed – the Yiddishists and the Hebraists. The supporters of Yiddish-language schools were in the majority: they had the backing of the political parties – the *Bund*, the United Party and *Poalei-Zion* – and the differences of opinion led to divisions among the teachers. In July, a conference of Hebrew teachers met in Odessa, with 137 delegates representing about 1,500 Hebrew teachers. This conference founded the Hebrew teachers' federation called *Ha-more* (The Teacher).

In 1918 in the Ukraine ruled by the RADA (Ukrainian Government) there were 270,000 Jewish children aged seven to eleven, 96,000 of whom were in secular schools, both Jewish and non-Jewish, while 174,000 children were apparently in *ḥeders*.[130] Various secondary schools were set up in this period, most of them offering four or five years of study, but a few offered seven years. The first Yiddish-language secondary school was founded in the Ukraine in 1918 by the 'League for Culture'. Day-schools were also established in various places.

With the Bolshevik take-over, in the regions under the new government's control administrative difficulties were raised against the *ḥeders* and the Hebrew schools. On 19 August 1918 the Jewish Commissariat for National Affairs announced that the language of instruction must be the mother-tongue (that is, Yiddish), and that Hebrew must not be taught in the first year in any secondary school and thereafter not for more than six hours a week. Existing schools were commandeered by the local soviets and handed over to the Central Bureau of Jewish Education in the Commissariat for Public Education, and in December 1920 a decision was taken to abolish the *ḥeders*. In this way secular schools were turned into Yiddish-language schools, and the *ḥeders* were closed down entirely; most of the children who had been learning in them stopped learning or were taught illegally. The Evsektsia and other Soviet government institutions began to try those running *ḥeders* and even to arrest the pupils. Not even schools affiliated to the *Bund*, the 'United' or the 'Folkists' were spared.[131] It was only among Bukharan Jews that Hebrew teaching continued – until half-way through the 1920s.

In 1918 a Soviet education network was created, which included two types of 'uniform, practical' schools: elementary schools for children aged eight to thirteen (five classes) and secondary schools for ages thirteen to seventeen (four classes). In 1930 elementary education was made compulsory: schools were now divided into three types: elementary (one to four classes); partial secondary (five to seven classes); and full secondary (ten years' study).[132]

In the years 1918 to 1923, the creation of a Yiddish school network encountered many obstacles. First, there was opposition from the local authorities (local soviets and trade unions, which dealt with setting up schools for different nationalities), because of political hostility to Jewish 'nationalism' or the majority population's withholding funds from the minorities in the various republics. Second, large sectors of the Jewish population were deterred from sending their children to Yiddish schools under Evsektsia supervision. Third, there was a shortage of text-books, since the old ones did not suit the Evsektsia programme and it was impossible at that time to bring out new ones. Fourth, it was difficult to find teachers with a communist ideology. Lastly, the poor standard of the Yiddish schools in the early days did not help to bring in a large influx of pupils, and many parents chose to send their children to Russian schools. In 1921 there were 100 Yiddish schools in Belorussia with 10,231 pupils, and in the Ukraine 300 schools with about 15,000 pupils.[133]

The main growth in the number of Yiddish schools came after the twelfth Communist Party congress and the beginning of the policy of 'Korenization' ('implantation' of the national minorities). In 1923 there were 98 Yiddish schools in Belorussia with 12,241 pupils, and in 1924 in the Ukraine 268 with 42,000 pupils. The period of growth began in 1925 and reached its peak in the school years 1931 to 1933. So in the Ukraine, the school network developed as follows: in 1926 there were 432 schools with 79,000 pupils; in the peak year, 1931, there were 831 schools with 94,872 pupils; in 1934 85,489 pupils were learning in Yiddish schools and thereafter the decline was evident, with only 73,412 pupils in 1935.[134] There are no data for the years 1936 to 1938, but according to one source, published in 1948, there were only 19 Yiddish schools in the Ukraine in 1939.[135] The proportion of Jewish children in the Jewish schools was 53% in the peak year, 1931, with 4,000 Yiddish teachers.

In Belorussia growth was swift in the years 1925 to 1933, the decline beginning later than in the Ukraine. In 1925 there were 140 schools with 19,085 pupils; in 1928, 190 schools with 26,000 pupils; in 1931, 262 schools with 33,000 pupils; and in the peak year, 1933, 339 schools with 36,501 pupils. From 1934 on there was a break in the publication of data. In 1937 the Yiddish newspaper *Der Emes* (Truth) stated that there were 30,000 pupils in the Yiddish schools.[136] The ratio of Jewish children learning in Jewish schools in Belorussia was the highest in the whole of the Soviet Union: 47.9% in 1926; 62.3% in 1930; and 64% in 1934; while in the Crimea, for example, in 1926, it was only 4.8%, and in Asia 5.3%.

The situation in the Russian Republic was different. In the most propitious years for Soviet policy, no Yiddish school network developed there. In 1929 there were only 33 Yiddish schools in the republic, with 3,573 pupils mainly in the Western areas and not in the main cities like Moscow and Leningrad. It seems that 1930 was the peak year, when 11,000 pupils were learning in 110 schools. As we have seen, this stemmed from the nationalities policy of the Russian Republic regarding the extra-territorial national minorities, a policy manifest in the negligible number of national soviets and law-courts in the republic. It can be inferred that the large Jewish migration into this republic led to the immediate transfer of Jewish children from Jewish schools to Russian ones, with all that this implied in consequences for the Jewish sense of national identity.

If we take the entire Soviet Union, the following picture emerges: in 1926 there were 509 Jewish schools with 70,482 pupils; in 1927, 800 Jewish schools with 107,000 pupils (a different source gives 642 schools with 94,063 pupils); in 1939 it appears that there were only 75,000 pupils in Yiddish schools. As regards the proportion of Jewish pupils in Jewish schools, in 1928 in the Soviet Union there were 411,711 Jewish pupils in schools, 29.4% of them in Jewish schools (31.8% in the Ukraine, 48.9% in Belorussia and only 7.9% in the Russian Republic).

The nature of Jewish schooling must also be considered and the Jewish content of their studies. From 1919 to 1940, 159 elementary school text-books were published in Yiddish.[137] What was in these text-books? The period 1921 to 1923 can be considered experimental, when the political–pedagogical policy for Jewish schools had not yet been worked out, and the curriculum was the same as before the Revolution or in the first year of the new regime. In this period, there were still text-books containing works by the classic authors in Yiddish – Bible stories re-told and reminders of the Holidays of Israel – but the proportion of the classics was decreasing. The share of Soviet Yiddish-language authors rose from 17% of the school material in 1921 to 33% in 1923, and literary passages from 6% to 16%.

Text-books underwent a significant change of content from 1924 to 1929. There was a more critical attitude towards the past, and a concentration on the favourable things in Soviet society as a whole and in the situation of the Jews. Passages from the classics were curtailed or even excised because of their 'hostile' ideological content, the passages in question being rephrased to make them fit 'Soviet reality'. The declared purpose was education for class-consciousness. About a quarter of most of the books was devoted to stories, memoirs and songs about Lenin and passages from his speeches. Other text-books were devoted to the 'Soviet fraternity of the peoples'. There was also a careful selection from non-Soviet writers: thus, for example, there was far less of Y. L. Perets, considered less *kasher* (accept-able) than of Shalom Aleikhem. Writers were particularly careful not to include material dealing with religion and Jewish traditional life. In the place of traditional history there was a subject called 'Knowl-edge of Society', with an admixture of Jewish history. When the anti-nationalist trend began to predominate, towards the end of the 1920s, attacks were made by the 'internationalists' against 'Yiddishism' and there were demands that the only Jewish history taught should be that of the Russian Jews. The purpose was to create emotional and intellectual resistance in the pupils to the 'outmoded' content of Jewish national–religious ideology.[138] The Yiddish language also had to be taught according to the general political principles of the period – solely as a medium.

The liberal approach to Soviet education came to an end between 1930 to 1939, and strict supervision was introduced, on the initiative of Stalin himself, both of the content of the curriculum and of teach-ing methods in the study of history in the schools and universities. This was the height of the anti-nationalist campaign among the min-ority nationalities and the beginning of the pre-eminently Russifica-tory trend. The previous a-religious approach in education became anti-religious. Chapters in the textbooks were headed: 'Against reli-gion – for socialist construction.' Jewish national content and themes were more and more restricted and the 'international' foundations of the Soviet Union were emphasized, until texts dealing with Jews and Judaism amounted to no more than 15% of the material. The study programme was changed in 1932 and 'knowledge of society' disap-peared from the curriculum. The subject history re-appeared, but there was no such thing as Jewish history. Reforms were made in Yiddish orthography to bring it closer to Russian and there were innovations in various terms and word-endings to suit the supposedly internationalist, but in fact Russificatory, line. If there was still any Jewish content left in the Yiddish school-books, it was anti-Jewish, against religion, against Jewish national elements and the tradition and history of the Jewish people.

Several reasons existed for the drop in the number of pupils in Jewish schools in the 1930s: the structural changes in Jewish society that we have already described, the migration from the traditional

Jewish areas to the Russian Republic, and the rise in linguistic and social assimilation, which we shall deal with later. We must first point to the difficulties facing Jewish institutions when they tried to prepare a reserve of teachers for the network of Yiddish schools. The 'Institute of Proletarian Jewish Culture' of the Academy of Sciences in the Ukraine managed to train only twenty-one graduates, nor were the pedagogical institutes in Vitebsk, Minsk and Odessa much more successful. Second, problems arose and multiplied in preparing curricula and text-books. Third, there were budget difficulties and difficulties arising from local authority counter-activity. Fourth, efforts were made to tempt teachers to leave the Jewish schools and go over to Ukrainian and Russian schools. Fifth, the lack of Yiddish institutions of higher learning had its effect. Finally, the purges of 1936 to 1938 included mass arrests of the Jewish intelligentsia, among them teachers, education supervisors, text-book writers, etc., with a consequent destructive effect on education. [139]

Literature, language and the press

In Russia before the October Revolution Jewish literature was written in three languages – Hebrew, Yiddish and Russian. We shall note briefly how this literature developed from 1917 to 1939, and give a resumé of the literature of the non-Ashkenazi Jews.

HEBREW LITERATURE AND PRESS

Hebrew literature was flourishing at the beginning of the twentieth century. Among the outstanding writers were: Yehudah Leib Perets, Ḥaim Naḥman Bialik, Shaul Cherniḥovsky, Zalman Shneur, Yaakov Fiḥman, G. Shofman and many more. From the angle of chronological development, three periods can be distinguished 1917 to 1919, 1920 to 1927, and 1928 to 1939. [140]

The harvest of this literature was reaped in the years 1917 to 1919, before it was cut down by the Evsektsia and before the Hebrew writers (among them Bialik) left the Soviet Union, with the help of Maxim Gorky, in 1921. In this sub-period 188 Hebrew books and periodicals were published out of a total of 343 for the whole period up to 1939. Of these 188 Hebrew publications, first place was taken by text-books and children's books: 85; second, periodicals: 31; third, *belles lettres* and criticism: 29; and religious writings: 15. Most of the Hebrew writers were published in Odessa, the main Jewish cultural centre in Russia (60% of all Hebrew publications). The second centre came into being in Moscow (about 15% of all publications).[141] The press and periodicals were important for fostering and disseminating Hebrew literature – *Ha'am* (The People), *Hashiloah* (The Messenger), *Darkenu* (Our Path), *Knesset* (Congregation), *Hé'avar* (The Past), *Ha-Mishpat Ha-ivri* (Hebrew Law) and *Hatkufah* (Our Time) – which were all shut down by the beginning of the 1920s.

From 1920 to 1927, Hebrew writing centred round a number of young authors, who were zealous Hebraists and at the same time pro-Soviet. They wanted to secure official recognition for the Hebrew language and literature, affirming it to be as 'progressive' as Yiddish. Writers and poets in this group were Eliezer Shteinman, Avraham Kariv, Gershon Ḥanovich, Shimon Haboneh, Moshe Ḥaiug (Plotkin) and others. They succeeded in publishing their work, in the following collections: '*Bereshit*' (Beginning) (Moscow-Leningrad, 1924, pp. 204); '*Tsiltsulei Shema*' (Loud Cymbals) (Kharkov, 1923, 100 copies only printed); and *Gaash* (Eruption) (Kiev, 1923, forty-seven pages of the poems of Mili Novak).

From 1928 to 1939 the only way of publishing books by Hebrew writers was to have them printed abroad. The greatest Hebrew poets in the Soviet Union lived in this period – Elisha Rodin and especially Ḥaim Lensky. Those who had not managed to emigrate to Palestine went through appalling sufferings. Most of them were arrested and disappeared (Lensky in 1934, A. Friman in 1934 and again in 1936, Ḥaiug and Zvi Pragerson after the war, Haboneh before, in 1927) or were consigned to psychiatric institutions for treatment (Rodin). On 21 April 1938 Lensky wrote from the concentration camp where he had been held for four years: 'I am physically and morally destroyed. I have only one aspiration left – to die quickly. I ask you Bitochka not to exert yourself on my behalf – my fate is sealed.'[142]

LITERATURE AND THE PRESS IN YIDDISH AND OTHER LANGUAGES

The Yiddish literature and press of the 1920s and 1930s sprang from the circumstances created by Soviet policy on the nationalities problem. In towns with a considerable Jewish population – like Kiev, Kharkov, Odessa, Moscow, Minsk and later in Birobidzhan – the best Yiddish writers and critics came together to work for the development of Jewish culture – Perets Markish, David Bergelson, David Hofshteyn, L. Kvitko and others.[143]

The Evsektsia censored over this development, but it nevertheless had a real share in fostering Yiddish literature. Though it prevented the use of 'nationalist' words – not precisely a creative function – the Evsektsia during the years of its existence supported and protected Jewish culture. The line followed by Yiddish literature up to the beginning of the 1930s was also influenced by the Jewish 'Proletarian Writers' Union', affiliated to the general 'Proletarian Writers' Union'.

The foundations of the new Yiddish literature after the Revolution were laid by the group *Eygens* in Kiev, in the years 1918 to 1920, which published collections containing the prose writings of David Bergelson, 'Der Nister' and A. Katsizne, and the poetry of David Hofshteyn, Asher Shwartsman, Perets Markish, Leib Kvitko and Yehezkiel Dobrushin. The literary genres governing their work were impressionism and post-symbolism; the central themes were the first World War, the Revolution, pogroms, urbanization and the internal changes in Jewish society. There was, of course, still a long way to go from the *Eygens* group to the Soviet Jewish literature of the relatively liberal 1920s.

Organization on more official and Soviet lines began in Moscow in 1921 and a literary monthly, *Shtrom*, was published there from 1922 to 1924. Among active members of this group were some of the Kiev people, Aharon Kushnirov and Ezra Fininberg. These writers accepted communist ideology and the bases of Soviet rule unquestioningly, but they claimed autonomy for themselves in their work. Clearly this independent stand was not acceptable to or accepted by the Evsektsia and its Commissar for Cultural Affairs, Moshe Litvakov, editor of the daily, '*Der Emes*'. Another group took shape simultaneously, of younger authors and poets, enthusiastic supporters of the Soviet regime like Itsik Fefer and Izy Kharik, leaders of the 'proletarian trend' in Soviet Yiddish literature. In 1925 a Jewish Section was formed in the Union of Proletarian Writers, which published a literary periodical, *Oktober*, in Moscow and another, *Der shtern*, in Belorussia.

The 'fellow-travellers', that is to say, those who were not members of the Union of Writers or of the Communist Party, published the literary periodical, *Neierd*, in Moscow, and in the Ukraine they centred round the periodical, *Di Roite velt*, which appeared from 1924 to 1933.

As the campaign against 'nationalist deviations' intensified in the late 1920s and the 1930s, accusations of 'nationalism' and 'chauvinism' were levelled at a number of Yiddish writers (Perets Markish, Shmuel Halkin, Ezra Fininberg, Shmuel Rozin, Leyb Kvitko, A. Cohen and others). In 1929 Markish was arraigned because his heroes were exclusively Jews and thus he made it seem as if it was only Jews who carried out the Revolution; moreover, his books were full of the spirit of the death of martyrs.

The themes increasingly used in Yiddish literature in the 1920s and 1930s were: the October Revolution; the Civil War and the defeat of the enemies of the new regime, internal and external; the pathos of socialist construction; and the joy of labouring and living in the first socialist state in the world. The Jewish background to these themes was the Jewish heroes' development in fighting the reactionary forces that still clung to the remote past by means of the *ḥeder*, the synagogue and the Jewish political movements (mainly the Zionist ones, but the *Bund* as well). Any Jewish national features in Yiddish literature grew fewer and fewer in the 1930s until they disappeared, ousted by praise and of the party and its leader, Stalin. Simplification prevailed to the point of primitivism and pathetic rhetoric. Then the change in the nationalities policy, which began in 1934 and reached a climax in 1938 and 1939 when the patriotic sentiments of the Russian and other peoples were conjured up to confront the dangers of war, opened new horizons for Yiddish literature. Typical of the atmosphere of the period was Der Nister's *The Mashber Family*, the first volume of which appeared in 1939, and Shmuel Halkin's plays, *Bar-Kokhba* (1938) and *Shulamit* (1940). The reversion to Jewish nineteenth-century history in *The Mashber Family* and to the remote past in Palestine in Halkin's plays marked the change of direction in Jewish literature in the war period, towards a feeling of the continuity and unity of the Jewish people.

While private publishing still existed, from 1917 to 1920, 767 Yiddish books appeared.[144] From 1921 to 1924, there was a decrease in Yiddish publications, both because of the disappearance of private publishing and because of financial difficulties. The nationalities policy was unclear, at least until 1923, and fewer funds were allocated for publishing works in the languages of the national minorities. A further factor in lowering the total number was the publication of relatively few text-books. Only 269 books appeared in these years, an average of 67 books a year. Then, from 1925 to 1932, Yiddish publication jumped to a record number of 2,801 books, that is to say, an average of 350 a year. The peak years were 1930 with 531 books and 1932 with 668. From 1933 to 1939, 2,650 books appeared, a higher total than that of the preceding years, but a substantial decline when compared with the years 1929 to 1932.

It was not only the number of publications by a national minority that was important, but also their content. In the first years of the Soviet regime most of the books in the minorities' languages – such as Yiddish, German and Polish – were coloured by political propaganda, and most of them were translated from Russian. They were mainly the works of Marx, Lenin and other communist leaders. Later in the 1920s and 1930s, there was an increase in the classics of the national literature, in original Soviet writing and in translations from Russian literature, and also in text-books and technical literature.

Of the original Yiddish publications, only 10% of the political and propaganda writing was written originally in Yiddish, whereas more than 70% of the *belles lettres* were original work. Among translated books were works of Russian and Soviet writers like Pushkin, Lermontov, Chekhov and Gorky, and almost half the original *belles lettres* were the work of Mendele Mokher Seforim, Y. L. Perets and, above all, Shalom Aleikhem. The art section, too, was mainly original. The education section comprised textbooks, mainly for the Yiddish schools. Finally, children's books – an important category – were mostly translated, generally from the Russian.

The publication of newspapers and periodicals also went through a number of phases, distinct from each other in quantity and in content. From 1917 to 1921, 328 Yiddish periodicals and newspapers appeared, an average of sixty-six a year; but many lasted only a few months: they were party and Jewish organization papers and most of them were liquidated in this period.

In the years 1922 to 1927, 156 newspapers and periodicals were published, an average of twenty-six a year. There are no data for the period 1928 to 1934, though this was certainly the peak period for the nationalities' press. In 1935, forty-one Yiddish papers and periodicals were published, and from 1936 to 1939 a decline began, both in quantity and quality, when leading papers began to be closed down: *Der Emes* (Truth) was closed in 1938, *Ofn sprakhfront* (The Language Front) in 1939, *Oktiabrl* (Little Oktober) in 1939. *Wissenshaft un revolutsie* (Science and Revolution) and were closed as early as 1936, *Yunge gvardie* (The Young Guard), *Farmest* (The Competition) and *Ratenbildung* (Soviet Education) in 1937.

We cannot discuss here whether Jewish literature and culture can survive when expressed in a non-Jewish language, but, for our purpose, every writer or artist of Jewish origin who considers himself Jewish and writes on Jewish subjects belongs to the Jewish national creation. Thus, in the 1920s and 1930s many works of considerable artistic quality were published by Jewish writers writing in Russian or Ukrainian or Belorussian.

The outstanding Jewish writers of the period who wrote in Russian, were Yitzḥak Babel, who published *Red Cavalry* in 1926 and in 1927 *Tales of Odessa*, an account of the life of Russian Jews during the pogroms and revolutions; and Ilya Erenburg, most of whose works in this period were on Jewish themes, most notably, *The Adventures of Lazik Roitschwanetz, Julio Jurenito, 13 Pipes, Rvach* and *Den vtoroi*. Other writers and poets publishing works on Jewish subjects were: Eduard Bagritsky, Iosef Utkin, Mikhail Svetlov, Iuri Libedinsky, Ilya Selvinsky, Venyamin Kaverin, Vasily Grossman, and many more.[145] In the Ukraine, writers on Jewish subjects were Natan Rybak, Leonid Pervomaisky and Savva Golovanivsky and in Belorussia Zmitrok Byadulya (Shmuel Plavnik).

From 1917 to 1937, individual writers and artists were able to express their national feelings within the permitted bounds of the regime. Whether they could do so as an organized group centred round newspapers and periodicals in the Russian language dealing almost exclusively with purely Jewish subjects, was a different question. From this point of view, there are two separate periods, the 1920s, and the 1930s.

The historical periodical *Evreiskaya starina*, founded by Dubnov, which brought together the leading Jewish historians, ethnographers, demographers and sociologists, continued to appear until 1930. The periodical *Evreiskaya letopis*, which appeared from 1923 to 1926, was important for the development of Jewish culture in the Russian language. In the 1930s the only important Jewish Russian-language periodical was *Tribuna*, the organ of OZET, which appeared from 1927 to 1937.

For the Jewish Russian-language press the most important years were from 1917 to 1920. No less than 84 Jewish newspapers and periodicals appeared in 1917–18 in Petrograd, 11 in Moscow, 9 in Odessa – representing various Jewish parties and organizations; in 1918–47, in 1919–31, and in 1920–19. In those years the Russian-language Zionist press held an important place – 41 newspapers in 1917, 24 in 1918, 17 in 1919, and 11 in 1920.

From 1921 on, the Russian-language Jewish press suffered a set-back because of the liquidation of the non-communist political parties and organizations. In this year only four Jewish papers in Russian remained. Very few non-communist papers appeared from 1922 to 1930, and those that did had to be authorized by the censor. There was *Gekhaluts*, organ of the legal *He ḥaluẓ* movement, *Evreiskaya starina, Evreiskaya mysl* and *Evreiskaya letopis, Voprosy biologiii patologii* and *Evreiskaya proletarskaya mysl*. As we have already said, with the ending of all non-communist publications the only Jewish publications in Russian were OZET's *Tribuna* and the paper of the Jewish Autonomous Region, *Birobidzanskaya Zvezda*.

Jewish culture appeared in other languages besides Yiddish, Hebrew and Russian: Jewish languages like Tati and Bukharan, and non-Jewish ones like the Georgian of the Georgian Jews. A leading writer in Georgian on Jewish themes was Herzl Baazov, whose main works appeared in the 1920s and 1930s: *The House of Hain* and *Itske Rozhinashvili*.

Various clubs and choirs developed in the 1920s among the 'Mountain Jews' and there was some literary activity. In 1928 a Jewish paper was published in Tati, called *Zakhimtgkash* (Workers), in the town of Makhachkala. Other papers appeared for brief periods, and in 1936 a Bureau was even set up of Tati Jewish writers, among them Sh. Rubinov and Y. Borukhov; but the decline of Jewish cultural activity, both in Georgia and by the Mountain Jews had begun in the late 1930s with the mass arrests among the Jewish intelligentsia. The first newspapers in the Jewish–Bukharan language appeared from 1921 to 1923: *Rosta*, and *Rushinoi* – the organ of the Evsektsia in Bukhara. Many books were published in Bukharan in the 1930s (thirty-seven in 1930, 177 in 1933). The most important writers in this language were Muhiv (Mordekhai Batchaev), Gabriel Samednarov, Iunatan Karaev, Yaakov Ḥaimov, M. Aminov, P. Abramov and Y. Mordekhaev. At the end of the 1930s writers and cultural activists were arrested and in 1940 the last three works in Bukharan were published.

The cultural revolution undergone by the national cultures in the Soviet Union did not spare the languages of the various nationalities. Immediately after the Revolution, it was proposed to transpose the different scripts of the various peoples in to Latin letters. Latinization would express internationalist aims and bring about a speedy cultural revolution. This revolution in scripts was also supposed to symbolize the break with the past, a step of particular importance for the eastern peoples with their ties with Islam and with Arab and Persian culture. The idea of Kyrillization rather than Latinization was not adopted at this stage, because of its tsarist–Russificatory associations. Jewish supporters of Latinization used the usual arguments in favour of Latinization: – being part of the process of internationalization, close to the proletariat both of the east and the west, a solution to problems of graphics, orthography and philology, and so on. Among the interesting arguments advanced were that Latinization would reduce expenses, and that writing from left to right does not block the light on the writer's page, or that it makes it easier to put down mathematical formulae. Among the 'scientific' Jewish arguments advanced by the supporters of Latinization were the following: the Hebrew alphabet constituted a vestige of religion, separated the Jewish proletariat from the Russian, and was not suited to Yiddish, which is not a Semitic language; and finally, Latinization would put an end to the claims of the supporters of Hebrew that they had an important role to play in Jewish culture and would help to bring the Jews into the cultural revolution which was taking place throughout the Soviet Union.

In spite of these efforts, the Latinization of Yiddish was not adopted, and the supporters of the 'language revolution' had to be content with small-scale reforms, such as the use of vowellized forms of Hebrew words in Yiddish (applied in the years 1929 to 1930); getting rid of the 'final' forms of five Hebrew letters at the end of words; and taking two letters used only in Hebrew out of the Soviet Yiddish alphabet. Other reforms in a variety of languages including Yiddish extended to adopting Russian terminology in many fields; these were reinforced with the passage in March 1938 of the law making Russian-language teaching obligatory in the schools of all nationalities.[146]

The Jewish Tati language and Bukharan could not hold their own against Yiddish, a language spoken by Jews all over the world. Tati was written in Hebrew letters until 1928, changed to Latin in the 1930s and to Kyrillic – i.e. Russian – in 1938. The Hebrew alphabet was replaced by the Latin one in the Jewish Bukharan language in 1931 to 1932, and Kyrillization was approved – but was not applied since Bukharan publications came to an end in 1940.[147]

Jewish art

Jewish art – in the widest sense – reached its peak in the 1920s and 1930s in the fields of the professional and amateur theatre, music, cinema, radio, painting and sculpture.

THE THEATRE

The theatre led the arts because of its influence over the public and because of the combination of literary–dramatic creation, music, ballet and lighting.

The continued existence of the most important Hebrew theatre of the Diaspora, *Habimah*, in the Soviet Union in the period when almost all the other Hebrew bodies were being abolished is one of the political anomalies of the 1920s.[148] The initiative for founding a Jewish theatre in Russia in 1917 came from Naḥum Ẓemaḥ. The theatre started with young actors who had only partial mastery of Hebrew. They had difficulty in finding money and a hall to appear in, but were lucky enough to gain the support of the greatest Russian theatrical producers of the day, Konstantin Stanislavsky, Evgeni Vakhtangov and Aleksander Tairov. The première of the first production by the *Habimah* theatre company took place on 8 October 1918; it consisted of four episodes based on stories of Y. L. Perets, Shalom Asch, Y. Z. Berkovich, and Yitzḥak Katznelson. The première of their second production, *The Eternal Jew*, was in December 1919; this play, by David Pinsky, deals with the destruction of the Temple and the flight of the *Shekhinah* (holy spirit) from the people of Israel. Though the play was not great drama, it portrayed the Jewish national spirit. *Habimah's* greatest success came from Ansky's play, *The 'Dibbuk'*, translated by Bialik and staged by Vakhtangov. The première took place on 31 January 1922 after lengthy preparation. Three hundred performances were given in the Soviet Union alone, and *Habimah* was praised by leaders of Soviet Russian culture like Maxim Gorky, Feodor Chalyapin, Konstantin Stanislavsky, and by the country's rulers – Anatolii Lunacharsky and Lev Kamenev – and above all by the Jewish and Russian public. This gave *Habimah* a backing that enabled it to resist harassment from the leaders of the Evsektsia, who made ironical attacks on the Hebrew theatre. The last plays put on by *Habimah* were *The Golem*, by Leivik, in March 1925, and *The Flood*, a translated version of the American play by H. Berger, produced by

Virshilov. The *Habimah* actors' troupe left the Soviet Union in January 1926 for a tour in Europe and the USA and never returned.

The Yiddish theatre had had no facilities or backing under the Tsars because of government policies. Internal Jewish factors were also not acceptable in a traditional society in the early stages of modernization. This situation changed after the Revolution – the Soviet government saw the theatre not just as an art form but as an educational propaganda instrument.

The founder of the first Soviet Jewish theatre was Aleksander Granovsky, who transferred his group from Petrograd to Moscow and set up his studio there at the end of 1918. The first sketches by the theatre (*Goset*) were put on in January 1919.[149] In 1922 it staged Goldfaden's *The Witch*. Repertoire problems hampered *Goset* and the other Jewish theatres from the outset: a compromise reached in the 1920s, a balanced mixture of plays from the outside world and Soviet ones was followed in the 1930s by complete imbalance. The classic Jewish playwrights whose work was most often produced were Shalom Aleikhem (his play *200,000* was very successful), Y. L. Perets (*Night in the Old Market* was a success, but was harshly criticized on ideological grounds), Mendele (*The Travels of Binyamin the Third*), Shalom Asch (*The Lord of Vengeance*) and the father of the Jewish theatre, Avraham Goldfaden (*The Witch*). The outstanding playwrights in the Soviet Jewish theatre were Veviurka (*137 Children's-Homes*), L. Reznik (*The Revolt*), Perets Markish (*Unworried*), David Bergelson (*The Ploughman*), M. Daniel (*Julis, Four Days*) and others.

Among the plays from the outside world put on in translation were *Uriel Acosta* by Gutzkow and Shakespeare's *King Lear*, which was the *Goset* theatre's greatest success, with Shlomo Mikhoels and Binyamin Zuskin in the main roles.[150]

The frequent tremors that shook the Soviet theatre did not spare the Jewish theatre, which had to tread carefully in the 1930s in its choice of repertoire and producers, use of experimental effects and so on. The Jewish theatre received some support from German anti-Fascist playwrights who came to the Soviet Union after 1933 – Bertold Brecht, Friedrich Wolf, Ernst Piskator, Vallentin, Granach, Reich, and others.

In the Ukraine, where half the Jewish population of the Soviet Union, with its rich literary and theatrical tradition, lived, private theatres already existed at the beginning of the 1920s – the 'Experimental Theatre' and *Kunstwinkel* in Kiev. It was not until 1925, however, that the decision was reached to establish a Soviet Jewish Theatre in the Ukraine. A state Jewish Theatre, run by Efraim Loyter, was founded in Kharkov, the Ukrainian capital, despite the fact the Kiev had a larger Jewish population. The theatre faced financial and management difficulties as well as a lack of actors. The plays put on were those of Soviet Jewish writers: A. Kushnirov (*Hirsch Lekert*), L. Reznik (*The Last Ones*), B. Orshansky (*Blood*), Itsik Fefer (*The Chimney-Sweepers*), E. Fininberg (*Young Men*) and others. Translated plays included *Professor Mamlock* (by Wolf), *Uriel Acosta* (by Gutzkow) and Shakespeare's *Merchant of Venice*.

In Belorussia, the foundation of the Yiddish theatre had to wait until 1926, in spite of various attempts made at the beginning of the 1920s to set one up in Minsk (where a theatrical studio was created). The theatre, founded in 1926 under M. Rafalsky, had a repertoire similar to that in the Ukraine; it was more to the left than *Goset* in Moscow, with the stress on revolutionary plays that put the spotlight on the contribution of the Jews to changes in society. Among the plays staged, or listed for production, were *Boitre* by Moshe Kulbak, *Sunset* by Yitzhak Babel, *Hirsch Lekert* by A. Kushnirov, *Botvin* by Veviurka, *Above and Below* by Bergelson, and *Thief* by Viktor Golovchiner, the theatre's producer. A new theatre created in Belorussia in 1928 was called 'The Wandering Theatre' and it visited more places than did the Minsk theatre.

In Birobidzhan, the fourth Jewish cultural centre, a Jewish theatre was set up in 1934 after many efforts; its first production was *The Party*, a piece put together from a number of Shalom Aleikhem's sketches. When Lazar Kaganovich visited Birobidzhan in February 1936, the theatre put on passages from Shalom Aleikhem's *Gold Miners* for him; Kaganovich said he thought the theatre ought to present heroic moments in the history of the Jewish people.[151] In August of that year the theatre was authorized to call itself the 'Kaganovich Theatre'; it developed between 1937 to 1939 with a bigger budget and a new producer, Moshe Goldblat. Among the plays put on in Birobidzhan were *The Ovadis Family* by Perets Markish, *The Haters* by Gorky and *The Wandering Stars* by Shalom Aleikhem.

How many Jewish theatres were there in the Soviet Union in the 1920s and 1930s? The answer depends on the definition of 'theatre' in Soviet terminology. The data given in the Soviet literature are not clear and are the result of a wish to stress the cultural 'achievements' of the Jews in the Soviet Union. At the height of Jewish artistic creation, at the end of the 1930s and the beginning of the 1940s there were eighteen Yiddish theatres: four in the Russian Republic (Moscow, the Crimea and Birobidzhan), two in Belorussia, and twelve in the Ukraine (Kharkov, Kiev, Odessa, Vinnitsa, Dnepropetrovsk, Kremenchug, Nikolaev and Kalinindorf).[152] In 1939, according to one Soviet source, there were twelve Yiddish theatres (in the cities of Moscow, Leningrad, Birobidzhan, Minsk, Kiev, Kharkov, Odessa, Zhitomir, Dnepropetrovsk, Baku, Tashkent and Simferopol),[153] while according to another source there were only ten.[154]

Among the non-Ashkenazi Jews there was apparently no professional theatre at this time, except for a Bukhanan Jews' theatre in Tashkent – but little is known of its repertoire or activities.[155]

CINEMA

There were no actual Jewish films in the Soviet Union, only attempts to create a Jewish cinema.[156] In 1925 the *Habimah* Theatre was invited to make a film of Shalom Aleikhem's *The Flood*, but it was never screened. Another Yiddish film made at this time was also a Shalom Aleikhem story, *Iddishe Glikn*, based on the Menaḥem Mendel letters, and starring Shlomo Mikhoels. In 1928 a third Jewish film was planned by Gricher-Cherikover, *Durkh trern*. In 1927, one of the best film producers, Grigori Roshal, planned to film *Hirsch Lekert*, and in 1930 a film to be called *The Man from the Little Town* was planned, with Binyamin Zuskin playing the leading role. In Birobidzhan a film about the region itself was planned, to be called *The New People of Birobidzhan* and produced by V. Korsh, again with Zuskin in the leading role. In the second half of the 1930s, when the Soviet Union still wanted to publicize the persecution of the Jews under the Nazi regime, two films were planned on Jewish themes, Leon Feuchtwanger's *The Oppenheim Family* and *Professor* (in German, *Dr*) *Mamlock*, based on the play by F. Wolf.

MUSIC

Music of Jewish composers on Jewish themes (and not music on Jewish themes by non-Jewish composers like Shostakovich) in the Soviet Union can be divided into three main categories: incidental music for plays, and so closely linked with the Jewish theatre; music for Jewish folk-songs or for songs by Soviet Jewish poets, suited to the small Yiddish stage; and music on Jewish themes by Jewish composers without any connection with literature or the theatre. Jewish composers who contributed to Jewish music in this period were Mikhail Gnesin, Yosef Akhron, Aleksander Krein, Lev Pulver, P. Shteinberg, Sh. Rabunsky and M. Milner, and there was a composer of Jewish origin, who wrote music mainly for Russian songs but who also contributed to Jewish music, Yitzhak Dunaevsky.

PAINTING AND SCULPTURE
The greatest Jewish painters and sculptors worked mainly for the theatre and in illustrating Yiddish books. Mark Chagall designed sets for the Jewish theatre in Moscow until he left Russia in 1923. Other artists who assisted the Jewish theatre were Natan Altman, M. Zhitnitsky, Rabichev, Jakob, Rabinovich, Shifrin, R. Falk, A. Tishler and many others. Jewish artists exhibited their works both in general art galleries and in Jewish ones, as well as in mobile exhibitions, which travelled from one town to another and brought art and painting to the Jewish population.

Jewish research institutes and museums

Research institutes, museums and libraries are important not only for research into the nation's past but also to provide training in fostering the national culture. In the 1920s and the first half of the 1930s a network of Jewish research institutions existed in the Soviet Union, most of them connected with Soviet scientific institutes and under the constant supervision of the government and the Evsektsia. Only a few succeeded in preserving their original ideological independence to the end of the 1920s.[157] These research institutes can be divided into Departments and Commissions of the Universities and Academies of Sciences; autonomous centres and institutes; and non-communist, private foundations.

DEPARTMENTS AND COMMISSIONS
In the universities, these were restricted in power, and dependent on their sponsor institutions. The Historical–Archaeological Commission of the Academy of the Ukraine in Kiev was active between 1919 and 1929 in research into Ukrainian Jewish history. Among the members working on this Commission was the historian Ben-Zion Dinur, until he emigrated to Palestine. The central personality was the Jewish–Ukrainian historian, Ilya Galant. In 1928 to 1929, the

Commission published two volumes in the Ukrainian language of researches into Jewish subjects.[158]

Another Jewish institute in the Ukraine in the years 1921 to 1925 was the Philological Commission of the Central Department of Jewish Education in Kharkov. This commission concerned itself with preparing Yiddish terminology for the natural sciences and for schools.

In Belorussia, a special Commission was set up in 1921 under Mikhail Rabinovich, to assemble Jewish books, manuscripts and archive material; but it existed for a short time only and the material collected was transferred to the Institute for Belorussian–Jewish Culture.

The greatest activity in such institutes took place in the Russian Republic. The principal bodies were: the Jewish Department for Regional Ethnographical Research in the University of Leningrad, active only from 1926 to 1927; the Scientific Society of the University of Moscow, active from 1928 to 1931; the Society for Research into the History and Economy of the Jewish Proletariat, part of the Leningrad Branch of the Russian Academy of Sciences, which existed for only one year, 1930; the Jewish Department in the Saltykov–Shchedrin Public Library, which lasted from 1931 to 1937 and did research and issued bibliographical publications; and the Bibliographical Congress of the Moscow Central Education Department held in 1923.

What characterized all these short-lived bodies was that attempts to transfer them to some other place would have led to their being closed down. Moreover, the change from the favourable nationalities policies of the 1920s led at the end of the decade to smaller budgets and to constant fear of the accusation of 'nationalist deviation'.

CENTRES AND INSTITUTES

These enjoyed some autonomy in their scientific work and were more active and longer-lived than the bodies listed above. One of the most important research institutes in the Soviet Union was the Jewish Academy of Science of the Belorussian Academy in Minsk, which functioned from 1924 to 1935. It went through a number of stages initially, changing from a Jewish department to a Jewish sector, before becoming a fully fledged institute. It had three main sections: historical, under I. Sosis; literary, under N. Oyslender; and linguistic, under M. Viner. In the late 1920s and early 1930s, in spite of internal disputes inside the Belorussian Communist Party and between the Belorussian Evsektsia and its Central Bureau in Moscow, the activity of the Institute was varied and wide-ranging. It issued periodical reviews and collections of scientific papers on the history of Israel and of Yiddish language and literature, such as *Zeitshrift* and *Roite bleter*, and prepared an atlas of Yiddish dialects and a complete scientific dictionary. Research was done on the Jewish guilds (artisans' companies) according to their logbooks and on the history of the labour movement in Russia. Some research was also carried out into Jewish folklore and theatre.

The Institute of Jewish Culture in Kiev functioned from 1929 until 1948. From 1929 to 1940, it had the following departments: Historical, Literary, Philological, Socio-economic, Pedagogic and Ethnographical. It had a number of auxiliary institutions: a library, a bibliographical centre, an archive of press and folklore. The Institute hoped to establish affiliated sections in the towns of the Ukraine and also in other republics: the Odessa section was set up in December 1929 and an attempt was made to set up another in 1932 in Birobidzhan. Professor Y. Liberberg visited Birobidzhan with this purpose, but was obliged to give up the idea because of lack of researchers and suitable conditions. Among the more important periodicals published by the Institute of Jewish Culture were: *Di Yidishe sprache* and *Wisenshaft un revolutsie*. The Institute organized scientific congresses, with the participation of researchers from all over the Soviet Union. Among their own senior researchers were Y. Liberberg, the principal until 1932 (when he went to Birobidzhan), Naḥum Oyslender, Eliahu Spivak, Y. Kvitni, Y. Hinchin and others. A heavy blow was dealt to the Institute early in 1936 as a result of the big changes in the nationalities policy and the purges in the Ukrainian Academy of Sciences. It underwent a re-organization, which in fact amounted to its being closed down, and what was called the 'Kabinet' was set up in its place. Of the one hundred or more workers there in 1935 and a budget of 650,000 rubles there now remained only a handful of people with a limited budget, increasingly dependent on the Academy to which the 'Kabinet' was affiliated.[159]

PRIVATE RESEARCH BODIES

It was still possible in the 1920s to set up private scientific institutions and bodies, but they were dependent on the goodwill of the government, which had the power to stop their work. The Historical–

Ethnographical Society in Leningrad, founded by the historian Sh. Dubnov, existed from 1918 to 1930, issuing the periodical *Evreiskaya starina* (Antiquities of the Jews). The Historical Congress of the All-Russian Directorate of the ORT (Association for handicrafts and agricultural labour among the Jews in Russia) was active in Moscow from 1925 to 1930 and published research in demography and the Jewish economy. The OZE (Society for maintenance of health among the Jews) was active in Leningrad from 1926 to 1930 and published brochures on biology and pathology. The OPE (Society for Spreading Enlightenment) continued to be active in the 1920s and published the periodical *Evreiskaya mysl* (Jewish Thought) and *Evreisky vestnik* (Jewish Herald).

Finally, the Commission for Research into Pogroms and Disturbances, under Y. Krasny-Admoni, functioned for a short time and was closed down at the end of 1920.

MUSEUMS AND LIBRARIES

Many museums and libraries were set up in the Soviet Union in this period and they also carried out independent research or assisted other research institutions.[160]

The Jewish Museums in Samarkand was established in 1923. It displayed exhibits such as cult objects, musical instruments, photographs of gravestones, medals and manuscripts. The Belorussian State Museum concerned itself with collecting Jewish pictures, drawings and books; it had a Jewish Department in Odessa, the 'Mendele-Mokher Seforim Museum', which functioned from 1924 to 1933.

The historical–ethnographical museum of Georgian Jewry was set up in 1933, with the aim of training workers for research into the Jews of the Caucasus in general and of Georgia in particular. From 1928 to 1939 the Museum prepared an exhibition on the theme, 'The Old Way of Life of Georgian Jews and the New'. In addition to cultural research work, the Museum also had to promote propaganda among the Jews of Georgia. The arrests, at the end of the 1930s, of people who worked in the Museum or were connected with it (like the writer Herzl Baazov) practically paralysed its work. The Director of the Museum was Aharon Krikheli.

Among the libraries was that of Birobidzhan, which was intended to become the Central Library of the Soviet Jews by the end of the 1930s. It possessed about 10,000 volumes in 1947.

To sum up, from the beginning of the Soviet regime the prospects for the survival of Jewish culture in the Soviet Union were poor, for the following reasons:

(1) Marxist–Leninist theory, with its refusal to recognize the Jews as a people, had little effect in the 1920s but was influential in the later 1930s.

(2) An extra-territorial minority scattered among the different Republics would inevitably have greater difficulty in creating a national culture than a territorial national minority endowed with a federative unit.

(3) The accelerated processes of urbanization and industrialization, together with internal Jewish migrations, modernization and demographical changes, discouraged the traditional attachment of Jewish parents to Jewish schools for their children and their concern for Yiddish culture generally.

(4) The Soviet regime was against the establishment of bodies intended to foster an independent culture.

Despite the difficulties a widespread network of Yiddish educational and cultural institutions did develop, as we have seen, because of the pragmatic policy of the Soviet leadership after it gained power in October 1917. By the end of the 1930s, however, the Hebrew and Russian branches of Jewish culture had been cut down and Yiddish rendered powerless by the wave of purges in which the Evsektsia heads and many leaders of Jewish culture were 'liquidated'.

INDEPENDENT NATIONAL ACTIVITY, TIES WITH WORLD JEWRY AND THE SENSE OF NATIONAL IDENTITY IN SOVIET JEWRY

The new Soviet regime, with its Marxist–Leninist ideology – which affirmed *inter alia* that the Jewish people did not exist – and its resolve to wipe out opposing institutions and parties and to prevent new ones being established, was by its very nature the decisive force governing both the continued activity of Jewish non-communist organizations, parties and institutions and the extent of the ties between Soviet Jewry and other Diasporas of Israel, including the *Yishuv* in Palestine. The fight waged by the new administration, on the initiative and with the assistance of the Evsektsia, and the change in nationalities policy, together with the socio-economic processes already described, finally forged a new national identity for Soviet Jews by the end of the 1930s.

The Bolsheviks end the independent activity of the nationalities

The February 1917 Revolution seemed to open a new era of independent Jewish activity, which had not been able to manifest itself under the tsars. The aspirations of many generations sought national expression in many different forms.

The October Revolution took place at a time when the Russian Jews were creating numerous political, ideological and cultural public organizations, whose nature and aims were bound to change Jewish life. This Revolution met with deep resentment from the Jewish public and with resistance on the part of most of the Jewish political parties and groupings. The Bolshevik Party was welcomed by only a small section of Jewish workers, mostly in the big cities, and its influence on the Jewish public in 1917 and 1918 was slight. This state of affairs began to change during the Civil War because, on the one hand, of the anti-Semitic character of the forces fighting against the Bolsheviks and on the other of the growing strength of the new regime and the solutions it was beginning to offer for the economic distress of the Jewish population.

We shall now consider briefly the activity of the Jewish parties and organizations under the Soviets and their tragic end.

THE NON-ZIONIST OR GENERAL JEWISH PARTIES AND
ORGANIZATIONS

The first victim of the new regime was the small group of 'bourgeois' parties among Russian Jews which disappeared after the October Revolution. The liberal Jewish parties had never been strong, either numerically or in voting power. The *Volkspartei* and the *Volksgruppe* (which received less than 5% of the total votes of the Jewish voters in mid 1917) collapsed when they were made illegal. The big Jewish Socialist parties, which had most influence, the *Bund* and the 'United', lasted a little longer.

The *Bund* Party and its leaders were fierce opponents of the new regime, fighting against the Bolshevik take-over of the state and the administration.[161] At the end of 1918, with the growing strength of the regime and the spread of the Civil War, the inner unity of the *Bund* gave way, and a number of branches, such as Bobruisk, Ekaterinoburg and Odessa created 'left *Bund*ist groups, which grew stronger until they split the Party and founded the 'Communist *Bund*' in the Ukraine and Belorussia. The Evsektsia was interested in the breakdown of the independent Jewish Socialist parties; it did everything in its power to strengthen the left-wing elements in the Jewish parties by promising them their autonomy if they joined the Bolshevik Party and followed the policy of its Jewish Section. On 28 February 1919, a Jewish Communist Party was founded in Belorussia, two-thirds of whose delegates were former *Bund* members. In April 1919 the 'Communist Union' was established in the Ukraine.

The 'United' Party, established in May 1917, went through the same process: strengthening the left wing, which inclined increasingly towards the Bolsheviks, then splitting away from the central and right wings. In fact, the split had already begun on 8 April 1919 with the establishment of the 'United Jewish Communist Party', which inclined towards unification with the 'Communist *Bund*'. In mid-1919 the leaders of the two pro-Bolshevik factions were ready to join the party in power, on condition that their members be admitted to the party as a unit.

The demise of the Jewish Socialist parties came in 1920 and 1921. At the twelfth congress of the *Bund*, which met on 12 April, two factions formed – the left under Esther Frumkin, and the Social Democrats under Rafael Abramovich. A majority of two-thirds of the delegates (forty-three out of sixty-six) supported unification of all the Jewish Communist Parties and were against challenging the Evsektsia. A parellel process befell the 'United' Party. On 9 June 1920 a union of the 'Communist "United"' with the *Bund* was agreed, the name *Bund* being retained; by a majority of forty-seven delegates, with twenty-nine abstaining, it was resolved to join the Russian Communist Party. There are no data on the number of members who joined the Communist Party but it was between six and eleven thousand.[162] Thousands of former *Bund* and 'United' members stopped all political activity. For the Evsektsia, this accretion of strength was decisive not only quantitatively but also qualitatively, since the heads of the *Bund* would soon take over all the influential positions and would remain at the head of the Evsektsia until it was 'dissolved' in January 1930.

The non-Zionist religious grouping, organized at the end of the war and reaching the peak of its activity in mid-1917, did not create a 'party' as such; it was a federative union of about fifty local and national groups (with names such as 'Israel the Eternal', 'Assembly of Israel', 'Keepers of the Law', 'Glory of Israel' and *Agudat* [League of] *Yisrael*). The anti-religious and anti-bourgeois campaigns of the new regime did not allow this group any possibility of survival, once Soviet rule was effectively established in most of Russia. The only organized activity that continued was that of the Hassidic *Habad* movement, headed by Rabbi Schneurson, who was arrested and finally forced to leave the Soviet Union. The *Habad* Hassidim worked in clandestine groups under the name *Tiferet Bahurim* up to the end of the 1930s, and even in the late 1940s despite numerous arrests among their members.

ZIONIST PARTIES AND ORGANIZATIONS

Before the October Revolution, the Zionist Movement was the most important public and political force in Russian Jewry, with around 300,000 active members in 1,200 towns, big and small. Like the non-Zionist Parties, it included different political–theoretical currents: the general Zionist or liberal, the socialist and the religious. The 'general' and 'religious' were the first to disappear. On its establishment, the Soviet regime made all 'clerical' and 'bourgois' parties illegal by legislative Act. The First Zionist Congress met in Moscow on 20 April 1920, with ninety delegates, some of whom were arrested and put on trial. Thereafter the only Zionist group that fought to maintain a legal existence (and an illegal one as well) was that of the socialists or people close to its theoretical basis.

The *Poalei-Zion* Party was theoretically the most firmly based on Marxist theory and the teachings of Ber Borokhov; it went through a process similar to that of the two non-Zionist socialist parties, the *Bund* and the 'United'. The *Poalei-Zion* was in a particularly difficult position: on the one hand, it was distrusted by the other Zionist parties because of its political radicalism and Marxist ideology; and on the other hand, the general socialist parties could not accept its Zionism.[163] Some leaders of *Poalei-Zion* joined the Jewish Commissariat established in the Narkomnats in 1918. A split formed in the Russian and worldwide *Poalei-Zion* in 1919, and deepening in 1920 as a result of the *Poalei-Zion* Congress in Vienna. In the Soviet Union, the extreme wing of *Poalei-Zion*, calling itself 'Left *Poalei-Zion*, founded the Jewish Communist Party and took an active part in Soviet government institutions. It attempted to join the 'Comintern' (founded in March 1919), but was faced with the demand to give up its Zionist platform, which it refused to do. In December 1922 the Jewish Communist Party split up, some of its members joining the Russian Communist Party and the rest continuing legally in the party until 1928.

The Labour-Zionist movement in Russia carried great weight because of its large membership and its activity in the '*Zeirei-Zion*' Party.[164] Differences of opinion were already evident at the second congress of the party, which was held in May 1917, and in spite of the adoption of a compromise party 'platform', the differences continued to exist. At one extreme were the supporters of socialist movements, such as the Social-Democrats, and at the other the 'toilers', *trudoviki* (workers), closer to the Social-Revolutionaries. The divergence between the two was seen again at the third congress in Kharkov in May 1920, attended by about forty delegates. Two parties emerged – the Zionist–Socialist Party and the 'Party of the Toilers – '*Zeirei-Zion*'. As far as theoretical identity with parties in Palestine at that time is concerned, the Zionist–Socialist Party was close to *Ahdut-Avodah*, while the 'Toilers' Party' was close to *Hapoel Ha-zair*. As we shall see, this split led to the break-up of the *He-Haluz* movement and of the Zionist–Socialist Youth Movement in 1923. In spite of the split, of arrests and harassment, both parties extended their membership and their activities to many towns in 1924 and 1925, at which time the membership of the Zionist–Socialist Party alone was about 4,000 (and of its youth section about 2,500 in 1923). In the 'Party of the Toilers – '*Zeirei-Zion*' – there were about 2,000 members from 1922 to 1926; and in its affiliated youth movements, such as *Ha-shomer Ha-zair* and *IVOSM* (the General Zionist Youth Organization in Russia) there were about 15,000 members in 1926. *Zeirei-Zion* operated clandestinely from its inception and continued to function until the beginning of the 1930s. On 24 May 1929 it set up a National Commission, which decided to intensify the party's work in small towns with large Jewish populations. In September 1934 the last central organizer of the party's activity was arrested and its activity ended.

The *Haluz* (Pioneer) Movement held a special place among all the Jewish movements and organizations established in Russia.[165] The idea of a grouping of Zionists who were sworn to put their beliefs into practice was put forward even before World War I, but could not be realized until the war was over. The attraction of *He-haluz* was the combination of the basic aim of universal revolution with a Jewish-national content. Removement began in the year of the Revolution, 1917, with the simultaneous and as it were spontaneous appearance of *Haluz* groups in various places. The ideological ties of this movement were with *Zeirei-Zion* in the first stage, and it was at the Conference in May 1917 that the idea was accepted of founding a federation of the *Ḥaluẓ* groups.

A *He-ḥaluẓ* Council met from 15 to 18 May 1918, with about twenty delegates. The meeting deliberated on the character and future path of the movement and decided to set up a United National congress of *He-ḥaluẓ* in Russia. The congress met in Petrograd from 6 to 9 January 1919, with thirty delegates participating. The second congress met in October 1920, and the third and last congress of the united *He-ḥaluẓ* met in January 1922, when all its members were arrested.

Until 1923, attempts were made to secure legalization for the *He-ḥaluẓ* movement, attempts that led to disputes among its leaders and to the split that occurred in September 1923. Before the split, the *He-ḥaluẓ* members numbered about 3,000, organized in sixty-five branches.[166] After it, the legal ('left – class') *He-ḥaluẓ* numbered about 1,600, a figure that rose at its peak to about 7,000. Members of the 'toiling *He-ḥaluẓ*' (now the right wing) had about 1,500 members in 1924, and in 1926, the peak year, about 9,000.

The most important settlement work done by the *He-ḥaluẓ* movement was the founding of agricultural units in the Crimea, the Ukraine and Belorussia. In 1925 there were seventy-nine such units, where 600 members were preparing themselves for emigration to Palestine.[167]

After the ending of the NEP, *He-ḥaluẓ* was abolished by official decree on 1 March 1928, and the paper, '*He-ḥaluẓ*', which had appeared since 1924, ceased to appear in 1926. Arrests of members of *He-ḥaluẓ* and of the other Zionist parties increased in the 1930s, but clandestine organized Zionist work went on until 1934.

Ties with world Jewry

The family, cultural and political ties of Russian Jews with world Jewry were of great importance in the tsarist period, as we have seen, and were even more important in the Soviet era, because of the nature of the new regime and its inclination to cut itself off from the outside world politically and ideologically.

In the relatively liberal 1920s, when the Soviet government wanted to increase its diplomatic and economic contacts with capitalist countries,[168] it was easier for Jewish organizations and individuals in Jewish communities in different countries to keep in touch with

Soviet Jews, but these contacts ceased in the 1930s and were even dangerous for Soviet Jews, because they could lead to accusations of spying and disloyalty to the socialist fatherland, a danger which became a reality in the purges of the later 1930s.

The ties between Soviet Jews and those in the rest of the world can be classified as follows: links with Jewish welfare organizations; links with Zionist political organizations; and links with 'progressive' scholars, scientists, writers and artists like Einstein, Leivik, Opatoshu, Brainin, and others. We shall deal here with the first two of these categories, since they were particularly important for the Soviet Jews in the Soviet Union and affected their sense of national identity.

TIES WITH JEWISH WELFARE ORGANIZATIONS

We have already noted that the Soviet government was both financially and politically interested in getting assistance from world Jewry, while the Jewish welfare organizations were interested in maintaining contact with the Soviet Jews and giving them as much aid as possible. Official cooperation began between the Soviet government institutions dealing with this matter and Jewish welfare organizations like the 'Joint', Agro-Joint, ORT and OZE.[169]

Visits of delegations from abroad, numerous in the 1920s, and the creation of special institutions in the Soviet Union to handle the grant of aid to Soviet Jews maintained contact between them and other Jews, mainly in the USA, a contact which had been cut off during the war and not renewed by the Soviet regime. The assistance to Jewish educational bodies for vocational training helped indirectly to preserve the Jewish national content of the educational programmes.

The work of the Jewish welfare organizations was faced with numerous difficulties in the 1920s, both because of the Evsektsia's being opposed to their presence and because of administrative and police surveillance. Often searches and arrests were made among the foreign employees of the welfare organizations and agents infiltrated their ranks. Members of ORT and Agro-Joint often had to turn a blind eye to the arrest of *ḥaluzim* (agricultural trainees) on the farms they were running. The atmosphere of terror in the later 1930s restricted contacts between Soviet citizens and foreigners, and in 1938 Jewish welfare organizations ceased functioning in the Soviet Union.

TIES WITH THE ZIONIST MOVEMENT AND THE YISHUV IN
PALESTINE

The main contacts between Soviet Jews and Jews in the rest of the
world were maintained by the Zionist Movement in the 1920s and
1930s. The Soviet leadership despite waging a fierce campaign from
the outset against Zionism and its influence over Soviet Jews, still
concerned itself with events in Palestine and kept in touch with various representatives of the Yishuv and leaders of the Zionist Movement, thus boosting the Zionist organizations within the Soviet
Union.

In 1921 Dr David Eder visited the Soviet Union and met a number
of Zionist leaders there. In 1923 there was a visit by *Histadrut* leaders
David Ben-Gurion, Meir Rotberg and Yehudah Kopelevich (Almog)
to the international agricultural exhibition; they met the leaders of
the Zionist and *He-ḥaluẓ* Movements and even tried to get their
various factions to cooperate with each other. In 1924 *Histadrut* leaders David Remez and Levi Shkolnik (Eshkol) also came on a visit. In
1925 renewed attempts were made to influence the Soviet authorities
to change their anti-Zionist line and allow Zionist work in the Soviet
Union.[170]

In addition to the official delegations that visited the Soviet Union,
either by invitation or at least with official authorization, emissaries
were sent to the Soviet Union to work illegally in the Zionist Movement there. The last two of these emissaries, David Horenshtein and
Shmuel Schneurson, reached the Soviet Union in 1927.[171] Some of
the leaders of the Soviet Zionist Movement also made illegal visits
abroad, to take part in Zionist conferences in Europe.

In the 1930s the leaders of the Zionist Movement and the *Yishuv* in
Palestine also had various contacts with Soviet representatives. Between 1932 and 1934 Ben-Gurion was in constant touch with the
heads of 'Intourist', hoping to get a visa to visit the Soviet Union, in
order to conduct economic negotiations in Moscow and to arrange to
bring Jews from Odessa to Palestine in Soviet ships. When the Soviet
Union joined the League of Nations, Naḥum Goldmann contacted
two senior Soviet diplomats in France and in the League of Nations,
Grigori Potiomkin and Marcel Rosenberg, hoping to secure improved relations between the Soviet Union and the Zionist Movement, but without result.[172]

The most important issue was of emigration of Jews from the
Soviet Union to Palestine.[173] At the time of the Revolution and the

Civil War, from 1917 to 1920, the borders were stil open and thousands of Zionists managed to leave Russia illegally. From 1920 to 1939, Jews emigrated from the Soviet Union in two main ways – emigration in accordance with the laws and regulations in force, or emigration by means of banishment. There are no data on the number of Jewish emigrants from the Soviet Union into Palestine in 1918 and 1939, but from 1919 to 1924 an estimated 20,000 Jews came in from the Soviet Union and an estimated 12,500 from 1925 to 1936.[174]

If we add Jews who emigrated from the Soviet Union to countries other than Palestine, the total number of Jews emigrating between 1919 and 1939 must have been about 70,000.

The sense of national identity

All Jews are aware that they belong to an ethnic group with common character traits, a common past and a common destiny. It is difficult to estimate the strength of this feeling of identification with the group, particularly in the Soviet Union, where published data are scarce. We shall discuss this question in chapter 4; here we shall seek to examine how modernization and Sovietization affected the Jews between 1917 and 1939.

As we saw when we dealt with Jewish demography, many Jews 'disappeared', that is to say, they did not declare their Jewish nationality in the population censuses of 1926 to 1939 – about 10%, while at the time of the 1897 census the proportion seems to have been 1 or 2%. During most of the later period – at least until the mid-1930s – the Jews felt that state anti-Semitism no longer existed and that they had nothing to fear from declaring Jewish nationality; therefore the 10% non-declaration among Soviet Jews must have been due mainly to assimilation.

Acculturation among the Jews began at the end of the nineteenth and the beginning of the twentieth century. Individual Jews adjusted to the Russian culture and way of life without losing their sense of national identity. In this way, they were able to live in an increasingly open society, enjoying the available education, professional advancement and daily contacts. The circle of Jews who underwent partial or complete acculturation grew as a result of social and economic changes in the Jewish population between the two World Wars, and was increased by the policy of Russification. Several indicators can help us to discern the changes that occurred in the Jews' sense of national identity between 1917 and 1939: mixed marriages, use of the Yiddish language, integration in the State apparatus, and emigration (in the sense of the wish to escape from the Soviet Union).

There were hardly any mixed marriages among Russian Jews at the beginning of the century, as conditions under the tsarist regime prohibited them. Even during the years from 1905 to 1917, the Jewish way of life in the closed religious–national communities of the Pale of Settlement was a barrier to mixed marriages. The Revolutions of 1917 and the establishment of the new regime with its ideology of 'the brotherhood of peoples', together with the demographic and economic processes at work, led to a significant increase in mixed marriages. In 1925 in the European part of the Russian Republic there were 18.83 mixed marriages for every 100 Jewish males.[175] In 1926 in this Republic there were about 21% of mixed marriages among the Jews, while in 1927 in the Ukraine of the Pale of Settlement the figure was 11.1%.[176] We have no data for the 1930s, but it is reasonable to assume that the ratio of mixed marriages rose in this period.

In 1926 nearly 25% of all the Jews in the Soviet Union declared that their mother-tongue was Russian, while in 1939 this proportion rose to 54.6%, having doubled in the course of thirteen years – and this at a time when there was still a network of Yiddish schools and research institutes, Yiddish books and newspapers, etc. This shows that the voluntary process of Russification of the Jews was swift; Sovietization – integration into the apparatuses of the party and administration – was, as we have seen, also swift in this period.

The wish of so many Jews to leave the country where they were born and where they had lived their lives in order to emigrate to some unknown country originated both from their rejection of the politico-economic reality in the Soviet Union, and from some 'positive' attraction to the country of their destination. There is no doubt that, in addition to the 70,000 Jews who succeeded in leaving the Soviet Union between 1919 and 1939, there were many thousands more, mainly in Zionist and religious circles, who wanted to emigrate on account of the restrictions on Jewish culture and religion and because they suffered great hardship for their faith.

So, on the eve of the outbreak of the Second World War, sections of the Jewish population of the Soviet Union were becoming assimilated: ties between individual and their ethnic group were weakening, and there was a transition from merely learning the Russian language to a mental and spiritual bond with Russian culture. The other aspect of the process of assimilation – indifference, even hostility to Jewish national culture – began to be felt increasingly in the 1930s, mainly in the Russian Republic and in the big cities of the other republics.

3

The years of destruction, 1939–1953

The years from 23 August 1939, the German–Soviet Non-Aggression Pact to 5 March 1953, Stalin's death, were the worst in the history of Soviet Jews, and were correctly called 'the black years', years of 'physical and spiritual holocaust', of 'anxiety and despair'.

As individuals and as a national minority, the Jews were the object of an intense hatred, both under the Nazi regime which sought their extermination, and under the Stalinist regime which regarded them with suspicion and hatred. Caught between two totalitarian regimes at the peak of their power, the Jews had to fight for survival. The period can be divided into three sub-periods: 1939–41, the years of German-Soviet friendship; 1941–5, the war years; and 1945–53, the post-war period.

In the first, relatively short, period, the Jewish population in the Soviet Union underwent far-reaching changes in its socio-economic composition, with the new western frontier increasing its number from three to five million. There was a certain softening in the official anti-nationalist line and a halt to the dissolution of Jewish cultural institutions. Moreover, the influence of Jews from Poland, Romania, and the Baltic States, with their strong sense of Jewish identity, was of immeasurable importance in reinvigorating Jewish national feeling, which had begun to fade under the impact of Sovietization in the late 1930s.

Then, in the war years, in the shadow of the Holocaust, and despite Jewish heroism in the army, the partisan forces and the ghettos, an equivocal official policy was pursued regarding the Jewish minority. This was manifested on the one hand by the establishment of the Jewish Anti-Fascist Committee and an increase in cultural activity, and on the other hand by official silence over the Holocaust, anti-Jewish discrimination, and lack of opposition to anti-Semitism.

In the post-war period, the anti-Jewish direction of Stalin's policy became increasingly evident, reaching its height in the years 1948 to 1953, when an official campaign was waged against Jewish nationalism, 'cosmopolitanism', and Zionism. In the last years of Stalin's life, Soviet Jews were faced with the greatest threat in their history: exile. Only Stalin's death saved them from this fate.

ANTI-SEMITISM

The Second World War unleashed popular anti-Semitism of a kind unknown even in tsarist Russia; it spread from areas conquered by the Germans and reached even the ranks of the partisans and the Red Army. The main reasons were:

(1) Like other emotional states of mind, anti-Semitism is intensified in times of crisis, and there had never been a graver crisis than the Second World War.

(2) In the search for 'the guilty', 'those responsible' for the disasters that had befallen the Soviet Union at the outbreak of war, the Jews were an ideal scapegoat.

(3) Nazi propaganda, presenting the Jews as the embodiment of everything that was wrong with the Soviet regime, spread anti-Semitism more widely than ever before.

(4) Territories with a multi-national population of about twenty-five million, largely influenced by the anti-Semitism current in the semi-Fascist regimes of Eastern Europe, were annexed to the Soviet Union.

(5) The official policy aimed at arousing the patriotic national feelings of the Russian and non-Russian peoples, in order to intensify the war effort, had some unfavourable effects, one of which was latent or semi-latent anti-Semitism.[1]

Official Soviet policy showed an almost total disregard for the existence of this rising wave of anti-Semitism. Still more disturbing was Soviet silence about the Nazi policy of exterminating the Jews;[2] Stalin mentioned Nazi Germany's anti-Jewish policy only once during the war years – at the beginning of the war.[3] This policy resulted from two closely related factors: the first was a complex of political, social and psychological considerations which required the anti-Semitic feelings of the population to be taken into account, supposedly for reasons of state; the second factor was the existence of the same anti-Semitic sentiments in the Soviet leadership, headed by

Stalin, as personal testimonies recently published in the West prove.[4] At a meeting between Stalin, Sikorski, Anders and Kot, held in December 1941 to discuss the establishment of a Polish army in the Soviet Union, there was unanimous agreement that Jews were cowardly fighters,[5] and in his conversations with President Roosevelt at Yalta Stalin made derogatory remarks about the Jews.[6]

Not only did the end of the war not end the anti-Semitic feeling current in the Soviet Union during the war, but it led to its intensification, especially in areas which had been occupied by the Nazis, for obvious reasons. The old factors which had given rise to anti-Semitism were now complemented by new ones, above all the fear of a sector of the local population which had cooperated with the Nazis that the Jews returning to their former homes would demand the return of their apartments and property. Those who had taken over the posts held by the Jews before the outbreak of war, especially in institutions of higher education, art and science, were afraid that the returning Jews would demand them back.

The authorities were of course aware of this danger. On the one hand, the regime feared that by being identified with the return of the Jews it would lose the population's support to the anti-Soviet nationalist movement, which was particularly strong in the Ukraine and Lithuania, and was exploiting anti-Semitism for its own purposes. On the other hand, they could not ignore the inherent dangers of a policy tolerating displays of anti-Semitism, because it would be difficult to compete with the nationalist movements without using anti-Semitism to promote government aims. Their considerations, therefore, were based on objective interests. The humanitarian aspect of the suffering of the Jews and the need to rehabilitate the victims of the Holocaust do not seem to have played any part in these considerations.

The official policy for the Jewish minority, as implemented after 1946, was based on the following principles:

(1) Limited and discreet moves against the more extreme manifestations of anti-Semitism.

(2) Allowing Jews to return to their former homes in liberated areas, but conducting propaganda to persuade them to remain where they had lived during the war.

(3) Admitting Jews to economic, educational and art institutions, but with certain restrictions; and not accepting them for political and security posts in the party or in government.

(4) Granting limited opportunities for the reconstruction of Jewish cultural life.

Even at this stage, however, there were signs that Stalin had decided upon a much more extreme anti-Jewish line. This manifested itself first in the systematic removal of Jews from positions they still occupied in the government apparatus, and especially in institutions connected with the conduct of Soviet foreign policy, such as the Foreign Ministry, the Ministry of Foreign Trade, the army and security services. Second, various steps were taken to restrict the activity of the Jewish Anti-Fascist Committee, the only representative Jewish body established during the war. Third, the campaign against 'Jewish nationalism' began to assume a more serious character than that waged against the other nationalities, because of the inferior status of the Jewish minority in the Soviet Union and the tenuous state of Jewish culture after the Second World War. Fourth, hints began to appear in the press and other mass media that the Jews constituted a foreign element, possessing dual loyalties, and capable in times of crisis of betraying the socialist motherland and going over to her enemies. Finally, the murder of Mikhoels, head of the Jewish Anti-Fascist Committee and director of the Moscow State Yiddish Theatre, on the 13 January 1948, made plain to all those who had looked forward to a revival of 'Jewish statehood' in the Soviet Union that their hopes were vain, and that they had to expect the worst.

Official anti-Jewish policy reached its harshest stage between November 1948, when the Jewish Anti-Fascist Committee was disbanded and nearly all its members arrested, and March 1953, when a show trial of Jewish doctors was to be held, and plans for exiling Jews were implemented. We shall deal with various aspects of this period later, referring here to only one aspect of this policy, which was perhaps less drastic than others but reflecting the 'spirit of the times', namely, the influence of anti-Semitic publications appearing in the Soviet press.

Scrutiny of articles, both 'serious' and 'humorous', published in the Soviet press between 1948 and 1953 reveals a distorted picture of the Jew. In the eyes of the general public, including the Soviet intelligentsia, a stereotype emerged, which could only foster anti-Semitism. The Jew was portrayed as generally corrupt; he regularly evaded military service, and this even at the most difficult point in the history of the Soviet Union (he was sent to the front but miraculously always reached the rear); he was not attached to any one place (he was an eternal wanderer incapable of attachment to any particular spot); he was unable and unwilling to work, his ambition being rather to make an easy living (a parasite by nature). As soon as he settled into a job, he brought in members of his family or acquaintances (family and community nepotism); his certificates were acquired through false claims or sharp practice; and promotion at work was the direct result of fraud. Thus the Jew was portrayed as exploiter, professional swindler, and smooth operator (although his Jewish origin was not explicitly mentioned, the reader was given numerous hints), frequently appearing as a villainous figure in literature (Shylock and Fagin, for instance), and naturally aroused loathing and revulsion, as well as jealousy and anger. From this it was a short step to hatred. The extent to which this propaganda was accepted, not only by ordinary people but also by representatives of the more 'cultured' classes, can be judged from various testimonies.[7] There were naturally many reasons why wide circles of the population absorbed anti-Semitism from above. We have already pointed to the anti-Semitic tradition in Russia, the Ukraine, Lithuania, and other nations, which was fed during the war by Nazi propaganda. But there was also the difficult economic situation, the housing shortage, hard working conditions, fierce competition for promotion, all at a time when expectations of better things had been disappointed; these were the factors which contributed to the growing hatred of foreigners, strangers, and all those whose situation seemed, rightly or wrongly, to be superior. If we add the existence of a totalitarian regime which created an atmosphere of anti-intellectualism and xenophobia, then the Jew seems an ideal target for this hatred; all the authorities had to do was to channel the people's wrath towards the Jews.

The question which we have to ask, but which is difficult to answer, is: how far are we justified in seeing official anti-Semitism as a direct result of 'objective needs', and how far did this policy spring from strong anti-Jewish feelings in the minds of the Soviet leaders, especially Stalin? Despite the 'need' to find a scapegoat for failures, the desire to assuage resentment by channelling it away from those responsible, and the other advantages that could be gained from an anti-Semitic policy, the government was strong enough to manage without the use of a weapon as potentially dangerous to the user as anti-Semitism, bearing in mind that the Communist regime proclaimed its policy of equality for all nations and all races. The regime could have abandoned anti-Semitism, but it did not; and we must conclude, therefore, subjective as well as objective interests were taken into account when an anti-Semitic policy was adopted.

If Stalin was anti-Semitic, as the foregoing analysis seems to show, it is important to examine why this was so. In analysing Stalin's attitude towards the Jews, it is possible to use the three clinical charts of anti-Semitic behaviour suggested by Rudolph Loewenstein: (a) the existence of an attitude of lurking suspicion, of wariness which, when reinforced, can become a feeling of loathing; (b) Judophobia, taking the form of mixed hatred and fear, loathing and contempt; (c) the 'paranoic' anti-Semitism of people who believe in an international Jewish 'plot' to enslave and destroy the Aryan world.[8] Of course, not everyone who has been aroused to anti-Jewish sentiments needs to pass through all three stages. It is reasonable to assume that most anti-Semites remain in one of the first two stages; some, however, may 'leap' to the paranoic stage. It seems likely that this 'theory of stages' holds good for Stalin, and we shall attempt to trace the roots of his anti-Semitism.

It is unlikely that Stalin had many encounters with Jews in his native town of Gori which would arouse anti-Jewish feelings. There were rumours, however, also to be found in Maxim Litvinov's diary,[9] that the young Stalin's anti-Semitism resulted from the fact that his father was in fierce competition with a Jewish shoemaker in the town. However, the Litvinov diary later proved to be a forgery; and even if Zinovyev's evidence in this book were not false, it is not really convincing. It is possible that Stalin may have become prejudiced against the Jews during his years of study at the theological seminary in Tiflis, since there is evidence that an extreme Jesuitical and Russificatory atmosphere prevailed in that institution.[10] On the other hand, we have the case of Anastas Mikoyan, a pupil at a similar institution who is not identified with Jew-haters.[11] At the beginning of his revolutionary activity, Stalin met only a limited number of revolutionaries of Jewish origin.[12] Thus, it was only from 1906 on, when he first went to the Stockholm congress, that meetings with Jews became more frequent. For the ambitious Stalin, suffering from an inferiority complex and consumed with jealousy, Bolsheviks like Kamenev, Zinovyev and Litvinov could have aroused feelings of hatred, but these would not necessarily take the form of anti-Semitism. Also, Stalin's hostile attitude towards the Menshevik faction, in which the Jews held an important place, still does not prove that this hostility sprang from an anti-Semitic background. Perhaps the only accurate reflection of Stalin's attitude to the Jews at this time is the following extract from his report on the party congress in London, which he published in 1907 in *Bakinsky rabochy*:

Not less interesting is the composition of the congress from the standpoint of nationalities. Statistics showed that the majority of the Menshevik faction consists of Jews – and this of course without counting the Bundists – after which came Georgians and then Russians. On the other hand, the overwhelming majority of the Bolshevik faction consists of Russians, after which come Jews – not counting of course the Poles and Letts – and then Georgians, etc. For this reason one of the Bolsheviks observed in jest [it seems, Comrade Aleksinsky] that the Mensheviks are a Jewish faction and the Bolsheviks a genuine Russian faction, so it would not be a bad idea for us Bolsheviks to arrange a pogrom in the party.[13]

The publication of this feeble joke in a Russia that had just been swept by a wave of pogroms seems to be more than merely bad taste, and Stalin's essay, 'Marxism and the National Question', published in 1913, is a concentrated attack on the Jewish nation, the *Bund*, and Zionism. Even though the ideas in this essay are similar to those in Lenin's articles on the subject, it is difficult not to feel that Stalin was making a special attack on the Jews. To sum up this chapter of Stalin's life, which ended with the Bolshevik victory in the October Revolution, in accordance with Loewenstein's scheme, it seems that at this time, suspicion and perhaps even subconscious rejection of the Jews were being aroused in him.

After the October Revolution, Stalin came into contact with a large number of Jews in the course of his various party and government duties. His dispute with Trotsky in 1918 had by the second half of the 1920s spread to include the most prominent party leaders of Jewish birth.[14] During this fight for control of the state, did Stalin recall Aleksinky's jest about the Jewish faction (by this time the 'United Opposition' in his party)? What is known, as we have already pointed out, is that he used anti-Semitism to promote his personal aims.

The evidence of Stalin's daughter, Svetlana Allilueva,[15] is very important, because it helps us to understand how Stalin's ideas changed from suspicion to hatred, contempt and fear.[16] It seems that the transition began in 1948, when Stalin, with his Russificatory tendencies, began to imagine that an international Jewish plot was being concocted against the Soviet Union.[17]

Even during the worst period of anti-Semitic policies, between 1949 and 1953, Stalin was careful not to express his feelings publicly. However, his anti-Semitic position was well-known among the Soviet leadership and rumours about it began to filter out to the general public both within the Soviet Union and beyond its borders.[18] Judging by the ruthless acts perpetrated by Stalin over a long period of time, it is clear that nothing would have deterred him from implementing his plan to exile Soviet Jewry to Siberia, and that only his death saved it from this fate.[19] Reports of partial exiling of Jews from various regions (mainly the Ukraine and Belorussia) had appeared in the West even earlier (*Jewish Chronicle*, 29 July 1949, 23 November 1951, and 9 May 1952) but it seems they were exaggerated or perhaps 'premature'.

THE CAMPAIGN AGAINST 'JEWISH NATIONALISM' AND 'COSMOPOLITANISM'

From the beginning of the regime, basic insoluble contradictions in the national problem of the Soviet Union necessitated a constant campaign against 'nationalist' deviations. Although campaigns against Jewish nationalism and Jewish cosmopolitanism were frequently carried out simultaneously, we believe that three main periods can be distinguished: (a) 1946–8, when a campaign was waged against all forms of bourgeois nationalism; (b) 1948–9, when the campaign was mainly against cosmopolitanism; and (c) 1950–3, which saw a campaign against both 'deviations'. Whereas in the post-Stalin era the anti-cosmopolitan campaign ceased almost completely (for reasons which we shall discuss later), the campaign against bourgeois nationalism flared up from time to time, affecting the Jews sporadically.

The campaign against Jewish nationalism, 1946 to 1948

The war period brought a relative relaxation of the struggle the authorities had been conducting against nationalist 'deviation', especially in the second half of the 1930s. This relaxation sprang from the need to unite all the Soviet peoples in the battle against Germany; but it also enabled the intelligentsia of the Soviet nationalities to exploit these circumstances by freer expression of their national aspirations. By 1944, however, the first signs could be detected both of an impending change for the worse and of a resumption of the campaign against nationalist 'deviations'.

In August 1944, the Central Committee of the Communist Party decided to improve ideological activity in the Tatar Autonomous Republic and to eliminate what were described as serious mistakes of a nationalist character made by historians and writers.[20] A similar criticism was levelled at the Bashkir Communists in January 1945.[21] In March 1945, the Kazakh historians were accused of nationalism because of the book, *A History of the Kazakh People*, which had been highly praised on its publication in 1943.[22]

At the end of the war, in May 1945, the attacks on bourgeois nationalism, particularly aimed at historians, writers, philosophers and artists, were extended to the European republics liberated from German occupation.[23] The fiercest campaign was conducted in the Ukrainian Republic, beginning in June 1946.[24] In 1947 and 1948, the campaign was intensified and its scope widened.[25] The targets of these attacks can be summed up as follows:

(1) Idealization of the past, by the glorification of epochs of special significance for a particular nation and 'exaggerated' portrayals of national heroes (e.g. the Tatar Idegei, the Kazakh Kenesary Kasymov, Shamil among the peoples of the Northern Caucasus, etc.).

(2) 'Insufficient' evaluation of the national fraternity between Russians and non-Russians, and sometimes even emphasis on the enmity between them, e.g. the 'incorrect' description of the war of 1812 in the play *Kakhim Turya*, whose author pitted Russian and Bashkir fighters against each other.

(3) 'Insufficient' appraisal of the influence of Russian culture on the culture of other nations.

(4) 'Failure to appreciate' the progressive aspect of the tsarist conquests (or, in Soviet terminology, the union of the non-Russian nations with Russia) which brought about the abolition of feudalism. Many Soviet historians had viewed the tsarist conquest as an absolute evil, or as a lesser evil in comparison with possible conquest by a neighbouring power. In this period both concepts began to be questioned, though it was only after 1950 that the new policy of considering the Russian conquest as an *absolute good* was adopted.

(5) 'Insufficient appreciation' of the decisive role of Russian in saving Europe from the Tatar yoke.

(6) Lack of emphasis on the enmity of states such as Turkey and Iran towards the peoples of the Caucasus and Central Asia.

(7) Acceptance of the 'single-stream' theory, which leads to disregarding the class war being waged within all nations. The increasingly fierce campaign against nationalist deviations, which included, as we have seen, the major nationalities of the Soviet Union, could not have passed over the Soviet Jews.

The signal for attacks on Jewish nationalism to begin came in Zhdanov's speech in August 1946 and the Resolutions subsequently adopted by the CPSU (Communist Party of the Soviet Union) Central Committee. The article which set the campaign in motion appeared on 24 September 1946, in *Eynikayt*, the organ of the Jewish Anti-Fascist Committee.[26] It emphasized that the Resolutions of the Central Committee immediately concerned Jewish theatre and literature. A number of important writers, poets and playwrights, such as Sh. Halkin, E. Fininberg, A. Sutskever and M. Pinchevsky were accused of producing works that were apolitical, devoid of ideas, and nationalist in character. On 10 October 1946, a critique of S. Verite's book *When the Earth Burned* appeared, accusing the author of being too preoccupied with Jewish history and of slandering the Soviet people.[27] Two days later, an article by the literary critic Y. Dobrushin, appeared, in which he appealed to Jewish writers not to confine themselves to a limited national framework but to describe the general social processes of the whole of Soviet society.[28] On 14 December 1946, writers and theatre and literary critics were called upon to write in the spirit of A. Zhdanov's speech.[29] The writer Itsik Kipnis was attacked here for the first time, though only because of his 'small town' approach. In April 1947 the campaign resumed; variety artists were attacked for continuing to provide their audiences with matter that was apolitical and devoid of ideas, and for romanticizing the old Jewish way of life.[30] In July and August 1947, a major campaign against Kipnis was conducted in the pages of the Jewish and Ukrainian press and at writers' conventions, which resulted in his being expelled from the Writers' Union and, later, in his arrest. The occasion for the attacks was a story which Kipnis wrote after the war called 'Without Giving It a Thought', which was published in full only in Poland.[31]

The signal for the attacks on Kipnis was given in the newspaper *Eynikayt*, in a leading article headed 'Nationalism in the Guise of Friendship of Peoples'. 'Only a nationalist', the article stated, 'is capable of placing Soviet awards and medals, which symbolize the honour, greatness and courage of the Soviet people, side by side with

... the Star of David. Jewish fighters would of course reject this award of Kipnis.'[32] The writer Leyb Kvitko, who had been elected at the end of 1946 to the post of Chairman of the Jewish Section of the Soviet Writers' Union, joined in the attacks two days later.[33] 'Kipnis was forewarned', wrote Kvitko, 'a series of critical remarks were addressed to him, but unfortunately he paid no attention to them. He allowed himself to ignore our criticism and went still further astray'.[34] On 15 September 1947, at a session of the Ukrainian Writers' Union convened to discuss Resolutions of the Central Committee concerning the journals *Leningrad* and *Zvezda*, A. Korneichuk, the Chairman of the union, attacked Itsik Kipnis in his opening speech for his bourgeois nationalist deviation. 'Kipnis', said Korneichuk, 'slandered Soviet man in the story he sent to the Zionist newspaper in Poland by wanting the Star of David – the Zionist symbol – to be worn alongside the Soviet Star on the breast of the Soviet soldier.'[35]

The strongest attack in the Ukrainian press came from two Yiddish writers living in the Ukraine, H. Polyanker and M. Talalaevsky,[36] who wrote, 'It would not hurt Kipnis to know that the five-pointed Soviet Star has long since overshadowed both the six-pointed Star of David, as well as Petlyura's Trident, and all the eagles and other nationalist emblems.'[37] On 17 October, at a meeting of Kiev writers, Polyanker once more attacked Itsik Kipnis,[38] and on 28 October Kipnis was accused of nationalist recidivism.[39] However, the culminating point in the campaign against Jewish nationalism in Yiddish literature was reached in an article by Haim Loytsker,[40] written in a Zhdanovite spirit and surpassing anything else written at this time in the Soviet press. The main points criticized in this article, and in many others that were to appear between 1946 and 1948,[41] were as follows:

(1) An apologetic and uncritical approach to questions of national heritage.
(2) Idealization of the past, expressed in the blurring of the class differences which existed among Jews just as they did among other nations.
(3) Disproportionate emphasis on the description of Jewish national sentiments.
(4) Exaggerated use of the word 'Jew' (*Yid*) in its various combinations.[42]
(5) Exaggerated and unnecessary use of Hebraisms.[43]
(6) The employment of national–historical and legendary–Biblical motifs (known in Soviet jargon as 'archaisms').[44]

(7) Nationalistic egocentricity in Yiddish literature; for example, only mentioning the evacuation of the Jews, whereas other nations also had to undergo this unpleasant experience.

(8) An even more dangerous nationalism, shown by constant references to the Holocaust and Jewish martyrology.

(9) Zionist nationalism such as, for example, that of Itsik Kipnis.[45]

A comparison of these points with the above-mentioned attacks on historians and writers of other nations proves (see pages 146–7) that, despite the similarity on a number of points, there are essential differences (for example, points 1, 2, 3 and 7). First, it is almost inconceivable that a critic of Ukrainian, Belorussian or Uzbek 'nationalism' would criticize the frequent use of the words 'a Ukrainian', 'a Belorussian' or 'an Uzbek'. Second, the other nations, even at the height of the campaign against bourgeois nationalism, were not required to sever themselves so drastically from their historical and cultural past. Third, no evidence has been found of any criticism of the other nations for mentioning their martyrdom under the Nazi occupation. Finally, the linking of internal bourgeois nationalism (i.e. within the borders of the Soviet Union) with an external national movement was not common at this period, except in the case of the Jews. Far more serious, however, was the difference in the consequences of the campaign against nationalism: no national culture was liquidated in the Soviet Union as a result of this campaign except that of the Jews. The liquidation of Jewish culture began at the end of 1948 and continued until the end of 1949.[46]

Since by the end of 1948 and the beginning of 1949 all the leading Jewish writers, literary critics and theatre workers had been arrested, which meant that the nationally oriented Communist Jewish intelligentsia had been liquidated, the full force of the campaign against nationalism was now redirected against the assimilated Jewish intelligentsia. The final attacks on Jewish personalities and institutions in the first half of 1949 were:

(1) The accusation of nationalism against David Bergelson, one of the best-known Yiddish writers who was, it seems, already under arrest.[47]

(2) The accusations against the critic Model, who praised the Jewish playwright Goldfaden, and against the stage director Golovchiner, who produced 'harmful and anti-patriotic plays' at the Yiddish theatre in Minsk (as a result of which the theatre was closed).[48]

(3) The accusation of nationalism against the journal *Der shtern*, which appeared in Kiev and was closed down at the end of 1948.[49]

Within the framework of the anti-cosmopolitan campaign (described below), attacks were launched on a number of writers, literary critics, composers and artists, because of 'nationalist and Zionist deviations', although they had never shown any interest in Judaism. In the Ukraine, the poets Leonid Pervomaisky and Savva Golovanivsky,[50] and the composer D. Klebanov, who composed a symphony on the subject of Babi Yar,[51] were arraigned for nationalism and Zionism. Among those who came under fire most frequently in the Russian Republic were the poet Pavel Antokolsky[52] and the writer Aleksandr Isbakh.[53] Nor did the literary critics responsible for the literature section of the *Large Soviet Encyclopaedia* escape attack for having dared to include 'all Jewish literature, regardless of where and under what political regime it was written'; even more serious was the fact that the 'Jewish literature' entry was allotted as much space as all the entries on Uzbek, Kirgiz and Georgian literature put together.[54] Jewish nationalism, Zionism and conspiring with world Jewry were the main charges in the trial of Jewish artists and writers in July 1952 and in the public attacks in the Soviet press in 1952 and from January to March 1953.

The anti-cosmopolitan campaign

Despite the similarity between the anti-cosmopolitan campaign and the campaign against bourgeois nationalism, there were a number of essential differences. First, it is important to examine the targets of this campaign of incitement. As we shall see, those attacked for cosmopolitanism were not specifically the national cadres of the different republics responsible for the education and culture of their nations, but some of the intelligentsia of the Russian Republic. Second, the most serious charge in the attacks on bourgeois nationalism was 'an excess of local patriotism', whereas in the anti-cosmopolitan campaign the main charge was 'a lack' or 'minimizing of national sentiments'. Third, the authorities' aims differed: the aim of the campaign against bourgeois nationalism was to weaken or liquidate, by pressure, intimidation and dismissals, the upsurge of national feelings that had occurred during the war; whereas the aim of the anti-cosmopolitan campaign was to liquidate foreign influences, which were also a direct result of the war, and to bring about the severance of the Soviet Union and her East European satellites from the 'capitalist West'.

1945 TO 1948

After the Second World War, Soviet patriotism, which since the late 1930s had become increasingly identified with Russian national-ism,[55] was one of the central topics discussed in all the media in the Soviet Union. In an article appearing in June 1945, the writer avers that 'Communism and a consistent, active and altruistic love of one's homeland are one and the same thing', whereas 'cosmopolitanism is an ideology alien to the workers. Communism has nothing in com-mon with cosmopolitanism, that ideology which is characteristic of representatives of banking firms and international consortiums, great stock-exchange speculators and international suppliers of weapons and their agents. Indeed, these circles operate according to the Roman saying: *ubi bene, ibi patria*'.[56] In his election speech to the Supreme Soviet on 9 February 1946, Stalin warned Soviet citizens that as long as capitalism existed there would also be wars, and that the Soviet Union must be prepared.[57] The meaning of his words was clear: the easing of tension at home and abroad was at an end, and once again two hostile camps faced each other.

The theoretical basis for this reorientation was produced by A. Zhdanov in his speech at the plenary session of the CPSU Central Committee in August 1946.[58] The session adopted the following Res-olutions: on 14 August, 'On the journals *Zvezda* and *Leningrad*'; on 26 August, 'On the repertoire of the drama and the means for improving it'; and on 4 September, 'On the film *A Great Life*'.[59] First, these Resolutions embodied glorification of the Soviet regime (which was a hundred times better than any bourgeois regime – according to Zhdanov), while at the same time stressing the superiority of the Russian people in science and culture; second, they inculcated a hatred of the 'decadent West', and especially the USA, blackening it in the eyes of the Soviet public; third, they attacked 'blind imitation' of and kowtowing to foreign culture; fourth, they attacked the ab-sence of ideas, apoliticism, individualism and pessimism in literature and art; finally, the Resolutions called for the utmost vigilance. Al-though the chief victims of Zhdanov's attack and the Resolutions of the Central Committee were two non-Jews, the satirist M. Zosh-chenko and the poetess A. Akhmatova, there were many Jewish names among those criticized, for example, the writers and playwrights Yagdfeld, Shtein, Varshavsky, Slonimsky, Khazin, Romm and Rybak. It is important, however, to emphasize that in these attacks there was no anti-Jewish tone, either explicitly or implicitly.

The campaign against toadying to the West went beyond literature and art, and the emphasis on the need to strengthen Soviet patriotism continued in the second half of 1946, becoming more marked in 1947. A leading article in the theoretical journal of the Communist Party stressed that: 'Traces of subservience to bourgeois Western culture have found expression also in insufficient appraisal of the independence of Soviet scholarship and in the bowing and scraping of certain of its representatives to bourgeois Western scholarship'.[60] This point was underlined vigorously in the debate on G. Aleksandrov's book, *A History of West European Philosophy*, in a speech by Zhdanov dealing with Soviet philosophy.[61]

Particularly relevant is the speech of the Chairman of the Soviet Writers' Union, A. Fadeev, at the eleventh plenary session of the Union.[62] Fadeev's attacks were focussed on *Pushkin and World Literature*, a book by the Jewish literary scholar, Y. Nusinov, which had appeared in 1941. 'In this book', declared Fadeev,

'there isn't a single word to the effect that the national war of 1812 took place ... The fundamental idea of the book is that Pushkin's genius does not express the uniqueness of the historical development of the Russian nation, as a Marxist ought to have shown, but that Pushkin's greatness consists in his being European, in his finding his own answers, as it were, to all the questions posed by Western Europe.'[63]

And Fadeev adds, 'Out of common courtesy to all things foreign, Nusinov had to place himself at Shakespeare's disposal in order to defend him against Tolstoy.'[64] Although there was no allusion in this attack to the Jewishness of Nusinov – 'the untiring defender of Western culture and disparager of great Russian culture' – nevertheless Fadeev's choice of Nusinov for this purpose was not accidental, since the Soviet intelligentsia knew that Nusinov was one of the most important scholars of Jewish literature. The labelling of Nusinov as a 'passportless wanderer in humanity' was also no accident, but the first sign of the anti-Jewish bias which the anti-cosmopolitan campaign was to adopt in 1948 and 1949.[65] At the same time, an equally serious attack was directed at B. Eikhenbaum for his essay on Tolstoy's *Anna Karenina*. 'Does one need a more glaring example', writes the author of the article, 'of lack of pride in the literature of our mother country, a better example of obsequiousness, of the lack of common respect for all things Russian which are so dear to us?'[66] The note sounded here, as we shall see, was also at the centre of the attacks on the 'Jewish cosmopolitans'. In September 1947, at the inaugural conference of the *Cominform*, Zhdanov stated categorically that the world was divided into two hostile camps.[67] He launched a strong attack on the United States' 'quest for world dominance'; the very concept of world rule was intended to weaken the progressive camp, and the Soviet Union at its head consistently supported the principle of national sovereignty. A call to condemn all manifestations of toadying to the West and its capitalist culture was sounded by V. Molotov in his speech on the thirtieth anniversary of the October Revolution.[68]

A number of writers and critics of Jewish birth who were later to be among the chief victims of the anti-cosmopolitan campaign immediately came forward in defence of the new anti-Western line.[69] The position taken by the writer Ilya Erenburg at the end of 1947 was significant. He could not, of course, disregard the new anti-Western policy and had to pay lip-service to it by maintaining that the Russians were not only pupils but also masters in the sphere of culture and science; but he firmly rejected the charge that one is bowing down to the West if one accepts its culture. 'It is impossible', he wrote, 'to "toady" to Shakespeare or Rembrandt, because bowing down before them cannot humiliate the worshipper'.[70]

In January 1948, the newspapers and journals continued to use the terms 'obsequiousness' and 'bowing and scraping' in their attacks on literary critics and scholars, to whose number the historians were now added for the first time.[71] At the end of February a strongly worded article appeared, bearing a title which was to appear in the newspaper columns almost daily for a whole year: 'The Cosmopolitans in Literary Research'.[72] But the beginning of the resurgence of the anti-cosmopolitan campaign came in June, with the appearance of articles by Paperny and Miller-Budnitskaya.[73][74] First, the term '*rootless* cosmopolitans' appeared for the first time in Paperny's article devoted to Vissarion Belinsky, one of the nineteenth-century literary critics most acceptable to the Soviet Union. Second, the author adopted Belinsky's approach to cosmpolitanism, quoting his harsh words: 'The cosmopolitan is a false, senseless, strange and incomprehensive phenomenon, a manifestation in which there is something insipid and vague. He is a corrupt, unfeeling creature, totally unworthy of being called by the holy name of man.'[75] Third, in this article an attack was directed for the first time at Lev Subotsky, then secretary to the board of the Writers' Union, who was later to be at the centre of the most vehement attacks. Finally, the article stressed the anti-national character of cosmopolitanism, not only as regards the Russian nation but as regards all the nations in the Soviet Union. It is probable that this 'liberal' approach was one of the reasons why Paperny himself was later attacked and accused of cosmopolitanism. On the other hand, for the first time in the Soviet press, Miller-Budnitskaya linked American cosmopolitanism (presented as the degenerate image of Hollywood) with the German-Jewish writer Leon Feuchtwanger, whom she compared with the 'first Jewish cosmopolitan' – Josephus Flavius.

This direct assault on cosmopolitanism in the various fields of literature and scholarship, e.g. biology, philosophy, history and philology, continued in the second half of 1948. The number of Jews among those attacked was constantly increasing, although no allusion to their Jewishness had yet been made. In this period also the expressions of contempt used to denote the cosmopolitans were heightened.[76] However, it seems that the ideological offensive was stepped up as a direct result of the deterioration of relations with the Western powers and the expulsion of Yugoslavia from the *Cominform*, and meetings and congresses were convened in the various fields of literature and scholarship for the purpose of condemning all kowtowing to the West. Among the most important were the meeting of the Ukrainian Writers' Union in July 1948;[77] the plenary sessions of the All-Soviet Academy for Agricultural Sciences from 5 to 9 August, when Lysenko attacked the theories of Morgan, Weismann, Mendel, and their Soviet supporters; and the sessions of the presidium of the Academy of Sciences between 24 and 29 August 1948.[78] The twelfth plenary session of the board of the All-Soviet Writers' Union which took place in December 1948 was especially important and prepared the ground for the real anti-cosmopolitan campaign from January to March 1949. The chief victims of the attack at this session were the theatre and literary critics, Yuzovsky, Borshchagovsky, Malyugin, Kholodov and Altman, who were labelled here, for the first time, 'a hostile group of theater critics'.[79] As we have seen, the anti-cosmopolitan campaign had been pursued vigorously in the years 1947–8, but only in 1949 assumed its extraordinary dimensions and outspoken anti-Jewish policy.

1949 TO 1953

The main ingredients for an all-out campaign against cosmopolitanism were present in 1948, but the decision to embark upon a campaign of such scope and severity (even for the Soviet Union) must have been taken at the highest level at the beginning of January 1949.[80] The signal for the new campaign was given in a leading article in *Pravda* on 28 January 1949 and in a second leading article in the organ of the Central Committee's Department of Propaganda and Agitation, *Kultura i zhizn*, on 30 January 1949.[81] The two articles were couched in the strongest terms and showed their real purpose in the emphasis in the headlines on the existence of an anti-patriotic group of theatre critics. There were no more attacks on 'individuals' or on 'solitary' literary critics, each responsible for his own errors; instead, it was an attack on an *organized group*, which had supposedly practised its anti-patriotic activity even after the important Resolutions of the Central Committee of 1946 to 1948 had been adopted, in an attempt to create a kind of literary *underground*. Under Soviet rule, and at this particular period, the accusation of group organization for purposes opposed to the accepted political line was most serious. 'This group, hostile to Soviet culture', as the articles put it, 'set itself the aim of vilifying the outstanding events of our literature and the best in Soviet dramaturgy.' The 'group' or 'tribe' of anti-patriotic critics included Yuzovsky, Gurvich, Kron, Kholodov, Borshchagovsky, Varshavsky, Malyugin and Boyadzhiev, most of them Jews, and all holding important posts in publishing houses, cultural institutions and literary journals. The discriminatory nature of these articles was shown first in the use of collective names, a device used in anti-Semitic literature at different periods – 'the Gurviches and the Yuzovskys'. Second, the question put by the article in *Pravda*: 'What notion could Gurvich possibly have of the national character of Soviet Russian man?', emphasized the alienation of the Jews from Russian culture. Third, the negative traits – hypocrisy, deceit, Jesuitry, contempt for the most lofty Russian national sentiments – of the critics under attack were stressed.

The campaign against the 'cosmopolitans' in the wake of these articles spread throughout the Soviet mass media – radio, press, literature, cinema, theatre, scientific and popular lectures, wall-notices at places of work. Since we have no statistical data on these media, apart from the press, it may be worth examining the campaign in this medium alone. We based our investigation on the fifty-six newspapers and journals at our disposal, selecting twenty-one complete sets for the years 1948 to 1953, of which nine were central and republic newspapers, and twelve were journals representing all areas of literature, art and the sciences.[82] In the whole of 1948 only twenty-three articles attacking subservience to the West and cosmopolitanism appeared, while the number of such articles reached its peak in February (forty-eight) and March (fifty-six) 1949. There was a sharp decline in April which was the result, it seems, of instructions from above to moderate the campaign both in quantity and quality.[83] The most active in the campaign were the newspapers *Literaturnaya gazeta* (twenty-six articles in twenty-four editions in February and March) and *Vechernyaya Moskva* (fifteen articles in February and March). Central organs like *Pravda* and *Izvestiya* confined themselves to giving directives and setting the tone for the rest of the newspapers. It is interesting that no anti-cosmopolitan attacks appeared in the newspaper of the Uzbek Communist Party, *Pravda Vostoka*; this paper confined itself to printing the articles which had appeared in the central press and 'contributed' nothing of its own – in contrast to the situation, for instance, in the Ukraine. Many of the articles which appeared in the newspapers and journals were reports of meetings of the party cells of scientific and higher educational establishments, special gatherings of writers' and artists' organizations, sessions of the academies for the sciences and the arts, and various reactions of the 'Soviet public'. Not all the hundreds, perhaps thousands, of meetings called at this period to condemn cosmopolitanism came to the notice of the public, but the many reports in the press and on the radio created a tense atmosphere of constant incitement and mutual distrust within the intellectual stratum of the Soviet Union. Among the members of the Party and Government leadership who took an active part in this campaign, apart from Zhdanov (who died in August 1948), were Khrushchev in the Ukraine, Gusarev in Belorussia, Pelshe in Latvia, and the ministers Bolshakov and Shcherbina.

As for the role of the Jews in this anti-cosmopolitan campaign, we have already noted that some joined in the campaign at the beginning, but as it assumed a more blatant anti-Jewish character, their number declined. It seems that this happened primarily because many of them became victims of the campaign (we have already mentioned Paperny and Shtein): second, the authorities probably saw no further need to use them for this purpose, as they wanted to emphasize that the Jews were to be found on one side of the fence only; third, it is likely that the Jews themselves were deterred from this distasteful activity, although this should not be exaggerated. Certain Jews who took an active part in the anti-cosmopolitan campaign were the philosopher and member of the Academy of Sciences, Mark Mitin; the journalist, David Zaslavsky, and the orientalist, V. Lutsky; there were also a number of Jewish writers, scientists and artists who were forced to participate occasionally in various meetings to condemn cosmopolitanism, but this was mainly by way of 'self-criticism'.

The attacks, which began with theatre and literary criticism, were extended in February and March 1949 to almost all areas of the arts and learning. Those whose names were published in the press were only a fraction of those denounced, but this small number included some of the greatest writers, artists and scholars of the Soviet Union at that time.

If one examines the *frequency of the denunciations*, it becomes clear that over 50% of those who were attacked more than three times were Jews; a considerable number of them were arraigned almost daily from January to March 1949, and at less frequent intervals thereafter. Some of the Jews accused of cosmopolitanism were attacked over a longer period than their non-Jewish counterparts. It seems that the intensity of the attacks was usually greater against Jews than against non-Jews.

No less important is the question of *sanctions*. There is no doubt that in the campaign of incitement very many Jews suffered not only morally and spiritually, but materially as well, and their suffering was out of all proportion to their real significance in the professions and positions they occupied.

After reading over 200 articles which appeared in the Soviet Union dealing with cosmopolitanism, the following conclusions can be drawn:

(1) The lightest sanction was a warning (*vygovor*), or a severe warning (*strogy vygovor*), which was issued to everyone attacked for cosmopolitanism by the establishments where they worked or the organizations to which they belonged.

(2) A stronger measure was the removal of the 'cosmopolitans' from various posts as, for example, from the chairmanship of committees (Kron from the Theatre Committee), from the editorial boards of newspapers and journals (Adelgeim from being chief editor of the

journal *Vitchyzna*; Kedrov from being chief editor of the journal *Voprosy filosofii*), or from the directorship of academic institutes (A. Trainin was removed from his post as head of the Law Institute and Subotsky from his post as Secretary of the Writers' Union).

(3) A still more serious measure was removal from professional organizations and frequently subsequent dismissal from work. There was a repeated demand that the following theatre and literary critics be removed from the Writers' Union: Yuzovsky, Gurvich, Boyadzhiev, Borshchagovsky, Altman, Varshavsky, Kholodov, Malyugin, Subotsky, Levin, Danin and Yakovlev; but it is not clear how many of them were actually removed. Demands, some successful, were made for the removal from the Composers' Union of the following composers and musicologists: Vainkop, Mazel, Zhitomirsky, Ginzburg, Shneerson, Shlifshtein, Ogolovets, Belza, Pekelis and Lobanova. Also removed from unions were the film director S. Yutkevich, and the cinema critics Oten, Volkenshtein, Manevich, and Lebedev.

(4) An extremely serious measure, and one that affected the family's economic survival, was the dismissal of those accused from their places of work. For writers or art and literary critics, this meant ceasing to publish their books and articles.[84] Some dismissals were published in the press, for example, those of Professor Goldenrikht, the writer Antokolsky, and the literary critics Yuzovsky, Levin and Broverman.[85]

(5) One of the most severe measures, often resulting in arrest, was the exclusion of the accused from the ranks of the Communist Party. The theatre and literary critics whose exclusion from the party was announced in the press were Yakovlev (Kholtsman), Altman, Kovarsky, Levin, Baskin and Danin. As regards the arrests, it is reasonable to assume that more Jews were arrested for cosmopolitanism than for bourgeois nationalism; but, proportionately speaking, only the arrests for bourgeois nationalism can be described as mass arrests.

These conclusions form additional evidence that the main object of Stalin's anti-Jewish policy from 1948 to 1953 was the liquidation of Jewish culture and its bearers, whereas with regard to the assimilated Jewish intelligentsia, the authorities were content to apply pressure and intimidation only – at least until the beginning of 1953.

We have already seen that cosmopolitanism was defined as a reactionary bourgeois ideology, hostile to national tradition and national sovereignty, preaching a neutral attitude to the motherland and to national culture. It is beyond the scope of this chapter to describe the attacks on cosmopolitans in all the mass media; instead, we shall note the central points of the campaign, while emphasizing its anti-Jewish orientation. First, there are the terms of contempt widely used to describe the cosmopolitans, mostly drawn from the classic anti-Semitic arsenal: they were persons without identity, nameless, without roots, bowing and scraping to all things foreign, passportless wanderers, etc. Second, there is the use of collective names, usually specifically Jewish: 'the Gurviches', 'the Levins', 'the Yagols', 'the Tsimbals', etc. Third, increasing prominence was given to Jewish names; when the surname sounded non-Jewish, the first name and patronymic was added. Fourth, from the latter half of February 1949,[86] another move was made in 'the removal of the mask from the true faces' of the cosmopolitans, when the press began using the anti-Semitic device of disclosing pseudonyms and the public discovered that Yakovlev was Kholtsman, Melnikov turned out to be Melman, Kholodov was Meerovich, and Burlachenko – Berdichevsky. At the beginning of March, each new edition of the newspaper uncovered more pseudonyms in almost all spheres of literature and art. However, from the beginning of April 1949, the disclosure of pseudonyms stopped for almost two years, and in 1951 we found only one disclosed in the Soviet press.[87]

Finally, the accusations levelled against the cosmopolitans revolved around alienation, kowtowing to imperialism and hatred of the Russian people. We shall restrict ourselves to pointing out the main themes: *Committing outrage to the Russian nation* – the critic Altman hates all things Russian. *Foul defamation of Russian man* – the poet Golovanivsky's poem 'Abraham' insinuates that the Russians and Ukrainians turned their backs on the Jews when they were being led off to their deaths by the Germans. *Insult to the memory of oustanding Russian writers* – the critic Levin even ranked Abram Gurvich (*sic!*) with Vissarion Belinksy, while the critic B. Byalik once asserted that the poet Mayakovsky was influenced by the poet H. N. Bialik. Such a comparison, of a Soviet poet of the Revolution with a reactionary and mystical Jewish poet, was said to be an insult to the memory of the patriot Mayakovsky. If we add that an extremely anti-Jewish atmosphere prevailed at conventions and meetings called to denounce cosmopolitans,[88] it is no longer possible to doubt that the anti-cosmopolitan campaign had acquired a totally anti-Jewish character. Most scholars dealing with this period do not query the anti-Jewish tendencies of the anti-cosmopolitan campaign,[89] but some disagree; in their view, as many non-Jews were denounced and as Jews also participated in the attacks on cosmopolitanism, the claim that the anti-cosmopolitan campaign was anti-Jewish in character is not proven. It is also argued that the anti-nationalist campaign waged in the Soviet Union was detrimental to many other nations, too.[90]

As we have already pointed out, it is important to distinguish between the campaign directed against bourgeois nationalism and the campaign against cosmopolitanism, despite a number of similarities.[91] Second, it is necessary to examine separately the situation in the European republics of the Soviet Union, namely, the Ukraine, Belorussia and the Baltic States, and in the Central Asian and Caucasian Republics. And finally, there is the quantitative factor: we must put into proportion the number of attacks on cosmopolitanism and their severity, both at the central, all-Soviet level and in the different republics.

The leaders of the republics were obliged to introduce the anti-cosmopolitan campaign, too, and did so without hesitation. Nevertheless, there were important differences between one republic and another, mainly as a result of local conditions. There is no doubt that, as regards the momentum of the attacks on cosmopolitanism and their vehemence, the Ukrainian Republic forged ahead (apart from the RSFSR – Russian Socialist Federal Soviet Republic), while in the republics of Central Asia and the Caucasus the campaign was conducted with little enthusiasm and sometimes even in comparative silence. What was important, however, was the question of *who* was attacked in the anti-cosmopolitan campaign. The victims of the attacks in the Ukraine and Belorussia, for example, were almost all Jews, while in the republics of Central Asia the percentage of Jews among those attacked was low. The reason was not only the presence of fewer Jews in these areas and the fact that they did not hold responsible posts in literature, art and the sciences; the amount of indigenous anti-Semitism, and the desire to exploit it for various purposes, also played a considerable part, particularly in the Ukraine but also in Belorussia and the Baltic Republics. The anti-cosmopolitan campaign in Central Asia, and to a certain extent in the Caucasus (chiefly in Azerbaidzhan), resembled the campaign against bourgeois nationalism in almost all respects, with its attacks on pan-Islamism, pan-Turkism and pan-Iranism,[92] and its incessant preaching of fraternal feelings for the 'Great Russian brother'; but in the European republics (and most prominently in the Ukraine) the anti-cosmopolitan campaign was used by some of the local intelligentsia, apparently with the support of the authorities, for other purposes; above all, they wanted to break the stranglehold of Russification, and, as it was impossible to attack the Russians directly, an opportunity presented itself to do so indirectly by attacking cosmopolitans whose attitude to Ukrainian or Belorussian culture was disparaging. It was also easier to attack 'cosmopolitans' of Jewish rather than of Russian origin, as the anti-Jewish quality of the campaign was obvious; and it was also possible to exploit the anti-cosmopolitan campaign in order to settle personal accounts with those Jews who had held important cultural posts in these republics.[93]

If we accept the view that the anti-cosmopolitan campaign became an out-and-out anti-Jewish campaign, the question arises why this was so. One principal reason was the lack of faith which Stalin, and evidently a sizeable section of the Soviet leadership, had in the loyalty of the Jews to their socialist motherland, especially if this loyalty were to be put to the test in the event of a war with the United States. This lack of faith apparently induced Stalin to decide that it was necessary to fight not only 'Jewish nationalism', whose protagonists were close to Jewish culture, but also 'cosmopolitanism', whose advocates were among the assimilated Jews. The transition, which began at the end of 1948, from the first campaign to the second can be more easily understood in this light, and also the apparent contradiction that the same persons were accused of both nationalism and cosmopolitanism almost simultaneously can be explained. Another reason was the benefit to be derived from the anti-cosmopolitan campaign by presenting it as a campaign directed against the Jews, hated as they were by large sections of both the Russian and the non-Russian population. It seems that anti-Jewish policy, as manifested in the anti-cosmopolitan campaign, was further influenced by internal struggles within the Party leadership, although even now it is difficult to establish which group supported the policy.

The campaign against Zionism and Israel

There is obviously a connection between the Soviet Union's policy towards its Jews and its attitude towards Zionism and the State of Israel – and this is against the background of its general Middle East policy; what is the connection? The complex questions that arise here have not, we believe, been answered satisfactorily.[94] Is there a direct correlation, positive or negative, between the Soviet government's policy towards Soviet Jews, Zionism and the State of Israel; in other words, do the events between 1946 and 1953 prove that a negative attitude towards Soviet Jewry inevitably leads to hostility towards Zionism and the State of Israel, or vice-versa? Are these correlations consistent or should we perhaps speak of points of contact only, a more general principle being difficult to deduce? Can one say that the factors determining the Soviet government's policy on these questions were internal, or was that policy linked to Soviet foreign policy?

The Ribbentrop–Molotov Pact of August 1939 led to Soviet annexation of territories with large Jewish populations, and mass arrests of Zionist activists in numbers which are difficult even to estimate.[95] In sum, then, we can say that up to the outbreak of war with Germany in June 1941 the Soviet Union maintained a consistently anti-Zionist line, which had its most extreme manifestations in the late 1920s and 1930s.

1941 TO 1945

After many years of almost total severance, rather shaky bilateral relations began to be formed, during the war, between official representatives of the Soviet Union and leaders of the Zionist movement and the Jewish *yishuv* in Palestine. While the first meetings were initiated by the Zionists (such as the meeting with the Soviet Ambassador to the United States, Umansky, on 17 July 1941; with the Soviet Ambassador to Britain, Maisky, on 13 October 1941; and with the Soviet Ambassador to Turkey, Vinogradov, on 6 January 1942), after 1943 the Soviets themselves began to contact the heads of the Zionist movement and respresentatives of the *yishuv* in Palestine. In all the meetings (such as the visit to Palestine of foreign service officials Mikhailov and Petrenko at the invitation of the 'V' League in August 1942; of Ambassador Maisky in October 1942; and of Novikov in August 1944), the Soviet representatives were concerned with gauging the strength of the Zionist movement and the *yishuv* and their influence on policy makers in the West. They were also interested in preparing data on the *yishuv* for their country's leaders in anticipation of the political decisions to come after the war.

The representatives of the Zionist Movement and the *yishuv*, for their part, raised the following issues:

(1) The release of Zionist Movement members confined in forced labour camps and prisons in the Soviet Union.
(2) The granting of permission to Jewish refugees from USSR-annexed areas, and those who had come from Nazi-occupied regions, to emigrate to Palestine.
(3) The extension of aid by Jewish organizations to these refugees.
(4) Discrimination against the Hebrew language and culture in the USSR.
(5) The establishment of some sort of Soviet representation in Palestine, in the same way as in Syria and Lebanon.
(6) Aid to the Soviet war effort of the *yishuv* and Jewish organizations.
(7) The possibility that the Red Army might blow up Nazi extermination camps in Poland.

The Soviet representatives' replies to these questions (except, of course, 7) were generally negative or evasive, and can be summarized as follows: no one had ever been arrested in the Soviet Union because of their nationality, or because they were Zionists, but only because of their connections with hostile political organizations abroad. All subjects in the territories annexed to the USSR had received Soviet citizenship and were satisfied with this state of affairs; there was no need to worry about these citizens, since the USSR had already concerned itself with them. As for Hebrew culture, the answer was that Yiddish culture already existed in the USSR and all Jews could benefit from it. The Soviet government was naturally prepared to be represented in Palestine, but the political situation had first to be clarified. As for bombing extermination camps, their reply was that the Soviet diplomatic corps had no right to give strategic advice to the leaders of the Red Army.[96] Moreover, it was clear from talks in this period between Soviet representatives and Americans and Arabs in the Middle East that the Soviets wanted to stress that their anti-Zionist policy would continue.[97]

The relations between the Jewish Anti-Fascist Committee and Palestine Jewry are particularly important as an indicator of Soviet policy towards Zionism during the war period. Although the Soviet authorities were interested in improving their country's image and in strengthening pro-Soviet sentiment among the Jews of the *yishuv*, they apparently did everything to discourage any connection between the leaders of the Jewish Anti-Fascist Committee and *yishuv* leaders. No meetings took place between Solomon Mikhoels and Itsik Fefer and representatives of the *yishuv*, even though they travelled through the Middle East *en route* to the United States and Canada in 1943. Similarly, relations between the Jewish Anti-Fascist Committee and the League for Victory were restricted, despite all efforts by the heads of the League.

It can be concluded, then, that from June 1941 until early 1945 the improvement in the situation of Soviet Jews was accompanied by only a minor improvement in the USSR's attitude towards Zionism and the *yishuv*. The reasons were the war, which demanded mobilization of all forces to fight against Germany, and the USSR's desire to obtain the support of world Jewry for this fight – but without any intention of changing basic policy.

FEBRUARY 1945 TO MAY 1947

The beginning of an improvement in the Soviet Union's attitude towards Palestine can be seen in February 1945 when Stalin agreed, together with Roosevelt and Churchill, that Palestine should be handed over to the Jews to be developed as their national home, and that Palestine should allow unrestricted Jewish immigration.[98] In the same month, this Soviet policy was openly expressed at the founding conference of the World Federation of Trades Unions, held in London. V. Kuznetsov, the head of the Soviet delegation, voted on behalf of his delegation for a resolution which determined, *inter alia*, 'that the Jewish people should be permitted to continue with the building of Palestine as a national home, as it has begun to do with great success by means of immigration, agriculture, settlement and industrial development'.[99] Even more important was Soviet consent to the emigration of Jews from Eastern Europe to Poland and to the Western-occupied regions of Germany and Austria, although it was obvious that it was the emigrants' intention to reach Palestine.[100]

On the other hand, the anti-Zionist tendency in official Soviet policy continued to find expression in the press and other information media. 'The programmes to found a Zionist–Jewish state in Palestine are supported by influential American circles', wrote the commentator K. Serezhin, disapprovingly, early in 1946.[101] He argued that the publication of Truman's proposal to bring 100,000 Jews from Europe to Palestine made the political situation still more complicated: the solution to the problem of the thousands of refugees was not dependent upon Jewish immigration quotas into Palestine, but upon the rooting out of Fascism, the liquidation of racism and its consequences, and the giving of aid to the Jewish population.[102] In the course of a still more violent attack, its tone recalling the calumnies of the twenties and thirties, the same author wrote: 'the leaders of Zionism have placed the interests of the Jewish people at the disposal of British imperialism... In the hands of the reactionary leaders of the Zionist Movement, the *yishuv* settlements have been transformed into an instrument of racist hate propaganda and chauvinism.'[103]

This argument was expounded clearly by V. Lutsky, an expert on Middle Eastern affairs, in a lecture delivered on 9 August 1946, which was also published as a special pamphlet by 'Pravda', the Communist Party publishing house.[104] The Jewish population in Palestine, he said, was under the influence of the bourgeois–Zionist nationalists, who were exploiting it for Britain's imperialist objectives. Lutsky also unintentionally used the 'classic' arguments of the British administration when he claimed that Palestine was over-populated and that its natural resources were non-existent ('one of the world's poorest countries'). While Soviet Russia and the Arab nations did not accept the imperialist mandatory system, the Zionists did so willingly, knowing that without Britain's help they would not succeed in realizing their programmes. One of the pamphlet's chapter-headings is also interesting: 'Palestine an Arab Country'; Lutsky described the Zionists in Palestine as oppressors of the Arab nation, having arrived there when it was already populated by another people, ending with the argument – later to be of prime importance in Soviet propaganda – that Zionism derived the concept of the Jews as a master-race from Fascism.[105]

It should not be thought, however, that these attacks on Zionism were only propaganda, aimed at influencing Arab leaders. That this was the official Soviet policy of the period is illustrated by an off-the-record remark by Aleksei Shevtsov, First Secretary in the USSR legation in Cairo, sharply attacking the *yishuv* leaders; he stated that the texts of Ben Gurion's speeches which had reached the Soviet Foreign Office were exactly like those of the Fascists.[106]

The deteriorating attitude towards Zionism in 1946 was accompanied by a deterioration in the situation of Soviet Jews after a speech by Zhdanov and the beginning of the campaign against local nationalism. However, in terms of the Soviet attitude towards the *yishuv*, this period may be described as one of probing, in the Arab world and the *yishuv* alike, to enable the USSR to decide 'which horse to back' in its rivalry with the Western powers, which entered a critical stage in 1947.

MAY 1947 TO MAY 1949

This is the most complex and difficult period to analyse. On the one hand, a pro-Israel policy finds expression in many areas, its outstanding manifestation being the role of Soviet influence in Israel's achieving independence. On the other hand, almost in parallel, we find an extreme anti-Jewish campaign being conducted in the name of the fight against bourgeois nationalism and cosmopolitanism which was at its height between November 1948 and March 1949. Was this really a double policy, differing internally and externally? Can it be said that what characterized Soviet Middle East policy as a whole, and its attitude towards Palestine in particular, was a series of partial improvised decisions, which were not even taken at the highest level? Or would it be more accurate to see in the Soviet–Israeli 'honeymoon' a kind of brief pause – a truce – in the USSR's permanent anti-Zionist and anti-Israeli policy, stemming from Soviet foreign policy in this period? An examination of the historical facts will help us to answer these questions.

Despite the fact that the architects of Soviet foreign policy, headed by Stalin, now primarily considered Central and Western Europe, they did not ignore the strategic and political importance of the Middle East, seeking bases there and ways of controlling the region. A decision was taken at the highest level, apparently just before May 1947, to support the programme for 'the establishment of an independent Arab–Jewish state, federal and democratic.... However, should it turn out that this solution is not implementable ... it will be necessary to examine a second proposed solution ... namely the partition of Palestine into two independent and non-dependent states – Jewish and Arab'.[107] The decision was announced by Gromyko in the General Assembly on 14 May 1947, and confirmed in speeches later delivered by Semion Tsarapkin on 13 October and by Gromyko on 26 November – this time with unequivocal support for the Partition Plan.

The principal factors which led to this decision were as follows:

(1) The Soviet leadership's disappointment, at the end of the 1930s, although mainly during the war period and following the establishment of the Arab League, with Arab nationalism, because of the latter's support first for the Fascist regimes and later for imperialist Britain. The Soviet Union apparently lost faith in Arab power to bring about the expulsion of the British from the Middle East, and against this background became convinced that it was the Jews who were capable of removing the British from Palestine.

(2) The increase in Soviet apprehensions that the United States was trying to increase its Middle East involvement, either alongside or in place of Britain.[108] This constituted a threat to the Soviet leadership's plans.

(3) The possibility of exploiting the distress of the Jewish refugees in Europe through the proposal to give them shelter in Palestine and thus to be rid of the problem of hundreds of thousands of refugees.

(4) The possibility of winning the support of world Jewry.

Active Soviet support in this period was manifested first in its consistent and continuous support for Israel's position in the international sphere in general and in UN institutions in particular, support which began with the above-mentioned speeches by Gromyko, and was reflected in the discussions in which representatives of the Soviet Union, the Ukraine, Belorussia and the East European states participated,[109] reaching a peak – which also signalled an incipient shift – in the vote on the admission of Israel as a member of the UN on 11 May 1949. Second, in aid to the *yishuv*, in the approval of the sale to Israel of Czechoslovak arms which played such an important part on the battlefield. Third, support for the emigration of refugees from the countries of Europe (except for the USSR) to Israel.

Nevertheless, scrutiny of the speeches on the Palestinian question by Soviet representatives in international institutions, together with Soviet press reports and political–scientific literature, reveals that this shift, though important in itself, failed to secure a parallel change in policy towards Zionism.[110] Even in the most relaxed period in Soviet–Israeli relations – from November 1947 to July 1948 – it was nowhere stated that the Zionist Movement was the national liberation movement of the Jewish people, which was the Soviet leaders' term for the Arab national liberation movements. At this time, in fact, the term 'Zionism' totally disappeared from the Soviet lexicon because of ideological–political unwillingness to rehabilitate a movement which had been so consistently attacked by the founders of the Soviet State. Had long term Soviet interests so demanded, the USSR leadership would have found a 'redeeming formula' to overcome ideological difficulties of this kind, as it did in the case of Titoism. However, it was apparently already clear to the Soviet leaders in this period that the political possibilities of exploiting the *yishuv* for the fight against British imperialism and for strengthening the Soviet Union's own position in the Mediterranean region would come to a swift end with the entry of the USA into the Middle East sphere, and its increasing influence (real or imaginary) on the State of Israel.

The first signs of a change in the 'neutral' attitude towards Zionism began to emerge in August 1948. A pamphlet by the Soviet Jewish orientalist, V. Lutsky, based on one of his lectures, stated, *inter alia*, that: 'With the support of England and the United States, the bourgeois Jewish nationalists have attempted to transform Palestine into a purely Jewish State, without taking into consideration the interests and rights of the local population.' Lutsky continued: 'The Soviet Union has rejected the programmes for transforming Palestine either into a Jewish state or into a purely Arab state.'[111] In the course of a review of M. Stürnsfeld's book, which was published in Stockholm, the Soviet commentator A. Kanunnikov wrote in early September 1948: 'In her description of the Jewish population's struggle for the establishment of the State of Israel, the author ignores the anti-imperialist national liberation movements of the Arab peoples.'[112] These, as we see, struck a totally new note in Soviet publications at this time. It was the writer Ilya Erenburg who expressed this tendency most clearly in his long article, 'Concerning a Certain Letter', which appeared in *Pravda* on 21 September 1948. It is interesting to note that yet another Jew, Izrail Genin, was also chosen to voice criticism of Israel.[113] The most violent attacks on Zionism, however, were interwoven with the campaign against cosmopolitanism and bourgeois nationalism.

The attitude adopted towards Israel by members of the Jewish Anti-Fascist Committee (not always identical, perhaps, with their true feelings) and given official form in the newspaper *Eynikayt*, was marked in the first place by the care taken not to deviate from the political line of the leading articles and commentaries that appeared from the beginning of June 1947 to 18 November 1948. Second, the main action taken by the Committee as an institution and in its own name was to send a formal telegram to Dr Chaim Weizmann on the establishment of the State of Israel.[114] Third, conspicuously few commentaries appeared in the newspaper, and these were written by a few people apparently assigned to the task: the writers Itsik Fefer,[115] David Bergelson,[116] A. Hindes[117] and G. Mindlin.[118] Fourth, There was almost complete agreement between the treatment of Israel and Zionism in the general press and in *Eynikayt*. In certain cases, however, the Jewish paper preempted the general press, for example, Itsik Fefer's sharp attack on the 'Joint' in February 1948.[119] Finally, it is important to note that after the appearance of Ilya Erenburg's article *Eynikayt* printed articles attacking those in the West who dared to oppose Erenburg's theses.[120] The targets were the leaders of Zionism, who claimed that 'Israel is allegedly the homeland of all the Jews in the world'. 'Soviet Jews', one article affirmed, 'will never desire to exchange their Soviet homeland'.

This period can be summed up by the following conclusions:

(1) Soviet support for the establishment of the State of Israel and Soviet aid in its War of Independence brought about some improvement in the Soviet leadership's attitude towards Zionism, so that Soviet attacks on Zionism ceased, and its existence was ignored, until August 1948.

(2) This improvement did not include issuing exit permits to Soviet Jews so that they could emigrate to Israel.

(3) There is a clear inverse correlation between the Soviet authorities' attitude towards Israel and their attitude towards Soviet Jewry; that is, a *pro-Israel* policy brought about a limited *anti-Jewish* policy (or aggravated the anti-Jewish policy that already existed).

The stages in this anti-Jewish policy were: (1) from the second half of 1947, the increasingly vehement attacks on Jewish nationalism, marked by anti-Zionist acts, such as the episode concerning the writer Itsik Kipnis; (2) the murder of Solomon Mikhoels, Chairman of the Jewish Anti-Fascist Committee on 13 January 1948; (3) the dissolution of the Jewish Anti-Fascist Committee and of most of the Jewish cultural institutions in November 1948; (4) mass arrests among the principal figures of Yiddish culture at the end of 1948 and the beginning of 1949; (5) an anti-cosmopolitan campaign with an anti-Jewish character, launched on 28 January 1949; (6) aggravated discrimination against Jews in various spheres.

At first sight this correlation appears strange: good relations with Israel, and efforts to improve them, seem to demand that Soviet Jews be treated in the same way as the other national minorities in the Soviet Union, and/or be allowed to emigrate to Israel, especially as the fate of the Soviet Jewry – a quarter of the Jewish people remaining after the Second World War – was extremely important to the State of Israel and the Zionist Movement. However, scrutiny of the factors affecting Soviet foreign policy towards Israel on the one hand and the weight of internal factors on the other demonstrates that a *positive-negative* correlation (a positive attitude towards Israel and a negative attitude towards Soviet Jewry) or a *negative–positive* correlation (negative towards Israel, positive towards Soviet Jewry) is far more 'natural' than a positive–positive correlation, which could only come about in the Soviet Union after a complete change in its attitude towards the Jewish nation generally and to its own Jews in particular.

The Soviet Union's foreign policy was worked out, as we have seen, on the basis of immediate political–strategic interests, anticipating a convenient international situation. However, the decisive factor was not the Soviet Union's foreign policy in the Middle East, but the need to deal quickly with a serious internal problem which arose mainly out of this foreign policy, but was influenced by other factors as well: the Holocaust, the shattering of the myth of the brotherhood of nations, official anti-Semitism, and so on. This new phenomenon was the Jewish national awakening, which found striking – and, in the USSR, very unusual – expression in spontaneous mass demonstrations in honour of the representative of a foreign – and not even socialist – country.[121] It is, moreover, reasonable to assume that even if Israel had changed its foreign policy and been consistently neutral, this would not have been sufficient to alter the course of events – unless Israel had become a communist state in the full sense, i.e. a Soviet satellite.

FROM JUNE 1949 TO THE BEGINNING OF APRIL 1953
This period was characterized by renewed Soviet attempts to expand its sphere of influence in the Middle East, though its efforts to gain both support and political advantages from the Arab world failed. This, then, is apparently one of the reasons why the Soviet leaders, despite their anti-Jewish and anti-Zionist policy, maintained correct, if cool, relations with the State of Israel virtually throughout the period. These relations were felt mainly in the position taken by the Soviet representatives in UN discussions – an aloofness from the Arab–Israeli conflict.

V. Lutsky, whose anti-Zionist and anti-Israel views are mentioned above, was one of the first to attempt, in the second half of 1949, to provide a theoretical basis for the need for a shift in Soviet policy towards Israel.[122] Lutsky averred, first, that Israel had not fulfilled its obligation to establish a democratic and independent state. Second, he noted that Israel's Zionist leaders had welcomed foreign capital and mortgaged their sovereignty, so that they could not carry on

without the support of imperialist states. Moreover, they were pre-
pared to join the aggressive Mediterranean bloc being established by
Britain and the USA. Third, they were simultaneously conducting a
policy hostile to the Soviet Union, as seen in their opposition to the
World Peace Conference and the movement which it established, and
demanding that the *Histadrut* leave the World Federation of Trade
Unions. Finally, from his analysis of the situation in the Middle East,
Lutsky concluded that the conditions had now been created in the
Arab states for a resurgence of the struggle for national liberation.
What Lutsky failed to state in this address, although it was noted by
Soviet commentators, was that the reactionaries in the Arab States
and the pan-Islamic organizations, such as that established by Nazi
agents in 'Al Azhar', the religious university of Cairo, in 1935,[123] had
played a delaying role in the development of the national liberation
movement in the Middle East. It was later stated – and this marked a
return to the Comintern policy of the 1920s and 1930s – that the
reactionary ideologies were: pan-Islamism, pan-Turkism, pan-Gan-
dhiism and Zionism.[124] But this sort of 'balance' did not continue for
long and increasingly harsh attacks were levelled against Zionism
after the end of 1949.[125]

The Rajk Trial, which took place in Hungary in September 1949,
during which a close connection was affirmed between Zionism and
the American espionage services, led to the anti-Zionist campaign
being widened to include the whole of Eastern Europe, reaching a
climax in the Slansky Trial in November 1952.[126] In the Soviet
Union itself articles began to appear in 1951, critical not only of
Zionism but also of the State of Israel. Zionism as a 'reactionary
national movement' was interlinked with 'Fascist methods of government and discrimination against the Arab population in Israel'.[127]
All this was insignificant compared to the campaign of incitement
and slander against Zionism, the 'Joint' and Israel, which began with
the announcement on 13 January 1953 of the discovery of the 'Doctors' Plot', and continued until Stalin's death on 5 March 1953.

The press and other communications media stressed, first, that the
Zionist movement was an organization embracing the whole world
(an idea taken straight out of the *Protocols of the Elders of Zion*). Second, they underlined the reactionary character of the Zionist movement since its foundation. In 1903 Herzl offered the tsarist Minister
of the Interior, von Pleve (the organizer of the pogroms) the assistance of the Zionist movement in the struggle against revolutionary

influences on Jewish youth. Beginning with Herzl, the leaders of Zionism had cooperated with the reactionary authorities, such as the Sultan of Turkey and the German Kaiser. The Zionist Jabotinsky, who organized a Jewish legion for the Allies, was connected with Petlyura. In the thirties many Zionist leaders (such as Abba Eban and Reuven Shiloah operated in the English espionage services and at the same time discussed with Mussolini the establishment of a Jewish state under the protection of Fascist Italy. Zionist organizations and the *Bund* in Poland cooperated with the Germans, while after the war Zionism became the stooge of Anglo-American imperialism. Third, Zionism was said to be undermining the foundations of the socialist regimes in Eastern Europe and in the Soviet Union itself, as revealed during the Rajk and Slansky trials, and by the confessions of imprisoned doctors. Fourth, to carry out its operations Zionism had established various organizations, in the guise of welfare institutions (such as the 'Joint'), and used them for espionage and subversion on behalf of the American espionage services. Fifth, it was asserted that Israel constituted a base for imperialism in the Middle East and a support for reactionary movements. Finally, particular notice was taken of an alleged close connection between the Zionist movement and Jewish millionaires, such as the bankers Lehman, Warburg, Morgenthau, and Blaustein.

This period, then, was characterized by the correlation between an internal anti-Jewish policy and an anti-Zionist and anti-Israel policy. Attempts made to draw closer to the Arab States were not always successful – hence the Soviet preservation of neutrality in UN institutions.

Jews on trial

ZIONISTS AND JEWISH NATIONALISTS

The Soviet Union's annexation, in 1939 and 1940, of territories in Poland, Romania and the Baltic states containing large Jewish populations, who had extensive organizations – Zionist, socialist, civil and religious – brought a wave of arrests, trials and mass exiles whose dimensions are difficult to estimate. The arrests were principally of activists in and sympathizers with the Zionist Movement and the *Bund* party. This campaign reached its height precisely when one might have expected it to be relaxed – after the outbreak of war between the Soviet Union and Germany. Thus the Polish *Bund* leaders Henryk Erlich and Victor Alter were imprisoned at the beginning of December 1941, were tried in secret for the second time and executed on 9 December 1941.[128]

In 1945 and 1946 there was another wave of arrests and trials in the Soviet Union, mainly of Zionist Movement activists and people trying to leave the Soviet Union by illegal means.[129] The common characteristic of all the arrests and trials at this time was that they took place against the background of the difficult war being waged by the authorities against the nationalist movements in the various European republics of the Soviet Union. In contrast to these movements, which had organized themselves for an armed conflict with the Soviet regime and for the attainment of full national sovereignty, no Zionist movement had such tendencies – which was of course wellknown to the internal security forces, who kept anyone suspected of Zionism under constant surveillance. Therefore, the arrests of many Jews who had just survived the Holocaust could not be attributed to the possibility that their Zionist activity might endanger the Soviet regime. The arrests stemmed from a continuation of the traditional anti-Zionist policy and a desire to intimidate Jews and deter them from any activity which might be interpreted as support for Zionism.[130]

From the middle of 1947 to October 1948 the persecution of Zionists in the Soviet Union was relaxed; but this did not mean that arrests and other administrative–police operations against the Jews ceased. Nevertheless, for all who believed in Zionism this was the best period in the history of the Soviet Union.

Against this background, the shift that now took place in Soviet policy on the Zionist question, signs of which had appeared earlier but were clearly visible in October and November 1948,[131] is all the more striking. Arrests were made from November 1948 until Stalin's death in March 1953, mostly of people showing affinity for the State of Israel who had dared to express publicly both their joy in its establishment and their desire to go to its aid.[132] People who maintained any contact with Israeli diplomats suffered particularly.[133] Most of the Jews imprisoned on charges of Zionism were sentenced secretly, before special boards (*Osoboe soveshchanie*), to long periods in prison.[134] The authorities also took administrative action against those accused of Zionism, such as dismissing them from employment, expelling them from their residences, and exiling them.[135] There were also reports, though their authenticity is difficult to judge, of arrests among Jewish officers who had served in eastern Germany in various military and civilian capacities. They were charged with expressing pro-Zionist views.[136]

TRIALS OF YIDDISH-LANGUAGE WRITERS AND ARTISTS

There is an interesting parallel between the trials of the 1930s and those that took place at the end of the 1940s and in the early 1950s. If, as we have seen, these Zionist trials largely resembled the anti-Zionist trials held in the 1920s and the 1930s, with the important difference that this time they also covered Soviet Jews of the younger generation (who had by now been raised and educated in communist theory), so the trials of the writers, artists and Yiddish-culture functionaries resembled in almost every way those by which the writers and Evsektsia functionaries were liquidated in the late 1930s. Nevertheless, there was a very important difference. The liquidation of the writers and Evsektsia functionaries in the 1930s might still be considered an integral part of the purges to which many communist leaders of other nationalities fell victim, while the attack at the end of the 1940s was directed mainly towards the liquidation of Jewish national culture.

We lack direct proof that the decision to liquidate Jewish culture in the Soviet Union was reached immediately after World War II, or at the outset of the campaign against Jewish nationalism, but there is no doubt that this campaign prepared the ground for it. The first sign of a clear anti-Jewish direction among the Soviet leadership was the murder in January 1948 of Shlomo Mikhoels, Chairman of the Jewish Anti-Fascist Committee, Director of the Jewish Theatre in Moscow and a prominent figure in Soviet Jewry.

From the course of events in the second half of 1948, it seems that a decision had been taken in October or November, at the highest level, to begin liquidating Jewish culture, which meant imprisoning all its principal proponents. The arrests were made in two waves, the first from the end of November 1948 until March 1949,[137] in which the leading figures of Jewish literature and art in the Soviet Union were arrested.[138] The second wave, which was smaller and complemented the first, took place in the first half of 1950.[139] Among those arrested and exiled to Siberia and other remote places were relatives of the writers and artists who had previously been arrested and tried.[140] It is difficult to give an authoritative list of everyone arrested in this period, but according to one drawn up by the Congress for Jewish Culture in New York after the twentieth congress of the Communist Party of the Soviet Union – a list which included those Jewish writers and artists who were arrested and disappeared in the 1930s and in the years from 1948 to 1953 – the 450 persons liquidated included 238 writers, 106 actors, 19 musicians and 87 painters and sculptors.[141] The compiler of another list of arrests,[142] which took place at the end of the 1940s, states: 'Within a few days 431 Jewish intellectuals were arrested and put in chains – 217 writers and poets, 108 actors, 87 artists and 19 musicians.'[143] It is important, however, to note that this assertion is not correct nor – which is more important – is the actual list, for although its compiler speaks of the arrests in the 1940s, his list includes many writers and artists who had either died during the war period or had not been arrested at all.[144] What is certain is that the arrests were on a very large scale and included most Yiddish writers, and some journalists, actors and artists connected with Jewish culture.

The majority of those arrested were sentenced, by the Special Boards of the MGB (Ministry of State Security), to ten years in forced labour camps. The main articles of indictment were: (a) bourgeois nationalism; (b) slandering the Soviet Union by spreading reports that there was anti-Semitism in the country; (c) espionage on behalf of Western powers. A minority, which included the most important writers and literary critics, the new Director of the Yiddish Theatre in Moscow, the former Deputy Foreign Minister and distinguished scientists – all of them leaders of the Jewish Anti-Fascist Committee – were interrogated over a long period, as if in preparation for a show trial.[145] If this is so, the question arises, why were the plans changed so that, instead of a show trial, there was one of the most secret trials ever held in the Soviet Union, a trial whose very existence is still questioned by some? The answer is that, despite his hostility to the Jewish people, Stalin was cautious in his foreign policy and in his use of anti-Semitism for political objectives and apparently still feared the effect which a large show trial involving leaders of Soviet Jewry might have. But this is only part of the answer. Those who planned the trial were influenced by the political advantages they thought they would gain from it. Since the aim which Stalin had apparently set himself in this period, as Khrushchev's statements at the twentieth congress and other sources show, was to conduct a large-scale purge among the Soviet leadership, it is hard to believe that a show trial of

Jewish writers could have served this purpose. Indeed, the preparations for the Doctors' Trial, which began in November 1952, demonstrate this. It is possible that the authorities' fear that the writers would not play their parts properly during the trial was also a deciding factor.

There is no doubt that a trial of the leaders of Soviet Jewish culture did take place from 11 to 18 July 1952,[146] but the central question, to which we cannot yet provide an answer, remains: who were the defendants and what precisely were the articles of indictment? From material published in the West since 1956, it is clear that there were between twenty-four and twenty-six defendants,[147] and that they included the writers Perets Markish, Itsik Fefer, Leyb Kvitko, David Bergelson, David Hofshteyn, and Shmuel Persov; the Director of the Jewish Theatre in Moscow, Binyamin Zuskin; the literary critic Yitzhak Nusinov; the former Deputy Foreign Minister and Chairman of *Sovinformburo*, Solomon Lozovsky; the scientist and member of the Academy of Sciences, Lina Shtern; and the Director of Botkin Hospital, Borish Shimelovich. Who the remaining defendants were is not clear.

The trial was held before the Military Collegium of the Soviet Union Supreme Court, the highest military tribunal. The main articles of the indictment seem to have been as follows:

(1) Armed insurrection with the aim of severing the Crimean region from the Soviet Union and establishing there a Jewish bourgeois and Zionist republic which would serve as a base for American imperialism (Article 58/II of the Criminal Code of the RSFSR, carrying a maximum penalty of death)[148] – a plan which had been put forward by the Americans in 1943 during the visit of S. Mikhoels and I. Fefer to the USA, and which was to have been implemented with the aid of Jewish organizations such as the Joint, the *Bund* and Zionist organizations.

(2) Espionage on behalf of foreign states (Article 58/VI of the Criminal Code, carrying a maximum penalty of death).

(3) Bourgeois nationalist activity and anti-Soviet propaganda (Article 58/X of the Criminal Code, for which, in accordance with Article 58/II, the maximum penalty in special conditions is death).

(4) Organization and activity forbidden by law (Article 58/XI of the Criminal Code).

After a week of deliberations, a verdict was handed down condemning twenty-three of the defendants to death; Lina Shtern received twenty-five years' imprisonment.[149]

As we shall see, the main charges brought against the leaders of the Jewish Anti-Fascist Committee in the Writers' Trial were to crop up again in different forms in the trial in Czechoslovakia and in the Doctors' Trial, which apparently had been meant to take place in March 1953. But first we must examine the economic trials of Jews during this period.

ECONOMIC TRIALS OF JEWS

It is only natural that Soviet Jews would be involved, as would citizens of other nationalities, in crimes of this kind in varying degrees; the researcher interested in the economic conditions of Soviet Jews must therefore investigate all the factors – economic, social, geographic and perhaps even psychological – working to produce such a phenomenon.

However, given the leaders' ability to make political use of every sphere of life and the regime's centralized control, the economic trials assume a new dimension. They can be transformed – whenever the Soviet authorities so desire – from what we previously called 'ordinary' trials into fully political trials. We must, then, examine when, how, and to what extent the economic trials were exploited by the authorities in their campaign against the Jewish minority.

From the few reports of economic trials appearing in the Soviet press between 1948 and 1951,[150] and from the more numerous articles dating from the second half of 1952 and early 1953,[151] it is clear that many Jews were involved in economic crime, including theft or sabotage of State property, speculation, giving and receiving bribes, evasion of work, and various fraudulent practices. Moreover, in trials reported in the press, the number of Jews exceeded that of non-Jews. The 'map' of economic crime encompassed all the Soviet republics, but it was the Ukrainian Republic that had a particularly high percentage of trials involving Jews.

It was in the Ukraine, too, that the most serious economic trial took place, in November 1952, after which there were many reports of Jews being arrested and tried.[152] In the first place, the defendants were tried not by a regular People's or District Court, but by a Military Court,[153] as in the secret trial of the Jewish writers conducted by the Military Collegium of the Soviet Union Supreme Court. Second, the indictment was in accordance with Articles 54/VII and 54/IX of the Ukrainian Criminal Code, which refer to 'activity of counter-revolutionary sabotage' in the sphere of commerce and supply, for which the maximum penalty is death. Third, the execution of three of the five defendants was intended to serve as a warning for the future. And finally, the fact that the three who were executed were Jews was also of special significance.

Exploitation of economic trials for political purposes, with the emphasis placed on the defendants' Jewishness, followed the announcement on 13 January 1953 of the discovery of the 'Doctors' Plot'. The press began to reveal the defendants' Zionist, *Bundist* or bourgeois–nationalist past, and to report that they were accused of having helped American and British spies to penetrate the factories they ran. The many *feuilletons* published in the Soviet press in this period fitted well into this campaign against economic crimes, with its anti-Jewish emphasis. Most of the Jews charged with economic crimes were factory and shop managers, warehousemen, doctors and lawyers, the doctors and lawyers being attacked with particular ferocity.

THE 'DOCTORS' PLOT'

The Prague trial of November 1952 and what was to have been the first show trial in the Soviet Union for more than fourteen years have many points in common. The similarity stems first from the fact that in Prague the ground was being prepared for the show trials in the Soviet Union itself, by testing the reactions of various Western circles, and perhaps by examining the potential of such trials and the political advantage to be gained from them in the conditions of the early fifties. Second, the Soviet advisers who prepared the Slansky Trial were high-ranking members of the Soviet security services and assistants of Ryumin, who was also in charge of preparing the Doctors' Trial. Third, during the campaign against the 'doctor–poisoners', the mass media relied on 'proof' drawn from trials which had taken place in Eastern Europe, particularly those of Rajk and Slansky. Fourth, there is evidence that witnesses connected with the Slansky Trial were to be used.[154] Fifth, the Slansky trial was for political murder with the aid of doctors, a charge which was to have been central to the Doctors' Trial. And, finally, some of the doctors were already in prison when the Slansky Trial opened.

The question arises, however, whether there is any need to look to Czechoslovakia for signs of what was about to occur in the Soviet Union. It is clear that at the end of 1952 and the beginning of 1953 the campaign against cosmopolitanism, bourgeois nationalism and

Zionism, and the employment of terror, reached heights that recalled the purges of the thirties.[155]

At the beginning of 1953, *Kommunist*, the central theoretical organ of the Central Committee of the Communist Party, published a 'call for vigilance', signed by Frol Kozlov. The main person attacked was the former *Bundist* and Trotskyite, Gurvich.[156] This article was a sign that a public campaign of denunciation of enemies, whose anti-Jewish character would be unmistakable, was about to be launched. But it was the Soviet news agency *Tass*'s communiqué on 13 January 1953,[157] announcing the discovery of the 'Doctors' Plot', that revealed Stalin's real plans. The charges were the murder of two prominent leaders of the Communist Party, Shcherbakov and Zhdanov, and preparations for the medical murder of the heads of the Red Army. Of the nine doctors arrested, six were Jews who had allegedly worked for 'Joint'.

Stalin's central aim – which had already emerged at the nineteenth CPSU congress in October 1952, where the decision was taken to alter the structure of the Politburo and enlarge it to twenty-five members – was to carry out extensive purges in the party and state machinery. The chief victims were apparently to be Beria, Molotov, Mikoyan and Voroshilov, that is to say, the surviving veteran leaders of the Communist Party.[158]

If Stalin had indeed decided on these purges, could they not have been carried out as in the 'Leningrad case', when Communist leaders like Voznesensky, Kuznetsov and Rodionov had been liquidated and thousands of their assistants imprisoned in absolute secrecy? More important for us, was it necessary to put Jewish doctors at the centre of the plot, and to present them as nationalists and Zionists operating as hired workers for American imperialism? These questions are answered below.

It was indeed possible to conduct large-scale purges which would include some of the Soviet leaders best known both in the Soviet Union and throughout the world by means of secret trials, but it would be difficult to do so, even in 1953, under Stalin's regime of terror. He therefore apparently decided to hold a series of show trials, modelled on the three show trials of the thirties and on those held in Eastern Europe between 1949 and 1952. Moreover, despite some drawbacks,[159] public trials had advantages from a political–psychological point of view, especially as the authorities wanted to confront the Soviet public with the grave danger threatening it from an enemy that would use any means to destroy its homeland. If the assumption that one of the main reasons for the show trials in the thirties was the threat of imminent war is correct, then a similar situation existed – so it seemed to Stalin – at the beginning of the fifties. It is difficult to determine to what extent Stalin's decision was affected by his natural vindictiveness, which apparently reached pathological dimensions at the end of his life and which was exploited during internal struggles within the ruling group – but it certainly had some effect.[160]

The selection of doctors as the link between the forthcoming trials was deliberate. In the first place, it is important to remember that Stalin knew that in the past doctors had acted on the orders of the security services (that is, of Stalin himself) to kill prominent Communist leaders such as Frunze and Kuibyshev.[161] Second, in the past, the accusation against doctors of the medical murder of various political leaders and public figures (for example, the Russian writer Maxim Gorky and his son Peshkov), which had served as grounds for prosecution in the trial of 21 March 1938[162] and in the Slansky Trial of November 1952,[163] had generally been believed, not only in the Soviet Union but also by Communist and Leftists in the West;[164] for, as Ilya Erenburg noted, suspicion and distrust of doctors can creep into the consciousness of even quite well-educated persons.[165] Third, for the reasons mentioned above, the traitorous acts of the doctors in the past could be linked with those of the present, especially since the names of the doctors Vinogradov, Vovsi and Kogan had been involved in one way or another in the 'Doctors' Affair' of the thirties.[166] Finally, in addition to the role the accused doctors were to play in the planned show trials, there was also the aim 'on the side' of liquidating a group of persons who had, in their years of work in the Kremlin, accumulated too much secret knowledge and so had become dangerous.

There were two reasons for putting Jewish doctors at the centre of the 'plot' and of the intended trial: it was necessary urgently to find a group, as homogeneous as possible, around which a web of accusations – all of them turning on acts of sabotage, espionage and moral corruption – could easily be woven. Since the Trotskyites had been eliminated in the thirties, and the Titoists were unsuitable, the choice fell on the Jewish doctors, with several non-Jewish doctors included as camouflage. What seems to have decided the issue was that Stalin saw in the trial a way to prepare the ground for exiling the Jewish population from the centre of the Soviet Union.

The propaganda campaign began immediately after the announcement on 13 January of the 'Doctors' Plot' and had become threatening by the end of the month and during February when daily articles, *feuilletons* and caricatures appeared, denouncing the 'Doctor–poisoners' and their Zionist–American instigators.[167] Behind the scenes, the authorities began to 'persuade' Soviet writers and scientists of Jewish origin to join the campaign.[168] The panic created among the public by the campaign was later described in Soviet literature,[169] most vividly in Vasily Grossman's description in his book *Forever Flowing*.[170]

THE JEWS IN SOVIET GOVERNMENT

We must examine the process which reduced the role of the Jews in Soviet government, to determine whether the factors operating in the previous priod continued to do so in the years 1939 to 1953, and to indicate what new factors emerged.

The Jews in the Communist Party and its central institutions. The last complete data on the national composition of the Communist Party are for 1927, when it had 49,627 Jewish members (4.34% of all party members).[171] The data for the period we are dealing with – this time only partial – are for the Ukraine, where in 1940 the Jews constituted 13.4% of Communist Party membership, whereas according to the 1939 census they represented only 4.9% of the total population. As the Ukrainian Jews constituted over half of the total Jewish population in the Soviet Union (50.8%),[172] and since the proportion of Jews in the Communist Parties of the RSFSR and Belorussia – the two republics with large Jewish concentrations – did not greatly differ from that of the Ukraine, Rigby concluded that the Jews constituted 4.9% of the Communist Party of the Soviet Union at that time. But one may question Rigby's calculations. While there is no doubt that the high proportion of Jews in the Communist Party in the Ukraine in 1940 is an important indicator – more useful for Belorussia, however, than for the Russian Republic – the proportion of 4.9% for 1940 appears to be too high. A proportion of 4.3%, as in 1927, or slightly less, is more likely.

As a predominantly urban population (according to the 1939 census, 87% of the Jews were town dwellers) constituting a professional and educated class from which the large majority of party members were recruited, the Jews were able to preserve their preferential position in the Communist Party, despite two impeding factors: the influx of national elements into the party, which began in the twenties and increased in the second half of the thirties; and the change for the worse in the treatment of the Jewish national minority, already quite marked in this period. (Lack of statistical data makes it difficult to estimate the influence of these factors.)

The profound demographic changes in the Soviet Jewish population after the war affected its proportion within the party. During the war years, the party widened its membership to make up for the losses it had sustained as a result of the purges, and to strengthen the morale of the army; indeed, the party grew by almost 50% (from 3,872,415 members and candidates in 1941 to 5,760,369 in 1945). As the majority of new members came from the army, and especially from the officer corps, one may assume that the proportion of Jews accepted into the party from the Red Army was fairly high, for two reasons: (a) It is estimated that Jews constituted 2.5% to 3% of the armed forces (about half-a-million out of a total of fifteen to twenty million soldiers),[173] whereas it may be assumed that after their extermination in the occupied regions they represented far less than the 1.8% of the overall population recorded in the 1939 census.[174] (b) The proportion of Jewish officers in the army was particularly high, because the Jews, being urban and well-educated, were an important source of recruits for the officer corps.

If these suppositions are correct, the Jews should at least have maintained their pre-war proportion in the party. We know, however, that from the outbreak of the war, and especially after 1943, Stalin and Shcherbakov pursued a policy of discrimination against the Jews, which was especially marked regarding promotions, the award of decorations, and appointments to various posts. Similar discrimination may have existed in acceptance of Jews into the party, but lack of data on the national origin of new party members in this period makes it difficult to draw justifiable conclusions.

Despite the purges, in which many Jewish communist leaders were expelled, Jews still occupied an important place on the Central Committee elected at the eighteenth party congress in 1939 – fourteen members and candidates, or over 10% of the Committee, were Jews.[175] From this point of view, their situation was no worse that it had been in the first half of the thirties. There was apparently a balance between those expelled from the defeated factions and those loyal to Stalin (including persons of Jewish origin), who were able to rise in the party hierarchy.

The shift towards the removal of Jews from the Central Committee began even before the outbreak of the Soviet German War. At the eighteenth Party Conference in February 1941, six members, among them two Jews (Antselovich and Litvinov), were transferred from membership of the Central Committee to candidacy, and fifteen candidates, among them two Jews (Vainberg and Zhemchuzhina, Molotov's wife), were expelled, while there were no Jews at all among the seventeen new members and candidates elected.[176]

As a result of Stalin's extreme anti-Jewish policy from 1948 to 1952, a decline occurred in the number of Jews on the Central Committee – from 10% of the Committee in 1939 to 2.1% in 1952.

During the years 1939 to 1953, only one Jew, Kaganovich, was still in the Politburo, the most influential body of the party. From the second half of the 1930s up to the late 1980s no Jew has been elected to the Secretariat.

The process which we have shown to be operating at the centre also took place in the republics.

The Jews in the Supreme Soviet of the USSR. In the 1937 Soviet elections, the first to be held after the ratification of the new constitution (December 1936), forty-seven Jews were elected to the Supreme Soviet out of 1,143 delegates (4.1% of the delegates of the two houses), whereas the Jews then constituted only 1.8% of the country's population. Since this session of the Supreme Soviet continued for nine years instead of the four fixed by the constitution, because of the war, it can be assumed that a number of the Jewish delegates did not serve their full terms (up to 1946) – either because they died or as a result of liquidations at the end of the thirties.

The shift in the representation of Jews was visible in the first post-war elections to the Supreme Soviet in 1946. It was not easily discernible in the party because the post-war elections to the Central Committee were not held until 1952. There was a steep fall in the number of Jewish delegates to the Supreme Soviet, compared with 1937. Only thirteen of the 1,139 delegates elected to the Supreme Soviet in 1946 were Jews, that is, slightly less than a 1% Jewish representation, whereas the decrease in Jews in the general population compared to 1939 was about one third (the post-war population was about 2,100,000). Another significant decline occurred in the last elections to the Supreme Soviet held during Stalin's lifetime, when the anti-Jewish campaign was at its peak, in the guise of the fight against cosmopolitanism and nationalism; thus in 1950 only eight delegates out of the total of 1,316 elected (0.6%) were Jews.

The Jews in the Soviet government. Between 1939 and 1953 the following Jews served as deputy premier: (1) Rozalia Samoilovna Zemlyachka (1939–43); (2) Lev Zakharovich Mekhlis (March–May 1941); (3) Lazar Moiseevitch Kaganovich (1944–53). Between 1939 and 1946, eight Jews still held the post of minister (though only four of them – Ginzburg, Vannikov, Mekhlis and Kaganovich – served in this capacity throughout the entire period) and four Jews held the post of deputy minister; whereas in 1947 their number fell sharply to two ministers and no deputy ministers at all. An additional Jewish minister (David Raizer) was added to the government in 1950, but he replaced (it is not known whether by coincidence or policy) another Jewish minister, Lev Mekhlis, who resigned (or was dismissed?) because of illness.

There is no doubt that in Stalin's last years, when anti-Jewish policy was at its height, many Jews were dismissed from their positions in higher education, art and culture. It is more difficult to discover how the purge affected the senior administrative cadres in central government institutions, although it certainly did affect them. The many trials, both open and secret, of the early 1950s, in which engineers and directors of economic enterprises were indicted, show that senior Jewish administrators did not escape the purges; but we cannot say definitively who was expelled from which Ministry, or when.

At all events, the ministries from which almost all the Jews were expelled were the Ministry of Defence (all branches, especially counter-espionage and other clandestine services); the Foreign Ministry, where as late as the 1940s a number of Jews still served (for example, Yakov Surits, USSR Ambassador to Brazil until 1946; and Boris Shtein, member of the Soviet delegation to the UN and holder of important posts in the Ministry until 1952); and the Ministry of Foreign Trade.

The falling curve of Jewish representation – starting at 1939 for the party and the government, and at 1937 for the Supreme Soviets – up to 1950 indicates the results of this process, but fails to answer one of the central questions raised here: was there a continuous decline in Jewish representation, or can one discern a discontinuous falling curve with turning points or divides? And if there are such divides, are they related to what we know from various sources about the Soviet leadership's policy on the Jewish question?

There seems to be a correlation between Soviet policy on the Jewish question and the decline in Jewish representation in virtually all the ruling institutions. The situation can be summarized as follows:

(1) *From 1939 to 1941*, following the change in the Soviet leadership's attitude towards the Jews and the liquidation of the network of Jewish institutions and influenced by the change in foreign policy after the Ribbentrop–Molotov pact, a policy of reducing the number of Jews in Soviet government seems to have been adopted. This is seen in Litvinov's dismissal from the post of Foreign Minister; in the restriction of Jewish representation on the Central Committee; and in the decline in the number of Jewish ministers. As part of this process, a number of Jewish delegates were also expelled from the Supreme Soviet.

(2) *From 1942 to 1945* two opposing tendencies were at work. On the one hand, the anti-Jewish policy which had begun at the end of the thirties continued and on the other the requirements of the war effort led to a few Jews, such as Litvinov and Antselovich, being restored to their former positions.

(3) It was *in the years 1946 to 1953* that the decisive shift occurred in Jewish representation in all the institutions of Soviet government; this confirms our conclusion that a correlation exists between policy on the Jewish problem and the proportion of posts allotted to Jews in the ruling institutions. In this period, which began with the change in internal policy (in 1946) and foreign policy (in 1947) and which has been named the '*Zhdanovshchina* Period', a systematic campaign was conducted against bourgeois nationalism, cosmopolitanism and Zionism, the principal victims being the Soviet Jews.

THE HOLOCAUST AND JEWISH HEROISM AS PORTRAYED IN SOVIET SCIENTIFIC LITERATURE AND THE PRESS

The portrayal of the Holocaust and Jewish heroism in the Soviet mass media is one of the most accurate gauges of official Soviet policy towards the Jewish question from the Second World War to the present time. This indicator is important because the attitude of the authorities – from the highest to the lowest – on a subject as sensitive as the Holocaust of Soviet and European Jewry, reflects their real, if hidden, intentions towards the Jews. At the same time, these official publications affect the Soviet Jewish population.

After the signing of the Ribbentrop–Molotov pact in August 1939, Soviet publications attacking Nazi Germany's extreme anti-Jewish policy ceased; such reports had been published, with greater or lesser intensity – in accordance with international practice – from Hitler's rise to power until 1939. Moreover, the beginning of the methodical extermination of European Jewry in countries already under German rule was not mentioned in any official Soviet publication. This silence, maintained for political reasons, was disastrous for the Jews – at least some of whom had not fled while there was still time because they were unaware of the fate in store for them at the hands of the Nazis.

It was to be expected that this short-sighted policy would change with the outbreak of the Soviet–German war in June 1941, but in fact the changes were only partial. First, it is important to note that the Soviet Russian-language press, as well as that of other languages, did not publish many reports on the extermination of the Jews in the occupied territories. Second, the reports that were published did not stress the fact that the Germans intended to exterminate the Jewish people, but implied that they would be content with enslaving and plundering the property of other peoples. Third, in the official publications that were mainly directed abroad, like the two appeals of 6 January and 27 April 1942,[177] made by the Soviet Foreign Minister, V. Molotov, to governments with which the USSR maintained diplomatic relations, the extermination of the Jews was mentioned only twice, and then in passing amidst lengthy reports dealing with German policy against the Russians, Ukrainians, Belorussians, Latvians, Moldavians, Estonians, and other nationalities. Another Soviet declaration, of 19 December 1942, was issued in the wake of the formal declaration made by the twelve countries fighting against Germany and its allies on 'the German policy of exterminating the Jewish population of Europe'; it stated that: 'In proportion to its small population, the Jewish minority in the Soviet Union had suffered particularly heavy losses because of the bestial bloodthirstiness of the Hitlerite devils.' This bald statement is insignificant compared with the detailed description of Nazi policy against the Russians, Ukrainians, Belorussians, etc.[178] Fourth, few of the reports of the 'Special State Commission for the Determination and Study of the Hitlerite Atrocities' (established in November 1942) concerned the Jewish Holocaust.[179] And, finally, in a trial of Nazi war criminals held in Kharkov in December 1943, following the liberation of the city, reference was made to the extermination of 'peaceful Soviet citizens', with no indication that the majority of those 20,000 citizens had been Jews.[180]

On the other hand, it must be emphasized that in Yiddish-language publications, in books and in many articles in *Eynikayt* – published by the Jewish Anti-Fascist Committee – the Holocaust and Jewish heroism occupied an important place.[181]

The question at once arises: what were the reasons for this dualism in official Soviet policy, concealing the Jewish Holocaust in publications in Russian and the languages of other nationalities, but underlining it in Yiddish-language publications? The answer is clear. The leadership feared that if Nazi propaganda about the absolute identification between Bolshevism and Jewry were to succeed, the Soviet policy of uniting all the nationalities in a war to the death against the German occupier would be undermined. The Soviet media (except those in Yiddish) therefore took pains to underplay the fact that the Nazis were directing their methodical acts of extermination principally against the Jewish population. However, this is only part of the answer for, as we shall see, the policy of concealment, and later of total silence, in the portrayal of the Jewish Holocaust continued after the war, when the danger from Nazi propaganda had passed. The unavoidable conclusion is that this dual policy was adopted because anti-Semitism existed within the Soviet leadership and also an innate unwillingness to recognize Jewish heroism and suffering.

The policy of concealment in the post-war portrayal of the Jewish Holocaust found expression in the episode of *The Black Book*. As soon as it was established in June 1942, the Jewish Anti-Fascist Committee decided to publish material on the atrocities perpetrated by the Nazis against the Jewish population in the occupied territories.[182] In 1943, apparently on the initiative of the writers Ilya Erenburg and Vasily Grossman, a 'literary commission' was formed to prepare a book of testimonies and documents on the Nazi extermination of the Jews;[183] but by order of the Deputy Director of the Sovinformburo, S. Lozovsky, the commission was dissolved (apparently in 1944), and preparation of the book was transferred to the Jewish Anti-Fascist Committee. The Committee set up a new editorial board whose members included the writers Ilya Erenburg, Vasily Grossman, and Konstantin Simonov; the literary critic A. Efros; the jurists A. Trainin and I. Trainin; and others. It was agreed between the Jewish Anti-Fascist Committee and Jewish circles abroad that *The Black*

Book would appear simultaneously in the Soviet Union (in Russian and Yiddish), the USA (in English) and Palestine (in Hebrew). The idea of forming a 'Black Book Committee' of all the groups interested in the publication was also mooted. In May 1946, the Presidium of the Jewish Anti-Fascist Committee announced that the Russian version of the book was ready for printing.[184] However, the authorities apparently opposed publication, and from time to time vetoed various sections of the book; finally, at the end of 1948, they broke up the type.[185] *The Black Book* was to have included (a) survivors' letters, diaries and testimonies; (b) descriptions and surveys by writers and journalists; (c) documentary material placed at the editorial board's disposal by the Soviet Governmental Commission for the Determination and Investigation of Nazi Crimes. Some parts of the book were published in English[186] and Romanian[187] editions.

A similar fate befell *The Red Book*, which was to have portrayed the part played by the Jews in the battles of the Red Army, and the history of Jewish resistance movements in the ghettos and partisan units. Ilya Erenburg, one of the initiators of the book, told a correspondent of the Yiddish paper *Morgn frayhayt* that the book 'contains much material underlining the heroism and valour of the Jewish fighters... It appears in the Russian language since it is of major importance that the Russian reader learn the full scope of the Jewish tragedy'.[188] One of the main objectives of the book was, as Erenburg's words imply, to refute anti-Semitic accusations heard during the war about the Jews' non-resistance of the Nazi occupier; this would explain why a significant part of the material was written by non-Jews. The real attitude of the authorities towards Erenburg's aims, noted above, was shown during the war. In mid 1944, Kondakov, an assistant of A. Shcherbakov (Chairman of the Sovinformburo and head of the Army Political Department), banned the text of Erenburg's call to American Jewry concerning the brutality of the Nazis. Kondakov argued that there was no need to mention acts of heroism by Jewish soldiers in the Red Army, because 'that is arrogance'.[189] *The Red Book* did not appear in the Soviet Union, but parts of the material assembled for it appeared in another book, entitled *The Brotherhood of the Partisans*, about Jewish fighters in partisan units, which was apparently not distributed either in the Soviet Union or abroad.[190]

From 1949 to 1953, Soviet policy on the portrayal of the Holocaust in the mass media and in historical and political literature, deteriorated still further, from partial concealment of the Holocaust and Jewish heroism to total suppression. These subjects were never referred to in the central Soviet press, nor in the local press. This policy was carried to such lengths that the authorities erased the mention of Jews from the few monuments erected after the war in memory of the Jewish victims of the Nazis.

JEWS IN SOVIET LITERATURE

When we review the treatment of the Jewish theme by non-Jewish Soviet writers during the war period, the first thing that strikes us is how few books there were on that subject. From this point of view, there was an improvement in 1946 and 1947, with the publication of works by T. Valednitskaya, P. Vershigora, G. Linkov, V. Nekrasov, I. Kozlov, A. Fadeev, V. Katlinskaya, I. Vilde, A. Fedorov, F. Panferov and V. Kataev. On the Holocaust itself, the most important book is Tatyana Valednitskaya's *Sun From the East*, devoted entirely to the portrayal of the Jewish ghetto in the city of Lvov, and its multifaceted life, until the extermination of all its inhabitants; but the Jewish tragedy is presented throughout as part of the general Soviet tragedy. The non-Jewish authors deal with virtually the same subjects as Soviet authors of Jewish origin, namely, the Jewish Holocaust and the attitude towards it of the local population. The non-Jewish writers stress even more that those who collaborated with the Nazis were traitors, army deserters, and members of nationalist bourgeois organizations. The majority of the population empathized with the tragedy of its Jewish neighbours but lacked the means to save them; while an active minority did do everything in its power to aid the fleeing Jews (as described in Kozlov's *In the Crimean Underground*). The Jewish resistance in the ghettos is hardly mentioned in these books; the exception is Valednitskaya's description of the spontaneous uprising in the Lvov ghetto by a Jewish populace lacking arms and without hope of victory. In contrast to this, the Jewish share in the partisan movement and in the Red Army was extensively related in the books mentioned above.

There is a difference between the works of non-Jewish Soviet authors and of their Jewish counterparts as regards the treatment of the Jewish national past. An analysis of the literature published during and immediately after the war shows that, in the works of the Russian, Ukrainian and Belorussian writers who dealt with the Jewish theme, the salient Jewish elements of national symbols, Jewish motifs, specific Jewish qualities, and the link with the past, are almost totally absent; and it is this which differentiates them from the works we noted earlier by Soviet writers of Jewish origin. It is therefore interesting to find such elements in a few works (mainly poetry), for example, the poems of the Russian A. Surkov,[191] the Belorussian M. Tank,[192] and the Ukrainians M. Rylsky[193] and P. Tychyna,[194] as well as in the prose of V. Panova.[195]

Incipient signs of the jettisoning of liberal policy were visible at the end of the war, and became still more obvious in August 1946 after Zhdanov's speech. The Jewish theme occupied an important place in the works of Soviet authors in 1946 and 1947, but anyone studying the official publication policy closely must have noticed a silence concerning the Holocaust in political statements and documentary publications. Moreover, it was also widely known that pressure was exerted behind the scenes by the administration to compel those collecting documentary material on the Holocaust and Jewish resistance efforts to cease their activities. This, it would seem, influenced many writers, mainly of Jewish origin, to drop Jewish subjects in general, and the Holocaust in particular. The fact that the continuation of Valednitskaya's *Sun from the East* was not published, despite repeated statements that it would soon appear, is perhaps the clearest external sign that this new policy had begun to take effect as early as 1946.

In L. Leonov's novel, *The Russian Forest* (1953),[196] where the author settles accounts with the enemies of 'the Russian forest' (Leonov's symbol for the Russian people), the Jewish timber merchant from Riga is presented as one of the principal enemies and the Jews are shown as hostile to the Russian people.

The only unmistakably anti-Semitic work known to us in the Soviet literature of the years 1948 to 1953 is V. Kochetov's novel *Zhurbiny*, which began to be published in 1952.[197] One of its most negative characters is Venyamin Semenovich, director of a cultural club and coordinator of its drama group. Kochetov portrays him as a man not without erudition, but over-ambitious, quarrelsome, and boisterous, despite the fact that he 'doesn't drink vodka'. He is a wanderer, accustomed to a gypsy life. The Second World War, Kochetov reminds us, is not reflected in the life of Venyamin Semenovich; he spends most of it in the rear in Kirgizia, where his main concern is how to get some sort of medal. He finally reaches the depths of baseness when he takes off from the city leaving his pregnant wife behind. All the stereotyped Jewish characteristics appearing in anti-Semitic *feuilletons* are concentrated in this novel.

There were two distinct periods in Soviet Stalinist literature from the point of view of its treatment of the Jews: 1941 to 1947 and 1948 to 1953, 1948 being a kind of transition year. In the second period, the Jewish theme was given less and less space by non-Jewish writers, and all but disappeared in the works of writers of Jewish origin. The reasons for this were of course political. During the 'black years' of the concentrated anti-Jewish campaign, it was dangerous even to deal with a Jewish topic, especially for those writers unremittingly attacked in the Soviet press. There may have been writers who were willing to take the risk, but it would have been clear to them that such works would not be published.

JEWISH 'AUTONOMY': RENEWAL AND DISAPPEARANCE

The first blow to the Birobidzhan project – which in any case had encountered numerous difficulties – was struck on August 1936, during the purges, when most of the leaders of the Jewish Autonomous Region were arrested on charges of Trotskyism, nationalism, and espionage on behalf of foreign powers. The second blow came in 1938, when all the special institutions that had dealt with Jewish settlement in the USSR since the mid twenties were closed down.

Nevertheless, after the purges and the annexation to the Soviet Union in 1939 and 1940 of new territories with a considerable Jewish population, fresh hopes arose for renewed development in the Jewish Autonomous Region. Plans to transfer thirty to forty thousand Jewish families to Birobidzhan were revived, but nothing came of them, and in fact very few Jewish immigrants arrived in the region between 1939 and 1941. With the outbreak of the Soviet–German war, immigration into Birobidzhan virtually ceased, to be renewed again only in 1945.

The old argument, whether a Jewish Republic should be established in Birobidzhan or in the Crimea, cropped up again at the end of the war. Interest in the Crimea was revived, due on the one hand to the expulsion of the Tatars from the Crimea because of alleged collaboration with the Nazis, and on the other to the feeling in the circles of the Jewish Anti-Fascist Committee that after the war the authorities would have to settle the survivors of the Holocaust in an area more suitable than Birobidzhan. However, the idea was quickly dropped when it became clear that the authorities had decided against it.

At the end of the war, when the new Five-Year Plan for 1946 to 1950 was being prepared, the Far East was assigned an important part in the rehabilitation of the population of the destroyed areas, and a place was found within this framework for a Jewish Autonomous Region. This fact was mentioned in the official Resolutions of the Council of Commissars of the RSFSR of 26 January 1946, and in an Edict of the Council of Commissars of the USSR of 27 January 1946, both of which dealt with measures for strengthening the economy of the Jewish Autonomous Region. Although these resolutions said little about the Jewish national aspect of Birobidzhan, they were sufficient to raise new hopes for Jewish settlement among Soviet Jewry. The parties most interested in the renewal of the programme of Jewish settlement in Birobidzhan were: members of the Jewish Anti-Fascist Committee, which had previously supported the establishment of a Jewish autonomous republic in the Crimea, but realized this project would not gain support from the authorities; many Jews who had survived the Holocaust and encountered hostile treatment from the local population when they returned to their former homes; and, it seems, a number of Soviet leaders who had previously backed the programme.[198]

The main internal factors influencing the Soviet authorities to agree to renewed emigration by Jews to Birobidzhan were the need to solve the problems in the Ukraine after disputes between the local population and Jews returning to their former homes; Birobidzhan's need for additional population; and the desire to divert the attention of Soviet Jews from Zionism and Israel. There were also external influences. First, there was the long-standing desire to prove to the world that the Jewish problem had found in the Soviet Union its only possible solution, that is, the socialist solution.[199] Second, the Soviet leaders wanted to exploit the issue of the renewal of Jewish settlement in Birobidzhan in order to win Jewish and general public support in the West. And finally, there was apparently also an attempt to use the Birobidzhan project to solve the difficult problem of Jewish refugees from Poland who had lived in the Soviet Union during the war.[200]

In its first stages, from 1945 to the end of 1946, Jewish emigration to Birobidzhan was disorganized and limited. However, in October 1946, after the authorities decided to organize the mass Jewish emigration in special trains (*eshelony*), the systematic registration of those interested in emigrating to Birobidzhan began.[201] In 1947 and 1948, twelve special trains arrived in Birobidzhan, bringing about 6,500 persons from the cities of Vinnitsa, Kherson, Nikolaev, Dnepropetrovsk, Odessa and Samarkand;[202] this immigration apparently totalled about 10,000. An exaggerated figure, more than twice this number of immigrants in eighteen months, was cited by Bakhmutsky, Secretary of the Birobidzhan District Communist Party.[203] The new immigrants to Birobidzhan included labourers, agricultural workers, and a high percentage of people with technical professions such as engineers, technicians, doctors, agronomists, and teachers. From this point of view, the post-war composition of the population differed from that of the first settlers in the 1920s.[204]

The arrival of the new immigrants, together with the change in Soviet policy on the Jewish Autonomous Region, breathed new life into Jewish cultural activity in the region, but it was not long before Jewish hopes for the revival of Jewish 'sovereignty' were dashed. At the end of 1948 and the beginning of 1949 the Kaganovich Yiddish Theatre, the Jewish publishing house, the periodical *Birobidzhan*, the library of Yiddish and Hebrew books, and the Jewish research institutions and schools were all closed down. The mass anti-Jewish purge carried out at this time in Birobidzhan, hitting especially hard at functionaries, writers and artists, was an even worse blow to the 'Birobidzhan project' than the purges of the thirties.[205]

The connection between the Jewish Autonomous Region and the outside world was severed between 1949 and 1953, and only rare reports reached the West of what was happening there.[206] The Soviet authorities ceased publishing reports related in any way to the Jewish nature of the region, their propaganda media being content with the efforts of the communist and pro-communist circles outside the USSR to refute 'anti-Soviet propaganda' and to describe the prosperity of the Jewish Autonomous Region and the contented life of the Jews living there.

Emigration to Birobidzhan, in the restricted form of the special trains, continued in the first half of 1949, but later (principally in 1952 and early 1953) the Jewish Autonomous Region became a land of penal exile, where Jews found guilty in the economic trials held during these years were sent to do forced labour. Moreover, in the months before Stalin's death, there were rumours that Birobidzhan would have to absorb a large number of the Jews about to be exiled from the European part of the Soviet Union. This plan was cancelled on Stalin's death on 5 March 1953.

JEWISH EDUCATION AND CULTURE

The principal phases of Soviet policy on Jewish education and culture between 1939 and 1953 will now be examined.

Jewish education.   Before the Soviet Union annexed the territories of the Western Ukraine in October 1939, there were only nineteen Yiddish schools in the country,[207] and the total number of Yiddish school pupils was about 75,000, accounting for only 20% of school-age children.[208] In the years 1939 and 1940 there was a quantitative increase and a renewal of Yiddish school activity in the regions annexed. Although there are no full data, the partial data show thirty Yiddish schools opened in Lvov,[209] and forty-three with 6,000 pupils, in Bialystok.[210] The subsequent mass exile of Jews from these regions and the pressure exerted on the Jewish population to send its children to general schools caused a drastic reduction in the number of pupils attending Jewish schools.

It seems that from 1941 to 1944 Jewish schools were maintained only in the Jewish Autonomous Region of Birobidzhan. Their precise number is unknown, since the central and local press stopped publishing data on them at the end of the 1930s.[211] The number of Yiddish schools in the Soviet Union after the war was insignificant. The limited number of schools in Birobidzhan included Jewish schools, a mixed (Yiddish–Russian) secondary school, and a mixed pedagogic technical institute (with a Jewish department and a Russian department, the former apparently being closed in 1947).[212] In Chernovtsy there were two Jewish schools (elementary and secondary) in 1945,[213] but they seem to have been closed quickly. In Vilnius and Kaunas (cities in the Lithuanian Republic) there were a school and an orphanage where the language of study was Yiddish. The Vilnius school was established in 1945[214] and apparently closed early in 1950.[215] In addition to its curriculum of studies, the Kaunas school formed a choir which appeared in the city with a repertoire of songs and readings.[216]

Jewish literature and press.   During and after the war the Jewish Anti-Fascist Committee was at the centre of Jewish cultural activity.[217] With other anti-Fascist organizations, it was established as part of the authorities' efforts to mobilize all possible forces for the war against Germany.[218] The Jewish Anti-Fascist Committee was established in May 1942 under the Soviet Information Bureau (Sovinformburo) with Solomon Lozovsky, Deputy Foreign Minister and Deputy Director of the Sovinformburo, as its head. Though it did not include Jewish personages and organizations from other countries (as the *Bund* leaders, Henryk Erlich and Victor Alter, had proposed to the Soviet authorities), and despite the restrictions imposed upon it, the Committee played a decisive role in developing Jewish culture. As the sole Jewish organization in the country, and because of the special nature of the war period, the Jewish Anti-Fascist Committee succeeded in uniting, for the first time in the history of the Soviet Union, the best writers, artists and researchers involved in Yiddish culture, and in bringing together writers, artists, scientists and public figures of Jewish origin who had until then been far removed from Jewish culture and activity.

Although most of the Committee's operations were aimed at the outside world, its leaders, the Yiddish Theatre actor, Solomon Mikhoels, and the writers Itsik Fefer, Perets Markish and others, unquestionably saw their principal task as fostering and disseminating Jewish culutre. The Committee's principal activities in this sphere were the founding of *Eynikayt* in June 1942; the concentration in Moscow of Jewish writers, journalists and artists previously dispersed throughout the Soviet Union; and the renewal of the operations of the publishing house, Der Emes. While the editors of *Eynikayt* endeavoured to underline the part played by Soviet Jews in the war against the Nazi enemy, they did not ignore the part of the Jews in the Allied armies and partisan movements. The newspaper dealt at length with the life of the Jewish communities on the home front, and with the Jewish contributions to science, industry and culture, laying particular stress on 'the Jewish theme'. But during and after the war reporting essays and articles centred around Jewish literary and artistic creation in the Soviet Union.

From 1942 to 1945, only fifty-eight Yiddish books and pamphlets were published in the Soviet Union,[219] because of war-time difficulties. Yet in 1946, a year after the war, there was no increase in Yiddish publications (only eighteen books). It was not until 1947 that a sizeable increase occurred, when the number of Yiddish books and pamphlets reached forty-nine.[220] It can be assumed that if the programme for 1948 had been realized the number of Yiddish books and pamphlets would have exceeded the forty-seven books actually published. In November 1948, however, the central publishing house, Der Emes, was closed down and the Academy of Sciences in the

Ukraine and the Belorussian Government ceased their Yiddish publications: Yiddish publishing in the Soviet Union was silenced until 1959. The circulation of Yiddish publications during and after the war, however, not only did not decrease compared to the 1930s but actually increased,[221] and about 85% of Yiddish books published between 1946 and 1948 were Jewish in content.[222]

After the war, three Yiddish-language literary-political periodicals played an important part in the dissemination of Jewish culture: *Heimland*, a literary–artistic and socio-political periodical published by the Writers' Union of the USSR in Moscow in 1947 and 1948 (a total of seven issues); *Der Shtern*, a literary periodical of the Jewish writers in the Ukraine in 1947 and 1948 (a total of seven issues); and *Birobidzhan*, a literary periodical published from 1946–8. These three periodicals had a larger circulation than the Yiddish literary monthlies at the end of the 1930s.[223]

In addition to original Yiddish literature and journalism, literature translated from Yiddish into Russian and other languages played its part in the dissemination of Jewish culture in the Soviet Union. The new Soviet policy of the second half of the 1930s led to an increase in the publication of Yiddish literature in Russian translation. From 1937 to 1941 alone, 120 such works appeared as against only thirty-one from 1932 to 1936. During and after the war there was again a sharp drop in Yiddish publications in Russian translation: twenty-one books between 1942 and 1945 and fifteen between 1946 and 1948. There were two principal causes for this decline: first, the inverse correlation between publications in Yiddish and their translations into Russian or other languages – that is, the authorities' decision to increase Yiddish publication led to a reduction in translations from that language; second, difficulties experienced during the war also had their effect.

The major themes of *belles–lettres* in Yiddish during the war, and to a lesser extent from 1946 to 1948, were focussed on a national awakening such as Yiddish literature in the Soviet Union had never known. This was the result of two interconnected factors: the shock of the Holocaust, and the Soviet authorities' liberal nationalities policy, which enabled Yiddish writers to express their innermost feelings. This they did through an extended discussion of the current topics of the war, such as Jewish heroism, the Jewish share in the victory over the Nazis, the destruction of entire Jewish communities, Jewish solidarity and Soviet patriotism, and the socialist brotherhood of nations; we find salient Jewish motifs, grief and deep affliction, anxiety for the future of the Jewish nation, adherence to symbols of the remote past and a rediscovery of religious and national motifs which had previously been rejected.

With the end of the war, and especially after the shift in Soviet policy in August 1946, Yiddish writers found themselves in a difficult situation. To retreat from their national position was virtually impossible, even had they wished to do so, for thousands of copies of their stories, poems and essays had been printed and their plays had been performed over and over again, and it is doubtful whether disavowal would have changed their fate. On the other hand, to continue with their creative work as before was not only dangerous but impossible under the stringent censorship of the Soviet regime, hence their difficult position and their search for a way out of this impasse.

The change in policy towards independent Jewish national existence in Palestine shown by the Soviet Union's vote of 29 November 1947 in the UN, and by its support for the establishment of the State of Israel, engendered new hopes among many Yiddish writers for a parallel change in the authorities' policy towards the Jewish national minority in the Soviet Union; but these hopes were quickly dashed. The decision to liquidate the vestiges of Jewish culture in the Soviet Union was apparently taken at the highest level of Government in the first half of 1948, but the authorities implemented their programme cautiously, mainly because of foreign policy considerations.

The first, most serious stage in the liquidation of Jewish culture came with the closing down of the Jewish Anti-Fascist Committee's organ *Eynikayt* on 20 November 1948, and three Yiddish periodicals in Moscow, Kiev and Birobidzhan immediately afterwards; the disbanding of the only Yiddish publishing house, Der emes, and the ban on Yiddish publications in the Ukraine and Belorussia. The second stage (as we shall see below) was the cessation of Yiddish radio broadcasts and the dissolution of the Yiddish theatre and actors' companies. The final trace of Yiddish literary works in the Soviet Union between 1949 and 1953 was a small number of translations into Russian and other languages.

Jewish national expression found a voice in Russia, especially during the war, in the works of writers of Jewish origin (Ilya Erenburg, Vasily Grossman, Pavel Antokolsky, Margarita Aliger, Lev Ozerov and others) who recounted the horror of the Holocaust as well as individual and group heroism in the war against Nazi brutality. However, after the war there was a decrease in works in the Russian language which included Jewish history. This is attributable not so much to sudden lack of interest on the part of the authors but rather to the Soviet authorities' extreme sensitivity to Jewish topics.

The renewed dangers for the Jews were felt very early on by Ilya Erenburg, and, as early as 1940, he expressed them in a poem about the wanderings and loneliness of tormented Rachels and Haims and Leahs.[224] Erenburg described in many articles and newspaper stories the Nazi atrocities against the Jewish populations,[225] and acts of heroism by Jews who revolted against the Germans, even when there was no chance of success. In 1946 to 1947 he wrote his great literary work *The Storm*, which described the war, the Holocaust and the tragedy of Babi Yar. One of the first writers to deal with Jewish martyrology at the beginning of the war was Vasily Grossman. While the Jewish theme was given only minor treatment in his first book, *Immortal Is The People* (1942), which described the panic-stricken retreat of the Red Army in mid 1941, he raised the question that hundreds of thousands of Jews were surely asking themselves – whether to remain or to flee. Grossman attempted to answer this question in his book *The Old Teacher*, which he wrote in 1942 and which was published the following year. In a small Ukrainian town, the Jews were unaware of the extent of the approaching disaster. The only person reading the situation correctly was the old teacher Rosental, who although he wanted to leave, delayed too long. Grossman was among the first to describe the relations between the Jews and the local population under the Nazi occupation. He attempted to make a clear distinction between the majority of the local population who took no hand in the persecution of the Jews, and a minority of nationalists, careerists and deserters who collaborated with the enemy.

It is this theme which is repeated in most of the literary works dealing with the war period. Among the few who dealt with the apathy of the local population when Jews were led to the slaughter was the Jewish–Ukrainian poet, Savva Golovanivsky, in his poem 'Abraham'. In Boris Gorbatov's book *The Undefeated* (1943), the theme of the local population's attitude towards the Nazi extermination of the Jews is dramatically conveyed, although it is idealized. His explanation of the reason for the Russian population's saving fleeing Jews is noteworthy: the acts of heroism performed in aiding Jews were not the result of communist ideology; rather, 'the smell of blood/ of Jews shot somewhere outside the city/ imposed a duty ... this was a duty of conscience'. The brotherhood of Soviet nationalities, which passes the test – perhaps because of strong family ties – is portrayed in the story '*Tamara* Savitskaya', by the poet A. Bezymensky, published only in Yiddish translation in 1944.[226] Expressions of shock at the Jewish Holocaust are found in works by the poets Ilya Selvinsky,[227] Leonid Pervomaisky,[228] Pavel Antokolsky,[229] Margarita Aliger,[230] Lev Ozertov[231] and Yakov Khelemsky.[232]

Descriptions of the mass murder of Jews carried out by the Nazis in the extermination camps, ghettos, villages and forests are contained in literary reports and in documentary collections of great historical importance, which were written and prepared for publication by writers of Jewish origin. These writers also related heroic acts by both solitary Jews and those in groups in their battle against the barbarous enemy in the occupied territories and in the ranks of the Red Army. These writers believed it was their duty not only to describe Jewish heroism as historical truth, but also to stamp out the rumours insinuating that the Jews were shirkers skulking in the rear, whilst the Russians and other nationalities were shedding their blood on the battlefield.

From the Jewish point of view, there is no doubt that the most important book is *Years of Life* (1948) by Aleksandr Isbakh, whose real name was Yitzhak Bakhrakh. The book, which to a large extent marked the end of a phase in the official publication policy on Jewish subjects in the Stalin period, was a collection of semi-autobiographical stories extensively portraying Jewish village life in the Pale of Settlement before World War I, beginning in 1911, and during and after the period of the Revolution. Through the history of the main protagonist of the book, the orphan Shtein, who traverses a long road from synagogue beadle to active communist, Isbakh succeeds in portraying the old way of life, the synagogue, anti-Semitism, and the relations between the various strata of the Jewish population, its parties and movements. Even though the author was critical of the Jewish religion (perhaps he had no choice in the matter), the fact that he described extensively Jewish festivals, prayers and customs – even quoting the words of the Zionist anthem *Ha-tikvah* – is remarkable. Isbakh was apparently misled by the new Soviet policy on the establishment of the State of Israel, and inferred that there would also be a shift of opinion in the Soviet Union regarding Zionism; but a few months after his book appeared, he was furiously attacked by the daily press and the periodicals.[233]

Jewish art and research institutions.   In the second half of the 1930s, with the beginning of the liquidation of Jewish culture, the number of these institutions decreased to ten.[234] With the outbreak of the Soviet–German war in 1941, several theatre companies were dissolved, whilst others, such as those of Odessa, Kiev, Minsk and Moscow, were transferred to remote regions. After the war they began to return to their permanent sites but some of them (especially in the Ukraine) encountered difficulties in getting their buildings back and in obtaining budgets.

In 1946 the following Jewish theatre companies were operating in the Soviet Union:

(1) *The State Yiddish Theatre in Moscow* which had about 100 actors and administrative personnel. It was headed by Solomon Mikhoels, until his murder on 13 January 1948. Its second director, the actor Binyamin Zuskin, was arrested at the end of 1948. A drama school under Moshe Belenky was attached to the theatre. Apart from Mikhoels, the teachers included stage directors and Yiddish-literature researchers.

(2) *The Shalom Aleikhem Theatre in Chernovtsy* which was headed by Grigory Spektorov until his death in early 1948, and thereafter by Moshe Goldblat.

(3) *The Yiddish Theatre in Odessa* under Efraim Loyter.

(4) *The Belorussian Yiddish Theatre in Minsk* under the artistic direction of Viktor Golovchiner.

(5) *The Kaganovich Yiddish Theatre in Birobidzhan*, with Alex Shtein as artistic director.

(6) *A Yiddish theatre company in Uzbekistan* founded in 1945, which apparently ceased functioning immediately after the war.

(7) Little is known of the Yiddish theatre companies in Kishinev (Moldavia) and Riga (Latvia), which were apparently very short-lived.

Apart from the permanent theatres, a further seventeen theatrical companies, nine professional and eight amateur, operated in the Soviet Union. Interestingly, more than half of them – ten out of the seventeen – were in the Ukrainian Republic, mainly because of the large Jewish population there, which had not yet assimiliated and still sought Yiddish culture. This explanation is supported by a similar situation in the Baltic Republics. The artistic standard of the permanent theatres and companies was not uniform. The State Yiddish Theatre in Moscow under Mikhoels attained a standard comparable to that of the best Soviet theatre companies; the theatres of the Ukraine, Belorussia and Birobidzhan also had significant artistic achievements.

The repertoire of the theatres in the final years of their existence is important in understanding the Jewish essence of Yiddish culture in the Soviet Union. In 1948 and 1949, the five permanent and professional theatres performed thirty-two plays, some of which had already been staged at the end of the war and immediately after, while others had their premières in 1948. Numerically, first place – some 41% (thirteen of the thirty-two) of all plays staged in this period – is held by original plays by Soviet Yiddish writers: *Freylekhs* by Z. Okun, a play permeated with Jewish folklore, was first performed on the stage of the Jewish Theatre in Moscow on 23 July 1945, and enjoyed great success; it received a state prize in 1946. Gershesnzon's *Herschl Ostropoler*, which also leaned heavily on Jewish folklore, enjoyed great popularity and was performed by all the permanent theatres and companies for a long period. More important in terms of content and literary–artistic values are Perets Markish's play *Revolt in the Ghetto* and Itsik Fefer's *The Sun Does Not Set*, both of which tell of the struggle of the Polish and Soviet Jews against the Nazis. Two plays deal with the restoration of Jewish life in the USSR after the war: *To Life* by Itsik Fefer, and Moshe Broderzon's *Holiday Eve*. The comedies *Exorcise the Devil* by Moshe Pinchevsky, *Other People* by O. Holdes and *It's Worth Living in the World* by I. Huberman are also interesting.

Second place is held by the two classical writers of Yiddish prose and drama: Shalom Aleikhem has seven plays and Avraham Goldfaden three. The plays of Shalom Aleikhem (even with their Soviet adaptations which had already begun in the 1920s) are among the finest of all Yiddish plays; they all have a salient 'social background' which is apparently one of the main reasons for their selection for performance in the Soviet Union.

The third group of plays comprises translations into Yiddish from Russian and other languages. Only two of the nine plays of this group have a Jewish content: *Zoriah Bilinkovich*, by Zinger and Vitenson, presented at the Yiddish Theatre in Moscow from 1949 until the theatre was closed down, and Linkov and Brat's *The Sighing of the*

Forests, also staged only at the Yiddish Theatre in Moscow in 1948 and 1949.

By the end of the war, or immediately after it, several plays with a distinctly Jewish character had already been withdrawn from the stage, the most well-known being Shmuel Halkin's *Shpilfoygl* and *Bar Kochba*, Moshe Pinchevsky's *I am Alive*, A. Levin's *Revenge*, and Gordin's *Mirele Efros* (staged from 1944 to 1946). Among the plays which were prepared but not performed because of their national content, David Bergelson's *Prince Reuveni* should be especially noted. Two other plays, which were prepared in 1948 and 1949 and also not staged, apparently for the same reason, were Perets Markish's *King Lampeduza* and Vasily Grossman's *The Old Teacher*. It seems that the other plays in this list were not performed for technical rather than for political reasons. The repertoire of the seventeen Jewish companies in those years was very similar to that of the permanent theatres.

The liquidation of Jewish culture in the Soviet Union, which began in November 1948, did not affect the Yiddish theatres and companies immediately, apparently because they presented the Soviet Union's culture to the outside world. At first only administrative measures were taken to restrict their activities, but on 12 March 1948 the Committee for Art Affairs attached to the Council of Ministers of the Soviet Union decided to cancel its financial support for 646 theatres, including the Yiddish Theatre in Moscow. The first sign of the imminent liquidation was the cancellation of government subsidies to the other Yiddish theatres, although allocations to theatres of other national minorities continued. The authorities then harassed the Yiddish theatres by sending them out on tours which were suddenly cancelled half-way through. Selling of subscription tickets eased the financial situation of the theatres, but with the first arrests of the principal figures of Jewish culture at the end of 1948, and rumours that Yiddish theatre-goers, not to mention permanent subscribers, also faced arrest, there was a drop in attendance at all the theatres not yet closed down. These difficulties led to many Yiddish actors, musicians and workers being discharged. The data on 'full halls' occasionally published in *Eynikayt* were certainly exaggerated. The decline in Jewish attendance at Yiddish theatres, which had begun in the second half of 1948, was greatly accelerated from early 1949.

First to be closed, at the end of 1948, was the Yiddish Theatre in Odessa. The Kaganovich State Theatre in Birobidzhan was shut down on 5 October 1949. The Yiddish Theatre of Minsk was closed in March 1949 after sharp attacks on its director, Viktor Golovchiner, for staging 'nationalistic' and 'cosmopolitan' plays. The Shalom Aleikhem Yiddish Theatre of the Ukraine in Chernovtsy was closed in September 1949. The last to be liquidated towards the end of November 1949, was the Yiddish Theatre in Moscow. We do not know the precise dates on which the companies were dissolved, but of the seventeen companies in existence in 1948, only four remained in 1949, and from 1950 to 1952 there was apparently only one Yiddish dramatic company in the whole of the Soviet Union, in Dvinsk.

The last Yiddish performances we know of in the Stalin period are: *Anna Guzik* in Georgia on 24 September 1950; *Sidi Tal* in Uzbekistan on 29 January 1951; and a group of Yiddish singers in Belorussia in June 1951. These isolated performances highlight the Jewish cultural wasteland in the Soviet Union following the liquidation of this culture in 1948 and 1949. As far as we have been able to ascertain, no Yiddish performances took place between 1952 and 1954.

During and after the war, Radio Moscow and local stations in Minsk, Odessa, Lvov, Kiev and Kishinev, broadcast special programmes in Yiddish intended for both Soviet and world Jewry. Apart from news and commentary, the broadcasts included literary and artistic programmes. The commentaries, in which the heads of the Jewish Anti-Fascist Committee participated, corresponded to political policy and changed as it fluctuated. In internal affairs this was noticeable in the policy on the nationalities, and in external relations, reflected the Soviet Union's attitude towards the State of Israel. The Yiddish broadcasts directed to American Jewry did not end with the liquidation of the Jewish Anti-Fascist Committee and the termination of Yiddish publications in November 1948, but continued until mid February 1949.

On the outbreak of the Soviet–German hostilities, the Institute for Proletarian Jewish Culture (by then called the 'Bureau'), together with the Ukrainian Academy of Sciences, was evacuated to Ufa, but was forced to leave its library and much of its archival material in Kiev. It did manage to preserve some important documents, such as the Jewish folklore archive and rare medieval Yiddish literature. In August 1942 the Jewish Bureau was transferred to Moscow, with the Ukrainian Academy of Sciences. Its limited staff in this period included E. Spivak (Director) and the researchers Loytsker, Maidansky, Beregovsky, and Shapiro. The Institute's departments were reduced considerably; those of history and literature were effectively abolished and most of the activity was concentrated in the folklore department.

In February 1944, the Bureau returned to Kiev with a small group of scientific workers from the former Institute and Bureau staff. It was given the status of an independent institution within the framework of the Ukrainian Academy of Sciences. Its staff was increased to twelve workers, but many of the senior scientists in Moscow and other cities also helped in its work.

Of the six departments existing in the 1930s only three were reestablished, those of language, folklore and literature; efforts to reestablish the historical department failed. In 1947 the Bureau formed a commission to perpetuate the memory of Jewish writers who had died in the war. Among the Bureau's permanent workers until it was closed in 1948 were E. Spivak, N. Oyslender, M. Beregovsky, M. Mezheritsky, H. Loytsker, A. Velednitsky and M. Maidansky. The Bureau's five-year plan (1946 to 1951) included research programmes, for example, into Jewish participation in the partisan movement, into thirty years of Jewish folklore and thirty years of Soviet Yiddish poetry; but in the end only a few articles were published in those Yiddish periodicals that still existed.

The Jewish Department attached to the All-Russian Society for Theatre was established in 1943. Headed by Professor Y. Nusinov, it enlisted Jewish dramatists, theatre researchers and theatre critics. Among its principal achievements were the organization of a series of lectures on the Yiddish theatre during the war and the preparation of a book on *The History of the Yiddish Theatre* (edited by Nusinov, Dobrushin, Oyslender, Lyubomirsky and Finkel).

The Mikhoels Bureau for the History of the Yiddish Theatre existed in 1946 and 1947. Its director was Naḥum Oyslender and its secretary Israel Serebryany. Within the Bureau framework there was also a Bibliographical Commission, which held a number of consultations. In association with the Der emes publishing house, the Bureau prepared the book, *Thirty years of the Soviet Yiddish Theatre*. It was closed down in 1947 before the liquidation of all other Jewish institutions.

A Jewish Department in the Belorussian Academy of Sciences was established by government edict in 1944, to prepare studies into the history of Jewish culture in Belorussia, especially on the Holocaust period. Nothing is known of the Department's activities; it apparently expired immediately after its establishment.

The Bureau for Yiddish Literature, Lvov, was a library rather than a scientific research institution; it had some 25,000 books, including 5,000 in Hebrew, and was directed by Yakov Honikman and Binyamin Valakh.

We can see, then, that post-war Jewish scientific activity in the Soviet Union was narrow in scope, irresolute and achieved little. The Soviet authorities were not interested in renewing Jewish cultural activity in the USSR but hesitated to close down Jewish institutions during or immediately after the war, hoping that this activity would die out.

During and after the war, the following museums operated in the Soviet Union:

(1) *The Historical–Ethnographic Museum of Georgian Jewry* (1933–51). This was founded to prepare young researchers from among Georgian Jewry who would engage in historical and ethnographic research on Caucasian Jewry in general and Georgian Jewry in particular. During 1938 and 1939, the Museum prepared an exhibition on 'The Old and New Ways of Life of the Georgian Jews'. Between 1940 and 1945 it published three volumes of studies and documents. It ceased to operate in the war years, but when hostilities ceased, the Museum staff, under Aharon Krikheli, began to collect material on the Jews of Kutaisi. In 1948, the Museum held an exhibition of Soviet Jewish culture and, in spite of country-wide liquidation of Jewish institutions in the Soviet Union, the Tiflis Museum apparently continued to function until the end of 1951. An American journalist, Harrison Salisbury, visited it on 26 May 1951 and saw an exhibition on Jewish heroes of the Second World War.

(2) *The Museum of Environmental Knowledge of the Jewish Autonomous Region, Birobidzhan* (1944–8). Founded in November 1944, its first director was G. Greenberg. It had four departments: nature study of the region; the history of the Revolution; socialist construction; and Jewish culture. The last-named department was devoted to the Jews and human culture, Jewish culture before the October Revolution, and the Jews in the war. It was closed down during the 'purge' in the region.

(3) *The Jewish Museum in Vilnius* (1945–8). Founded at the end of the war, it had about 3,500 books, and material on the history of the Jewish theatre, of Jewish social movements, and of the Soviet period in Lithuania during 1918 and 1919, material which included rare periodicals and newspapers. The Museum was closed down at the end of 1948.

After the war, departments of Yiddish literature functioned in a number of libraries in the Soviet Union (in Moscow, Leningrad, Kharkov, Lvov, Minsk and Kherson). All of them apparently ceased regular operation.

JEWISH RELIGION

After a brief period from 1933 to 1937 when Stalin relaxed the anti-religious campaign, it reverted to its previous severity in 1938. Several rabbis, among them one of the senior rabbis of the Soviet Union, Rabbi Medaliah, were accused of the gravest crimes; a press communiqué stated that under the guise of religion they had allegedly executed tasks for the Fascist secret services, mainly by sending agents to disrupt the construction of socialism in Birobidzhan.[235] The rabbis were also accused of running underground religious schools and of illegally baking and selling *mazot*.

The outbreak of the Soviet–German war in June 1941 led to a change in the authorities' attitude towards the religions, because of the patriotic stance adopted by the Churches and the need to unite against the enemy; the Soviet desire for Western support also played an important part in this change of emphasis. Steps were taken to ameliorate the situation of the Jewish religion. The Moscow community which, since the imprisonment of Rabbi Medaliah, had been without a rabbi, was given a new one, Rabbi Shlifer, and at the same time rabbis were appointed in Moscow and in other cities, where religious congregations were reestablished and had had their previously requisitioned synagogues returned to them. The change in attitude *vis-à-vis* the Jewish religion was also shown when Rabbi Shlifer was appointed a member of the Jewish Anti-Fascist Committee, representing Jewish religious institutions. In this capacity, he issued appeals to world Jewry and, together with Rabbi Chobrutsky, press releases.[236] The requests of the Jewish Community Council in Moscow for representation on the 'Council for the Affairs of Religious Cults' (established in the summer of 1944) were, however, rejected, on the grounds that the Jewish synagogues, unlike churches and mosques, were not organized on a hierarchical basis, and lacked a central organizing body. Nevertheless, the changes that had taken place, together with the shock generated by the war, caused many Soviet Jews – among them young people and soldiers in uniform – to flock to the synagogues.

The positive attitude towards religion – including the Jewish reli-

gion, although this was granted fewer privileges than the others –
continued in the immediate post-war years; but the intensification of
the 'Cold War', the increasing isolation of the Soviet Jewish population from world Jewry and Israel, and the anti-Semitic campaign
masked as a war against nationalism and cosmopolitanism, must all
have contributed to the reduction in synagogue attendance, to the
reluctance of those who did attend to express themselves freely there,
and to the fear of being caught having any contact with Israel Embassy personnel or with the few tourists who managed to enter the
Soviet Union in this period. Arrests of the rabbis and their families
added to the fear which paralysed Jewish religious activity. The sole
activity permitted, in which a number of rabbis, including Rabbi
Shlifer of Moscow and Rabbi Shekhtman of Kiev, participated, was
connected with the political activity of the 'Clergy for Peace'. At
times, the authorities required the rabbis to join in the defence of
Soviet anti-Jewish policy; an illustration of this is the statement by
Rabbi Shlifer, after the publication of charges against Jewish doctors
in January 1953,[237] in which he argues that these accusations had
been directed against the doctors not because of their Jewishness but
because of their criminal acts.

Several questions emerge at this point: how did it happen that,
despite the unrelenting anti-Jewish policy from 1948 to 1953, there
was as yet no propaganda campaign in this period against the Jewish
religion? How is one to account for the fact that, as far as is known,
there was not one book or article published in this period attacking
the Jewish religion, whereas dozens of articles condemning Jewish
cosmopolitans and nationalists were being published daily? Why does
the period differ so greatly on this point from other periods in Soviet
history when the Jewish and other religions were an important, if not
a central, target? The main reasons for these strange phenomena
were:

(1) The Soviet leadership decided to continue the liberal policy
vis-à-vis the various religions in the Soviet Union, and so could not
easily conduct a campaign against the Jewish religion only. (The
exception was the Catholic religion, which came under heavier attack than any other religion in the USSR; but this was caused by
external factors, i.e. foreign policy considerations, and not by any
general anti-religious policy in this period.)

(2) With the liquidation in 1948 and 1949 of all Jewish institutions
in the Soviet Union, Jewish religious congregations remained the

only surviving Jewish representative institutions, and to have liquidated them would have placed the authorities in an embarrassing
position *vis-à-vis* the outside world.

(3) The already depressed situation of the Jewish religion in the
Soviet Union – in terms of number of synagogues functioning (about
100 in the entire country), the number of rabbis, and the number of
worshippers – probably made the authorities consider it of too little
importance to justify a strict anti-religious campaign.

(4) The authorities needed to use the rabbis for propaganda purposes, especially within the various peace organizations established in
the Soviet Union after 1949.

(5) It is possible – and we have confirmation of this from later
periods – that the authorities saw the existence of official synagogues,
open to all, with rabbis, *gabbaim* and *shamashim* (beadles), all of whom
had to report to the ruling power on synagogue activity, as preferable
to worship in private homes, where the possibilities of police supervision were *ipso facto* more limited.

4

The post-Stalin period, 1953–1983

The post-Stalin period is perhaps the most complex of all. Elements of Stalin's policy mingle with previous policy in so complicated a way that it is hard both to separate them and to trace the connections between them. The variables are numerous: the struggle for power inside the country itself; relations with the other socialist States and with the West; internal pressures by anti-Stalinist forces; attempts at reform of one kind or another; and the entanglements of Soviet Middle Eastern policy.

The relatively large quantity of material available to the researcher for this period can also be a hindrance. It provides a basis for comparison with the Stalin period, but it is difficult to master the whole field. Contemporary historical events also make it difficult for the researcher to achieve the necessary objectivity in treating such a sensitive subject.

Periodization is also a problem. It is possible to refer to sub-periods by the names of the leaders – Khrushchev, Brezhnev, Andropov – or to refer to sub-periods according to internal developments in Soviet Jewry; but both methods are one-sided. What is needed is a combination of developments connected with the overall nationalities problem in general and of the extra-territorial national minorities, including the Jews, in particular.

In the various sections of this chapter, the following periods will be discussed

(1) The first transition, 1953 to 1955.

(2) The Khrushchev period, 1956 to 1964.

(3) The second transition, 1965 to 1967.

(4) The Brezhnev–Andropov period, 1968 to 1983.

THE SOVIET CREED REGARDING NATIONALITIES AND ITS
CONSEQUENCES FOR THE JEWS

Soviet theory on the nationalities problem developed over the years, and influenced the policies adopted. These interactions were more significant in the 1920s than in the period we are reviewing, but the new leadership in the post-Stalin period wished to return to Leninism, and to the practices of the Lenin period, affecting discussions on nationality theory as well as other areas. The nationalities' problem now became paramount and the leadership had to search for solutions.

This does not apply to the first transition period, from 1953 to 1955, when the orthodox Stalinist creed was still in force: not only was there no criticism of Stalin's nationalities creed or policy, there was also continual praise for his genius.[1] The attack on 'nationalist deviations', and on 'cosmopolitanism' in particular, was kept up, but gradually became less menacing.[2] It was even admitted that the campaign against cosmopolitanism had been exploited for improper ends and had done great harm to Soviet literature, but no-one as yet questioned the need to combat the crime imputed to those authors, of 'toadying' and 'kowtowing' to the West.

The twentieth CPSU congress in February 1956 was a turning-point in many ways, particularly in deliberations on the nationalities problem. The beginning of de-Stalinization was marked by less use of terror. This also applied to the systematic terror that had been used to repress the cadres of the different nationalities. There was a partial rehabilitation of nationalities that had been banished from their territories and a mainly symbolic extension of the rights of the Republics regarding the administration of justice, education and the economy.

This changed policy on the nationalities, pursued in the 'Back to Lenin' period, was also supposed to mark a revision of Soviet historiography. This could be seen in a reappraisal of the Shamil movement and of the Muslim Miuridists and a re-evaluation of the tsarist conquests – in Soviet terminology: 'the unification of the non-Russian peoples with Russia'. At the same time, Stalin's writings on nationality were re-issued as late as 1961. His dogmas on how nations come into being and on what constitutes a nation were still considered authoritative, as were his views on regional languages representing an intermediate stage before their final absorption. After 1961 there was increasing criticism of Stalin's ideas, and attacks on his teaching about the nationalities were voiced at scientific congresses devoted to the problem. The main points discussed by the researchers were the burgeoning *rapprochement* and even intermixing between the nationalities, the significance of these processes and their interaction. Were they natural and spontaneous? Should they be fostered by deliberate party policy? What was the final aim and what intermediate stages must the Soviet Union go through in the spheres of language, economy, demography and federalism?[3]

Khrushchev's deposition (15 October 1964) had no immediate effect on Soviet policy on the nationalities. In the transition period from 1965 to 1967 it was precisely the uncertainty on the issue that allowed for the development of new ideas and for a break away from routine and the set party lines.

The main discussion on the meaning of 'nationality' began in the January 1966 issue of periodical, *Questions in History*,[4] and soon developed into a wide-ranging debate on the theoretical, methodological, historical and current political aspects of the nationalities problem. This discussion continued for more than two years without visible party interference or influence.

A new phase in the discussions began with the invasion of Czechoslovakia by the Warsaw Pact forces in August 1968. Thereafter, the question of socialist internationalism was constantly in the headlines and was the focus of the deliberations on the nationalities problem in the Soviet Union. In the Brezhnev–Andropov period (1968 to 1983), the new policy on nationalities was reflected in the encouragement of Soviet patriotism, which was once more identical with Russian patriotism and with the old campaigns against foreign influences in culture and literature. Even the ghost of 'cosmopolitanism' hovered about from time to time.[5] Theoretical disquisitions emphasized the future final absorption of the nationalities. Brezhnev stressed that the different peoples' should fit in with each other, while Andropov held that assimilation and final absorption would solve the nationalities problem in the Soviet Union.[6]

What was the contribution of Soviet theoreticians and researchers to clarifying the status of the Soviet Jews as a national unit? Two contradictory attitudes crystallized. The first, and most interesting, was that of the ethnographer, S. Tokarev.[7] It marked a change, at least in academic research, in the perception of the Jewish question.[8] Tokarev's definition of ethnic groupings made possible the inclusion of the Jews in the category of a nationality: first, his definition was the broadest of all the general formulae propounded on the subject in the Soviet Union; second, Tokarev rejected the notion of 'attributes' and preferred to use the more flexible term, 'social relations'; third, Tokarev is one of the few researchers, if not the only one, to include common origin and religion among the characteristics of an ethnic group, features that had been rejected by Lenin and Stalin as 'subjective' and 'non-material'. As regards the importance of territory in the creation of ethnic groupings, Tokarev stressed that the existence of a territory is essential at the beginning of the development of every people, but thereafter sharing a territory can become less important, and may even disappear without the group's ethnic unity being weakened. The author gave as examples peoples who have lost part of their territorial unity, and also peoples who are dispersed throughout the world, such as the Armenians, the Jews and the gypsies. Finally, Tokarev supported his argument by affirming that the Jews' ethnic community is firmly based on religion. The philosopher I. Tsameryan has a different attitude to the Jewish question. He declared that Tokarev's reliance on the Jews as proof of the relative unimportance of a common territory had no foundation, since there was in fact no single Jewish people. The ethnographer V. Kozlov shared this view: many Jewish groups, he wrote, no longer had anything in common, apart from some notions, often vague, about their common origin and destiny.[9]

The official Soviet attitude negating the existence of Jewish nationality was illustrated in the formal classification of the population into ethnic groups. The highest category of stable ethnic groups with the most developed national consciousness was a 'nation' (*natsia*); a 'people' (*narod*) was a general term for ethnic groups of various kinds. Jews were not in either of these categories, nor even in that of a 'small people' (*narodnost*), a term for peoples living in Siberia and the northern Caucasus each numbering about 80,000. The Jews were generally referred to as 'nationals' (*natsionalnost*). This term is used almost exclusively for Jews; it is based on the registration in their identity certificates (as enacted on 27 December 1932), and is politically significant, since it reflects the authorities' intention to regard the Jews as individuals and not as a collective body conscious of its national unity. A further down-grading of the Jews in the hierarchy of Soviet nationalities took place at the end of the 1960s, when the ethnographer Kozlov propounded a new order, beginning with the most numerous people, the Russians; going on to peoples constituting an absolute majority in the towns and the villages of their Republics and ending with national minorities such as the Yukagirs – and other small groups, which he called the '*ethnos*'es; this last group was where the Jews belonged, together with the Assyrians and the gypsies.[10]

The basic argument concerning the Jews, however, usually went like this: historic circumstances had placed the Jews where they were, with their specific social structure, and they had had no possibility of developing into a nation.[11]

Tsameryan more recently outlined a new approach on the classification of the peoples living in the Soviet Union. The Jews are not explicitly mentioned, but it is clear that they are considered to be an extra-territorial national minority like the Poles, Germans, Hungarians and Romanians.[12] According to this classification, besides 'nations' (*natsia*) and 'small peoples' (*narodnost*), there are national groups and *ethnos*es cut off from the main bulk of their nation and living in an international environment. If a group like this is relatively large and its members live close to each other, then, says the author, it does not differ in essence from a socialist nationality such as the Poles, Germans and Hungarians; but other national groups that are dispersed in the regions of other nationalities will assimilate with the people among whom they live.

Tsameryan refuses to consider subjective traits, accepted by some Soviet researchers, such as cultural experience, character, psychology, consciousness of a common origin. According to him, the Germans in the German Democratic Republic, for example, are a different people from the Germans in Western Germany. From this it is, of course, possible to infer that the same principle applies to the Jews in the Soviet Union and the Jews in Israel and other countries.

The ethnographer Y. Bromlei had a different approach, although his typology of ethnic groups was similar. At the top of his pyramid he put the *ethnikos* – an ethnic group with settled traits of culture and psychology and with a sense of separate identity distinguishing it from other groups.[13] Bromlei devotes special attention to nationalities with exiled sections outside the territorial framework of their *ethnikos*. He does not refer to the Jews, but his approach holds good for them, as a dispersed people with a national centre in the State of Israel. Part of an *ethnikos* may be swallowed up by the people among whom they live, the indicator for this being over ten per cent of mixed marriages, but according to Bromlei this is not inevitable.

By doing away with the need for territory and allowing the importance of a sense of national identity, researchers tend to include Jews in the category of a nationality, but, with a few exceptions, the conclusions concerning the Jews are varied. The final judgment is always the following: the Jews have not reached the stage of development of a nationality, the corollary being that they have no prospect of reaching it in the future. This distorted logic stems from the Marxist–Leninist refusal to regard the Jews as a nationality. This approach was reinforced by government anti-Jewish measures, which will be described later in this chapter, and by the researchers' efforts to prove that the Jews had been absorbed to such an extent that they would soon disappear as an independent ethnic entity.

The nationalities problem is also studied by historians and journalists who concern themselves with the history of the Jews in general and Zionism in particular and adopt the Stalinist theory. Vostokov sees the idea of the existence of a Jewish people as 'reactionary'; the idea appeared in the programme of the Zionist Movement in Russia and was adopted at its seventh congress in 1917.[14] He argues that the Zionists wanted to establish an independent Jewish State within the Russian framework, a state where the Jews would live in accordance with Jewish religious law.

One of the anti-Zionist propagandists, Evseev, dealt at length with the existence of a worldwide Jewish nationality and its significance.[15] The Jews can be defined simply as an ethnic group, but Evseev finds this definition inadequate. He concludes that it is impossible to find an unambiguous solution: one may speak of ethnic groups, not of one single Jewish ethnic group, of separate groups in every country in every continent.

Zionism (and one author adds the *Bund*),[16] by supporting the concept of a 'worldwide Jewish nationality', freed the concept of nationality from its identifying characteristics (territory, language, economy, culture) and substituted voluntary idealism.

The efforts of Soviet propagandists to disprove the central contention of Zionism – the existence of one Jewish nationality – arguing from Stalin's definition of nationality, were not only theoretical but had a political purpose: to justify cutting Soviet Jewry off from other Jewish communities in the world and especially from the State of Israel. These writers' desire to carry out the task laid upon them led to frequent contradictions: for example, despite emphasizing the essential difference between Soviet Jews and those of the USA, resulting from the different economic systems and political regimes of the two countries, they demonstrated that an identical assimilation process existed in both countries, as Jews stopped speaking their mother-tongue, distanced themselves from their national culture and frequently entered into mixed marriages. The propagandists also argued that a solution based on national cultural autonomy, which had been rejected by Lenin, would be retrogressive, stressing that Soviet Jews enjoyed linguistic and cultural rights without having a fixed territorial base. On the one hand, they affirmed that the Soviet authorities had no objection to allowing Soviet citizens of Jewish origin to emigrate to Israel under the 'reunion of families' arrangements; and, on the other hand, they attacked the Jews who decided to do so. While they affirm continually that Soviet Jews have freely chosen assimilation with Russian culture and that there was no compulsion in this matter, they attack the most irreproachable Jewish Communists for any expression of national sentiment, however fleeting.

The dissident movements, which reached their peak of activity in the late 1960s and in the 1970s, were also preoccupied with the general nationalities problem and the specific Jewish problem. The principal dissident movements were: neo-Leninist, Socialist, democratic, and nationalist.

Neo-Leninists such as Roy Medvedev, Piotr Grigorenko and the historian Kosterin based their ideas on Lenin's interpretation of Marxism, adding some concepts of their own. They discern the democratic elements in Lenin's teaching and ignore the élitist ones, neglecting the need to reconcile Lenin's teaching with different circumstances. Their (dissident) *Political Diary*,[18] criticizes the policies of Stalin and Krushchev: it condemns the lack of consideration given to the justifiable national claims of the various nationalities, but also comes out against various nationalist manifestations in the republics. As for the Jewish question, Roy Medvedev wrote a memorandum in May 1970, covering Soviet Jewry and the Middle East Arab-Israeli conflict.[19]

Social-democratic circles criticize the present Russification policy, demanding the establishment of a real Federation which would recognize the national minorities, including the Jews. These circles also condemn Soviet support for the Fascist regimes of the Arab states.[20]

The democratic movement represented by Sakharov, Orlov, Tverdokhlebov and Chalidze has received more publicity in the West than any other movement because of its outstanding leaders and its unconventional activities. It is not an organized body with a declared ideology, but the nationalities problem has been considered in a number of the movement's *Samizdat* publications,[21] and its 'platform' states *inter alia* that: 'Many peoples and especially the Ukrainians, the Tatars and the Jews, aspire to political, cultural and economic self-determination, but this is not yet within their reach because of opposition from those in power.'[22] The movement considers that the way to bring about national liberation is to make Soviet society democratic. The UN should be charged with responsibility for securing the right to self-determination for all the nationalities in the Soviet Union. The Soviet administration is attacked for discriminating against Jews in admissions to institutions of higher learning and to a range of posts and for abolishing cultural autonomy. All the leaders of the democratic movement support the Zionist movement and the State of Israel.

The nationalist Russian dissidents, both Slavophiles and neo-Fascists,[23] are generally hostile to the Jews, considering them to be a foreign element, absorbing and destroying Russian culture. The neo-Fascists also attack every element of Jewish nationality and religion; they are especially indignant at the contention that Soviet Jews are a minority oppressed by the Russians, when they seem to have a monopoly of science and culture.

Among the dissidents in the different nationalities – the Ukrainians, Lithuanians, Georgians and others – there is sympathy for Jewish national claims. The Ukrainian Ivan Dziuba has this to say on Babi Yar: 'As a Ukrainian, I am bewildered and shamed that anti-Semitism exists among my people too. Ukrainians and Jews have had a similar, bitter historic fate. Their best leaders have always called for understanding and friendship between them and they must pledge themselves to work for a different future.'[24]

ANTI-SEMITISM

Between Stalin's death and Khrushchev's rule, there were important changes in the government's use of anti-Semitism, and still more changes under Khrushchev and his successors. These changes were inextricably connected with the government's efforts to master internal pressures – the rise of a liberal trend in the intelligentsia and the emergence of the dissident movements. We shall attempt to unravel the motives of official anti-Semitism in the different sub-periods and to trace its results; we must also scrutinize the various forms of popular anti-Semitism and the Soviet public's attitude in the matter.

Official anti-Semitism

In the first transition period, 1953 to 1955 steps were taken to improve the status of the Jewish population. First, the doctors' trial, which was to have been held on 15 March 1953, did not take place and the doctors were released. Political prisoners in prisons and concentration camps began to be released and there was less frequent use of terror. Second, Jews who had been dismissed from their posts during the anti-cosmopolitanism campaign were gradually reinstated. Third, publication of anti-Semitic articles was stopped. Fourth, there was some improvement in the conditions for Jewish religious practice. Finally, relations with Israel and contact between Soviet Jews and their relations abroad were resumed.

How did this partial change come about? Was it the result of general political changes in this period, or a changed line on the Jewish question, or both? To answer these questions, we must examine the ideology of Stalin's close associates, who fought for the succession after his death. In his last years, Stalin kept final decisions in his own hands, but was influenced by the stratagems of his close associates.

As we saw in the last chapter, the Party leaders closest to Stalin were Zhdanov, Malenkov, Beria, Molotov, Kaganovich and Khrushchev, followed by Voroshilov, Mikoyan and Bulganin.

As regards Kaganovich, it is hard to believe that he would want to support an anti-Jewish policy, but he seems to have done nothing to block it.[25] Molotov and Voroshilov had Jewish wives (Molotov's wife, Zhemchuzhina, was arrested on a charge of Jewish nationalism and sentenced to banishment) and were anti-nationalists, but not anti-Semites.[26] Opinions are divided about Zhdanov's attitude to the Jews. He had close family and political ties with A. Shcherbakov, who implemented anti-Semitic measures in the army during the war, and was himself an instigator of the campaign against nationalism and 'cosmopolitanism', the main victims of which were Jews. On the other hand, he was known to have consistently and energetically supported leaders of Jewish origin in the Popular Democracies.[27] Zhdanov died in August 1948, and all his associates were 'eliminated' in 1949 in the 'Leningrad Affair', and it seems that his influence did not affect Jewish affairs during this period.[28] The two leaders who had most influence on Stalin and carried out the new policy after his death were Malenkov and Beria. After the war Malenkov was involved in a struggle with

Zhdanov for superiority in the party leadership, and both of them were apparently ready to use anti-Semitism for their own ends. The most extreme anti-Semitic policy in the history of the Soviet Union was pursued between 1949 and 1953, when Malenkov was at the peak of his career, and there is evidence that he made anti-Semitic pronouncements.[29] Nevertheless, Malenkov helped to bring about the change in policy that we are examining. It follows that, as long as Stalin pursued an anti-Semitic policy, Malenkov's personal interest coincided with his anti-Jewish sentiments, but not in the state of political change after Stalin's death. Where Beria stood is the most complex question of all and little is known about it. If we ignore the rumours that he was himself of Jewish origin, we can throw light on his real attitude to the Jewish issue, from 1941 on Beria was directly involved in Stalin's 'Jewish' line and was an initiator and executor of the idea of setting up the 'Jewish Anti-Fascist Committee', to mobilize support from Jews all over the world; however, he was still head of internal security at the time of the murder of Mikhoels, though his position was already weakening, and he was responsible for the purge in the Ministry of the Interior, which he headed. Against these considerations, there are reasonable grounds for the claim that during his leadership of the Georgian Communist Party and afterwards, when he still had decisive influence there, he consistently defended Georgian Jewry.[30] Whatever the final judgment on Beria's relations with the Jews in Stalin's time, one thing is not in doubt – in the four months from March to June 1953, when Beria's influence on policy-making was decisive, major decisions were reached on the nationalities problem in the direction of extending rights which also benefited the Jews. In this confusion over policy towards the Jews during the years 1953 to 1955 the objective factors were predominant, in contrast with earlier periods, and facilitated the limited changes for the better in the situation of Soviet Jewry.

Khrushchev only achieved full control over the party and the government (though never on Stalin's scale) in 1957, when he liquidated the so-called 'anti-party group', but by 1955 his influence was already decisive on all important issues. The new political leadership that came into being after the twentieth Party congress left the totalitarian regime intact, but the partial liberalization we have already indicated (and the halt to terror) meant changes for the Jewish population. What concerns us here is how this liberalization affected both official and popular anti-Semitism.

Khrushchev had been concerned with the Jewish question since

Boleslaw Bierut on 22 March 1956, Khrushchev told a meeting of the Central Committee of the Workers' United (Communist) Party, "'I believe that in Poland, you too are suffering from an abnormal composition of the leading cadres, as we have suffered from it...'" Looking hard at the chairman of the meeting, Roman Zambrowski, who was born Zukerman, he concluded, "Yes, you have many leaders with names ending in -ski, but an Abramovich remains an Abramovich, and you have too many Abramoviches in your leading cadres.'"[37]

On his second visit to Poland in the same year, on 19 October, when he wanted to persuade the Polish leadership not to hand over power to Gomulka, Khrushchev shouted as he got off the plane: 'Are you going on helping the Jews?!' In his talks with the Polish leadership some hours later, he explained his outburst, saying, 'The Red Army shed its blood to free Poland, and now here you want to hand over your country to the capitalists plotting with the Zionists and the Americans'.[38] This time he replaced 'Zhid' with 'Zionists' but the intention remained the same.

Khrushchev and several other party leaders received a French socialist delegation in May 1956, a Canadian Communist delegation in August 1956, and in April 1958 the French journalist, Serge Groussard.[39] No reports of these meetings were published in the Soviet Union itself, but the reports published abroad appear to be trustworthy. According to these reports, Khrushchev made a number of remarks about the Jewish people in general and Soviet Jews in particular, and the close connection between them. His distorted picture was based on a series of half-truths such as: after the liberation of Chernovtsy, the streets stayed dirty and when the Jews were asked why they did not clean them they answered that the non-Jews whose work it was had fled from the city; thousands of tourists go abroad from the Soviet Union every year; in one year only three did not return and all three were of course Jews; a Jew was appointed to an important post and he at once set about surrounding himself with assistants of Jewish origin; the Soviet Government put a large region with ideal conditions for settlement at the disposal of the Jews, but after a short period of enthusiasm they all fled from Birobidzan; Jews are individualists incapable of working in industry and public enterprises; the Jews were given the possibility of having their own schools but they preferred to send their children to non-Jewish schools; according to Khrushchev, Stalin was right to refuse to give the Jews the

Crimea to settle in, because of the danger that in wartime the region would become a bridgehead against the Soviet Union; Israel was ungrateful (for Soviet past support) and was in the service of Western imperialism.

No Soviet leader, not even Stalin, wanted to admit to being an anti-Semite and Khrushchev needed to show that it was wrong to accuse him of anti-Semitism. Proof that he was mainly an 'unconscious' anti-Semite is perhaps to be found in his use of the traditional arguments, such as: many of my colleagues in the government are Jews (Kaganovich, Vannikov, Mitin); General Yakov Kreizer is my best friend; my oldest son married a Jewess so my grandson is half-Jewish... The Soviet authorities denied the accuracy of these reports, which were published abroad, but there were sufficient declarations by Khrushchev published within the Soviet Union to prove that his quoted statements were not chance remarks but part of a deep-rooted attitude and with a political purpose.

In a talk with an American reporter, Henry Shapiro, in November 1957, Khrushchev[40] revived the Stalinist watchword, 'rootless cosmopolitanism', which had been used in the Soviet authorities' fight against the Jewish intelligentsia. In March 1963, in an address to the veteran writers and artists of the Soviet Union in the presence of most of the party leaders,[41] Khrushchev distinguished between 'good' and 'bad' Jews, giving as an example of the latter the treachery of a Kiev Jew named Kogan, a *Komsomol* member who betrayed his comrades and was rewarded by the Germans with the post of interpreter on the staff of von Paulus at Stalingrad.[42] Khrushchev must have known the truth about this affair and was thus not serving any state interest but venting anti-Jewish feeling. The affair was exploited by nationalist anti-Semitic writers, and the book by P. Gavrutto, *Clouds over the City*,[43] which appeared in 1965, included one of the most extreme anti-Semitic stories in Soviet literature up till then, describing how the traitor Judah (Judas Iscariot) Kogan handed over to the Germans a thousand of his comrades in the underground movement. That the whole affair had been invented was proved in August 1966 by Ariadna Gromova, who found, after careful research, that the name Kogan did not appear among those who had betrayed the Kiev underground and that the Kogan referred to by Khrushchev and Gavrutto had fought in the war against the Germans and could not have been an interpreter on the staff of von Paulus.

Khrushchev attacked Evgeni Evtushenko after the publication of his poem, *Babi Yar*, in *Literaturnaya gazeta* on 19 September 1961,[44] and openly supported the virulent criticism of the poet by writers and critics.[45] We must conclude that he was hostile to the Jews, despite public disclaimers given both when he was in power and, later, in his memoirs. Probably the best explanation was given by Erenburg to a reporter, A. Werth: 'He [Khrushchev] had lived too long in my – though not his – native Ukraine and had been infected with the kind of visceral anti-Semitism that is still very far from having been stamped out there.'.[46]

In addition to the influence of his years in the Ukraine and his time in Moscow at Stalin's side, Khrushchev was affected by his relationship with the Jews in the party leadership and in particular with the Kaganovich brothers and Lev Mekhlis, who were among Stalin's closest associates.

Whatever the reasons, Khrushchev's anti-Semitism was very different from that of Stalin in his last years. It was not pseudo-scientific, rational, or ideological anti-Semitism; it was not even political anti-Semitism inspired by particular interests. It was really 'popular anti-Semitism', based on traditional prejudice against the Jew as one who evokes suspicion, envy and hatred.

Other leaders in the post-Stalin period, such as Kosygin,[47] Brezhnev and Andropov, said little on Jewish affairs. They stressed their opposition to anti-Semitism, but their policies towards the Jews show their attitude to be essentially the same as Khrushchev's. Brezhnev's declaration to the twenty-sixth congress of the Communist Party in March 1981 is interesting: he put anti-Semitism and Zionism side by side as 'nationalist deviations'.[48]

Despite the leaders' views and the use of anti-Semitism to promote political aims, there were the following deterrents to extreme measures during most of this period: (1) The current Marxist–Leninist ideology was fundamentally opposed to discrimination on grounds of nationality and race. (2) The use of terror declined and increasing importance was given to the judicial network, charged with preserving the rights of the individual, including his national rights. (3) The authorities refrained from using the anti-Semitism weapon, lest they should be unable to control it. (4) There was internal pressure from sections of the population (mainly liberal circles, which we shall consider later) against anti-Semitism. And (5) the decisive factor – there is constant external pressure: the authorities wanted to preserve their socialist image and to camouflage actual anti-Semitic policy by describing it as a legitimate campaign against Jewish nationalism and clericalism.

How then did anti-Semitic policy manifest itself in the Khrushchev and post-Khrushchev periods? Full answers will be given later in this Chapter; here we shall briefly outline the different forms of official anti-Semitism.

PROPAGANDA IN THE MASS COMMUNICATIONS MEDIA

All the communications media in the Soviet Union – the press, publishers, radio, television and cinema – are state institutions under permanent internal surveillance (in the apparatus of the institutions themselves) and external control by the censors. Nothing can be published – stories, articles, news – that goes counter to the Communist Party policy, as laid down by the leadership. Nevertheless, even under Stalin, and certainly in the more liberal period after his death, differences can be discerned between publications, which stem from the differing attitudes of those in charge and from the strength of the power supporting them in the party and government leadership.

After a short break during the transition period from 1953 to 1956, vignettes of various kinds reappeared in increasing numbers in the press after 1957.[49] In these feuilletons the Jew appeared again as the stereotype from Stalin's days: narrow-minded, hypocritical, unscrupulous, ready to commit any fraud or villainy to get material advantages of any kind (such as better housing, easier and better-paid jobs, diplomas, etc.). From time to time the Jews were also represented as malingerers, evading army service, using the old war-time jokes about Jews who did their fighting in Tashkent.

This kind of thing was provided from time to time in the other mass media, at first over the radio and on television and then, from the second half of the 1970s, in full-length films (usually made to look like documentaries), such as the film 'Merchant of Souls', released on 22 January 1977, modelled on Nazi anti-Semitic propaganda films. A film put on in Odessa, 'Overt and Covert', opened with the attempted assassination of Lenin by Fanny Kaplan and *inter alia* showed how Hitler came to power with the help of Jewish capital.[50]

Under the guise of fighting religion and Zionism, caricatures appeared in the daily papers and the 'humorous' quarterlies; there are also reports that these anti-Jewish caricatures were put up on the notice-boards in work-places. An astonishing number of caricatures appeared from the 1960s onwards. Between 5 June 1967 and 5 June

1972, 1,107 anti-Jewish caricatures appeared in forty-four Russian newspapers dealing only with the Arab–Israeli conflict,[51] but the papers with the largest circulation, *Pravda* (7.5 million copies), *Krasnaya zvezda* (the Red Army paper, 2.5 million copies) and *Izvestiya* (*c.* 8 million copies) also published and distributed them widely. A Norwegian researcher who studied the Soviet Press found 1,709 anti-Jewish caricatures from 1967 to 1980, 55% of which showed Zionists (=Jews) corrupting the world with the aim of ruling over it; in 45% Zionism was linked with capitalism, in 33% with US imperialism and in 10% with Nazism.[52]

Another means of spreading anti-Jewish propaganda was through lectures in universities, cultural institutions (clubs, meeting halls, concert halls, and so on) and in work-places, lectures that are heard by millions of people in conditions where the anti-Jewish message can be put over with greater emphasis because what is said is not for publication. However, the most dangerous anti-Semitic propaganda is probably to be found in the sphere of *belles lettres*.

Soviet literature was necessarily affected by changes in the political climate – the relative liberalization under Khrushchev; the conflicts between the different trends and forces in the Communist Party and the intelligentsia; the criticism of the 'cult of personality'; greater variety in possibilities and forms of expression; the contradiction between a more liberal policy on the nationalities question and the continued discrimination against given minorities, including the Jewish national minority; and the spread of outside influences as a result of the breach in the 'iron curtain'.[53] Most of the works with blatantly anti-Semitic tendencies appeared, as was to be expected, in the publications of the Stalinist–conservative Russian-nationalists, who had influential patrons in the Communist Party leadership and in government institutions – the periodicals *Oktyabr*, *Znamya* (connected with the Defence Ministry), *Molodoya gvardiya*, *Moskva*, *Ogony-iok* (for young people) and *Nash Sovremennik*, and the publishing houses Voienizdat (of the Army) and Sovremennik.

Two novels by Nikolai Chukowsky, *The Wanderer*, published in 1956 (although written by 1932), and *Variya*, published in 1958, feature characters, clearly meant to be Jews, who are shown in a bad light. Mishka in *The Wanderer* is after money; he has no homeland and no ideals; he becomes rich through black market transactions and runs away from army service to wander through many countries, including Palestine, so as to get richer still, until he is killed by border 'passers', who steal even his gold teeth. The second most important character, Lazar Kravitz, betrays his comrades, who are defending Petrograd, and the woman he loves, and kills one of his commanders as he tries to desert to the enemy.[54] Even less attractive Jewish characters are found in the novel, *The Return*, by N. Ilyina.[55] A journalist, Roizman, born in Odessa, reached the city of Kharbin, where he started a paper and used it to blackmail people. Utterly unprincipled, he lives for one thing only, to get rich (the *leitmotiv* in all the Soviet anti-Semitic writings), and he soon reaches the land of his dreams, the USA. In the gallery of villains in this novel, Roizman is one of the shadiest characters. Unlike the 'White' Russians abroad, he despises his Russian homeland. Possibly the aims of these authors may not be exclusively anti-Semitic, but there is no question about it in the trilogy, *The Rachevsky Sisters*, by the Ukrainian authoress Irena Vilde (Darya Drobiazko), published between 1955 and 1959; a second edition of 150,000 copies was issued in Lvov in 1965. Practically every character in the book is a profiteer, but one is worse than all the rest; Suleiman, a figure taken straight out of the 'Protocols of the Elders of Zion'. A usurer and a hypocrite, he is an agent of the Polish police (the action takes place in the Carpathians on the eve of World War II) and a sadist. His attempt at rape fails because he is impotent, and he furiously tears up the Book of Psalms, just as he used to tear birds apart when he was a child.

When the trials of Jews for economic crimes reached their climax in 1962, an author named Tevekelyan (an Armenian with a Chekist past) published a story describing how Jews named Katz, Zeldiner, Shechtman and others were engaged in profiteering and smuggling gold and silver during the Civil War.[56]

One of the most extreme anti-Semitic novels was published in the Ukraine during the Khrushchev period: *The Paths of Life*, by A. Dimarov.[57] The story takes place in the period after the October Revolution, with digressions to earlier periods. The Lander family, who had been sworn enemies of the Ukrainian people from the earliest times, were put in charge by their Polish overlords not only of lands and property but also of the Churches. They were even worse than the Tartars who invade, despoil and then go away, for the Landers stayed there for ever. Solomon Lander had a wonderfully developed flair for choosing the right Party and for knowing when to desert it. He is described by Dimarov as a *Bundist*–nationalist, a member of the Social-democratic Party (not of the Communist Party as he should have been), a Trotskyist and an agent of the secret services, all roles that are hated by a large section of the Ukrainian people.

In 1964, 50,000 copies of a book called *And Life Again*, by G. Makhorkin was published.[58] The author describes a Jewish family named Krauze, whose members rivalled each other in baseness and cruelty. The father ran an institute for foreign languages in the Ukraine and was getting ready to leave the city when the Nazis arrived; immediately, he began to work as an interpreter in the Gestapo (this was to recall the 'traitor' Kogan who was supposed to have been an interpreter on the staff of von Paulus). During interrogations he behaved with greater cruelty than the Nazis. The younger brother, Daniel, who began his 'career' as an informer even before the outbreak of war, is captured by the Germans and he too becomes a traitor–*provocateur*, handing over people in the underground resistance to the Germans. He is put through a special course in sabotage and is sent to the Soviet Union to carry out spying and sabotage operations. While infiltrating, he kills a fisherman who has saved his life, but is caught and pays the penalty. Just to 'complete the picture', Makhorkin adds that, after the liberation, the mother of the family falsely accuses a Ukrainian, Zrobeiko, of collaborating with the Nazis, and this innocent man is condemned and sent to a prison camp.

It is inconceivable that books of this type could have gone on being published for so long and in such quantities without political authorization. At the same time, other books appeared during this period, condemning anti-Semitism with the utmost vigour. On the whole, anti-Semitic literary publication did not show any change in the post-Khrushchev period, in the transition years from 1965 to 1967, or in the Brezhnev–Andropov period, although the quantity and virulence of the material published actually increased. The important difference was the absence of any counterweight in the form of condemnation of anti-Semitism or moral rehabilitation of the Jews. Another work by Tevekelyan appeared in 1966,[59] which fitted into the sequence of attacks on the Jewish religion in the communications media. The main character, Solomon Moiseevich Kazarnovsky, is a pious Jew, scrupulously observing Jewish religious rules and living modestly as a pensioner not far from Moscow. He is also the head of a dangerous gang and does not shrink from ordering the murder of a suspect in his gang. They specialize in stealing icons from old churches to sell abroad. A kind of Satanic force – or is it simply his racial character? – impels him to accumulate more and more riches, which he does not need and which bring him no benefit.

The 1970s saw the appearance of books by I. Shevtsov,[60] in which almost all the villains were Jews – profiteers, spies, thieves, murderers – belonging to the Jewish intelligentsia. One character, Nahum Holtser, is a drug-dealer and of course owns 'Zionist literature'. He gives drugs to his beautiful Russian girl-friend and brings about her death. Finally he murders his own mother, because she was Russian; otherwise he certainly would not have done it. All this leads to the major theme: in propaganda in the West, the supposed writer, Holtser, is turned into a dissident hero, suffering under the Soviet regime because he is a Jew.

A different literary genre flourished in the post-Khrushchev period: the short story about revolutions which took place before the establishment of the Soviet regime. Conservative–nationalist authors attacked those 'enemies of the people' who were of Jewish origin, such as Zinovyev and – especially – Trotsky, who brought disaster to Russia. Kochetov, who was for a long time editor of *Oktyabr* and was experienced in the political–literary Stalinist tradition, was cautious in his references to Zinovyev's Jewish origins, but his young colleague Zakrutkin saw no need for such reticence.[61] Zakrutkin resorted to all the usual propaganda methods to emphasize Trotsky's Jewishness, calling him contemptuously 'Yudushka' (i.e. Judas Iscariot). He stressed the first name, Judah, of the 'Trotskyist' Stern, a member of the White Guard who attempted to assassinate the German Embassy Counsellor von Twardowsky in 1932 (wounding him) in order to bring about a war between Germany and the Soviet Union. In his book, Trotsky's friends and supporters have Jewish names and are depicted as treacherous weaklings, incapable of understanding Russia. Finally, Zakrutkin recalled how much Hitler enjoyed reading Trotsky's autobiography and even learned a good deal from it.

Shevtsov also depicted Trotsky as the most treacherous and dangerous of the enemies of the Soviet Union. Anatoli Ivanov and Mikhail Kolesnikov described Trotsky, the adventurer, saboteur and Freemason (the symbol of the 'Jewish world-conspiracy'),[62] who was responsible for introducing violence and terror into Russia. Recently, historical figures such as Rasputin, have been presented as puppets manipulated by the Jews in their efforts to destroy Russia. An example of this new technique is a story by Valentin Pikul of Latvia, published in *Nash Sovremennik* in 1979.[63]

ANTI-SEMITIC PROPAGANDA IN ECONOMIC TRIALS

We have already seen that 'economic crime' in the Soviet sense led to economic trials. In the post-Stalin period, these trials lost their political content and less publicity was given to them, but they were increasingly exploited as anti-Semitic propaganda.

From 1954 to 1957, publicity given in the press to economic trials declined and the anti-Jewish line was less prominent. In 1958, when the campaign against the Jewish religion revived, the anti-Jewish trend also intensified in the press reports on economic trials. In 1961 and 1962 the policy on economic offences veered from being relatively liberal towards imposing heavier penal and administrative sanctions; on 5 May 1961, a Decree even laid down the death penalty for a number of economic crimes. There were about thirty-four trials involving Jews in 1961 and 112 in 1962; the peak year was 1963, with 145 trials, and 1964 saw a slight decrease to 109. A reversal came only in 1965, when Khrushchev was deposed and the new leadership decided that publicity should not be given to the sentences.[64] After 1966 and 1967 less publicity was given to economic crimes and the number of trials dropped to an average of about twenty-five a year.

In the 1970s the trials of Pinkhasov, Laviev and others were used as anti-Jewish propaganda in the campaign against Jewish emigration. The main charges in the cases involving Jews were: independent production of goods using materials stolen or illegally purchased, and their sale on the black market; theft of state property; dealing in precious stones and foreign currency; offering and/or accepting bribes; forgery of documents and falsified production reports, either for private profit or to fulfil imposed quotas. The high percentage of Jewish accountants, comptrollers of stores and inventories, and middlemen, originated from the official policy of discrimination against Jews in education, as we shall see later; but this does not explain the prominence given in the media to the fact that the accused were Jews. This stress was especially obvious between 1961 and 1964; as well as pointing out that the accused were Jews, the reports turned the trials into show pieces. In 1962, a trial in the town of Frunze in the Kirgiz Republic went on for several months and was conducted not by the Supreme Court of the Republic, as was customary, but by the Supreme Court of the Soviet Union, with the local and the national press publishing almost daily reports on the course of the trial and commentaries about the accused Jews. The papers highlighted the prosecution's stress on the connections of the accused with relations, tourists and banks in the West, that is to say, their foreignness and disloyalty to their country. In many of these trials, the Jewish religion and Zionism were introduced deliberately, because most black-market deals were concluded in synagogues, often with the help of the rabbi and the beadle, and because there were connections with tourists from Israel and members of the Israeli Embassy. If the family name of the accused did not sound Jewish, his first name and that of his father would be given in full; and the press had no qualms about denigrating the accused.

There were official denials, some of them by Khrushchev himself, that the economic trials were anti-Jewish; but it is clear that there was an anti-Jewish policy from 1961 to 1964, and again in 1967, evidenced by the difference in the degree of publicity given to the trials in different periods. It seems that once the authorities had decided to eliminate economic crime, they found it convenient to use popular anti-Semitism to disguise economic shortcomings and deflect popular dissatisfaction away from the leadership.

DISCRIMINATION IN GOVERNMENT, EDUCATION AND EMPLOYMENT

Statistical data on discrimination against the Jews will be given later in this chapter. Here we shall briefly outline how this discrimination worked and what anti-Semitic aims were.

As regards Jewish representation in government, the situation was static from 1953 to 1956, with only a slight fall in Jewish representation. From 1957 to 1964 the decrease was more marked, but less dramatic than between 1946 and 1953. From 1965 to 1970 there was a slight rise in Jewish representation on the Supreme Soviet and in government institutions; thereafter, the situation once more appeared static.

Given the urban nature of the Jewish population and its high level of education, the Jews could play a much more central part in the Soviet system than they do today. Even now, they have more Communist Party members than any other nationality in the Soviet Union, in proportion to the size of the Jewish population there: but discrimination against them has led to a reduction of their numerical ratio in all government institutions. Moreover, there are offices that have been *judenrein* since the 1950s, when the Jews were removed from them in Stalin's time: the security services, the Foreign Affairs Ministry, the Ministry of Foreign Trade, and the top ranks in the army.

According to evidence that has accumulated since the mass Jewish emigration from the Soviet Union, there is clear discrimination against the Jews in admissions to important posts in security, science and the national economy, and Jews feel that they are denied promotion simply because they are Jewish. At one time an identity certificate was sufficient to indicate the nationality of the person concerned, but today he has to produce data on his parents; that is to say, persons who are not registered as Jews on their identity certificates can also be targets of the 'in depth' discrimination against Jews.

The policy concerning higher education seriously affects the Jews. Discrimination existed under Stalin from the 1940s onwards, but was circumscribed because of the urgent need for experts in science, especially the natural sciences. In the 1950s the cadres of the different nationalities were expanding in higher education, and Soviet leaders explained that it would be necessary to reduce the number of Jews employed and even to establish some quotas.[65] This was not a system of *numerus clausus*, like that in tsarist Russia and in a number of East European countries in the 1920s and 1930s, but rather a policy that was inconsistent, both as regards the different periods and as regards the field concerned. A number of prestigious institutes were closed to Jews by the 1950s, such as the Institute of External Relations, which trains Soviet diplomats, and the highest Party study centre, automatically blocking their access to certain careers. The most important universities in the main cities (Moscow, Leningrad, Kiev and Kharkov) began to restrict the admission of Jews to certain faculties and departments in the 1960s, and from the 1970s onwards Jews found it hard to gain admission to a number of departments in these universities.[66] The systems introduced to classify applicants were 'improved' and elaborated to such an extent that many Jews made no attempt to look for somewhere else to study, either in the same city or in a distant province.

Popular anti-Semitism

By 'popular' anti-Semitism we mean prejudice, and hostility among the population to the Jews living among them. Did widespread anti-Semitism of this kind exist in the post-Stalin period in the same way in the earlier periods? Few observers will argue that popular anti-Semitism has disappeared from the Soviet scene; the Soviet leaders themselves admit that vestiges of it remain in the Soviet Union.[67] No serious researches have been undertaken to study this, and it is doubtful whether there will be any in the foreseeable future;[68] in their absence it is hard to evaluate the size of the phenomenon, its social and geographical distribution and the way it has changed (if at all) under the influence of changing factors, psychological, social, economic and historical. Furthermore, there has not yet been any comprehensive research into this subject outside the Soviet borders. Some surveys dealing with the emigration of Soviet Jews, have asked questions about anti-Semitism and its influence on the decision to emigrate; but what is referred to is anti-Semitism in general and not 'popular anti-Semitism'.[69] We have therefore to rely mainly on Soviet literature and on information from Western reporters, members of student delegations and tourists. There is also testimony from emigrants from the Soviet Union which appears in the Jewish *Samizdat* and in the petitions that have been sent to leaders both within and outside the Soviet Union and to international organizations.

Popular anti-Semitism is expressed in words and in actions; words may be less serious but are more widespread: the use of insulting terms about Jews, accompanied by sporadic acts of violence in public, in work-places and study centres, in communal housing, and so on.[70] The Jews are accused of taking the best jobs, eating the bread of the Russians and dreaming of Israel; they are also often accused of being arrogant and despising the people round them. Less frequently they are even told, 'It's a pity Hitler didn't kill you all off'.[71] The insulting terms *Abrasha* etc., reiterated by hooligans and drunks (but not only by them) are the equivalent of 'Jew-boy', 'Jewish face', 'cursed Jew', and so on.

Actions, if less widespread, are more serious: acts of vandalism in synagogues and cemeteries and blood libels reminiscent of tsarist Russia. Some exceptionally serious instances, sometimes involving local authorities, are given below.

(1) *The Malakhovka affair* on 4 October 1959 began when leaflets were posted on the walls of apartment blocks and public institutions, signed by a body calling itself 'Hit the Jews and save Russia', the notorious slogan of the 'Black Hundreds'. It ended with the burning down of a synagogue and of the house of a Jewish cemetery watchman, whose wife died in the fire. The authorities at first tried to deny that the incident had happened, but in the end stated that those guilty of arson had been caught and tried.[72]

(2) *The Tskhakaya affair* in May 1962 also involved the burning

down of a synagogue, this time in Georgia. In spite of requests by local Jews, the authorities did nothing to trace the criminals.

(3) *Blood libels and pogroms in Dagestan and Uzbekistan.*[73] On three occasions, Jews were accused of drinking the blood of Christians or Moslems for religious cult purposes. The first case, in August 1960, was perhaps the most serious, because it was reported in the official Communist Party paper with the approval of one of the editors, and only angry reactions, both local and from abroad, led to the printing of a 'correction'. In 1961 a pogrom against the Jews occurred in Margelan (Uzbekistan), and another at Passover 1962 in Tashkent (the capital of the republic). The local authorities remained passive during the attacks on Jewish homes but reacted angrily against Western 'libels'.

The causes of popular anti-Semitism among Russians and other Soviet peoples are similar to those affecting the Soviet leadership and there is no doubt that State anti-Semitism nourishes popular anti-Semitism. Insofar as there are differences, the manifestations of popular anti-Semitism are more spontaneous and uncontrolled, more irrational and also briefer; unlike State anti-Semitism, where political aims control what is done and for how long. Popular anti-Semitism would certainly be less evident if its sources were not encouraged by the leadership, instead of being combatted energetically as in the late 1920s.

The liberal intelligentsia and anti-Semitism

Popular anti-Semitism is not confined to 'workers and peasants'. There is evidence that it exists among the millions of white-collar workers in the bureaucracy and the technocracy. Most Jews belong to this stratum of Soviet society and are constantly in contact with it in places where they work, live or gather together. They awaken feelings of inferiority, envy and anger among some members of this intelligentsia, feelings which often turn into hostility towards Jews in general. This hostile attitude is essentially the same as popular anti-Semitism, except that it takes more 'refined' forms.

We shall look now at the intelligentsia in its narrow sense, the intelligentsia that has always felt itself to be the conscience of Russia, protesting against discrimination and social or national injustice: writers and scholars, like those in tsarist Russia who called on lovers of freedom and justice in Russia and in the world to protest against the pogroms and libels involving the Jews. The Soviet intelligentsia was crushed by Stalin and silenced for many years, but after his death, and more particularly after 1956, with the disclosures of the twentieth congress and the events in Poland and Hungary, isolated voices began again to be raised against anti-Semitism.

Evgeni Evtushenko was among the first. As early as 1955 he referred by implication to anti-Semitism in the Soviet Union in his poem, 'Winter Station'.[74] The authoress Valtseva followed in the footsteps of Korolenko and attacked the anti-Semitism prevalent both in official circles and in the security services. G. Nikolaeva (in 1959) and Yuri Bandarev (in 1962 and 1964) revealed the consequences of Stalin's 'anti-cosmopolitanism' campaign in infecting large numbers of the Soviet peoples.[75]

In the end, the fight of the liberal intelligentsia against anti-Semitism in general, and official anti-Semitic policy in particular, came to be symbolized by the affair of Babi Yar, which aroused intense emotions and stimulated debate.[76] On 10 October 1959, Kiev-born writer Viktor Nekrasov for the first time publicly raised the question of the absence of a monument in Babi Yar.[77] He attacked the Kiev municipal council's 'wicked' plan to make a public park and football field there, instead of putting up a monument to the victims of Nazism. He did not specifically name the Jews, speaking rather of 'Soviet people'; but his attack made a great impression and evoked a widespread response from the public. Evtushenko's poem, written after he visited Babi Yar, was published in September 1961 in *Literaturnaya gazeta*, after much debate by the editorial board of the Writers' Union. He discarded all disguise and tackled the question of putting up a monument in Babi Yar by attacking the anti-Semitism that had generated the atrocities of the Nazi conquest.[78] Publication of the poem was important because it brought into the open the existence of anti-Semitism in a socialist society in spite of, or perhaps because of, the official statement that it had disappeared. Evtushenko went further, declaring that anti-Semitism had become dangerous in the Malakhovka affair with the revival of the slogan of the 'Black Hundreds'. Contradicting the official line, Evtushenko spoke of the Jews as one people, a nation with a continuous history of suffering from the Exodus from Egypt to the present time. He violated yet another taboo in his poem: he broke the 'conspiracy of silence' over the Jewish Holocaust that had been maintained by the government for so many years, by hiding the extermination of the Jews under descriptions of general Fascist anti-Soviet actions.

The poem 'Babi Yar' angered the leadership and infuriated Russian–nationalist circles. People were found who argued that to return to the theme of anti-Semitism in the Soviet Union in 1961 was an act of treachery to communist internationalism; and who were especially outraged by Evtushenko's speaking of 'the Jewish people', which was quoted as revealing his petit-bourgeois approach.[79] These attacks went on for several months, until the twenty-second Communist Party congress, and even during the congress itself. From the end of 1961, however, the attacks stopped and throughout 1962 Evtushenko was able to resume reading his poem at mass meetings, where he was enthusiastically received. Support came from Shostakovich, who wrote his 13th Symphony for the poem in 1962; he himself composed on Jewish themes and was deeply concerned over the fate of the Jews.[80] Apparently under pressure from the authorities, and on Khrushchev's instructions, Evtushenko agreed to two changes in the text of his poem: among the victims of the Nazis, he added Russians and Ukrainians as well as Jews; and he added an entire line of verse to the effect that under the tsars Russian workers had actively opposed pogroms.

Since the 1970s, protests against anti-Semitism, disguised as the fight against Zionism and the Jewish religion, have come mainly from democratic dissidents, but also from humanists within the Soviet intelligentsia; an example is Professor M. Korostovtsev's statement at the convention of Humanist Institutes of the Soviet Academy of Sciences in February 1976, in which he attacked 'people who spread newspaper anti-Semitism'.[81] Such expressions, and the support they receive from student circles and from part of the intelligentsia are encouraging, but they do not affect official policy or erode popular anti-Semitism, which is still nourished by state anti-Semitism.

THE JEWISH SHARE IN GOVERNMENT

Did the new Soviet leadership in 1953 intend to change the Stalinist policy of discrimination against Jews in government? Or was there a decision to carry on limiting Jewish representation to a minimum, in line with the system of nationality quotas? How far was policy affected by anti-Semitic sentiments?

To answer these questions, we shall follow the method used in the previous chapters and survey the place of the Jew in the party, the soviets and the administration.

Jews in the party

Only partial data have been published for the years from 1953 to 1975 regarding the number of Jewish members and candidate-members in the Communist Party. It is therefore difficult to discern the policy in this matter in different sub-periods. Estimates for the early 1960s vary from 1.7% to about 3% of Jews in the party.[82]

In 1976, full data on the party's nationality composition were made public for the first time since 1927. As regards the Jews, it emerged that they comprised 1.9% – 294,774 of the 15,638,891 Communist Party members and candidate-members.[83] Among Communist Party members, Jews were the sixth largest nationality, after the Russians, Ukrainians, Belorussians, Uzbeks and Tatars; their proportion was therefore higher not only than that of the general population but also of the urban population.

In order to explain this state of affairs against the background of the anti-Jewish policy of reducing the Jews' representation in party institutions and government, one must examine in greater detail the available data on the republics where, according to the 1970 census, some 20% of the Jews were living – Belorussia, Uzbekistan, Georgia, Moldavia and Lithuania. In 1962 in Belorussia there were 16,000 Jewish Communists (6.4% of all party members and only 1.4% of the population). By 1978 the number of Jews there had risen to 17,900 (3.3% of all party members); that is to say, although there was an increase of about 12%, in comparison with the general increase the ratio of Jewish Communists had fallen to about half.[84] In Uzbekistan in 1953 there were 4,691 Jewish Communists (3.3% of all party members); in 1962, 6,147 (2.5%) and in 1964, 6,659 (2.3%); in Georgia in 1969 there were only 2,150 Jewish Communists, constituting 0.7% of all the Communists in the republic, compared with 1.2% of the whole population. In Moldavia in 1963 there were 4,463 Jewish Communists (6.4% of all communists) and in 1967, 5,662 (5.7%); this shows an increase of 27% in only four years, but also a definite decline in the proportion of Jewish communists. Finally, in Lithuania in 1953 there were 2,055 Jewish Communists (5.7% of all Communists), in 1962, 2,280 (3.4%) and in 1977, 2,232 (1.5%),[85] that is to say, the sharpest decline in comparison with the other Republics; this was apparently the result of increased emigration from this republic.

We can conclude from these partial data that in the years from

1961 to 1978 there was an absolute increase in the number of Jewish communists, from 240,000 to 298,000, but a percentage drop from 2.5% of the total party membership to 1.8%. This process accelerated later, mainly from 1978 to 1981, both on account of Communist Party policy and of the rise in Jewish emigration from the Soviet Union.

The high proportion of Jews in the Communist Party, despite the policy of discrimination against them, was due to a number of factors: (a) Jews had been active in the Party since the 1920s; (b) they figured mainly in the technocracy and the bureaucracy; (c) there was a high percentage of Jews in the urban population, from which most party members were drawn; (d) there was a high percentage of Jews in the educated stratum; (e) many Jews hoped that membership of the party would help them achieve a professional career.

In this period there was an interesting development in the standing of Jews in the Communist Party leadership, as compared with the previous period: Lazar Kaganovich remained in the Politburo until 1957 and was expelled during an internal power struggle (the 'anti-party group') and not on nationality grounds. The number of Jews in the Communist Party Central Committee went down from five in 1952 to four in 1956 (apparently because of the death of Lev Mekhlis in 1953); the biggest fall occurred at the twenty-second congress in 1961, when only one Jew remained on the Central Committee, Venyamin Dimshits – representing only 0.3% of its members. A change took place at the twenty-fourth congress in 1971, when the writer A. Chakovsky was co-opted onto the Central Committee, and in 1976 two more Jews were added at the twenty-fifth congress: Georgi Tsukanov and Lev Volodarsky. At the twenty-fourth congress, moreover, two Jews were appointed to the Party Control Commission, General David Dragunsky and the Secretary of the Birobidzhan Party, Lev Shapiro. This change in Jewish representation at a high level originated apparently from Brezhnev's desire to stress his support for the Jews in the Helsinki era and as part of the campaign against Jewish emigration from the Soviet Union. Active Jews were also deliberately chosen for the Central Committee and the Control Commission (Volodarsky, Chakovsky, Shapiro and Dragunsky). Possibly the change was encouraged by the campaign against nationalist elements in the leadership, which led to the expulsion of Shelest, Polansky, Shelepin and Voronov; certainly two Jews acted as personal advisers to Soviet rulers – Tsukanov advised Brezhnev and Arbatov advised Andropov.

the 1930s; impulsive and quick-tempered, enjoying talking to newsmen and to delegations of all sorts, he often publicly voiced views opposed to Stalin's on the Jewish question. A brief outline of his pronouncements may help us to understand the complicated motives determining policy regarding the Jews in the post-Stalin period.

Khrushchev did not make any statements about the Jewish question to the press from the time he was chosen First Secretary of the Ukrainian Communist Party in 1938 until he took over the leadership of the country in 1955. The reason was not caution (although this, too, influenced him), but the existence at that time of a policy of only making statements on the Jewish question when it became necessary to answer critics abroad. Nevertheless, there are records of such statements by Khrushchev from reliable sources which throw light on his real attitude. For example, late in 1939, after the annexation of the Western Ukraine to the Soviet Union, Khrushchev spoke to a vast crowd in Lvov. He declared *inter alia* that the Red Army had liberated the peoples oppressed by Poland – the Ukrainians, the Belorussians and the Jews. When the interpreter translated the word 'Jew' into Polish with the customary *Zhid*, Khrushchev turned and rebuked him: 'Oh Comrade, Comrade! I don't like them either, but to call them simply "Yids" out of the blue in front of all these people, that's no good'.[31]

On 1 March 1944 Khrushchev delivered a speech at the opening session of the Ukrainian Supreme Soviet dwelling on the atrocities of the Nazi occupation and the war of the peoples of the Soviet Union in general, and of the Ukraine in particular; but he did not mention the Jewish victims of the Holocaust.[32] Moreover, in a private conversation Khrushchev maintained that the Jews had had no share in the partisan movement.[33] He even proclaimed that the Jews would have to stay in the places where they were living, since they were not welcome in the Ukraine.[34] In reply to an appeal from Ilya Erenburg to intervene and prevent Babi Yar from being turned into a marketplace, Khrushchev wrote: 'I advise you not to interfere in something that is none of your business. Better write some good novels...'[35]

From 1956 to 1964, Khrushchev did not change his attitude. In his 'secret' speech to the twentieth congress, he spoke about Stalin's crimes against the party leadership and against various nationalities, but ignored the suppression of Jewish culture and the liquidation of its leaders, even when referring to 'the Doctors' Plot', whose anti-Semitic implications were clear.[36] At the funeral of the Polish leader

We do not have many data on the standing of the Jews in the party leadership in the different republics. In the Ukraine, Spivak and Birenbaum served as Secretaries of the Region Committee; Dragunsky was a Central Committee member in Armenia; Zimanas was a member of the Central Committee in Lithuania. In Moscow in 1965 three Jews were among the 178 members appointed to the city Party Committee, in Leningrad three out of 122. In the lower ranks of senior officials of party institutions, a few Jews still held various posts, but their presence only illustrated how steeply the number of Jewish office-holders had fallen during and after the Stalin period.

Jews on the soviets

The representative institution comprising the Supreme Soviet of the USSR, the Supreme Soviets of the Republics and the local soviets has only a minor influence in policy-making. As we have seen, in the last years of Stalin's rule the share of the Jews on these bodies was drastically reduced.

In the first election, held about a year after Stalin's death, the situation remained much as it had been in 1950, with a slight decrease from eight to seven Jewish delegates on the Supreme Soviet of the USSR (0.52% of all the delegates). Khrushchev adopted a policy of distributing delegates to the Supreme Soviet according to nationality quotas, as became clear in 1958 when the number of Jewish delegates was fixed at five out of 1,384 (i.e. 0.36%); this policy was maintained until 1970, when there were five Jewish delegates, that is, 0.32% of the total number. In 1974 (the ninth assembly), six Jewish delegates were 'elected' (0.39%): L. Groisman, V. Dimshits, G. Zimanas, Y. Khariton, Lev Shapiro and Aleksander Chakovsky. In the elections to the tenth Supreme Soviet in 1978, however, only four Jews were 'elected' (Dimshits, Khariton, Shapiro and Geller).[86] All the same, the representation of the Jews was still better than that of other national minorities without federative status, such as the Germans, Poles, Greeks and Koreans, who had one or two delegates each; but if one takes into account that the Jews were endowed with a federative unit (the Jewish Autonomous District of Birobidzhan, which sent five delegates to the Supreme Soviet, usually two of them Jews) and that their socio-demographic structure was that of an urban population with a high proportion of educated members, they were obviously under-represented.

As regards the Supreme Soviets of the Federal Republics, the autonomous republics and the local soviets, the only data at our disposal are for the years 1959 to 1975. In 1959, fourteen Jewish delegates were 'elected' to the Supreme Soviets of the Federal Republics, out of a total of 5,312 delegates; that is to say, only 0.26%, with only one in the Russian Republic and one in the Ukraine, while in the Lithuanian Republic, which had a negligible Jewish population, there were three Jewish delegates. In 1963, thirteen Jews were 'elected' (0.23%) and in 1967 and 1971, 19 (0.33%); that is to say, in the Khrushchev period the Jews were represented by less than a quarter of their proportion of the whole population, a share that rose to a third under Brezhnev. This under-representation was certainly influenced by the general quota policy, together with local pressures in each of the republics. Thus, for example, in the Moldavian Republic, where there was no Jewish representation at all, one Jew was 'elected' in 1975, Abba Gokhbergen.[87] In the autonomous republics, Jewish representation was among the lowest in all the representative institutions in the Soviet Union. In 1959 there were only four Jews on these bodies (0.15%). From 1963 to 1967, there was an increase to eleven delegates (0.38%) and in 1971 another decline, to nine delegates (0.30%).[88]

The local soviets which, with the Executive Committees elected by them, constitute the local administration, have elections every two years. In 1959 7,624 Jewish delegates were elected, 0.42% of this body. In 1963 there were 7,490 (0.38%), in 1965, 8,124 (0.4%), and in 1969, 6,619 (0.32%); this decline continued with only 4,591 delegates in 1975, constituting 0.2% of the total delegates on local Soviets.[89] Thus under Khrushchev Jewish representation on this body was static while under Brezhnev it declined to half. If we compare the situation of the Jews in this sector of local authority with that of the other nationalities, we find that the Jews come last. To take only one year, 1971, there were 77 Russian delegates for every 10,000 people, 136 Latvians, 103 Hungarians, 71 Germans, 69 Poles, 77 Greeks and only 28 Jews. Clearly there is deliberate discrimination, as well as a difference in the structure of the population (the Jews being exclusively urban) and its geographical distribution (concentrated mainly in the big cities), which also affect Jewish representation on the local authorities. It is odd that Soviet propaganda stresses that thousands of Jewish delegates are elected to the soviets in the USSR.

Jews in government and administration

Although policy-making is in the hands of the supreme party institutions, the government and the senior officials in the various ministries have great influence on public life.

The senior post of Deputy Prime Minister has been held since 1962 by Venyamin Dimshits, but his influence cannot be compared with that of other Jews in the past, such as Lazar Kaganovich or Lev Mekhlis. He is mainly a technocrat with qualifications in economics and technology, though he has his place in the party leadership as a member of the Central Committee.

Until Khrushchev took over in 1957, there were many Jews in government posts. Important ministers in this period were L. Kaganovich, B. Vannikov and D. Raizer. From 1958 to 1961 there was no Jewish minister in the government for the first time in the history of the Soviet regime, and only one Jewish Deputy Minister, Dimshits. By 1964 there were three more Deputy Ministers, Yuli Bokserman, Leonid Glikman and Avraham Levinsky,[90] but under Brezhnev the number decreased from three to two, Glikman and Levinsky.

There is little information on the situation in the Republics. Regarding Jewish Ministers in the 1950s, we know of the Minister of Health in the Esthonian Republic, A. Goldberg, and the Minister of the Fishing and Food Industries in the Lithuanian Republic, E. Bilavichus. Deputy Ministers were L. Popierno, Deputy Minister of Building in Belorussia, and I. Bulat in the parallel post in Moldavia.

Data on senior officials are sporadic and partial. Nearly all the senior officials of Jewish origin were expelled from all sections of the Ministry of Security (and especially from the counter-espionage services, where Jews held important positions in the 1930s), the Interior Ministry and the KGB, and from the Foreign Ministry, where there was still one Jew in the 1960s – L. Mendelovich, head of the Latin-American Department. In the economic ministries (including the Central Planning Commission), the following Jews were serving in the 1960s (and perhaps even in the 1970s); M. Eidelman, A. Babichkov, S. Ginzburg, L. Volodarsky, N. Turin, M. Levitan, L. Meizenberg, I. Ravich, L. Rimsky and Y. Shendler. Very few Jews remained among senior officials in the republics. In the Russian Republic in the 1960s four Jews were heads of departments, among them the Deputy Attorney-General of the RSFSR; Aharon Kogan. There were three Jews in senior posts in Belorussia (one of them being the Deputy Director of Gosplan, P. Shvarzbund) and in the Ukraine, with its large Jewish population, only two.

In the army the number of Jews holding high rank decreased steadily under Stalin's anti-Jewish policy after the war ended. In the 1950s, obituary notices in the Press indicate forty-three Jewish generals of the rank of Major-General or higher. In Khrushchev's time, the two most famous Jewish Generals were Y. Kreizer and D. Dragunsky. In the post-Khrushchev period, a number of Jewish Generals held teaching posts at the Military Academy but there were none on the General Staff or on unit Staffs. The Generals in the Academy were A. Tsirlin, M. Milshtein, I. Rabinovich, I. Rogozin and A. Shatsky.

This survey of Jews in government from 1953 to 1983 can be summed up as follows:

(1) From 1953 to 1955, the situation remained static, with a slight decline in Jewish representation in some government institutions.

(2) Between 1956 and 1964 there was a change of direction (though less extreme and dramatic than from 1948 to 1953), Jewish representation being curtailed in the Party Central Committee, the Politburo and the administration, and, less obviously, in the Supreme Soviet of the USSR.

(3) From 1965 to 1977 there was an increase in Jewish representation on the Central Committee, an apparently calculated decline on the Supreme Soviets of the republics and in the local authorities, and an almost static situation on the Supreme Soviet of the USSR.

(4) Since 1978 there has apparently been a further decline of Jewish representation on the Supreme Soviet of the USSR and also on the Supreme Soviets of the republics.

The main conclusion is unavoidable: that there was a consistent policy of reducing the number of Jews to a minimum in the party, on the soviets and in the administration, even if there is no proof of the existence of a plan to implement this policy. The combination of State and popular anti-Semitism facilitated its pursuit.

The various Jews who held government posts did not, of course, represent Soviet Jewry's national interests; the contrary may well be the case. Many, perhaps most of them, would have wished to part with the right to be considered as Jews, though they knew that they were 'elected' as representing the Jewish 'quota'. The only link most of them had with Judaism was that they were born Jews, and for this reason they always tried to keep their distance from Jewish affairs. In the new Soviet regime, however, most of them were forced to become involved in Jewish affairs, and even to establish an anti-Zionist body, as we shall see later.

JEWISH 'AUTONOMY' IN ECLIPSE?

After Stalin's death, the Jewish Region of Birobidzhan was the only remaining example of Jewish 'autonomy' or 'statehood'. It is therefore important to review the changes in Jewish life that occurred there at this time.

The first change was the end of the secrecy that surrounded the Autonomous Region in Stalin's last years. In June 1954, Harrison Salisbury of the *New York Times* visited the region, and on his return wrote two articles.[91] In August of the same year, the Israeli Ambassador to the Soviet Union Sh. Elyashiv visited Birobidzhan.[92] From 1955 news reports from the region began to appear in the world press, compiled from Jewish Communist sources,[93] but the information was slight and obviously attempting to conceal the almost total lack of Jewish education and culture in the region. In the Soviet Union, news about Birobidzhan only began to appear after the beginning of 1958, when Radio Moscow recorded and broadcast a series of foreign-language talks devoted to the region, in which some of the Jewish inhabitants took part.[94] On 6 August 1958 an article by V. Pakhman appeared in a Communist Party organ in the Russian Republic, describing the happy life of the Jews in Birobidzhan.[95] In 1959, 3,000 copies of an official collection of special articles in Russian appeared, marking the twenty-fifth anniversary of the founding of Birobidzhan.[96] Khrushchev had, however, made a dismal judgment (not reported in Russia) a year earlier, in a talk with a French reporter: 'We are forced to admit that Jewish settlement in Birobidzhan has ended in failure. They arrive with a burning flame in their hearts and later they leave one after another.'[97]

In 1959 there were only 14,269 Jews living in the Autonomous Region, 8.8% of the population of the region and 0.7% of the Jews in the Soviet Union. Compared not only with the Autonomous Republics but even with the other Autonomous Regions, this was the lowest percentage in the whole of the Soviet Union; for example, South Ossetians constituted 65% of the total population of their Autonomous Region and 15.6% of their nationality, and Adigeans

23% of the population and 8.6% of their nationality. Moreover the Jewish population in Birobidzhan mainly comprised the older age-groups, so that by 1970 their number had dropped to 11,452 – 6.6% of the population of the region, and by 1979 to 10,166 – only 5.46% of the population.[98] More than 90% of them were concentrated in a narrow strip in the north of the region and over 70% in the town of Birobidzhan itself.

A second indicator of how far (or how little) the 'Jewishness' of a region preserves its nationality is the number of Jews whose mother tongue is Yiddish. In 1959, 39.2% of the Jews in Birobidzhan stated that Yiddish was their mother tongue, in 1970 only 17.2% and in 1979 13.4%; that is to say, a drop of two-thirds in twenty years. The reasons for this were not only the trend towards language assimilation in the Soviet Union, but also the non-existence, since the late 1940s, of Yiddish schools. To change this situation – and to counter the demand by Zionist circles for permission to teach Hebrew – Yiddish has been made a special subject in a number of schools in the region in recent years.

In the Khrushchev years, Yiddish cultural life in the Autonomous Region was in an enfeebled state. There was no Jewish theatre, no museum of Jewish art, no other Jewish activity. The Yiddish newspaper (the *Birobidzhaner shtern*) had a limited circulation and unimpressive content. In the Municipal Library there were about 10,000 Yiddish books, out of a total 120,000. About eight Yiddish authors lived in the region and there were occasional performances by visiting artists.

The Jews' share in party institutions and in the region's administration was also much lower than it had been in the 1930s and 1940s. In the 1950s and 60s there was not a single Jew at the head of the region and its districts, whether in party or in government institutions. Of the seventy-five members elected to the Party Central Committee of the region in 1963, 10% were Jews, and of the ninety-nine delegates on the region's Soviet, elected in March, 1963, about 12% were Jews.[99]

Observance of the Jewish religion was as poor in Birobidzhan as in other parts of the Soviet Union. There was only one synagogue in the whole region, a small hut, with no resident rabbi. Nor was there a Jewish cemetery. In 1967 there was a Soviet survey of 300 Jews in Birobidzhan who were considered to be 'religious', and only eight told the questioner that they were observant believers; there were only forty-three persons in the Jewish congregation, the youngest of whom was aged 63.[100]

After Khrushchev, changes were at first slight, but there was more cultural activity – a Yiddish theatre troupe was created, more Yiddish artists gave readings, or recited or sang, and there was more about Jewish subjects in the local newspaper. A new booklet of articles was published in 1965 entitled 'The Jewish Autonomous Region'.

From 1968 to 1983 there was a limited revival of Jewish activity in the region, and evidence of the administration's increased concern for the Jews there. We have already referred to the opening of classes for Yiddish in the secondary schools. The Jewish theatre's activity was also expanded: it was given the title 'People's Theatre' and received a larger grant than the amateur troupe. The repertoire of the theatre was mainly the plays of Shalom Aleikhem, Goldfaden, Daniel, and the Birobidzhan writer, Buzi Miler ('Nothing falls from heaven'). There are now a few radio programmes in Yiddish (five times a week – consisting of news, reports, talks by the staff). In October 1970 the local newspaper doubled in size from two pages to four, and since 1971 it has appeared five times a week instead of three. A new 'Musical Chamber Theatre' was established in July 1977, with forty-five professional actors from various cities of the Soviet Union (not all of them Jews).[101] The director of this theatre, Yuri Sherling, himself an actor and musician, was one of the directors of the famous Moiseev Ballet. The Musical Chamber Theatre, which represents a considerable financial investment, was established for purely political purposes, as a cultural show-piece to impress all the Soviet Jews; but it turned out that the directors of the theatre wanted to use the Russian language, since most of the Jews in the Soviet Union, and non-Ashkenazi Jews in particular, do not understand Yiddish, and even thought of putting on shows for foreigners in English. These ideas have not been put into practice, however, and two musical productions have been so far staged, in Birobidzhan and in various cities outside the region.

In the political field, the Jews' share has been increased both in the region's local government institutions and in the governing bodies of the Russian Republic (to which each region belongs). In 1970, Lev Shapiro held the highest post, First Secretary of the Region. Yosef Bokor was First Deputy to the President of the Region Executive Committee, and Yosef Vergilas, Avraham Kramer and Yakov Goldman were Deputy Heads of the Executive Committee.

At the beginning of the 1970s there were two Jews on the USSR Supreme Soviet, Valdimir Feler and Mikhail Abelman, instead of one, as in the previous period, and from 1975 there were two more, Lev Shapiro and Rahel Geler. Lev Shapiro was on the Supreme Soviet of the Russian Republic at the beginning of the 1970s and Mark Kaufman from 1978.

From 1959 onwards, rumours were heard within the Soviet Union and abroad that a government plan existed to banish Soviet Jews to the Autonomous Jewish Region; these rumours were denied by Soviet government leaders and described as anti-Soviet libel.[102] The argument has also been heard in the West that the Jewish Autonomous Region was only preserved because of the constitutional difficulties involved: this is, of course, baseless, since Khrushchev had no difficulty in 1956 in abolishing the Federal Republic (that is, the highest-ranking federative unit) of Karelia-Finland. The Jewish Autonomous Region continues to exist for political propaganda purposes, as an alternative to the Zionist solution and as a potential area for the transfer of the Jewish population should such a policy be adopted in the future.

From the internal Jewish point of view, there were many reasons for the failure of the Birobidzhan project:

(1) The choice of Birobidzhan for the Jewish Republic, instead of, for example, the Crimea or the Ukraine.

(2) The relatively satisfactory situation of the Jewish population in the western regions of the Soviet Union in the 1930s, which meant that few volunteered to go to Birobidzhan.

(3) The feeling that the Soviet Union was progressing towards an amalgamation of the peoples, rather than stabilising them and promoting their survival in the future, which led many Jews to embrace 'internationalist' solutions.

(4) The lack of consistency in official policy on Birobidzhan, the few resources put at the disposal of the project during the critical periods of the late 1930s and the 1940s, the frequent changes of direction on the part of the authorities, and the purges of 1936 to 1937 and 1948 to 1952 together wrecked the undertaking in its early stages.

Finally, a central factor in deciding the fate of the project from the Jewish national viewpoint may have been the absence of any spiritual tie between the Soviet Jews and Birobidzhan; while the establishment of the State of Israel and the Zionist national revival awakened those sentiments that had no place in Birobidzhan.

THE FIGHT AGAINST ZIONISM AND ISRAEL

The political changes in internal Soviet policy after Stalin's death could not fail to affect policy towards Zionism and Israel. The following survey of developments in this policy in the various sub-periods attempts to mark their correlation with official 'Jewish policy'.

1953 to 1955

This was the period of transition to a new foreign policy, which also manifested itself in Soviet–Israeli relations. Diplomatic relations were renewed on 21 July 1953 after negotiations which lasted for months.[103] Soviet objectives in the Middle East remained as they had been in the era of Stalin – to develop relations with the Arab States and Egypt. Egypt now seemed to be pursuing a 'progressive' policy and was a convenient base from which to extend Soviet influence to other Arab countries. The new Soviet leadership attempted at first to play the role of intermediary in the Arab–Israeli conflict, but when this was seen to have no hope of success, because of the increasingly wide gulf between the parties, the policy changed to one-sided support for the Arab states, in general and for Egypt in particular.

Relations with Israel had reached their nadir between January and March 1953, and efforts to improve them took the following forms: renewing diplomatic relations; raising the respective diplomatic missions to the rank of embassies in August 1954; improving trade, with a proposed barter deal, citrus for crude oil (bilateral trade rose from $150,000 in 1950 to $3,120,000 in 1954);[104] granting emigration permits to about 600 Jews between 1954 and 1956.[105]

Other signs were, however, even more disquieting than in the Stalin period. The Soviet representatives at the UN used their veto for the first time on 22 January 1954, and again on 29 March, to demonstrate their unreserved support for the Arabs.[106] In September 1955, Czechoslovakia signed an arms trade agreement with Egypt, with Soviet support, marking the beginning of active Soviet involvement in the Middle East on the side of the Arabs; this arms deal laid the basis for close Soviet political, military and economic cooperation with Egypt and Syria.[107] At the end of December 1955 Khrushchev told the Supreme Soviet of the USSR,

We understand the aspirations of the Arab peoples fighting for their complete liberation from foreign rule, and so we are bound to condemn the actions of Israel, which has been a threat to its Arab neighbours from the first days of its existence and has pursued a hostile policy towards them. This policy clearly does not serve Israel's interests and those who carry it out are backed by the well-known imperialist powers. They want to use Israel as a tool against the Arab peoples for the purpose of merciless exploitation of the natural resources of the region.[108]

These contradictory tendencies – renewed relations with Israel and some improvement in the conditions of Soviet Jews on the one hand and support for the Arab states in the Arab–Israeli conflict on the other – were also reflected in the treatment of Zionism. The communications media's anti-Zionist propaganda did not cease, but it was reduced in this period both in quantity and in virulence.[109] The KGB's war on Zionism was carried on, however, with undiminished vigour, special attention being paid to the Zionist nuclei that were beginning to form in the cities and their contacts with the Israeli Embassy in Moscow. On 11 July 1955, twenty-one people were arrested in Moscow, Leningrad and Malakhovka, after prolonged observation; they were tried secretly in Moscow in January 1956 and given prison sentences of from two to ten years. There were more arrests and trials of Zionist groups in 1956, in Kiev, Odessa and Latvia. The charges against them were the most serious that could be framed (under Clauses 58/10 to 12 of the Criminal Code) – anti-Soviet activities, since they had received and distributed Israeli newspapers and literature, celebrated Israeli holidays such as the Day of Independence and disseminated Zionist propaganda among the Jewish population. In August 1956, three members of the Israeli diplomatic mission were expelled from the Soviet Union: they had been in contact with those on trial, Kahat, Sela and Levanon.[110] No news reached the West about these trials, because Israel followed a deliberate policy of restraint and did not publicize the anti-Zionist and anti-Israel line taken in the trials, hoping to reduce the tension and eventually improve relations with the regime.

Between Stalin's death and Khrushchev's affirming his hold on power, there was a correlation between the renewal of relations with Israel, the end of the press campaign against Zionism, and the partial improvement in the condition of the Jews, marking a change from the previous period and especially from the situation prevailing from 1949 to 1953. What is interesting is the connection between the three variables – Israel, Zionism and the Soviet Jews – in both periods. (In the years 1947 to 1948 unique conditions made the situation rather different.) Conclusions regarding correlation between Soviet policy towards the Arab States in the period we are dealing with and towards Israel/Zionism/Soviet Jews are less clear cut. A change of policy in Soviet relations with Egypt and Syria was signalled in 1955, but it was not yet sufficient to change Soviet foreign policy towards Israel. In other words, in this period the internal factors remained dominant.

November 1956 to October 1964

Signs of a deterioration in Soviet–Israeli relations could be discerned in August 1956, with the nationalization of the Suez Canal and the consequent closer *rapprochement* between Egypt and the Soviet Union. The Israeli Sinai Campaign and the Soviet desire to exploit it to strengthen the Soviet Union's position in the Arab countries led to a serious deterioration in Soviet–Israeli relations. The crisis was reached in the Note from Soviet Premier Marshal Bulganin to Israeli Premier David Ben-Gurion, of 5 November 1956, which stated *inter alia*, 'The Government of Israel is criminally and irresponsibly gambling with the fate of its people. It is sowing seeds of hatred of the State of Israel among the peoples of the East that cannot but have consequences for the future of the State of Israel and that throw doubt on the survival of Israel as a state.'[111] On 7 November, the Soviet Union unilaterally cancelled the crude oil agreement of July 1956,[112] and on 10 November threats were voiced that if military operations were not called off and the invading forces withdrawn from Egyptian territory, Soviet volunteers would be despatched to the area.[113] The Soviet Press denounced the English–French–Israeli action, and prominent Soviet Jews were mobilized for the campaign against 'Israeli aggression' – Jews of all types, from the assimilating intelligentsia, persons connected with the Jewish cultural and military élite like General Yakov Kreizer and the writers and scientists, Deborin, Mints and Rybak, to religious personalities and heads of congregations, both Ashkenazis and non-Ashkenazis (Georgians and Bukharans).[114] In the 'public appeals' issued by these people the main theme was that reactionary Zionism would lead Israel to a catastrophe from which only the 'progressive Israeli people, opposed to aggressive war', could save her. Israel took the brunt of the attack on the 'three aggressor States'. From January to March 1957 official Soviet representatives and communications media went on repeating that the Straits of Tiran were Egyptian territorial waters and attacking the USA for supporting Israel's contention that the Gulf of Akaba should be proclaimed an international waterway.[115] The Soviet Ambassador to Israel, Abramov, returned to his post in April 1957, but this did not improve relations between the two States.[116] An extreme anti-Israel campaign began at the end of July 1957, rising to a peak after the 'International Youth Festival' in Moscow in August, where a large delegation from Israel was received with enthusiasm by large numbers of Soviet Jews, in scenes reminiscent of the demonstrations of pro-Israeli feeling in 1948. The anti-Zionist and anti-Israel campaign went on to assume an anti-religious tone directed against Soviet Jews.[117]

It was in August that the Soviet leaders launched this campaign. The Israeli Cultural Attaché, E. Hazan, was arrested by the Secret Service when he was visiting Odessa and charged with distributing anti-Soviet propaganda among Soviet citizens. The KGB tried by persuasion and by threats to get him to 'cooperate' and immediately after this affair he had to return to Israel.[118] An article in *Pravda* by the former *Bundist*, David Zaslavsky, attacking 'the diplomat from Lilienblum Street', underlined the fact that the authorities would not tolerate contacts between Israeli diplomats and Soviet Jews.[119] The press and radio campaign concentrated on the 'Zionist propaganda' which had misled some Soviet citizens and persuaded them to go to the 'Israeli paradise', and now they were disappointed and begging to be allowed to return to the socialist fatherland.[120] Khrushchev himself argued, on several occasions, that the Jews were not interested in leaving Russia but, on the contrary, 'many who had reached Israel were requesting permission to return'.[121] Every report that appeared in the West about the mass emigration of Soviet Jews to Israel was immediately denied as a conspiracy to undermine the friendship between the Soviet Union and the Arab countries.[122] This was not sufficient, however: many young Jews openly expressed their intention to emigrate to Israel, contacting the Israeli Embassy, distributing Israeli literature, and meeting in public places, such as synagogues and concert-halls. From 1959 to 1963 the combined anti-Israel, anti-Zionist and anti-Jewish pressure reached an extraordinary level, recalling 'the dark years'. The campaign was conducted on two fronts simultaneously – one of secret arrests and trials of Jews who expressed attachment to Israel and wanted to go there; and the other of propaganda in the media: new books and pamphlets (seven books in Russian between 1959 and 1964, dealing with Israel and Zionism, and others on Israel and the Jewish religion),[123] innumerable articles in the central and local press, and 'live' treatment on the air. This propaganda dealt with four main themes,

(1) an account of the State of Israel as a bridgehead held by imperialism;
(2) unreserved attacks on Zionism;
(3) denunciation of Israeli diplomats and tourists;
(4) the disenchantment of immigrants with the 'Israeli paradise'.

THE STATE OF ISRAEL

From its inception, the State of Israel practised a policy of mass expulsion of the Arabs from their lands, about a million people in all.[124] This theory appeared as early as 1957 and was affirmed with increasing frequency in nearly all the books and articles, together with a revised version of the War of Independence. Israel consistently pursued a policy of blowing up houses, murdering Arabs, expulsions by force of arms and border provocations, all with the aim of extending its territory at the expense of her neighbours. Israel's foreign policy towards the Soviet Union and the Soviet bloc was, as Khrushchev said, one of 'absolute ingratitude'.[125] Israel worked hand-in-glove with the imperialist countries, contributed to clearing the name of the Third Reich by accepting restitution payments from Germany, and acted as an agent of imperialism on the African continent. Israeli socialism was a myth created by Israeli propaganda; in fact great inequality existed there, with much unemployment and bankruptcies that often ended in suicide. The *kibbutz* was attacked even more fiercely than the socialist parties and the *Histadrut* (Trades Union Federation); it was described as a labour camp where idealistic labourers were exploited by Wall Street capitalists. Finally, Israel was said to be conspiring, under US inspiration and guidance, against 'progressive' regimes in the Arab world.[126]

ZIONISM

Although much of the propaganda campaign was directed against the Jewish religion, the attacks on Zionism between 1959 and 1964 – whether in the religious context or directly – were reminiscent of the anti-Zionist campaign of Stalin's last years, and in some instances even surpassed it in malignancy.

The main attack was the same as in the 1920s: Zionism was a bourgeois, reactionary nationalist movement directed against communism. Anti-communism was the watchword uniting Zionism, the Jewish bourgeoisie, clericalism and world reaction. Zionism fostered the mistaken belief in a worldwide Jewish nation.

New names were added to the list of reactionaries with whom the Zionists supposedly collaborated, such as Kerensky (head of the Provisional Government in Russia in 1917), the 'White' Generals Denikin and Kolchak, and the Fascists Mussolini, Hitler and Eichmann.[127] Israel's Premier David Ben-Gurion supposedly declared that Zionism inflames anti-Semitism in the world in order to increase immigration into Israel.[128] Jewish organizations, such as the 'Joint', were also attacked and there were repeated references to the ties connecting Zionism and Israel with Jewish and non-Jewish capitalists throughout the world.[129]

ISRAELI DIPLOMATS AND TOURISTS

Attacks on Israeli diplomats, such as those noted above, began in the second half of 1957 and were repeated throughout the whole period. They were directed against every member of the Embassy, except the Ambassador. Among those singled out for special treatment were Levanon, Yaakov Sharet, Hazan, Halevi, Agmon, Eliav, Gat and Zimrat. These attacks appeared in most of the Soviet newspapers, but those in the Trades Union paper, *Trud*, the Odessa paper, *Znamya Kommunizma*, and other local papers were the most vehement.[130]

The 'anti-Soviet activities' were described in detail. Israeli diplomats, students and tourists distributed anti-Soviet literature in synagogues and public places. They were accused of enlisting spies among the Jewish population, of receiving secret documents and issuing instructions for acts of provocation against the Soviet regime. The press would publish letters from Jews demanding that Israeli diplomats' criminal activities be stopped, and an Israeli diplomat would be expelled as *persona non grata*.

DISENCHANTED IMMIGRANTS TO ISRAEL

The Soviet leadership opposed the emigration of Jews and other national minorities. Khrushchev made many declarations regarding the Jews, which were published inside the Soviet Union.[131] The main thesis was that Israel was in the imperialist 'camp', a tool in the hands of American reactionaries, who could easily initiate spying and provocation by Israelis; since there is no such thing as one Jewish people, there is no connection between Soviet Jews and Jews living in Israel; Soviet Jews have no wish to emigrate to Israel and those who do so are bitterly disappointed and want to return to their Soviet fatherland; the time has not yet come to permit Soviet citizens to emigrate, but the government is prepared to allow 'reunion of families' on a humanitarian basis.

Khrushchev adopted a different policy on 'repatriation' – the return to their countries of prisoners-of-war and foreign citizens.[132] The Soviet leadership never recognized the Jews as candidates for such repatriation, except once, between 1957 and 1959, when about 30,000 Jews of Polish origin were repatriated to Poland. The Israeli leadership either did not know about or did not choose to press the possibilities of this 'repatriation' by demanding that all Jews be allowed to return to their homeland.

From 1954 to 1964 there were only 1,452 immigrants into Israel from the Soviet Union, and only 224 from 1957 to 1960. This small-scale emigration produced a disproportionately noisy propaganda campaign in the Press and in declarations by Soviet leaders. One of the usual methods of discouraging emigration was the publication of letters from emigrants from the Soviet Union who had been disappointed – a method also employed in the 1930s to discourage German emigrants to Germany and Canada. Similar letters were now published from emigrants who had gone to Israel and returned, expressing their joy at being home again and warning the Jews against being misled by Zionist propaganda into hasty actions. Numerous articles appeared in these years under headings such as 'Tears in "Paradise"', 'We paid dearly for our mistake', 'A foreign land', 'The Truth about the "Promised Land"', etc.

This propaganda, aimed at cutting off contact between Soviet Jewry and Israel, was accompanied on the one hand by acts of harassment, threats and even arrests of Zionist activists or of any Jews suspected of having connections with the Israeli Embassy, and on the other by severe restrictions on the grant of exit permits. The government also hoped to impress the Arab countries with the firmness of the Soviet anti-Israel stand, a concept that had had considerable influence at the time of the Suez crisis.

A partial relaxation occurred in tourism and cultural exchanges, but this hardly affected basic Soviet anti-Israel policy under Khrushchev. Nor did relations with Israel improve when Soviet–Egyptian relations deteriorated after the declaration of the Egyptian–Syrian 'United Arab Republic' in February 1958 and the revolution in Iraq in July 1958, or as a side effect of ideological disagreements with 'progressive' Arab leaders. The *rapprochement* with the Arab States was by now an accepted element of Soviet foreign policy, because of their strategic, economic and demographic importance and revolutionary potential in the Middle East and the 'third world'.

November 1964 to May 1967

Khrushchev's deposition in October 1964 and the rise of the Brezhnev–Kosygin–Podgorny 'collective leadership' did not change Soviet policy on Israel and Zionism; but there were minor amendments in style, which for a short time affected Soviet Jewry and Soviet–Israeli relations.

The Israeli Ambassador to Moscow, Katriel Katz, made the following entry in his diary in December 1965:

One notes a certain improvement in the style of relations with the Embassy; no members of our staff have been accused recently of 'bad behaviour'; our Information Service release pleading for wider liberalization in the grant of exit permits was not rejected right away as 'intervention in (their) internal affairs' – and their reminder that by now over a thousand persons have emigrated was meant to indicate that a move has been made towards us.[133]

The first sign of this improvement in relations between the Soviet Union and Israel, and to a lesser extent in the attitude to Zionism, was a decrease in the number of propaganda articles on the subject of Israel and Zionism and a softening in their tone.[134] Attacks on Israeli diplomats did continue, and even referred for the first time to Ambassador Yosef Tekoa by name, but they were not as aggressive as before.[135] Another sign of improvement was in cultural relations: there were exchange visits of scientists and scientific delegations and an increase in the number of Israeli tourists visiting the Soviet Union.

What was most important was the increase in the number of Jews who emigrated to Israel, rising from 891 in 1965 to 2,046 in 1966. In the first half of 1967, before emigration stopped because of the Six-Day War, 1,406 Jews emigrated. A formal declaration had been made by Soviet Premier Kosygin in December 1966, which was even published in the Soviet Press,[136] according to which emigration permits would be given to all who wished to rejoin their families. Soviet Jews took this to mean that emigration was now legal, and a number of Jews who came to the OVIR (Visa Office) to apply for exit permits produced copies of the newspapers containing Kosygin's declaration.[137]

These moderate improvements in the situation were the result of changes both in the Soviet Union with the take-over by the new Soviet leadership and the debates on the policy to be pursued, and in Israel, with the replacement of Premier Ben-Gurion, whom the Soviets regarded as anti-Soviet, with the less radical Levi Eshkol. This process was soon to be blocked, however, by more important factors. Internally, Soviet anti-Israel policy was dictated by unwillingness to change the traditional attitude to the Jewish national minority, either by extending full cultural rights to its members or by granting them freedom to emigrate from the Soviet Union. There was a danger that very large numbers of Jews would ask to emigrate, despite all the obstacles, and this strengthened the resolve of those Soviet leaders opposed to any liberalization in this matter. The final hardening of the anti-liberal line coincided with the war on the dissident movements marked by the trial of the writers Sinyavsky and Daniel in February 1966.

In the same month, February 1966, a *coup* brought the 'new Ba'ath' to power in Syria. This coincidence had great political significance and far-reaching consequences, since factors within the Soviet Union and in the Arab states were reacting with each other.

The years 1965 to 1967 were thus characterized by a partial improvement in Soviet–Israeli relations, which left no real mark on the Soviet leadership's attitude to Zionism and Israel. At this time, then, as in the first transition period (1953 to 1955) there was a positive correlation between Soviet–Israeli relations and Zionism–Soviet Jewry, as against the negative correlation of the Khrushchev years (1956 to 1964).

June 1967 to 1983

There is no place here for analysis of the events in the Middle East from May 1966 to June 1967, and the role played by the Soviet Union. What concerns us is the outcome of the Six-Day War, as regards Soviet–Israeli relations and the situation of Soviet Jewry.

The first step was the breaking-off of diplomatic relations with

Israel by the Soviet Union and the other socialist countries – with the exception of Romania. The next measure was the despatch of arms and military instructors to Egypt and Syria, and the grant of large-scale economic aid. The third step was a severe anti-Israeli and anti-Zionist propaganda campaign, launched by Kosygin in his address to the United Nations in New York and in his many subsequent appearances. Finally, Jewish emigration was banned; only 229 immigrants reached Israel from the Soviet Union in 1968.

In addition to these direct results, the Six-Day War had serious consequences in other Eastern European countries, particularly Poland and Czechoslovakia in 1968. In Poland, a violent anti-Zionist, anti-Israel and anti-Jewish propaganda campaign ended in the expulsion of the remaining Jews from the country.

We shall now outline the anti-Zionist campaign in the Soviet Union and Soviet official policy on Israel from the Six-Day War to the present day.

SOVIET–ISRAELI RELATIONS

Since the second half of the 1950s, the Soviet leadership had been planning an Arab empire under Soviet protection, a plan disrupted by the Six-Day War. The Soviet Union did not shelve the project, but continued to foment the Arab–Israeli conflict by supporting the Arab States, directly and indirectly; it even sent Soviet pilots to fight against Israeli planes in the War of Attrition. The Arab–Israeli conflict served Soviet interests by increasing Arab dependence on Soviet aid, helping to remove US influence and contributing to a radicalization of the Arab States themselves.

Improved relations between the Soviet Union and the West in 1971 led to an attempt by the Soviet leadership to improve relations with Israel, at least partially, by meetings with Israeli representatives. This was reported, but the anti-Zionist attacks in the Soviet Press continued. The Soviet aim may have been to induce Arab leaders to adopt a more pro-Soviet stance by the threat of a change in Soviet policy towards Israel. These tentative moves failed, and the Soviet Union suffered a diplomatic setback in 1972 with the expulsion of almost all its military instructors from Egypt.

The October 1973 War allowed the Soviet Union to return to Egypt and the Middle East in greater force and to assume an active role in the international arena, but expectations that relations with Israel would be renewed after the Middle East Peace Conference, held in Geneva in December 1973, disappeared when the Soviet Foreign Minister, Gromyko, stated that this could only happen if there were 'significant progress' in contacts between Israel, the Arab States and the PLO.[138] A Soviet government proposal of 1 October 1976, to convene a second Geneva Conference and adopt a given agenda for a solution of the Middle East conflict, failed, although Israel agreed to take part in such a conference with its original composition – that is, without the PLO.[139]

The visit to Israel of President Sadat of Egypt, made without the Soviet Union's assistance, and the signing of a Peace Treaty between Egypt and Israel on 26 March 1979, were criticized in the Soviet press.[140] The political line was maintained unwaveringly into the 1980s, while the situation in Afghanistan and Poland, and relations between the Soviet Union and the USA, deteriorated.

The Lebanese War produced a fresh wave of attacks on Israel and its 'policy of aggression', and the successive changes in the Soviet leadership in the early 1980s had no effect on the anti-Israeli policy of the Soviet Union.

THE ANTI-ZIONIST CAMPAIGN

Our reviews of this subject during earlier periods have shown the permanence of the anti-Zionist campaign, and at any given moment it should be possible to discover why the campaign was being conducted in a particular way. The reasons for a heightening of the campaign are of paramount importance. Anti-Zionist campaigns are not planned in advance but are discussed and initiated by the leaders when the need for such a campaign arises.

From the beginning of the 1970s, special bodies were set up to deal with the Jewish question, both in the Central Committee Departments and in the Security services, and their decisions were supposed to be applied by governmental bodies (the Ministries of the Interior and of External Affairs). However, even if a decision to wage a campaign is taken at the highest level, it is not necessarily carried out in the same way by all the institutions involved, as substantial differences often exist between them. The execution of such a campaign is complex, and a search for an exclusive cause will almost certainly produce a mistaken evaluation of Soviet policy on the Jewish question in general and on Zionism in particular.

It is possible to regard the period after June 1967 as a high-level anti-Zionist campaign, manifested in the quantity of mass-media material condemning the Zionist movement, in the wide range of anti-Zionist measures and in the violence of the attacks. Yet this campaign, too, as we shall now see, has been irregular in its intensity.

To deal first with anti-Israel and anti-Zionist books: a total of 22 such works appeared between 1967 and 1969 (7 in 1967, 5 in 1968 and 10 in 1969).[141] From 1970 to 1974 – the peak years – 134 books were published (in 1972, at the climax of the campaign, 31, and in 1973 32). From 1975 to 1979 there was a decline – only 30 books in all, an average of 6 a year, as in the period from 1967 to 1969. In 1980 there was a sudden wave of anti-Zionist publications, with 28 books in that year and 19 in 1981. It is interesting that many were published in Western languages, English, French, Spanish and German; that is to say, they were intended for propaganda abroad and not for internal needs; in 1970, for example, 11 of the 19 books published were in these languages.

Since writing and publication take time, it is not possible to discern peaks in the campaign during a given year. An indication is, however, given by the Soviet press, through an anthology of its reports published in the West as *The Jews and the Jewish People*. This collection shows that events with internal or external repercussions for the Soviet Union give rise to increased anti-Semitic propaganda. In this period, we found the following foci: the Six-Day War and the events of the months from June to December 1967; Zionist activity in the Soviet Union and the involvement of Israel, together with the War of Attrition from July 1969 to July 1971; the October 1973 war; the Helsinki Accords and activity centred on them in 1975 and 1976: and, finally, in 1979, the change in emigration policy and the events in Afghanistan, Poland and the Lebanon, which created international tension. The peak years for the publication of articles on Israel, Zionism and Soviet Jews were 1967, with 110 articles, 1970 with 332, 1972 with 253, 1976 with 199, and 1979 with 185. The total number of articles on these subjects published between 1967 and 1980 was 2,262.[142] The themes of this propaganda were similar to those of the preceding period, but the emphasis differed: the stress on the reactionary nature of Zionism reached a climax in the years 1970 to 1972, declined from 1974 to 1978 and rose again after 1979. The most serious accusation was the comparison of Zionism with Nazi racism, which was at its height in 1970, with ninety-six references. In the preceding period, the Zionists were accused of having collaborated with the Nazis; now Zionism itself was being treated as a Nazi movement. Another serious accusation was that the Zionist movement carried out sabotage and espionage on behalf of the USA in all the socialist countries.

In previous periods, Jews had helped to write anti-Zionist books, articles and 'letters to the editor' in the press, during the campaigns against 'cosmopolitanism' and against the 'Jewish doctors' conspiracy', and at the time of the 1956 Sinai war. A new element was introduced now: organized appearances of supposed 'representatives of the Jewish public', not only in Moscow but also in cities like Riga, Kishinev and Tiflis. The range of Jews involved was wider than in previous campaigns: those well-known in the army, science, art, the economy; religious and secular Jews; party members and non-party members; all drawn from those republics with concentrations of Jews. This organizing of 'representative Jews' was closely connected with the reactions of Jews in Israel and the West to repressive measures against Soviet Jews marked by the first Leningrad trial in December 1970, measures that led to the setting up of the Brussels Conference for the Defence of Soviet Jewry in February 1971.

In 1983 the Soviet Union started what seems to be a new phase in the use of Jews in the fight against Zionism when eight eminent Jews called for the establishment of an 'Anti-Zionist Committee'.[143] This declaration was signed on 1 April by Jews active in Jewish affairs in official institutions, among them General Dragunsky, whose name had been well-known since the 1950s; Zimanas and Zivs, who had from time to time defended Soviet 'Jewish' policy; and Kolesnikov, an anti-Zionist writer. The proposed Committee was created on 21 April, presided over by Dragunsky, and among its members were the Jewish deputy chairmen, Zivs, Kolesnikov and Mark Krupkin (assistant editor of the *Novosti* publishing house) and a non-Jew, Igor Belaev. Rabbi Fishman of Moscow stated that he would join the Committee, but after his death there was no further co-option of any representative religious Jews until 1985, when Rabbi Shaevich joined the Committee. Nor were there any representatives from Birobidzhan, or from the non-Ashkenazi Jews, or the Yiddish 'establishment' surrounding the periodical, *Sovietish heimland*. From the beginning, differences of opinion arose among the Committee's members on how to define Zionism and how to fight it. Belaev and Solodar wanted extreme measures, while Zivs and Zimanas were more moderate, and Dragunsky remained in the middle.[144]

Anti-Zionist harassment and arrests.   One aim of the propaganda campaign against Zionism was to frighten the Jews, so that they would want no part in Zionist activity. In its fight against those who still dared to work for the Zionist cause, the regime resorted to drastic measures. Many Zionist activists had been waiting to emigrate, since the beginning of the 1970s. The number of those 'refused' was estimated, in the early 1980s, to be about 10,000. Many Zionist activists were dismissed from their employment and forced to take any kind of work in order to earn a living and avoid arrest as 'parasites'. Zionists and their families were kept under constant secret service surveillance, arrests being made from time to time to maintain pressure and inconvenience. Hooligans from the underworld of crime were sent to harass the activists. If any complaints led to the hooligans' arrest, they were at once released by the security services. Telephones in the activists' homes were cut off and telephone conversations stopped, especially with people abroad. KGB officers constantly exerted pressure on Zionist activists through threats and promises. Zionist activists were arrested and tried in large numbers.

The series of political trials of Zionist activists opened with that of Boris Kochubievsky in Kiev on 13 May 1969, on a charge of conducting anti-Soviet propaganda.[145] Four main trials were held in Leningrad, Riga and Kishinev, between December 1970 and June 1971, on charges of hijacking a plane, betraying the fatherland, anti-Soviet activity and slandering the Soviet Union: thirty-three people were charged and sentenced (two death sentences were commuted to life imprisonment after mass protests in the West). From 1972 onwards, the trials were mostly of individuals and not of groups, and some of the sentences were harsh: Yitzhak Shkolnik of Vinnitsa, seven years' imprisonment; Leonid Zabolishensky of Sverdlovsk, six years' imprisonment; Mikhail Shtern, seven years' imprisonment. In 1977 Anatoly Shcharansky was sentenced for spying and treachery to ten years' imprisonment and ten years in a forced labour camp.

From 1969 to 1983, eighty-seven people were tried, in sixty trials, on charges such as treachery to the fatherland, espionage, aeroplane hi-jacking, anti-Soviet propaganda, possession of fire-arms, refusal to serve in the army, betrayal of State secrets, hooliganism, parasitism, distributing drugs, and economic crimes. The trials were held in different towns in the Russian Republic, the Ukraine, Moldavia, Latvia, Dagestan, Georgia and Tadzhikistan; for some reason, no such trials were held in this period in the Belorussian and Lithuanian Republics, where there was much Zionist activity.

If we compare the anti-Zionist trials with the anti-German trials of 1974 to 1979, we find that there were more trials of activists of the German nationalist movement (twenty-five, as against twenty-one anti-Zionist trials), but as this was the peak of German activity, the difference is not substantial. The Germans accused were tried on relatively less serious charges, such as illegal demonstrations, petitioning, and anti-Soviet propaganda, and their sentences varied from three months to three years. As well as the different structure and areas of activity of the two nationalist movements, the difference in the way they are treated is influenced by the widespread view that Jewish nationalist–Zionism is a conspiracy against the Soviet Union and the socialist bloc, unlike the limited Soviet–German campaign for emigration.[146]

EMIGRATION POLICY

In the transition period from 1964 to 1967 the Soviet leadership began an 'agonizing reappraisal' of emigration, and began to realize that exit permits must be granted to a limited number of Soviet citizens from a few minority nationalities. The political volte-face occurred in March 1971, when the leadership apparently decided to permit emigration from the Soviet Union. The anti-Zionist campaign had reached its climax early in 1971, and here, as it were, was an 'anti-climax', a decision contrary to the main thrust of the campaign, marking victory for Zionism and the failure of the Soviet policy of intimidation.

The change of policy on emigration was the result of the Soviet government being offered an opportunity to get rid of Zionist activists at not too high a price: international pressure, supported by a number of Communist Parties in Western Europe, encouraged the Soviet leadership's desire to improve its relations with the West, in order (among other considerations) to receive certain economic advantages. Conditions were in favour of allowing emigration, and from 1971 to 1973, 61,436 Jews, 9,064 Germans and about 4,000 Armenians emigrated from the Soviet Union. In 1974 and 1975, as a result of the October War and the failure of Soviet–USA negotiations on most-favoured-nation treatment, the total of emigrants decreased to 20,628 in 1974 and 13,221 in 1975. The levels of German emigration in these two years prove the international influence on Soviet calculations on emigration: the number of German emigrants increased to 6,541 in 1974, compared with 4,493 the previous year.

From 1976 to 1979 the number of emigrants from all the national minorities increased, reaching a peak for the Jews in 1979 and for the Germans in 1977. In this period, 111,182 Jews, 36,659 Germans and about 4,000 Greeks and Koreans emigrated from the Soviet Union. The higher numbers were the result of the 1975 Helsinki Conference on human rights and the Soviet desire to improve relations with the USA; internally, the leadership hoped to complete the emigration process at one stroke.

In 1980, and especially in 1981, the reversal began. The policy now was to restrict the number of emigrants, whether Jews or of other nationalities. In 1980 there were 20,412 Jewish emigrants, in 1981 9,448, in 1982 2,760 and in 1983 less than 1,000, with the downward trend continuing. The reasons for the reductions are clear: emigration policy continued to be an instrument for securing Soviet aims in political, military or economic negotiations with the Western powers. The control of emigration of those national minorities with strong links with the outside world – Western Germany, Israel, and indirectly the USA – cannot induce a change in the policy of those countries, but can warn that a worsening of relations with the Soviet Union will directly affect the scale of emigration. No single factor influences Soviet emigration policy; every deterioration in international relations in the direction of the 'cold war' and every aggravation of the internal situation leading to increased terror against liberal or dissident forces will bring about the closing of the Soviet Union, and reduce the flow of Soviet citizens leaving the country, whether as emigrants or as tourists.

If a new climate is to be created similar to that prevailing at the beginning of the 1970s, many conditions will have to be met, both in Soviet–Western relations and in internal Soviet policy. First, there must be an improvement in Soviet–US relations. Second, the emigration movement must be strengthened among the Jews and the other 'emigrating' national minorities, who have to make sacrifices to be able to emigrate; and finally, vocal support is needed from both governments and the public in Western countries. Only a combination of these factors could produce a change, since the Soviet leadership, for reasons of prestige, the economy and security, and from fear of other nationalities' being infected by the 'contagion' of emigration, continually finds additional grounds for restricting the right to emigrate.

DEMOGRAPHIC AND SOCIO-ECONOMIC PROCESSES

The Jewish population – size and distribution

The demographic processes in Soviet Jewry were accelerated during and after the Second World War. The evacuation of the Jewish population was not to save it from the Germans; many Jews were evacuated as part of an overall policy affecting members of the party and government economic and military institutions. According to the calculations made by Yosef Tenenbaum, about four million Jews were in areas of the Soviet Union occupied by the Nazis, 1.5 million of whom managed to escape; therefore there must have been about 2.5 million Jews in the free part of the Soviet Union;[147] but according to the Soviet demographer Y. Kantor, there were no more than two million Jews in the free sectors.[148] This means that the percentage of the Jewish population's losses was between 12.5% and 15% of the total Soviet population's losses (between 2.5 and 3 million out of a total of about 20 million).[149] About 1.6 million Soviet Jews were murdered by the Nazis, about 200,000 fell fighting in the Red Army and the partisan forces, and the rest died naturally or from illness and starvation caused by the war.

THE SIZE OF THE JEWISH POPULATION, 1959 TO 1979
According to the first population census after the war (in 1959), there were 2,267,000 Jews in the Soviet Union, constituting 1.1% of the entire population, as compared with 1.8% in the 1939 census and an estimated 2.5% in 1940.[150] If we add 15%, to represent those Jews who concealed their nationality, this brings the Jewish population to about 2,607,000. This is close to the total reached by calculating the estimated annual natural increase at an average rate of *c.* 1% (2.5 million in 1946, together with an increase of *c.* 350,000 up to 1959), minus the emigration of some 200,000: this gives the figure of 2,645,000 Jews in 1959.

   At the beginning of 1965, according to the official Soviet estimate, the Jews numbered 2,400,000.[151] This indicates an average annual natural increase of 1%, and accordingly when the 1970 census was taken, the Jewish population should have reached 2,505,000; but the census revealed that only 2,151,000 persons declared themselves to be Jews. The disappearance of *c.* 350,000 Jews can be explained in the first place by an increase in the number of Jews who did not declare themselves, because of the anti-Jewish and anti-Zionist propaganda campaign. Second, the latest censuses reveal an aging population (in 1959, 18.6% of the whole Soviet population were over the age of 50 and in 1970 20.6%). Third, it is important to note that the natural rate of increase is lower in the urban population, to which nearly all the Jews belong; and, finally, local falsifications may occur, so that the registration is not exact.

The apparent decline in numbers continued from 1970 to 1979, when a new factor was added; the emigration of about 125,000 Jews. In the most recent census (in 1979), the number of declared Jews was only 1,811,000; if those who did not declare themselves as Jews – about 10% – are added, it follows that at the beginning of the 1980s the Jews numbered about two million (0.7% of the population of the Soviet Union, in comparison with 0.9% in 1970). Due to this loss of about 17% in the years from 1959 to 1979, the Jews have moved from eleventh to sixteenth place in the list of Soviet nationalities.

The number of Jews in the Soviet Union will continue to decrease, even if there is no mass emigration, because of smaller families (3.2 persons in 1979 and fewer than 3 today), the aging of the Jewish population (for example, about 25% of the Jews in the Russian Republic were aged over 60 in 1970 and only 12% of the general population), low fertility and the process of assimilation – in addition to factors affecting the Soviet population generally, whose natural rate of increase fell from 1.68% in 1960 to 0.94% in 1970 and apparently fell still further in 1979.

DISTRIBUTION BY REPUBLICS

There were 875,000 Jews living in the Russian Republic in 1959, only slightly fewer than in 1939, in contrast to the great fall in the Jewish population of the Ukrainian and Belorussian Republics in the same period. In 1970 the number of Jews in the Russian Republic was down to 808,000 (0.6% of all the inhabitants) and in 1979 it was 701,000 (0.5%); nevertheless, in the period under review, the Russian Republic headed the list of republics with Jewish populations, having about 38% of all the Jews in the Soviet Union.

In the Ukrainian Republic, where about half the Soviet Jews were living in 1940, there were 840,000 in 1959, 770,000 in 1970, and 634,000 in 1979 (1.3% of the entire population of the Republic), just over a third of all the Jews in the Soviet Union. It was in the Belorussian Republic that the largest decrease occurred between 1939 and 1979 – from 375,000 to 135,000 (1.4% of the whole population of the Republic). Today the Jews of Belorussia constitute 7.5% of all the Jews in the Soviet Union, as compared with 12.5% in 1939. The main reason for this change was the migration of the Jews from Belorussia to the Russian Republic and the other Republics.

In the western Republics (the Baltic Republics and Moldavia), all of which were annexed to the Soviet Union in 1939 and 1940, the processes of Jewish absorption were slower than in the other Republics: there were 161,807 Jews in 1959, 164,000 in 1970 and only 128,000 in 1979. This decrease was due mainly to mass Jewish emigration to Israel between 1971 and 1979.

In the border republics of the south and the east (three Caucasian and five Asian), there were 164,000 Jews in 1939, only 5% of all the Jews in the Soviet Union; in 1959 there were 240,000 Jews there; in 1970 254,000; and in 1979 *c.* 190,000 (178,000 in the Caucasian Republics, in Tadzhikistan and in Uzbekistan and some 12,000 in the other Republics, for which there are no data).

The reasons for the changes in the distribution of the Jews between the censuses of 1939 and 1979 were on the one hand dispersion and on the other continued migration from the Ukraine and Belorussia to the Russian Republic.

DISTRIBUTION BY SEX AND AGE

Before the Second World War, there were 1,102 women for every 1,000 men in the Jewish population, while in the general population there were 1,087 women for every 1,000 men. The war losses led to a serious imbalance between men and women in the country.[152] According to the 1959 census, there were 1,220 women for every 1,000 men: that is to say, between 1939 and 1959 the number of women for every 1,000 men in the general population increased by 133, while in the Jewish population there were 1,200 women for every 1,000 men, an increase of only 98. The reasons for the difference were that in the Jewish population relatively more men survived than women, not because of any lesser participation of Jews in the war against the Nazis but because there were more Jewish men than women in the partisan movement (who remained alive), and it was mainly men who were mobilized in the Red Army in the areas later conquered by the Nazis, and some of these survived as well. In the 1970 census, there were 1,177 women for every 1,000 men in the Jewish population; this time, in comparison with the population as a whole the imbalance between the sexes was higher among the Jews.

As regards distribution by age, according to the 1959 census among the Soviet population as a whole it was as follows: 0–15 30.4%; 16–49 51%; over 50 18.6%. We do not have data on the Jewish population for the whole country. In the Russian Republic, where apparently the Jewish population was older than in the other Republics, in 1970 in the age group 0–15 there were 11.2%; 16–49, 46%; and over 50 42.8%. Thus in 1970 there was already a serious aging of the Jewish population, which increased in subsequent years.

URBAN AND RURAL POPULATION

The process of urbanization of the Jewish population accelerated towards the end of the Second World War because the Jewish settlements in the Ukraine, Belorussia and the Crimea were wiped out and the few Jews from the Jewish agricultural areas who remained alive did not return to agriculture.

In 1959 only 4.7% of the whole Jewish population lived in rural areas, some of whom were not occupied in agriculture but lived there because of the difficulty of finding housing elsewhere. The rural population was divided as follows, by Republics: Russian Republic – 45,079; Ukraine – 30,280; Georgia – 7,752; Belorussia – 5,590; and Uzbekistan – 4,421. By 1970 there was a further substantial decrease in the Jewish rural population; it was reduced by 56.6% and constituted 2.1% of the Jews in the Soviet Union. This change was caused by the continued migration from the villages to the towns, the high rate of Jewish assimilation, and changes in the administrative status of rural areas that had been transferred to urban areas. This process continued in the 1970s and the Jewish rural population decreased to only 1%.

An important aspect of the process of urbanization of the Jews in the Soviet Union is their concentration in the big cities. In 1959 in Moscow there were 239,246 Jews and in 1970 251,500 (3.6% of the inhabitants of Moscow); in Leningrad 168,246 and 162,087 (4.1%); in Kiev 153,466 and 152,000 (13.9%); in Odessa in 1970 116,280 (13%); in Kharkov in 1970 76,211 (6.2%); in Dnepropetrovsk in 1970 68,776 (8%); in Tashkent in 1959 50,445 (5.5%).[153] These data show that educational and cultural centres for the Jewish population are needed in those quarters of the big cities where the Jews are concentrated. Such centres do not, however, exist because the Jewish population has been assimilated but because the authorities are unwilling to set them up.

DIVISION BY COMMUNITIES

In 1926 non-Ashkenazi Jews constituted only 2.5% of all Jews in the Soviet Union. No data on non-Ashkenazi Jews were published in the 1939 census, but it can be assumed that they constituted about 3%. In 1959 they numbered about 110,000 – about 4.9% of all Soviet Jews, and in 1970 some 130 to 140,000 – about 6.5%.[154] The increase in their relative numbers in the Jewish population can be explained by their having suffered relatively fewer losses in the Holocaust (only the 'Mountain Jews' were affected) and by their higher rate of natural increase. It also appears that the percentage of those concealing their Jewish nationality was lower than among the Ashkenazi Jews.

The Georgian community numbered 21,471 according to the 1926 census, and 36,000 in the 1959 census – an increase of 64% in 33 years. This approaches an annual increase of 2% and is higher than the national rate of increase of the Georgian population (less than 1.5%). If the average natural increase in the years 1959 to 1970 was the same as in the preceding period, the declared Jewish population of Georgia numbered about 44,000 in 1970, and the total population, including those who did not declare themselves, about 48,000. In 1982 the number of Georgian Jews can be put at about 30,000 (if one takes into account a natural increase of about 12,000 and the emigration of about 30,000 in the years 1971 to 1981).[155]

The 'Mountain Jews' (the Tati), who also live in the Caucasus, numbered about 26,000 in 1926, and according to the 1959 census approximately 30,000. This relatively low increase among a population known for its high rate of natural increase (about 15% in 33 years) was the result of the losses inflicted in the Holocaust. To this datum should be added, however, Jews who do not appear in the census as 'Mountain Jews' because of the lack of clarity in Soviet terminology, which failed to distinguish between the 'Mountain Jews' and the mainly Moslem Tati tribe (with a Christian minority). In 1970, before the great emigration, the number of 'Mountain Jews' can be put at about 44,000 and in 1982, after the emigration of about 11,000, at about 40,000 (44,000 plus 7,000 natural increase minus 11,000). About half the 'Mountain Jews' were concentrated in the Autonomous Republic of Dagestan, most of them in the town of Derbent.

The Bukharan Jews, living mainly in the Uzbek Republic in the districts of Samarkand, Fergana and Bukhara, numbered about 19,000 in 1926 and according to the census about 28,000 in 1959. In 1970 there were about 35,000 Bukharan Jews in the Soviet Union, if one assumes that their high rate of natural increase had declined in the 1960s; in 1982, after the emigration of 15,666 between 1971 and 1981, they numbered about 26,000.

The smallest non-Ashkenazi community is that of the Crimean Jews, or Krimchaks. They numbered 6,383 in 1926 and in 1959, after the Holocaust, only 2,000. It is not known whether any of them emigrated, but their rate of assimilation is high and very few of them appear to have declared their Jewish nationality in the 1979 census.

Socio-economic processes

From the second half of the 1950s, partial data began again to be published on the educational and occupational status of the different national minorities, including the Jews. It is thus possible to examine the main processes that occurred among the Jews in the socio-economic sphere, even if only for certain years, in the period from 1939 to 1979.

THE JEWS IN EDUCATION

In all the countries where Jews live, their high level of education is one of their most important socio-economic characteristics and is particularly important in the socio-economic structure of the Soviet State.

According to data on 95% of all the Jews in the Soviet Union, in 1939 for every 1,000 persons aged ten or over there were 330 Jews with more than seven years' schooling (that is, high school and above), while in the general Soviet population there were only 83 and in the urban population 181. In 1959 there was a further significant increase – 1.7 times – in the number of Jews with secondary or higher education (from 330 to 566 in every 1,000). In that year, in the republics where 88% of Soviet Jews were living, 21% had partial or complete higher education, 10.2% had college-level vocational training, 14.8% had full secondary education and 15.8% had incomplete secondary education; that is to say, about 62% of the Jews in those republics had partial secondary education or higher. In comparison with the general urban population in the country, the Jews had 4.4

times as many persons with higher education and twice as many with secondary or vocational college education. If we turn to the other republics (the Caucasian and Asian Republics, where non-Ashkenazi Jews with a relatively low educational level lived), it emerges that in the whole of the Soviet Union less than half the Jews had less than secondary schooling, while among the general urban population the percentage was as high as 83. By the 1970 census this ratio had changed, and had changed even more by 1979 – the proportion of people with education had increased greatly among all the nationalities. According to the 1970 census, there had been a further rise in the percentage of Jews with seven years' schooling or over: in the Russian republic, for every 1,000 aged ten or over, there were 824 with seven years' schooling or more, in the Ukraine 747, in Belorussia 710 and in Moldavia 660; in the whole Soviet Union, the number of Jews with education from incomplete secondary schooling to higher education can thus be put at about 760 for every 1,000, of whom 239 had higher education.[156]

In 1935 Jews constituted 13.3% of all students in the country (74,900 out of 563,000). It is estimated that in 1956 there were 84,000 Jewish students (*c.* 4.2% of all students). The first official datum is from 1960 to 1961, when there were 77,177 Jewish students studying in institutions of higher learning (3.2% of all students). Between 1964 and 1967 there was a considerable increase in the number of Jewish students, which now stood at 110,000, but their percentage of the whole student population was down to 2.6%. The figures were static from 1968 to 1970, and from 1970–1 there has been a steady decline both in absolute numbers and in the percentage of all students. In 1970–1 there were still 105,800 Jewish students, but in 1976–7 there were only 66,900 (1.4% of all students) – less than the Jews' ratio in the urban population (which was 1.5% in 1970). Vocational training presents a similar picture: from 1961–2 to 1976–7, the number of students in these institutions rose by 95%, but among the Jews it dropped by 40% from 44,116 to 33,300 and their ratio fell from 1.9% to 0.7%.[157]

Differences exist between the republics, and sometimes even from one city to another, according to the local perception of the policy on how the student body was to be divided up among the nationalities in the Soviet Union. Moscow is a good example with its considerable Jewish population. Thus in 1970 there were 19,508 Jewish students in Moscow University; in 1974, 19,895; in 1976, 12,049 (1.88%); in 1977, 11,531 (1.8%) and in 1980 only 9,911 (1.57%).

The way students are divided up among different systems in the universities can serve as a partial indicator for Soviet policy on Jews in higher education. In the year 1960–1, 46.1% of Jewish students in the Russian Republic were learning in day classes, compared with 39.8% of Russians and Ukrainians; in evening classes, Jews were 13.5%, Russians 11.9% and Ukrainians 7.8%; in correspondence schools the Jews were 40.4%, Russians 41.3% and Ukrainians 52.4%. The situation was far worse from the Jewish point of view in the Ukrainian Republic in the same year, where 19% of all students studied in evening classes (the least convenient system and the least generous with grants): 13.2% were Ukrainians and 8.7% Jews.[158] There was also a decline in the number of Jewish *aspirants* (candidates for doctorates who received grants) from 4,945 in 1970 to 3,456 in 1973 – a 30% decrease in three years.

What caused so significant a decline, both absolute and relative, in the number of Jewish students? There were both objective and subjective reasons. To the first class belong the 'aging' of the Jewish population: the decrease in the size of the 20 to 29 age-group who were the candidates for higher education (from 121,000 in 1959 to 88,000 in 1970 in the Russian Republic), and the mass emigration of 270,000 Jews between the years 1969 and 1980, a high percentage of whom were in the student age-group. Among the subjective causes were the various forms of discrimination against Jews in education – being barred from certain institutions and having restricted admission to others. This policy was rationalized as promoting the equality of the different strata of the population and particularly (under Khrushchev) of 'workers and peasants', and of the various nationalities – the Russians, Ukrainians and Belorussians as against the Georgians and Armenians.

VOCATIONAL TRAINING

The number of Jews of secondary school level in vocational training in 1957 was 368,000 out of the total of 6,821,600 workers (5.4%); Jewish workers with a secondary education (not vocational) numbered 260,000 (9.3%). In 1964 the number of Jewish workers with vocational training and secondary education was about 482,000, but their ratio in the total of workers in both classes had gone down to 4.3%. If we take Jews with secondary education only, the percentage decline was greater, from 9.3% to 7.1%. In 1975 there was a further increase in the absolute numbers of Jewish workers with secondary education to 385,000 and with higher vocational training to 180,700; but their percentage share was down to 4.1% in the first category and 1.4% in the second, a downward trend in the average annual growth.

SCIENTIFIC WORKERS

This term applies to all those employed in universities, research institutes and scientific academies and affiliated institutions.

The number of Jews among scientific workers in 1950 was 25,125, 15.5% of all scientists. As a result of Stalin's anti-Jewish policy, in 1955 they numbered 24,620 (11.04%). From 1956 to 1961 there was an average annual increase of some 2,000 to 2,500 Jewish scientific workers, the highest on record, and so their percentage was only slightly smaller: 8.5% of all scientific workers. From 1963 to 1970 there was again an average annual increase of some 2,500 Jewish scientific workers, but from 1971 on there was a perceptible slowing down in the absolute growth of the number of Jewish scientific workers, to an average of 1,300 a year. By 1975 their percentage was down to 5.7%, which was still relatively high, but it would certainly have been higher still if there had not been anti-Jewish discrimination. This policy also barred scientists of Jewish origin from secret or particularly 'sensitive' research institutes, but this is not reflected in data published in the Soviet Union.

Among scientific workers with a doctorate (the highest degree awarded in the Soviet Union), the Jews constitute the second largest national group after the Russians, and twice the size of that of the Ukrainians, who have a population twenty times larger.

The social composition of soviet Jewry – breadwinners with academic education

No statistics have been published on the occupational distribution of Soviet Jews for the years 1940 to 1980. Partial data have, however, been published since 1962 on Jews in a number of academic professions, in order to show in propaganda abroad that the Jews hold important posts in prestigious occupations and thereby to counter 'Zionist propaganda' on discrimination against Jews.[159]

From Soviet publications of 1962 to 1964 it seems that Jews were 14.7% of all the doctors in the Soviet Union (78,000 Jewish doctors) or 24% of all employed Jews having an academic education, while the percentage in the general population was only 12%. The figures published for 1978, however, show the Jews as 3.4% of all doctors, a steep drop in this profession. This resulted both from the increase in the number of doctors in the Soviet Union and the emigration of Jewish doctors (about 3,000 doctors reached Israel and others went to the USA and other Western countries), and also from the discrimination over the admission of Jews to medical schools.

In the mid 1960s, Jews constituted 8.5% of all authors and journalists, about 3,700 persons and 1% of all Jewish breadwinners; in 1977 their ratio was down to 6.5%. Among actors and artists, Jews constituted 7.7% and in 1977 5.2%. In Belorussia Jews constituted 12.1% of the members of unions among authors, painters, composers, architects and film-makers: 140 out of the total of 1,154 'creative workers'.[160] Although the Jews still have an important place in Soviet literature and art, it would seem to be less so in posts in cultural institutions where there is direct contact with the population; the authorities are encouraging Jews to concentrate instead on the natural sciences and scientific research. In the legal profession, the share of the Jews has decreased from 10.4% in 1964 to 6.7% in 1977.

It is important to determine what percentage of the Jewish population is active, that is to say, the percentage of breadwinners (men aged from 16 to 60 and women from 16 to 55). As we have seen, in 1970 there were 527,000 Jewish breadwinners with higher or postsecondary vocational education. It emerges that about a million Jews belong to the 'active' population, some 47% of all the Jews in the Soviet Union. This was similar to the overall percentage in the Soviet population in that year (47.7%) but lower than the percentage in the urban population (52.1%).

The Soviet practice is to divide up the 'active' population according to the following social strata: workers, officials, *kolkhoz* members and 'others'. These data are not particularized for the nationalities (including the Jews), except from Lithuania. The data from Lithuania give the following social distribution among the Jews: 44.5% workers (Lithuanians 52.1%, Russians 58.2% and Poles 70.1%); officials 55.3% (Lithuanians 17.8%, Russians 36.5% and Poles 8.3%); and only 0.1% *kolkhoz* members. There are of course considerable differences between Lithuania and the other Republics, especially the Russian and Ukrainian which are the two most important ones, from the point of view of the Jewish population concentrated there. These data, therefore, can only serve as a partial indicator. They show that Jews belong mainly to two broad social categories:

officials (which include scientific workers and those in the teaching professions) and workers, while their ratio in agriculture is negligible. Since more than half the Jewish population has higher or vocational education, it can be inferred that the ratio of official to workers is higher in the Soviet Union as a whole than the 55:45 ratio in Lithuania.

From the point of view of standard of living, the majority of Jews are middle and high-level earners (directors, or members of the academic professions: teachers, engineers, chemists, architects and occupied in the arts), since they are an urban population with relatively small families, a high percentage having higher education, and are constantly striving to improve their living conditions.

EDUCATION AND CULTURE

As we recorded in the previous chapter, Jewish education and culture in the Soviet Union ended in the late 1940s, and its last surviving representatives vanished in the early 1950s. Would this state of affairs change in the post-Stalin period? Would the efforts of Jewish circles in the Soviet Union and outside it succeed in renewing one or more of the Jewish national linguistic forms?

Jewish education

After 1953, no move was made in this sphere until the twentieth CPSU congress in February 1956. Then the question of Jewish education and culture began to be raised in meetings of Soviet leaders with Western statesmen. The inclination of official Soviet spokesmen like the Minister of Culture Furtseva and L. Ilyichev of the Ministry of External Affairs was to deny the existence of any such problem in the Soviet Union,[161] as can be seen in the correspondence between Professor Katsh and the Deputy Minister of Education of the Russian Republic, A. Arsenyev.[162] Professor Katsh asked why there were no Jewish schools in the Soviet Union, to which Arsenyev replied, 'Under Soviet Law every parent has the right to send his child to a class where all subjects are taught in his mother tongue ... This right also applies in full measure to persons of Jewish Nationality.' Obviously the facts were otherwise: all the attempts made by Jews in appeals to the Soviet central government institutions to open classes for teaching in Yiddish or to receive permission to teach the language privately had failed. The appeals were rejected for a variety of administrative reasons; for example, since the Jews were dispersed all over the Soviet Union it would be very expensive to establish Yiddish schools; the Jews were not really interested in sending their children to Jewish schools, and of course the Soviet leadership would not force them to do so, for they would simply rise up in revolt. The first of these arguments is hardly convincing, since the Germans, Poles and other extra-territorial minorities are widely dispersed and nevertheless the Germans, Poles, Hungarians and Greeks were able to open schools or classes in the various republics for learning their mother tongue, while others – and the Jews among them – had no such possibility. Thus, for example, there were Polish schools in the Ukraine and in Lithuania, but not in Belorussia, with its considerable Polish population. Germans could learn in their mother tongue in Kazakhstan, in the Russian Republic and in Kirgistan, but not, for some reason, in the other Republics. In Kazakhstan in the 1960s, for example, about a quarter of the German children learnt in their mother tongue in special classes.[163] The second argument is stronger, for in the period when Jewish schools did exist, many Jewish parents preferred to send their children to Russian schools. There were, however, many Jewish parents who even now would have sent their children to Jewish schools if they had existed, both because of the Jewish national revival and because of the existence of open or hidden anti-Semitism in the general schools.

A change of direction has been seen in recent years regarding learning Yiddish, at least in the Autonomous Jewish Region of Birobidzhan, apparently as a result of the government's bitter fight against the Zionist movement and the demands of the activists to be allowed to learn Hebrew. Three Yiddish classes were opened in secondary schools in Birobidzhan in 1980, one in *kolkhoz* Waldheim and two in Birobidzhan city, with twelve teachers teaching in this language. According to recent publications, it is intended to increase the number of Yiddish classes in the region. A Yiddish-language textbook of 298 pages has been published in Khabarovsk, and a new Russian–Yiddish dictionary has also appeared.

If this is the position with regard to Yiddish, which is officially recognized as the national language of Soviet Jews, what can devotees of Hebrew expect, when a war has been waged against the language by the authorities since the 1920s? The paradoxical status of Hebrew is that, on the one hand, it is taught in a number of universities (Moscow, Leningrad and Tiflis) and in theological seminaries (including the Yeshivah Kol Yaakov) as a Semitic language, while, on the other hand, Jews who want to are not allowed to learn it, neither officially in any Soviet educational institution nor privately.[164] As we shall see, the fight for the right to learn and teach Hebrew has become one of the foremost signs of the vitality of the Zionist movement in the Soviet Union since the late 1960s. Long before that, small groups or individuals had begun learning Hebrew, and by the early 1970s there was a considerable network of Hebrew classes in many cities with large Jewish populations. There are no statistics as a whole, but in Moscow alone there were some 1,000 people learning Hebrew in 1980 with about 60 teachers, and about 40 teachers were known to be teaching in other cities.[165] A 'Hebrew Study Week' was held in Moscow from 5 to 11 March 1979 and there was a similar event in Leningrad. The police and the KGB have busied themselves in recent years in combatting Hebrew studies in private homes – breaking into houses, carrying out searches and arresting people. Those arrested are charged with keeping anti-Soviet publications, which refers to nothing but Hebrew–Russian dictionaries (one published officially in the Soviet Union in 1963, edited by P. Shapiro) or text-books used as teaching aids. Hebrew teachers are accused of parasitism, despite their work permits having been refused.

Literature and the press

The revival of the Yiddish press and literature was slow in the post-Stalin period but finally succeeded, due to the new political situation inside the Soviet Union, combined with pressure from Communist and progressive circles in the West. There was also support from liberal Soviet writers and artists.

In 1954–5, one small work by Shalom Aleikhem was published in Russian translation and two poems by Aharon Vergelis, translated by Evtushenko, in *Novy mir*. The first sign of an altered official approach was the rehabilitation of the poet Perets Markish in December 1955,[166] after which various other writers who had been executed in Stalin's day had their names cleared.[167] Yiddish authors, many of whom had only just been released from forced labour camps, appealed to the Union of Soviet Writers to support a renewal of Yiddish publishing.[168] The Secretary of the Union, Aleksei Surkov, told the editor of the Jewish Communist paper in New York, Haim Suller, that a programme was under way to establish a Yiddish publishing house, a newspaper and a literary quarterly and to convene a nation-wide congress of Yiddish authors and 'cultural activists'.[169] At the end of 1956 there was a rumour that a Yiddish weekly would soon appear, which was intended to become a daily paper. A variety of individuals and official bodies recommended meeting some of the demands for a renewal of Yiddish culture, to silence anti-Soviet propaganda in the West.[170]

Technical difficulties, such as lack of Yiddish type, are not an acceptable explanation of the delay in publishing books until 1959, when selected writings of Shalom Aleikhem came out (with a preface by Vergelis); of the postponement of the appearance of a literary periodical until 1961, when 25,000 copies of *Sovietish heimland* were printed (reduced in 1965 to 16,000 and in 1979 to 7,000); and of the failure to produce a Yiddish daily newspaper. The intention of the authorities was clear – to hold up these developments as long as possible, in the hope that in time the pressure from abroad and in the Soviet Union itself would die down.

From 1959 to 1964 – from the publication of the first Yiddish book to the deposition of Khrushchev – only 7 Yiddish books appeared (5 *belles lettres* and 2 socio-political works). From 1961 to 1963 no Yiddish books were published, but when the new leadership took over 16 books came out in the next three years. In 1968 only 2 books appeared, but in 1969 there was a record number for the whole period – 9 books. The 1970s saw sporadic publications, due perhaps to technical reasons rather than to any deliberate policy. Thus in 1970 4 Yiddish books appeared (10,000 copies of each), in 1971 7 (18,000 copies), in 1972 only 3 (9,000 copies), in 1973 6 (10,000 copies) and in 1974 5 books (7,000 copies). There was a rise at the end of the 1970s: in 1978 8 books appeared (17,200 copies) and in 1981 there were again 8 (11,700 copies).[171] Soviet announcements concerning the number of Yiddish books published since 1959 are not accurate; according to one Soviet 'expert' on Jewish affairs, Rukhadzhe, in the last decade alone 124 works appeared,[172] while the *Novosti* Agency speaks of 85 books and 148 translations from Yiddish into Russian in the last 20 years. The confusion results from the desire to prove the 'flourishing' state of Jewish culture in the Soviet Union; for this purpose the number of Yiddish books published is added to translations from Yiddish and even books written on Jewish themes. The quantity of translations from Yiddish into Russian has decreased since the 1970s.

The main forum for Yiddish literature is *Sovietish heimland*, mentioned above, which began to appear in January 1965 as a fortnightly periodical and was later turned into a monthly. It published the works of over a hundred Jewish writers, most of them now aged over sixty. With the emigration to Israel of about twenty writers and the deaths in the last decade, the circle of Yiddish writers has dwindled. Most of them live in Moscow, in the Ukraine and in Birobidzhan. The absence of Yiddish schools has restricted the development of a new generation of Yiddish writers, and few remain. The publication of translations from Yiddish literature into Russian and other languages is the only way these works can reach the younger Jews, who do not speak Yiddish.

Yiddish literature in the 1960s and 1970s revolved round two main themes: the Jewish and the general Soviet ways of life, glorifying the achievements of the regime; or recalling the pre-Revolutionary past (particularly in the novels of Nathan Zabara and Eli Shekhtman and the period of the Holocaust. As the Israeli critic Shmeruk notes, 'these works are neither innovating nor searching nor combatant. They do not seek new stylistic or artistic expression, nor have they anything new to say'.[173]

As for the Yiddish press, so rich and extensive in the 1920s and 1930s, and even in the 1940s, there is today only Vergelis' *Sovietish heimland*, and the daily paper, *Birobidzhaner shtern*, which began to appear at the end of the 1960s in 12,000 copies, a low-level sheet concerning itself very little with Jewish themes. In comparison with other extra-territorial national minorities, such as the Germans, whose population was similar in number to the Jews, or the Poles or Hungarians with smaller populations, the Yiddish press is inferior: since 1957 the Germans have had a weekly paper, published in Moscow, a daily paper appearing in Kazakhstan, a newspaper appearing in the Russian Republic and a literary-social annual appearing in Moscow. In 1960 there were six Polish and five Hungarian papers, and in 1967 four Polish and six Hungarian. Between 1946 to 1956, 2,417 German books were published, 1,287 Polish and 719 Hungarian.[174] Even if we take into account that these books were intended not only for Soviet Germans, Poles and Hungarians but also for these nationalities outside the Soviet Union, the figures are revealing, emphasizing as they do the difference between the official attitude to the Jews and to the other national minorities in the same category.

Besides the official policy towards Jews, the revival and development of Jewish culture has been hampered by the absence of a central Jewish body, like the Evsektsia of the 1920s and the Jewish Anti-Fascist Committee of the 1940s, which, even within the narrow limits set by the Soviet regime, were able to make use of rights granted to national minorities. Vergelis and the 'Anti-Zionist Committee' for all their pretensions have no representative status and are simply tools used by the government for propaganda for the outside world.

The best Jewish writers and poets in the Soviet Union, who had written on Jewish themes during and after the war, in Russian or Ukrainian, such as Antokolsky, Aliger, Svetlov, Khelemsky and Golovanivsky, neglected these subjects in the post-Stalin period and returned to general themes. The exceptions were Vasily Grossman, Ilya Erenburg and Boris Gorbatov, and they have been joined by younger writers.

Life in the Pale of Settlement was described in a story published in 1961 in a collection of Y. Taif's stories for children.[175] The autobiographical work by A. Burshtein, *Spring*, recalls the 'Dreyfus affair' and the deeds of Jewish revolutionaries.[176] Another well-known children's writer, Sh. Marshak, also reverts to the 'Dreyfus affair', and describes his experiences in his grandfather's home, and learning Hebrew.[177] Erenburg's memoirs constitute one of the most vital testimonies that have appeared in recent years on the Jewish question in the Soviet Union, and are partly devoted to Jewish life in Moscow and Kiev in tsarist Russia.[178] A book that spans the life of Russian Jewry is the novel, *The Tsimbalists*, by David Halkin.[179] In his novel, *Aleksei Gaidash*, published in 1955, Gorbatov described a simple Jewish shop assistant named Yuri Dimshits, who resembled the good soldier Schweik. He enlists in the army, is shaken by this change in his life but finally comes through his ordeal with honours. The author criticizes the Jewish religion 'which supports the Brodskys and the Rothschilds', and argues that in the Soviet Union there is no need to hide the fact that you are Jewish, and that you can get any job, but this novel marks an improvement in the treatment of Jewish themes. In 1978 another book on a Jewish theme came from the Jewish author Anatoli Rybakov (Aharonov), *Heavy Sand*, describing the life of the Jews in Belorussia and the Ukraine from the beginning of the century until the Second World War.[180]

Very few works by Soviet Jewish writers deal with the Holocaust. People were afraid to write about this, since such works were either not published or caused their authors endless difficulties. An example is Vasily Grossman's *Life and Fate*, which was never published in the Soviet Union, despite all the author's efforts, and has only recently been published abroad. Among the few works on the Holocaust that were published was the poem by A. Selvinsky, 'Judgment Day', written in symbolic language.[181] Two other poems on the Holocaust were those of Semion Lipkin, 'Tien Shan', and Boris Slutsky, 'How they murdered my grandmother'.[182] (Lipkin also published a Jewish-national poem on his bond with the State of Israel, 'The letter "I"'). 'Children in Auschwitz' was the title of a moving poem by Naum Korzhavin,[183] and a book by Yitzhak Meras, *Stalemate with Death*, published in Lithuanian in 1963 and in Russian in 1966, made an immediate impact. The story of Jewish resistance fighters against the Nazis was described in a novel by the Jewish–Ukrainian poet, Leonid Pervomaisky, who raised the question of the attitude of the authorities to the Jews during the war; he recounted the heroism of a Jewish soldier, Shreibman, who destroyed a German tank, but the decoration for bravery was given to someone else after his death, on the assumption, says the author, that 'the dead have no need of fame'.[184]

Erenburg's story, *The Thaw*, was about Jewish life in the Soviet Union after the Second World War and dealt *inter alia* with the 'Doctors' Plot'. An interesting book by Lev Sheinin, *Wolves in the Forest*, described a profiteer and confidence trickster, who changed his (Jewish) name of Bokor to Bukashvili (a Georgian name), then to Bokashian (an Armenian name) and finally to Bukov (a Russian name) according to his sphere of operations – at times it is better to be a Jew than a German and sometimes vice-versa.[185]

No doubt many books on Jewish themes by authors of Jewish origin which could not appear in official publication were passed from hand to hand after the war in restricted circles. Some were published in part in the *Samizdat* anthology, *Collected Poems on Jewish Themes*, by well-known poets like Slutsky, Imber, Marshak and Emmanuel Kazakevich. Younger poets whose works came out in *Samizdat* were N. Korzhavin, already mentioned, Y. Brodsky and A. Galich.[186] From the point of view of Jewish themes, a special place is held by Pasternak's *Dr Zhivago*, where the author devotes many pages to reflections on the question of Jewry and Christianity, the reasons for anti-Semitism and ways to overcome it.[187] Vasily Grossman,

whom we have already referred to, published material on Jewish
themes in *Samizdat,* and Yuli Daniel (son of the Yiddish writer Meiro-
vich) in his book, *This is Moscow Calling,* has a Jewish character, Margolis, who declares that if the day of 'open murders' comes and there
are pogroms, he will fight – 'Another Babi Yar there will not be!'[188]

Among Georgian Jewish writers and poets in the post-Stalin period
who published their works mainly in *Samizdat* are Ḥaim Iashvili, who
combated assimilation and fought to preserve Jewish national culture, Avraham Mamistvalov and Georgi Kuboshvili.[189]

An average of one or two books a year are published in the Tati
language. A 'Mountain Jew' writer of this period, Khizgil Avshalu-
mov, described events in the Second World War. Various Tati authors collaborated in the literary yearbook in Tat, *Svetinu* (Our
Motherland). The works are written in Russian and translated into
Tat, which is of course one more sign of the high degree of assimilation among the Jewish intelligentsia. No books have been published
in the Bukharan language since 1940. Bukharan writers and poets
today can only publish their works in Tadzhik and Uzbek.

The arts

After a break of a number of years, a reading of the works of Shalom
Aleikhem in Yiddish and Russian by the actor Yitzḥak Rakitin, the
first performance of its kind, was held in Tashkent in February 1955.
In Moscow in August of that year Shaul Lyubimov and Sidi Tal
began to appear in concerts of Yiddish songs. In 1956 in Vilna and
Dvinsk, the first amateur theatrical troupes came together after a
break of six years: four such troupes were formed in 1957 – in Tallin,
Lvov, Tashkent and Leningrad. A total of 20 groups were created in
the decade from 1956 to 1967, 10 professional, 6 amateur, 3 choirs
and one ballet group. Some of these only lasted a short time and
others went through various changes of their members, home towns
and so on. The most important were the drama group of Benyamin
Shvartser in Moscow, established in 1962, the Birobidzhan theatre,
established in 1967, and the 'Jewish People's Theatre' in Vilnius,
established in 1960. From 1968 to 1978 the following theatres were
established: the 'Jewish People's Theatre' in Kishinev (the Sidi Tal
troupe), managed by Reuven Levin (died 1972), which was reorga-
nized in 1976; the Theatre Circle in Kiev, which apparently lasted
only a short while; and the crowning glory – the Jewish Musical

Chamber Theatre in Birobidzhan, set up on 10 November 1978 under the direction of Y. Sherling, with forty-five professional singers and dancers, many of them non-Jews.[190] From time to time Soviet sources publish information about the number of spectators at Jewish theatrical performances; for example, the Vilnius Jewish theatre was said to have put on 450 shows for 500,000 spectators.[191] The official figures are exaggerated, but many Jews do stream to these performances, including young people who do not know Yiddish.

The repertoire of the Jewish theatres in this period differs little from that of the late 1940s: shortened versions of plays by Shalom Aleikhem (*Tuvia the Milkman, Wandering Stars, Two hundred thousand, The Tragic Practical Joke, People*); Goldfaden's *The Witch, Herschele Ostropoler* and *The Wise Men of Helm* by Gershenzon; stage versions of Jewish folk tales (*Happy Beggars, Holiday Greetings,* and *In an Unlucky Hour by Saktsier*). *Green Fields* by Perets Hirshbein was a novelty, and so were *Boytre* and *People are Good* by Moshe Kolbak. The Birobidzhan Musical Chamber Theatre put on a ballet, 'The Man Saved from the Ghetto', to music by Arnold Schoenberg. The Vilnius Theatre put on a play about the Holocaust by Hirsch Kanovich, *The Day of the Police*. Among translated plays, Lermontov's *Spaniards* shows sympathy with the Jews.

As far as is known, the professional level of most of the theatrical troupes is fairly low and there are few professional actors among them. At times the authorities' aim is propaganda and they instruct a group to put on something representing Jewish cultural life in the Soviet Union – the performance itself being living proof of its existence; but from the viewpoint of their national value, the theatres are more important as meeting places where Jews come together and know that Jewish culture is supposed to be there.

Among non-Ashkenazi Jews, only the 'Mountain Jews' finally succeeded in establishing a choir in the city of Nalchik; it started in 1959, was closed down in 1966, but revived in 1967.

Plays on Jewish themes are staged from time to time in Russian, Ukrainian and Belorussian theatres and in other languages; they are plays such as *The Diary of Anne Frank, The Life of Janusz Korczak, The Kiev Dossier* by Vadim Sobko (on the subject of Babi Yar), *The Time of the Tailors* by Bauman, and *Uriel Acosta* by Karl Gutzkow.[192]

A number of attempts to produce films based on Jewish national material have failed because of determined opposition from the authorities. The Jewish film producer, Leonid Trauberg, wanted to make a film of Shalom Aleichem's *Tuvia the Milkman*, and another producer, Mikhail Kalik, wanted to do Shalom Aleikhem's *Wandering Stars* and Yitzhak Meras' *Stalemate with Death*, to which we have already referred – but without success.[193]

On the other hand, as we have shown when discussing the anti-Zionist campaign, the authorities had propaganda films made on Jewish themes such as, *In the family of friendly peoples*, *Merchants of Souls* and *Birobidzhan 1970*.

Soviet Germans have had their own radio stations since the 1960s in every republic where they are numerous (Kazakhstan, Kirgistan and the Russian Republic), broadcasting a variety of programmes of talks and music for hundreds of hours each month. There has, however, been no revival of the Yiddish broadcasts that existed until 1949. Since 1956 a few Yiddish broadcasts have been made over the general Soviet radio and television services, mainly programmes of singers and groups with a repertoire of folk-songs and songs by Jewish poets. Political propaganda broadcasts in Hebrew for overseas listeners are given over Moscow radio's 'Peace and Progress' programme.

Jewish music is represented by the composer Moshe Veinberg (a relative of Shlomo Mikhoels), who composed his sixth Symphony with a boys' choir (in 1963) and his eighth to the words of the Polish Jewish poet, Julian Tuwim. Music for Jewish folk-songs and stories is still being composed by Z. Kompanieets, R. Boyarskaya, L. Kogan and M. Beregovsky, and in 1976 a record was issued of Vergelis' poems set to music by S. Shebstarov.

Few works by Jewish painters on Jewish themes have been exhibited in the Soviet Union. Among such events were exhibitions, held in Moscow and Leningrad in 1959 and 1960, of the works of L. Krivitsky, Y. Hanun and M. Klainsky. Painters like I. Gladsky and S. Rubashkin held exhibitions in private homes. Tanhum Kaplan painted illustrations for the works of Shalom Aleikhem, some of which have been published in the Soviet Union.[194] Works of the following outstanding Jewish painters and sculptors have been shown in general exhibitions: Z. Azgur, Y. Itkind, M. Zhitnitsky, Z. Tolkachev, A. Tyshler, E. Neizvestny, R. Falk, V. Tsigal, B. Kratko and P. Shabtai. Jewish painters depicted scenes from small Jewish towns and the old Jewish way of life; they painted Jewish figures such as Shalom Aleikhem, Mendele, Mikhoels, and the Jewish sculptors made statues of them. They depicted the Holocaust, the death camps, Jewish heroism, and Jewish life after the war.

Academic institutes and Jewish history

All Jewish research institutions were abolished at the end of the 1940s, but in the post-Stalin period, when the main fight was waged for the revival of cultural and artistic activity, there was no demand to found institutes for research into the history of the Jewish people. There was no discrimination against the Jews in this matter – the other extra-territorial minorities had lost their research institutions in the 1930s. In the Soviet Union today, research on Jewish subjects can be undertaken only by individual researchers in the universities, the official research institutes and the Oriental Department of the Soviet Academy of Sciences.

The fields of research in Jewish subjects are: the Hebrew language as part of the study of the Semitic languages; the Bible and Jewish religion; history of the Jews and Palestine. Since the 1950s, the non-Jewish professors G. Sharbatov and K. Starkova, and the Jewish professors, B. Grande, Y. Vinikov, A. Rubinstein and Y. Amusin have been working in the field of Hebrew studies. The emphasis in their studies is on the Hebrew of the Bible and the Middle Ages, but they also study modern Hebrew from the point of view of development of the language through 3,000 years of Jewish history. In 1964, the study of Semitic languages, including Hebrew, was discussed at length by the Soviet Academy of Sciences.[195] Research in Hebrew is also carried out at Tiflis University. Boris Gaponov worked for many years on translations from Georgian into Hebrew. P. Shapiro's Hebrew–Russian dictionary, which has already been mentioned, is very important; it was published in 1963, after many years' work.

In the 1950s the following researchers concerned themselves with biblical studies, despite the government's fight against religion: Y. Kryvelev, M. Altshuler, M. Belenky, M. Krutik, G. Livshits, and M. Shakhnovich. Y. Amusin has published two books on the period of ancient Jewish history concerned with the Dead Sea manuscripts. A. Varshavsky brought out a popular book on the same subject, and K. Kovalov and M. Kublanov published a book about the discovery of the manuscripts. G. Livshits devoted years of study to the class struggle in Judea and the revolts against the Romans, and his book was published in 1957; he also wrote a book on the Kumran manuscripts. The complete Kumran texts were published by Amusin in 1971. Three non-Jewish researchers concerned themselves with the history of the Khazars and its Jewish aspects: M. Artamonov (his book was published in 1962), L. Gumilov (1966) and S. Pletneva (1976). Articles on ancient history and on the Middle Ages appeared in *Palestinsky sbornik* (Palestinian Collection), which is published in Leningrad.

There has been no research at all on modern Jewish history, judging from the publications from the 1950s to the 1970s. There was, however, a collection of eighteenth- and nineteenth-century Jewish writings in Georgia, published by Babalikashvili in 1971, and a book by Panavas on the fight of the Bolsheviks against the *Bund* (1972).

The policy of silencing any description of the Holocaust and of Jewish resistance continued after Stalin's death. Then, after 1955, books began to be published in the Soviet Union, giving testimonies and accounts of events during the Second World War and sometimes including a few lines or pages of reports and memoirs on the Holocaust and Jewish heroism. The publication in 1960 of the *Diary of Anne Frank*, with an introduction by Ilya Erenburg, was especially significant. In 1963, the diary of a Jewish girl of the Vilnius Ghetto Masha Rolnikaite was also published. Much war material was published in the Soviet press, with occasional references to the Holocaust and to Jewish resistance. The capture of Eichmann, and his trial in Jerusalem, also highlighted the destruction of European Jewry and the need to set up a memorial to the Jewish victims.[200] As well as propaganda against the State of Israel of the type written by Evseev, Korneev and Begun, a few books with a more scientific basis did appear, although they too were strongly anti-Zionist. Two similar books, both called *The State of Israel*, appeared, one was written by K. Ivanov and Z. Sheinis, 150,000 copies of which appeared in 1958 and 1959, and the other by G. Nikitina, published in 1968 by the Institute for Asian Peoples of the Soviet Academy of Sciences.

When there are no Jewish schools, no research institutes and no books on Jewish history, where can Jewish students learn the story of their people, including the history of the Soviet Jews? It might be thought that an important source would be books of general history and of Russian history in the schools, but, as we shall show, accurate references to the history of Israel in these books are few.[201]

In text-books available between 1940 and 1953, there were short sections of two or three pages on the Kingdom of Israel and Judea. From 1954 to the present day there has been nothing at all in the text-books by S. Kovalov and P. Korovkin on the ancient history of Israel. Moreover, even the name 'Israel' has disappeared and in its place the authors prefer to use 'Palestine'. In the book by Mishulin (in use from 1940 to 1953) the word 'Jew' appears eighteen times, in Kovalov and Korovkin's book it appears only once. In the history of the Middle Ages by A. Agibalova and D. Donskoi, published in 1977 and intended for the sixth class there is no trace of Jews, and no mention of the persecution by the Inquisition. The Jews have disappeared almost completely from text-books on Russian and Soviet history – there is no mention of anti-Semitism in tsarist Russia, pogroms, or the Beiliss trial. Since the early 1970s there has been a new trend towards mentioning Jewish themes in a few restricted instances in the worst possible connotation, such as the opportunism and nationalism of the *Bund* Party which opposed Lenin and the revolutionary forces. When the text-books deal with the Second World War and the Fascist regimes in Europe, there is no mention of their anti-Semitism or of the extermination of European Jewry.

Young Jews who want to learn their past history have to turn to the libraries of Moscow, Leningrad, Kiev and Riga, for books published before the Revolution and in the 1920s, or else to turn to the Jewish *Samizdat*; but few manage to find this material and their past either remains unknown, or is brought to them in a distorted form in anti-Zionist propaganda publications.

RELIGION

As a unifying force which has not yet been completely Sovietized, religion is essential to Jewish national survival, both because of its content and because of the Hebrew language of its observances. It is the last barrier to the final absorption of the Jews into the Soviet Union.

Under Khrushchev, the Soviet leadership's attitude to religion in general and the Jewish religion in particular was complex and underwent numerous changes between 1954 and 1964. First, in contrast to the relative liberalization pursued in certain spheres, the policy on religion was to restrict the few rights that had been reluctantly granted during the war. Second, anti-religious propaganda was revived, after being in abeyance in the previous period. Third, anti-religious periodicals were again issued, as in the 1920s and 1930s.

1954 to 1958

Resolutions adopted by the Central Committee on 7 July 1954[202] were supposed to inaugurate a propaganda campaign against reli-

gion, and the communications media at once began the task. A few
months later, however, on 10 November,[203] another Central Committee Resolution was made public, criticizing writers in the Press
and lecturers dealing with religion for overdoing their unjustified
attacks on the clergy. This resolution did not of course stop the anti-
religious propaganda, but thereafter the campaign was conducted in
lukewarm fashion. The change in the general atmosphere in the
country gave the Jewish religious leaders the courage to stand up for
their legal rights; for example, the head of the Leningrad Jewish
congregation complained of illegal police interference in synagogue
activities. In May 1957 there was another change, this time towards
intensifying anti-religious propaganda.[204] The first and most striking
manifestation of this policy was the holding of a seminar for anti-
religious propaganda, when the Jewish religion was attacked with
special vehemence by a Jewish member of the Academy of Sciences,
Mitin, who had attacked Zionism under Stalin. Action against religion in general and against Jewish religion in particular revived in
1958, when for the first time after a break of several years eleven
books of propaganda against Judaism appeared.

Nevertheless, this was one of the least difficult periods for the maintenance of Jewish religious life in the Soviet Union. First, contacts
were renewed with world Jewry. Rabbi Shlifer of the Great Synagogue in Moscow, who began to be seen as the Chief Rabbi of Soviet
Jewry, although there is no such post, sent New Year greetings and
good wishes to the Jews in England (in 1953); invited the Chief
Rabbi of Israel to visit the Soviet Union in 1954; and sent his blessing
to a rabbinical convention in Israel.[205] In 1956, after an interval of
many years, a delegation of Rabbis from the USA, headed by Rabbi
David Hollander, visited Moscow, Leningrad, Kiev, Odessa and
Georgia. Rabbi Shlifer accompanied the delegation, which was welcomed with great emotion by thousands of worshippers. These Rabbis even met Khrushchev and spoke to him about the position of the
Jwish religion.[206] Rabbi Shlifer even wrote to the President of the
World Jewish Congress, Naḥum Goldmann, on the need to create
links between Soviet Jewry and the Jewish community in the
world;[207] but it seems that, under pressure from the authorities,
Rabbi Shlifer had to announce that there had been some misunder-
standing in this matter.[208] In 1956 the Rabbis of 'Agudat Yisrael'
and 'Ha-poel Ha-mizraḥi' were invited to visit the Soviet Union,[209]
and the climax of this renewal of international contacts was Rabbi

Shlifer's visit to Paris in that year to be present at the unveiling of a monument to the six million victims of the Holocaust.[210] Rabbi Shlifer's appearance in this delegation, which also included the Jewish General David Dragunsky, and his speech in Hebrew on the need for world peace, created a tremendous impression. To some extent it was reminiscent of the visit of Shlomo Mikhoels and Yitsik Fefer, of the Jewish Anti-Fascist Committee, to the USA and other countries in 1943.

Second, it was in this period that an event of the greatest importance for the practice of the Jewish religion in the Soviet Union took place: the establishment on 6 January 1957 of the *Yeshivah* 'Kol Yaakov' attached to the Great Synagogue in Moscow. News that a *Yeshivah* would be opened had already reached the West in 1955; the story was spread abroad in 1956 and this apparently prompted the Soviet authorities to permit its establishment.[211] This was the first time since the establishment of the Soviet regime that permission was granted for the creation of a Jewish theological institution to prepare Rabbis. When the *Yeshivah* opened, ten students enrolled; in 1958–9 their number rose to 15 (6 from Georgia, 5 from Moscow, 2 from Tashkent, 1 from Minsk and 1 from Dnepropetrovsk), aged between 20 and 54 years of age. Study in the *Yeshivah* took place for eight hours a day, four of them to be devoted to prayer. The condition for admission to the *Yeshivah* was the presentation to the Yeshivah Secretary of proof of a sufficient knowledge of Talmud, Torah, the Prophets and the *Shulḥan Arukh*. Naturally the authorities had complete control over the authorization of living quarters in Moscow for pupils from outside the city and in general over how many pupils should be admitted and who they should be. For the first period, eight teachers taught in the *Yeshivah*, three of them Rabbis – Shimon Trebnik, Ḥaim Katz and Yaakov Kalmanzon. The money to run the *Yeshivah* came from donations, like the upkeep of the synagogues.[212]

Third, in 1956 Rabbi Shlifer published a 'Peace Prayerbook' of photogravures of pages from old prayer-books and festival prayers. A number of emendations were inserted and a 'Prayer for Peace' was added. 30,000 copies of this prayer-book were printed. In 1957 it was announced that a new prayer-book would be printed in Leningrad, according to the Ḥassidic tradition, but it never appeared.[213]

Fourth, although there is no central representative body of religious Jewry for the whole Soviet Union, as is customary in other religions, Rabbi Shlifer, until his death on 31 March 1957, and

Rabbi Levin after him were recognized as Chief Rabbis of Soviet Jewry. This could be seen not only in formal ceremonies but also in their influence on the elections of rabbis and synagogue secretaries in cities outside Moscow and in their settlement of disputes between the 'group of 20' synagogue founding members and the management of the synagogue (disputes that were often instigated by the authorities, to give them an excuse to intervene).

Finally, the Rabbis were involved in public-political life almost as they had been under Stalin. From time to time they were called on to sign political declarations with which they did not always agree.[214] It is interesting that the March 1955 appeal against atomic warfare was addressed to world Jewry, that is to say, to an entity whose very existence was denied in the Soviet Union. Among those who signed the declaration condemning 'Anglo-French-Israeli aggression' in 1956 were Rabbis and secretaries of Georgian and Bukharan synagogues, that is to say, those living nearest to the Moslem and Oriental peoples of the Soviet Union.

However, this partially favourable attitude to the needs of religious Jews did not last long. The first signs of change were perceptible in 1957 and 1958. The reasons for the reversal will perhaps be more readily understood once we have examined the measures that were taken, in spite of the leadership's desire to improve relations with the West, where supposed 'Jewish influence' entered into its calculations.

1959 to 1964

In contrast to the preceding period, this was one of the worst periods for the Jewish religion in the Soviet Union. In every sphere connected with the survival of the Jewish religion, there was a determination to restrict Jewish religious observance to a minimum: there was an unprecedentedly violent and large-scale propaganda campaign, mass closure of synagogues, confiscation of Jewish cemeteries, harassment over circumcision and even over the baking of unleavened bread for the Passover.

THE ANTI-RELIGIOUS CAMPAIGN

The Resolution adopted by the Communist Party Central Committee in November 1958 to launch a concentrated and properly organized campaign against religion gave the signal for the communications' media to attack the clergy for breaches of Soviet law in religious matters, for their harmful influence in society and in some instances for subversive activity against the State.[215] The most violent and vicious attacks were directed against the Jewish religion. The number of articles written on these lines increased from year to year: 40 in 1960; 73 in 1961; 72 in 1962; 57 in 1963; 72 in 1964.[216] If we compare these figures with the total of anti-religious articles published – 460 in 1960; 345 in 1961; 447 in 1962; 439 in 1963; 429 in 1964,[217] we find that between 15 and 20% of all the anti-religious articles in the Soviet Press were directed at the Jewish religion and not at the main religions in the country – Provoslav, Moslem and Catholic. We have no data on the number of radio and television programmes directed at the Jewish religion, but to judge by those recorded in the West they were more virulent than the articles in the Press.

Special seminars were organized in this period for propagandists in the anti-religious campaign. Characteristically, the attack on Jewish religion always heralded an additional attack on bourgeois nationalism or Zionism. Moreover, there were special seminars for propagandists dealing exclusively with the Jewish religion.[218] In this period, fifty-four books were published against the Jewish religion in Russian alone. The editions of these works reached 100,000 copies, an enormous number even on the Soviet scale. Trofim Kichko's work, *Judaism Unmasked*, published by the Ukrainian Academy of Sciences in 1963, received worldwide publicity and evoked sharp reactions in the West and even in some Western Communist Parties. It was no different in structure and content from other works of the kind, but the lavish illustration of the book in the *Stuermer* style, and its publication under the highest scientific imprimatur in the Soviet Union went too far. The storm that blew up over this book forced the Soviet Communist Party leadership to criticize it, but the criticism was lukewarm and referred only to 'a number of inaccuracies' and mistakes that made it possible to interpret certain passages as anti-Semitic in spirit.[219] The author's collaboration with the Nazis during the war and consequent expulsion from the Communist Party was not mentioned.[220]

The media attacks described the Jewish religion as reactionary, teaching its followers to live on other people's money and by unethical practices, since the commandments not to commit crimes referred only to crimes against Jews. The Jewish religion was a creed of 'the chosen people', similar in every way to the Nazi doctrine of the superior race. It was also hostile to the Soviet Union and a tool of imperialism. The rabbis always collaborated with reactionary forces and fomented Jewish nationalism.

SYNAGOGUES CLOSED

Before we can calculate how many synagogues were closed down in this period, we must first clarify the definition of a synagogue, how one can be established and how it can be closed down under Soviet law. According to the various relevant Soviet laws of the years 1918 to 1929, with only slight changes in the new law in force since 1975, every citizen who reaches the age of 18 is permitted to join with other worshippers for the satisfaction of his religious needs. Religious 'leagues' are established according to the number of worshippers – they may be 'leagues' if the number is not less than twenty, or only a 'group' if less than that. Worshippers who have formed a league submit a request to the regional or municipal Executive Committee of the Soviet for permission to open a house of prayer; this Committee does not make decisions, but notes its opinion and sends the request to the Executive Committee of the next level, until it reaches the Council of Ministers of the Autonomous Republic or Soviet Republic. These bodies contact the Soviet Government's Council for Religious Affairs, which decides whether to grant the desired permission.[221] Thus from the very outset the worshippers find administrative barriers in their path before they even get a permit to establish a house of prayer. Other obstacles they face are the need to find a place available for the purpose of establishing a house of prayer and the need to obtain permits from the health authorities, the police, etc.

The Jewish prayer houses in the Soviet Union can be put into three categories: (1) a synagogue built specially for the purpose; (2) a small prayer house, generally in a private home; (3) a temporary prayer group (*minyan*) meeting in a private home, sometimes functioning with the knowledge of the authorities but in danger of severe penalties for a breach of the law.

Official Soviet statements on the number of synagogues in the Soviet Union are confusing, sometimes intentionally so, the data referring at one moment to fixed synagogues (in the first category) and at the next to mere *minyans*.

In 1926, 1,103 synagogues were still open in the Soviet Union, in 1945, 500 and in 1954 only a hundred or so,[222] the figure given by Rabbi Shlifer. If this figure is accurate, it indicates that immediately after this, from 1954 to 1958, there was a big increase in the number of synagogues, since according to the Soviet Union's report presented to the United Nations there were 450 synagogues in 1959,[223] but according to a different Soviet source there were only 150 in 1960.[224] This last figure seems to be nearer the truth, and will serve as a basis for comparison with the figures for the years 1961 to 1965. In January 1964 Moscow radio stated that 150 synagogues were functioning in the Soviet Union, half of them in the Ukraine and Moldavia; but in the same year an official spokesman, Dogorozhny, who had been Deputy Chairman of the Soviet Council for Religious Affairs, stated that there were 100 synagogues.[225] The data published for 1963 and 1964 were 96 and 97 synagogues,[226] but other estimates in these years put the number somewhere between 60 and 70 (19 of them in the Caucasus, 5 in the Baltic Republics, 13 in the Asian Republics, 17 in the Russian Republic, 3 in Belorussia and 2 in Moldavia).[227] Even if we take the official figures, we find that more than fifty synagogues closed down between 1958 and 1965.

High-ranking official Soviet spokesmen, such as the Deputy Prime Minister of the Soviet Union Kozlov or the Soviet representatives at the UN, firmly deny that anything is done to restrict the number of synagogues in the Soviet Union.[228] Synagogues – like churches, mosques and all other houses of prayer – can be closed down under Soviet law if the religious league dwindles away; if there has been a breach of the laws dealing with religious affairs, failure to observe the conditions of the contract, refusal to carry out legal instructions from government bodies; if the prayer house obstructs urban building plans; or if the site is needed for public purposes. This last clause was the one most frequently invoked when closing down synagogues.

The way the ground is prepared for closing down a synagogue is reminiscent of the 1920s. The first phase is a campaign in the local press and in lectures at work-places against the illegal and criminal activities of the heads of the synagogue, who are said to be carrying out black market deals on the premises or spreading Zionist propaganda. In the second phase, 'Letters to the Editor' from 'all ranks of the public' appear in the newspapers, some of them from former worshippers and heads of synagogues, calling for these 'nests of corruption' to be wiped out and the community cleansed of 'the abomination of religion'. Finally, the authorities 'respond' to these appeals from 'the public' and close down the prayer house. Furthermore, during the preparatory propaganda period, the police arrest some of the '20' and the synagogue heads on accusations of abusing their posts, doing illegal business, or plotting with representatives of capitalist countries (= tourists and members of the Israeli Embassy staff). A less elaborate system of intimidation is for the authorities to make frequent changes in the management of the synagogue (the head of the congregation and his deputy, the synagogue Secretary and other office-holders) while the police force their way into homes where there are *minyans*.

Although the Kol Yaakov *Yeshivah* was not closed, the number of pupils dropped to four in 1963 – students from outside Moscow were not given permits to live in the city.[229]

We do not have full data on the closing down of prayer houses of other religions for comparison, but from partial data it emerges that in the Ukraine alone from 1959 to 1964 about 10,000 Orthodox churches and about 800 Baptist churches were closed down,[230] sufficient evidence that under Khrushchev a harsh anti-religious policy was pursued, to reduce the influence of religion to a minimum.

RELIGIOUS OBSERVANCE

The difficult situation of Jewish religion in the period under review was also shown by the obstacles placed in the way of those wishing to carry out the prescribed religious observances.

The Soviet authorities were particularly against the baking of unleavened bread for the Passover (*mazot*) in the synagogues. From 1957, it was forbidden in the cities of Kharkov, Odessa, Kiev, Rostov, Kishinev and Riga, and from 1961 the ban was extended to the whole of the Soviet Union.[231] In 1962 a veto was declared and many Jews were forced to bake *mazot* secretly. If they were discovered, they were accused of illegal trading and given heavy sentences.[232] The despatch of *mazot* from abroad (mainly from Israel, the USA and England) also met with difficulties: people receiving packets were forced to return them and even to write letters protesting against these 'acts of provocation'.[233] As a result of world-wide protests, however, in 1964 the authorities decided to allow religious congregations in Moscow, Leningrad and Tiflis to bake *mazot* again.[234] According to Soviet Jews closely associated with the Great Synagogue in Moscow, in this city alone about 80 tons of *mazot* are baked every year, that is to say, supplies for about 25,000 to 30,000 persons, or 10% of the Jews in Moscow. There are also difficulties in obtaining the palms and citrus (*lulav* and *ethrog*) needed for the Feast of Tabernacles, and these are generally sent from Israel and the USA.

A more serious problem is the systematic destruction of Jewish cemeteries by local authorities, on the grounds that the area is needed for public use; the Jewish communities are not given other land instead. The Jewish cemetery in Moscow was confiscated in this way in 1963. There is also widespread vandalism – the smashing of grave-stones by hooligans – and little evidence that the police try to stop it.[235]

Police, administrative and propaganda measures are also taken against the practice of circumcision – the existence of this ceremony is apparently taken as a direct challenge to the official policy of absorption. The few people who still perform circumcisions in the Soviet Union do so at the risk of their lives. It is also difficult, though not forbidden, to celebrate *Bar Mizvah* and *Bat Mizvah*, and it is practically impossible for youngsters to prepare themselves since there is a legal prohibition on the teaching of religion to a person under eighteen.

There are no authoritative data on the number of worshippers in the synagogues on the Sabbath and on holidays in this period, but from the descriptions that have appeared in the Western Press it seems that a very limited number take part in prayers on the Sabbath eve and on the Sabbath and that they are mainly old people. Things are better in the synagogues of the non-Ashkenazi Jews, with their stronger tradition and close family ties. According to Rabbi Levin in 1965, a few hundred people took part in Sabbath prayers, and during the week there were between 100 to 150.[236] During periods of religious persecution, it is easier and less dangerous to hold *minyans* in private houses in the big cities. Since the early 1960s the synagogue has become a place of 'national assembly' for young Jews, very few of whom come there for religious reasons. Rejoicing in the Law (*Simhat Torah*) has become the most popular festival for them. In 1961 journalists estimated that 12,000 people came together in Leningrad,[237] and in Moscow in 1964 some 50,000 celebrated the festival.[238] The authorities attempted to interfere with these mass meetings, but without success.

WHY THE WAR ON RELIGION?
What were the reasons for the volte-face on religion after the relatively liberal policy pursued from 1948 to 1954? Why was the fight against all the religions from 1959 to 1964 so relentless?

First, what was described in official propaganda as the 'vestiges' of religion were not useless relics of the past, but had become live phenomena with increasing influence over Soviet young people and even over Communist Party members. To wipe out this plague, Khrushchev took an extreme line on the religious question, even while he was pursuing a relatively liberal policy in other spheres. This general assertion is, however, an insufficient answer, because it does not explain the difference in quantity and in violence between the general anti-religious propaganda and that directed against the Jewish religion.

Second, there were specific reasons for the anti-Jewish policy pursued under the cloak of the general anti-religious policy:

(1) In the second half of the 1950s, the synagogue had turned into the centre where Jews met legally, and this included many young people. These meetings fostered and manifested the awakening of the Jewish sense of identification, which was increasingly taking on nationalist forms and thereby seriously endangering the basic Soviet policy for the absorption of Soviet Jewry.

(2) The synagogue had also become the only fixed point where Soviet Jews could meet Jews from Israel and from the rest of the outside world (tourists, rabbinical delegations, Israeli Embassy people, etc.). The importance of these meetings to both sides was understood by the authorities, who used every possible means to limit them as much as possible, or at least to keep watch on them.

(3) In the eyes of the Soviet authorities, then, the synagogue had become a danger. It kept nationalism alive and reinforced loyalties or ideologies outside the Soviet Union.

(4) The decisive factor was the close link between the Jewish religion and Jewish nationality in its Zionist and Hebrew-language manifestations. Possibly the anti-Semitic tendencies of Khrushchev himself, and of others in the Soviet leadership, led to the use of the anti-religious weapon to persecute the Jews.

1965 to 1967

The basic anti-Jewish policy did not change after Khrushchev's deposition, but in the transition period there were some improvements in the situation. Whether it was the desire to change the image of the Soviet Union in the eyes of the world or the result of external pressures, the new leadership relaxed the propaganda campaign against the Jewish religion and abolished some of its measures.

The number of articles in the press dealing with the Jewish religion – 72 in 1964 – dropped to 37 in 1965 and to 29 in 1966; but as a result of the Six-Day War and the breaking-off of relations between the Soviet Union and Israel, there was another steep rise in 1967. The tone changed, too – the attacks were less vehement and less coarse. Firstly, more 'scientific' articles were published and fewer of the notorious *feuilletons*, and personal attacks on religious personalities ceased. As many books against the Jewish religion were published as in the previous period, but they had a more 'scientific' and less controversial trend; examples are Yosef Kryvelev's, *The Book about the Bible*, and *Bible Stories* by the Polish author, Zenon Kossidovski.

The Jews were promised that the veto on baking *mazot* would be abolished and it did become easier to obtain *mazot* in many towns, although there was not enough to satisfy the demand.[239] Rabbi Levin announced that the Council for Religious Affairs had authorized the publication of a new prayerbook in three volumes, with 10,000 copies, but it did not appear and instead 3,000 copies of the old 1956 prayer book were printed.[240] The council also promised to allow an increase in the number of pupils in the Kol Yaakov *Yeshivah* by the admission of twenty new pupils from all over the Soviet Union; but this promise was not kept either, and since 1963 the *Yeshivah* has functioned in a very narrow framework.[241]

Finally, it is important to note that there has been no real improvement as regards Jewish cemeteries or circumcision, and even the few rights accorded in 1965 and 1966 were cancelled in 1967.

1968 to 1983

This period, from Brezhnev to Andropov, combined elements from the previous two periods – a worsening of the situation of Jewish religion and continued attacks on it on the one hand and gestures of goodwill directed towards the outside world on the other.

THE CAMPAIGN AGAINST THE JEWISH RELIGION

While the main anti-Jewish propaganda in this period was aimed at Zionism, the Jewish religion was not forgotten. The theme was the usual one: Zionist ideology is based on the reactionary Jewish religion, and the Zionist movement works in close cooperation with the Rabbis.

In 1968 Kichko (we have already referred to his *Judaism Unmasked*

of 1963) produced a new book, *Judaism and Zionism*. In 1969, three
books appeared on Jewish religion, among them *Contemporary Judaism
and Zionism*, by P. Mayatsky, another anti-Semite of the Khrushchev
era. Reacting to increased Zionist activity, Soviet anti-Zionist propaganda produced seven works on the Jewish religion in 1970. In 1970–1
there was a partial truce, connected perhaps with the government's
renewed attempt to organize rabbis, synagogue secretaries and other
synagogue workers for the fight against Zionism, as was done under
Stalin in 1952 and under Khrushchev from 1955 to 1957. Khrushchev
mobilized them for the campaign against atomic weapons and for the
condemnation of the Israeli Sinai operation. This time the round-up
was much more systematic and better organized, calling a 'Conference
of Representatives of the Rabbinate of the Jewish Religious Congregations in the Soviet Union'.[242] A special brochure on the conference was
published in Russian, English, French, German and Spanish. Tass
Agency noted: 'This conference was convened in order to give expression to the protest against the provocative actions of the international
Zionist organizations and against their defamatory statements about
the situation of the Jews in the Soviet Union'.[243] The most productive
years for Soviet anti-Jewish religious publications were 1973 and 1974:
seven in 1973 and nine in 1974. It is interesting that the word 'Zionism'
appears in the titles of these works, *Judaism in the service of Zionism*,
Prophetic Zionism, *A critique of the ideology of contemporary Judaism and
Zionism*, and so on. From 1975 to 1981 there was a drop in the number
of publications against the Jewish religion, except for 1980 when three
books appeared. In the other years there were only one or two, the
total number being eleven.

There was a substantial difference between the themes of these
books and those of the Khrushchev period. They include all the
general elements of the anti-religious campaign in the Soviet Union
with the addition of specific Jewish aspects such as the 'chosen'
people, racialism, collaboration with imperialist and reactionary
forces throughout history, the 'immorality' of Jewish religion, hatred
of the non-Jews, etc.

SYNAGOGUES, RABBIS AND HEADS OF RELIGIOUS
CONGREGATIONS

Official Soviet publications on the number of synagogues in the Soviet
Union in this period are as confusing as the previous ones, deliberately
mixing up synagogues, *minyans* and temporary prayer groups.

In 1967, according to official publications, there were 97 synagogues open, but as we have seen only 67 functioning synagogues were known in the West. In 1976 one publication stated that there were 92 registered synagogues, 80 of them in State-owned premises, as well as a number of *minyans*. Twenty of these 92 synagogues were in Georgia.[244] Another source stated that there were 180 synagogues in the Soviet Union as well as several *minyans*.[245] In 1980–1 one source speaks of 91 synagogues[246] and another gives 93.[247] As before, the confusion stems from the lack of a clear definition of a synagogue as a fixed place of worship as distinct from a religious congregation, or else from the desire to show how good the situation of the Jewish religion is in the Soviet Union. It would seem that the real number of synagogues decreased from 67 in 1965 to 60 in 1980 and about 50 in 1983.[248]

The question of the rabbis in the Soviet Union is equally complicated. The older generation of rabbis from the 1930s and 1950s has died out. The Kol Yaakov *Yeshivah* which was supposed to prepare the future rabbis, did not stand the test, and it was in fact closed from 1967 to 1971. It started up again in 1972 with between eight and twelve pupils but did not solve the problem of the serious lack of rabbis, since there were not even enough teachers to teach all the subjects in this *Yeshivah*. The Soviet authorities in charge of religious affairs came to the conclusion that if the pupils were not sent abroad to study, or if rabbis were not brought to the Soviet Union from abroad, there would soon not be a single rabbi in the whole of the Soviet Union, and they chose the first solution. Ten pupils went abroad in the 1970s to the Jewish religious seminary in Budapest: among them were Adolf Shaevich, today the Rabbi of the Moscow congregation; Menahem Ridel, today Rabbi in Riga; Isak Fuks, Yuri Kerzhnevich, Mikhael Polezhitkov and A. Nudel. Moreover, for the first time in the history of the Soviet Union, a Soviet citizen was given permission to study theology in a capitalist country: at the end of the 1970s two pupils went to Yeshivah University in New York to study for three years and serve as rabbis on their return home.

In the meantime, however, the position as regards rabbis got steadily worse, and of the forty properly qualified rabbis who still officiated in 1965 only five are left now (two Ashkenazis in Moscow and Riga and three non-Ashkenazis in Georgia and Uzbekistan) – five, not fifty as Soviet sources state. There are no exact data on how many rabbis there are altogether – apparently some thirty to thirty-five available for the fifty synagogues still open.

Official intervention in the internal affairs of the synagogues through the Council for Religious Affairs, both on the all-Soviet level and locally, has increased over the last decade. In addition to granting permits for everything, big and small, connected with the number of *Yeshivah* pupils, the quantity of *mazot* that may be baked, receiving religious works from abroad, publishing religious works and yearbooks in the Soviet Union, and so on, the authorities also interfere in appointing rabbis and heads of the congregations, although this is, according to Soviet law (including the new one of 1975), an internal affair for the worshippers alone. Thus, for example, the head of the Moscow Jewish congregation, Shalom Rosen, was dismissed in 1971 on the pretext that Ephraim Kaplan had been elected; but in fact it was probably because he authorized a ceremony in memory of the Warsaw Ghetto rising. In 1978 the head of the congregation, Shlomo Kleinman, was replaced by Yaakov Mikelberg, because he had wanted to take control of all religious affairs in Moscow and appear in the guise of 'spokesman for Russian Jewry'. In 1980 Mikelberg was replaced in his turn by Boris Groem,[249] Deputy Head of the Council for Religious Affairs. V. Kuroedov makes no secret of these interventions in his newspaper articles and in his book, published in 1981,[250] in which he stated that it was the Council for Religious Affairs that chose the Rabbi of the Great Synagogue in Moscow. According to him, religious personnel must not only be loyal to the Soviet State but must also actively defend its policies, internal and external – that is to say, defend its anti-religious policy, aimed at wiping out all the religious institutions in the Soviet Union.

Since the early 1970s some rabbis and other religious office-holders have been permitted to take part in conventions and delegations abroad, in the context of the policy of getting them to act for political purposes. In 1970 Rabbi Levin visited the Jewish community in Belgrade. In May 1976, Rabbis Fishman and Shaevich were members of the delegation of religious personnel from the Soviet Union that visited New York. In the same year, a delegation of Soviet rabbis took part in a convention of community leaders from Eastern Europe, held in Budapest. As against this, the request from heads of the Great Synagogue in Moscow to take part in the deliberations of the World Jewish Congress was rejected.

RELIGIOUS OBSERVANCE
How many Jews in the Soviet Union observe the prescriptions of Jewish religious law and believe in the Jewish religion? No official

Soviet body can answer these questions. From time to time, however, fragmentary data are published, based on surveys, researches and statistical material assembled by the Council for Religious Affairs, which may serve as indicators of the state of religious observance in the Soviet Union in the most recent period.

In Esthonia, a third of the population (450,000 people) are practising. In the Soviet Union the Lutherans are estimated at 300,000. In the Karakalpak Republic, with its Muslim population, only 20% of the women and 23% of the men were atheists in 1972. The number of Lithuanian Catholics is put at about two million, that is to say, the great majority of the Lithuanian population.[251] The Baptists are especially active in the Soviet Union and their number is put at half a million or more.[252] In the five districts of Moldavia, where a survey was held in 1974, 9.2% declared themselves active atheists, 39.9% said they were 'passive atheists' (that is, they do not take an active part in the anti-religious campaign), 13.8% inclined to non-belief, 7.5% inclined to belief, and 29.2% declared that they were practising. In 1979 there was another survey in the same districts, according to which the number practising had dropped to 25%. In Belorussia 15.4% of the urban and 26.8% of the rural populations are practising.[253] These partial data show that the ratio of religious persons in the Baltic Republics and Moldavia, which were annexed to the Soviet Union in 1939 and 1940, is relatively high, ranging from 10% to over 60%, and relatively lower in Belorussia, only part of which was annexed to the Soviet Union.

The situation of the Jewish population in the original Soviet regions (that is, without the Baltic Republics and Moldavia) is largely different, as its atheistic trends were already marked in the 1920s and 1930s. According to official Soviet publications, in the 1970s the number of observant Jews was somewhere between 50,000 and 60,000, that is to say 2.5 to 3% of the entire Jewish population and about 5% of the breadwinners. Surveys carried out in the Russian and Ukrainian Republics give from 3 to 6% of the Jewish population as observant, in the Baltic Republics 5 to 9%, in Moldavia from 7 to 8% and among the Jews of the Caucasus and inner Asia 7 to 12%.[254]

In a survey carried out among Jews in the Soviet Union by B. Fein and others, it is stated: 'Only 7% of those questioned defined themselves as religious; 53% said that though they were not observant Jews, they respected the religion; 17% displayed a definitely atheistic approach; ... 21% said they went to synagogue from time to time'.[255]

In a survey carried out by the Hebrew University in Jerusalem, among 2,080 Jewish immigrants from the Soviet Union, 8.3% answered that they were religious.[256] From the partial data recorded here, it appears that the ratio of religious Jews in the Soviet Union is somewhere between 5 and 7%, and it is doubtful whether the religious revival of recent years among Soviet Jews, including the younger generation, has changed this proportion significantly.

How many Jews came to pray on week-days, on the Sabbath and on religious holidays in the 1970s? On this too we have only partial data. In Novosibirsk with a Jewish population of 11,200, there would be from 100 to 200 Jews taking part in holiday prayers (that is, 1 to 2%); in Kuibyshev with 16,000 Jews – 150 to 400 (1 to 3%); in Leningrad with 160,000 Jews – 2,000 to 2,500 (less than 2%); in Kishinev 800 to 900 (3% of the adult population).[257] An Israeli visitor to the Soviet Union in August 1979 found only a few *minyans* in Moscow on weekdays; on the Sabbath there were about 350 men, mostly elderly. In Leningrad on the Sabbath there were about 100 and in Kiev about 80.[258] The picture was different on the High Holidays, especially at the New Year, the Rejoicing in the Law and Passover. Thus for example in 1981 in Moscow about 5,000 Jews came to the Passover services and there were about 20,000 at the Rejoicing in the Law.[259] Clearly, most of the people who come to synagogue on the High Holidays are not religious at all, but by this participation of theirs they are demonstrating their national sentiments, which have no other channel of expression in the Soviet Union.

In this period there was a shortage of prayer-books and religious accessories, though there was some improvement in this respect early in the 1980s, with the help of world Jewry (mainly the USA, Canada and Romania). The Moscow congregation continues to publish its yearbook in Yiddish and Russian, with the dates of the High Holidays and other Jewish religious material.

According to data from 1976, there are thirty-nine institutions that bake *mazot* and make candles. In Moscow in 1977 160 tons of *mazot* were baked and in 1978 170, and 75 tons each for Leningrad and Kiev and 30 tons each for Vilnius and Riga. A problem that has remained unsolved is the discouragement. *Bar Mizvah* celebration is still not easy to arrange in synagogues and is sometimes held in secret in the home.

The mass emigration from the Soviet Union covered a considerable percentage of religious Jews, which means that their number in the country will steadily decline. The disappearance of rabbis, slaughterers and circumcisers must mean a drastic reduction in religious observance, although the few synagogues that still remain will certainly continue to exist, because the government wants them to do so for propaganda purposes.

NATIONAL IDENTITY: THE NATIONAL MOVEMENT AND CONNECTIONS ABROAD

The term 'national identity', in use in research on nationality and in publicistic writing, is so vague that it produces misunderstandings. In research on nationality problems this is, however, too useful a term to be ignored and it can assist us to a better understanding of the Jewish question in the Soviet Union, for the socio-cultural processes we have recorded also reflect states of mind and ideological attitudes.

Researchers distinguish between two types of identity: public and personal. Public identity covers objective elements in the individual as perceived by others and the individual's subjective perception of his image in the eyes of others. Personal identity is the individual's image of himself – is private estimation of his qualities. Another important term for this analysis is 'identification' – the extent of the individual's wish to be numbered as a member of the Jewish people, to act as part of it and for its sake. We see Jewish national identity as awareness of belonging to this ethnic entity with its common past, common characteristics and common destiny. Jewish national 'identification' underpins this sense of belonging and finds expression in a number of different ways.

The term 'Jewish national movement' is generally used to indicate the Zionist movement in the Soviet Union, but it covers other national elements as well, such as *Hassidism* and other religious groups, and Yiddishist–nationalist circles. The term 'movement' indicates a fairly large number of Jews in different towns who proceed to organize themselves for common purposes in accordance with a common set of ideas and who work to achieve their aims in a variety of ways.

As regards contacts with Jews in Israel and the rest of the world, we shall attempt to measure their importance for Jewish national identity in the Soviet Union, for preserving Jewish culture for those who wish to stay there and for facilitating emigration for those who see no other solution to their national difficulties.

Jewish-national identity in the Soviet Union

Among quantitative and other indicators at our disposal especial importance attaches to the population censuses (1959, 1970 and 1979) and the surveys carried out in Western countries among Jewish emigrants from the Soviet Union. We shall examine the public Jewish-national identity (without distinguishing between the objective and subjective elements mentioned above) and national identification.

PUBLIC JEWISH-NATIONAL IDENTITY

In the Soviet Union this type of national identity is expressed quantitatively in two sets of statistical data: population censuses and registration on identity certificates (according to Clause 5 of the Order, still in force of the Supreme Soviet of December 1932); the latter is not made public.

A population census asks what nationality someone belongs to and what his mother tongue is. Although this declaration is made voluntarily, there is no doubt that it does not always express the Jew's feeling of identification with his people but his public identity as perceived by others, in this instance the Soviet government authorities and the environment. This identity is imposed from outside, and the person who is questioned either shows that he accepts it or else tries to reject it. In the population census of 1959 2,267,814 persons declared themselves Jews and in 1979 only 1,811,000.[260] Thus over twenty years the Jewish population decreased by 456,814, for two reasons: (1) a negative rate of natural increase among Soviet Jews, due to the age-composition and the aging process of this population, and (2) the process of assimilation that produces a stratum of 'marginal' or 'disappearing' Jews, registered as Jews on their identity certificates but not declaring themselves as Jews in the census. Even if we adopt a higher figure (based on partial statistical material and indirect calculations) of a negative average annual rate of increase of 0.5%,[261] about 41,000 Jews are still missing, who apparently preferred to hide the fact of their being Jewish. It is important to know whether there was a rise or fall in the number of these 'marginal' Jews in the twenty years from 1959 to 1979, as a consequence of the Jewish national revival on the one hand and of rising anti-Semitic propaganda and anti-Jewish discrimination on the other. We shall shortly be dealing with the process of assimilation and shall examine this issue more closely. At this stage we must pass on to our next set of data.

If we had at our disposal the statistical data from the 'Clause 5' registration on the identity certificates, we could calculate the number of Jews who chose to conceal their identity. Since these data are not published, however, we have to utilize the partial material published on mixed marriages and the offsprings' choice of nationality, and surveys on this point carried out among Soviet Jews.

Mixed marriages are an important element in evaluating national identity. This is amply evidenced by Soviet researchers' treatment of mixed marriages as a principal lever in the process of mixing nationalities. From partial data published in the Soviet Union on mixed marriages between Jews and non-Jews (mainly Russians), it emerges that in the 1960s in Latvia the rate was *c.* 35%, in Kharkov 29.6% and in Belorussia 23.7%.[262] The estimates in 1979 for mixed-Jewish families in the three republics where 82% of Soviet Jews are concentrated were: Russian Republic 33%; Ukraine 19%, Belorussia 14%.[263]

From partial data published in the Soviet Union, we learn that from 1960 to 1969 the percentage of offspring of mixed Jewish-Russian marriages who chose Jewish nationality was as follows: in Makhachkala 28.4%; Vilnius 14%; Tallin 10%; Riga 6.7%; in Ordzhonikidze and Cherkask the percentage was nil.[264] Even if the Jewish national revival in the 1970s and the mass emigration that took place in this period brought down the proportion of the offspring of mixed marriages who preferred Russian nationality to Jewish (thereby also condemning themselves to staying in the Soviet Union for good), the percentage was still high. This means that the percentage of Jews registered as such on their identity certificates will steadily decrease, leading to a further aging of the Jewish population. In a survey carried out among Soviet Jews by Fein and others, more than half of those questioned stated that the existence of external Jewish traits such as an accent or facial features 'did not bother them', but many confessed that they would have preferred to hide their national identity. Furthermore, 60% would have liked to have the nationality clause eliminated from their identity certificates, and 50% would have preferred to decide for themselves, if it were possible, what should be written there.[265] The Soviet authorities, however, have not eliminated the 'nationality clause', on pragmatic grounds and in flat contradiction to the declared aims of their own nationality policy,

thus unintentionally helping to strengthen the public national identity of the Jews and other national minorities. Since Soviet Society
draws a clear distinction between Jew and non-Jew, the circle is
closed and can only be breached by illegal means, or by the second
generation of offspring of mixed marriages. The Jews are obliged to
identify themselves with their Jewish nationality. How deep is this
national identification and how is it manifested?

JEWISH-NATIONAL IDENTITY AND IDENTIFICATION IN THE SOVIET UNION

The degree and depth of Jewish-national identity cannot be
measured because of the absence of any surveys or research on this
subject in the Soviet Union itself. Partial surveys carried out in Israel
and the USA can only serve as indicators. An important source is the
Samizdat, both Jewish and general. Officially published Jewish *belles
lettres* and memoirs have already been cited in our sections on Jewish
culture. These publications, taken together, represent only a part of
the Jewish population, and what is absent is an expression of what
may be termed 'the silent majority' of the Jews in the Soviet
Union.[266]

It is possible to classify the Soviet Jews into four main groups:

Assimilated Jews. This group includes all those who want to cut
themselves off from being Jewish, but are unable to do so both because they are registered as Jews on their identity certificates and
because they are known as Jews to those around them; they constitute
the majority of the Jews in the Soviet Union, especially since the
emigration of about 265,000 Jews. This population can be subdivided
into 'ideologists' and 'pragmatists'. Those who assimilated for ideological reasons, who believed that the Soviet regime was itself the
solution of the Jewish national problem, were represented over a long
period by Ilya Erenburg. When the Nazis reminded Erenburg during
the war that his mother's name was Hannah, he reiterated the creed
which he stood by to the end of his life, 'I am a Russian writer, but as
long as there still remains one anti-Semite in the world, if I am asked
my nationality I shall declare with pride, "I am a Jew."'[267] This
position is represented today by the author, Lev Kopelev, a researcher into German literature. The dilemma he, and many like him,
faces is that on the one hand he cannot escape from being a Jew,
because 'the street' reminds him of it and the government does not

care to free him from it, and so he answers questions about his nationality with pride: 'Jewish'; but on the other hand he affirms bluntly on his own account: 'I have never found in my conscious mind anything which would link me to the nationalistic ideals or religious traditions of Jewry.' He admits that in his 'irrational' unconscious mind, however, things are different.[268]

The type of Jew who is assimilated but still on the brink of two societies is represented by Larissa Bogoraz-Daniel. She does not feel that she is Jewish, that is to say, she has lost the sense of emotional identification, unlike Erenburg and Kopelev, and she regrets it. She knows that she has a genetic connection with Jewry but lacks any deeper attachment – to a language, tradition, culture or specifically Jewish history. According to these traits, moreover, she is Russian and yet not Russian, and she concludes sadly: 'I am an alien in this country, someone without a fatherland, without a nationality, without a country of my own.'[269]

Jewish sensibility is almost always awakened among assimilated Jews at times of crisis, when they are trapped by their environment, as in the Second World War or during the 'dark years' of anti-Jewish war waged by the authorities. Jews who are completely at home in the Russian or Ukrainian culture and language will suddenly feel that not only they but everyone else hears the cry 'Hear, O Israel!' When the danger is over, the Jewish symbols begin to disappear, the hidden Jewish feelings again become blurred, and these Jews' love for Russia's forests and landscapes, language and culture is restored.

The 'pragmatic' Jew, who is still in the process of acculturization is less alienated than the ideological assimilationist; his identification with the environment is not as complete and so it is easier for him to continue to identify himself, at least partially, as Jewish. This heterogeneous group has in the past constituted a potential reserve for the other groups and will continue to do so in the future.

Communist–National Jews. This group is dwindling, because of the destruction of Jewish culture on the one hand and on the other the rise of the Zionist idea as the sole solution for the Jewish problem in the Soviet Union. Only the 14.2% of the Jews who declared in the 1979 census that Yiddish was their mother tongue belonged ideologically to this group: knowledge of Yiddish and claiming it as the mother tongue was not exclusive to such Yiddishists as Aharon Vergelis. The group was weakened further by the emigration of a large number of Yiddish writers and artists to Israel. If there were to be a sudden, radical change in Soviet policy on Yiddish education, which seems unlikely, this could produce a revival of the Yiddishist ideology, as embodied by the Evsektsia in the 1920s, which would mean a renewed fight against Zionism and the solutions it offers.

Religious Jews. In the sections dealing with the Soviet Jewish religion, we saw that the number of religious Jews in the Soviet Union is between 70,000 and 100,000, which is lower than in most of the national minorities in the Soviet Union. Their national identity depends on whether they are Orthodox, traditional, or activist-religious Jews.

To the first of these sub-groups, the Orthodox, belong elderly Jews concentrated in the western, rural republics and in the Caucasian and Asiatic Republics. These Jews place religion above all other national considerations and they are prepared to live in the Soviet Union as long as they can go on observing the ritually prescribed practices of Judaism. If there were no such possibility, they would be prepared to emigrate, but not necessarily to Israel. To the second sub-group belong in the main non-Ashkenazi Jews, for whom religion is part of the community-congregational identity and family identity, which are still very strong. The third sub-group of religious activists includes Jews imbued with a conscious mission, working to extend the religious network in the Soviet Union: these are the Ḥassidim, mainly of the 'Ḥabad' persuasion, who, having adopted 'policy of neutrality' towards the Soviet State are able to maintain closed organizations and circles. There are also many young people among the Ḥassidim, some of whom are 'naturally' religious because they were born and grew up in religious families, and some of whom came to the Jewish religion through personal conviction. Some turn to Israel, but others prefer to live in Ḥassidic communities in the USA and Canada.

There was ferment among Soviet young people when the Communist idols were broken in the 1950s and the search for new faiths formed the background for the ideas spread by Father Alexander Men and his 'Judeo-Christians'; but his influence on Jewish youth in the Soviet Union was very limited.

The Zionist national group. Zionism did not come to an end in the Soviet Union when the legal movement was banned and its illegal forms wiped out. At the end of the 1920s, a Soviet Jew with a Zionist national identity was distinguishable from the three classes already described, not only by his strong identification with Erez Yisrael and the dispersed Jewish people and his view that Hebrew was the only national tongue, but also, and mainly, by his belief that Zionism represented the radical solution for the Soviet Jews.

It is difficult to measure the Zionist potential in the Soviet Union, because conditions there are constantly changing. For the short term, one can possibly make a rough estimate: 265,000 Jews have already emigrated from among the 650,000 who received application papers from Israel in the years 1968 to 1982. (About 70% of those who left did not go to Israel.) According to these figures about 100,000 Jews are ready to leave the Soviet Union for Israel, but the position is not straightforward, and the number of unknowns is so great that mathematical calculations are practically excluded in this field.

SOCIO-CULTURAL PROCESSES AFFECTING JEWISH NATIONAL IDENTITY

To reach a better understanding of Jewish national identity – both in its public, collective form and in the sphere of personal identification – we must consider the socio-cultural processes at work under the impact of complex internal and external factors. Every national minority in a multi-national society, where the dominant culture and language is that of another people, must undergo a process of assimilation. It is useful to note three main stages in this long and often indirect process – acculturation, assimilation and absorption.

Acculturation. This term means adjustment to the way of life and the culture of the majority without loss of national identification – an adjustment which enables the Jews to live in modern society and reap its fruits in education and professional advancement and in the necessary daily contact with the surrounding society. Acculturation in this sense demands certain conditions: the existence of a national culture, at least on a small scale, with a certain power of attraction; a bond, more or less strong, between the national minority and its own culture; a hostility, or at least indifference, to their culture on the part of the majority, to whose culture the minority is adjusting. Jewish acculturation may, then, be tested according to the degree of adjustment to the Russian language and Russian culture and to the degree of integration into the apparatuses of the government and the economy.

To take the Russian language: one may say that all the Soviet Jews know Russian to some extent. This assumption is confirmed by the reduction in the proportion of Jews who declared that their mother tongue was Yiddish, from 21.5% in 1959 to 14.2% in 1979. Knowledge of Russian culture is more restricted, and differs not only between one republic to another but also between one district and one social stratum to the next. As regards integration into government, we have already noted that while the Jews still have an important place, surpassing that of the other extra-territorial minorities, they are being steadily pushed aside from the positions and functions they have previously filled.

Assimilation.   If this manifests itself in a weakening of the bond that the individual feels with his ethnic group, then the Soviet Jews have long since passed from the stage of acculturation to that of assimilation of ideas and attitudes. They have made the transition from knowing the Russian language and culture to conscious attachment to them, a feeling that they cannot live without them. This is not all. Assimilation strengthens their indifference and sometimes even hostility to Jewish national culture, about which they know little. In the social sphere, it strengthens their capacity to merge into their surroundings, a capacity evidenced by mixed marriages. Socio-cultural assimilation is strongest among Jewish intellectuals, especially those occupied with the social sciences or holding state posts among Communist Party and Komsomol members; geographically, they are especially strong in the Russian Republic, the central Ukraine and Belorussia.

Absorption.   This indicates the disappearance of the personal bond and of the wish to belong to the Jewish people. There is a sizeable but unknown percentage of Jews in the Soviet Union who have already been absorbed completely, usually into the Russian people, but sometimes into the Ukrainian and other peoples. To this category belong the offspring of mixed marriages, who succeed in erasing their official nationality and merging more or less into the surrounding society; they 'disappear' as Jews, as far as the government is concerned: as Mendes-France put it, they have no sense of being Jewish. At the same time, as Sartre observed, it is not only the subjective feeling that is decisive, but also the environment, and in the Soviet Union today the environment is permeated with nationalism, sometimes expressed by apprehension that, even when totally absorbed into the population a Jew remains a Jew, an alien element liable to enfeeble the defensive power of the nation into which he has been absorbed.

CAUSES OF JEWISH NATIONAL REVIVAL

It is a mistake to think that the national revival is identical with emigration to Israel. Its outcome is to be seen in the search for a way out of the impossible situation of leading a Jewish national life in the Soviet Union, a search that may lead the Jewish energies released into new channels. Not every Jew who emigrated from the Soviet Union did so for nationalist reasons; many, or perhaps most, of them emigrated on political grounds or because they wanted to improve their economic position.

Forces of repulsion. Surveys and interviews carried out among Jewish immigrants from the Soviet Union in Israel and in other countries have revealed a tendency to discount the unfavourable factors that influenced their national awakening and their decision to emigrate from the Soviet Union and to stress the factors of attraction. This was especially noticeable when people were individually questioned about the existence of anti-Semitism in the Soviet Union. A high percentage of those questioned stated that anti-Semitism existed; but when the question was put personally, the individual concerned tended to answer that he personally had not been affected by it and that this had not influenced his decision to emigrate. Nevertheless, the unfavourable factors undoubtedly accumulated over the years until they represented a powerful repulsive force. There were five main factors.

(1) *The trauma of the past.* The long history of the Jewish people is etched into its collective memory and affects the course of its actions. The change in Soviet policy in the late 1930s – the end of the fight against anti-Semitism, the strangling of Jewish culture and the closing down of Jewish administrative institutions – was the first blow. A deeper shock was inflicted during the war by the revelation of the Soviet population's hatred of those Jews massacred by the Nazis; even harder to bear was the Soviet government's policy of pardoning collaborators on the one hand and its unwillingness to allow the Jews to perpetuate the memory of those murdered in the Holocaust on the other. The realization that the famous Soviet 'fraternity of peoples' was a myth and the distrust of the Soviet regime's goodwill towards Soviet Jewry were unquestionably influential in reviving Jewish na-

tional consciousness. The worst was still to come, however, during the
'dark years' of mass arrests and the sustained war on nationalism,
Zionism and 'cosmopolitanism'.

(2) *Discrimination in the present.* Though the new leadership headed
by Khrushchev saved the Jews from the danger of progroms and mass
deportation, it did not (as we have seen) free them from the operation
of latent anti-Semitism, both popular and official.

Among Soviet Jews, the feeling of being discriminated against is
both individual and private, national and public. The Jews feel anti-
Semitism personally as regards admission (that is, non-admission) to
institutions of higher education and to government institutions and
professional advancement. From the public and national angle, the
Jews feel that they are discriminated against in comparison with
other nationalities.

(3) *Anti-Semitism and mass media propaganda.* We have already described popular and official anti-Semitism, and shall only note here
that the surveys carried out in Israel and the USA among the Jewish
emigrants from the Soviet Union indicate this factor (ranging from
20 to 70% of those questioned) as the impelling motive for the Jewish
national revival and emigration from the Soviet Union.

(4) *Dissatisfaction with the Soviet political and economic system.* This is
not a specifically Jewish phenomenon, but on account of unfavourable factors affecting them and the special sensitivity of the Jewish
intelligentsia, it goads the Jews to take action, as shown by their
adherence to the dissident movements. In internal politics they are
affected by the inadequate liberalization, the absence of the most
elementary civil rights, the continuation of police repression and the
unrelenting anti-Jewish and anti-Israeli policy. In foreign relations,
the Jews were especially outraged by Soviet intervention in Hungary
in 1956 and in Czechoslovakia in 1968, and possibly in Afghanistan
as well. In the economic field, there is widespread opposition to
corruption and to anti-Jewish economic trials.

(5) *Increased nationalism of the Great Russians and other peoples.* Much of
Soviet Jewry was inclined to accept Soviet internationalist solutions.
Perhaps more than any other people in the Soviet Union, they believed that they would be in the vanguard of the process of *rapprochement* and integration of the peoples, and they drew inspiration from
the official ideology and pronouncements. However, in the 1930s and
1940s, the rise in Russian nationalism, and that of the other peoples
as well, faced even the most assimilated Jew with the question: must

the Jew alone be 'a-national'? Must he be the only one to renounce his national identity and give up his feelings towards his own people? The weight of this argument must increase in the coming years, as nationalist circles in the Communist Party achieve increasing influence.

Forces of attraction. Attraction to the Jewish people and to Israel is an important factor in the process of national revival among Soviet Jews; but the process has only affected some of the Jews in the Soviet Union and so far the results, in the form of carrying out the Zionist ideal, are limited.

(1) *Meeting Jews from abroad.* The years 1939 to 1941, when the Soviet Union annexed areas where some two million Jews were living, provided contact with Jews from the 'outside world', which Soviet citizens had been denied since the 1920s. This meeting infused new vigour into Soviet Jewry's dwindling national consciousness. In the post-Stalin period, and mainly in the 1960s, the Soviet frontiers were opened to a stream of visitors – journalists, tourists, delegations, artists, athletes, etc. – and Soviet Jews were able to get more reliable information on what was happening in Israel and among Jews in the rest of the world. The Jewish revival was spurred by the emotional excitement over the large Israeli delegation at the 'International Youth Festival' in 1957 and by concerts given by the few Israeli artists who visited the Soviet Union.

(2) *The State of Israel and its efforts on behalf of Soviet Jewry.* When the State of Israel was established in 1948, with the support of the Soviet Union, it had an extraordinary effect on the Jewish public and more particularly on the disillusioned generation that suffered so much from official policy and from the hostility of the surrounding population. The State of Israel immediately became the symbol of a swift solution to the problems of the Soviet Jews. Its very existence was a light in the darkness. Active in world affairs, the State of Israel was especially important to Soviet Jews in times of distress and crisis, since it implanted the feeling that they were not isolated but had some international support.

(3) *National–cultural activity.* Jewish cultural activity, initiated by the Jews themselves, was very important in underpinning the Jewish national identity and providing ways of identification with the Jewish people: the Jewish theatre and its amateur troupes and choirs, comprising hundreds of people, which entertained a public of many

thousands; newspapers and books, both those in Yiddish, published officially, and in Hebrew in the *Samizdat*; Hebrew lessons (these too reached thousands of people); the mass assemblies at High Holidays in the synagogues; action undertaken since the 1950s concerning Holocaust sites and commemorating its victims; and work for the Zionist cause, which we shall now describe.

The Zionist national movement

The Jewish national movement is wider in scope than 'plain' Zionism; it covers both Yiddishist nationalists and religious circles that are not even Zionist, all of whom strengthen Jewish national identity. We shall concentrate here on the Zionist movement on which we have more complete data.

The organized Zionist Movement disappeared from the Soviet scene in the second half of the 1930s. The arrests of Zionists under Stalin's regime, from 1936 to 1945, paralysed all Zionist activity, even of isolated individuals. During the war, however, Zionist groups of the *He-ḥaluz* Movement from the annexed territories were active in the Soviet Union, though apparently any connections between them and original Soviet Zionists were few and ineffectual – except in places of detention and forced labour camps.

When the war ended and Soviet Jewry was shaken by the scale of the Holocaust, Zionist activity increased and became more overt. Two types of Zionist groups operated, without any connection between them: organized Zionists from earlier days in the annexed territories, working to assemble their surviving members, and move them from the Soviet Union to Poland and Romania, for eventual emigration to Palestine (activity later called the *Brekha*);[270] and new Zionist groups, mainly in the Ukraine, Moldavia and the Baltic Republics, organized by young Jews disillusioned with the Soviet regime, who had come to see the Zionist idea as the solution for the Jewish problem in the Soviet Union.[271] The establishment of the State of Israel and the initially pro-Israeli policy of the Soviet Union gave an impetus to the Zionist revival, illustrated both by efforts to help the new State in its fight for existence by trying to join its army, and by the organization of Zionist groups in many Soviet cities. By 1948, however, and especially in 1949, there was a wave of arrests of veteran Zionists, some of whom had only just been released from prison, and of new Zionists as well, which ended Zionist action until 1953.

No research has been done on Zionist activity in the Soviet Union in this period, and many people believe that the Zionist Movement began in the Soviet Union after the Six-Day War. It is true, however, that there is an essential difference between Zionist activity between 1953 and 1967 and that between 1968 and 1983.

Disappointment over Soviet policy towards the Soviet Jews and towards its socialist neighbours (especially Berlin in 1953, Poland and Hungary in 1956) reinforced the change in the atmosphere: during the period of 'the thaw', thousands of prisoners from the forced labour camps had been released, among them many veteran Zionists; there had also been more possibilities of meeting members of the Israel Embassy staff (in synagogues, at concerts, at public events and vacation spots) and freer listening to Western radio stations including *Kol Israel le-Golah* (Voice of Israel to the Exile). This was the background to the foundation of the first isolated, local Zionist groups in the post-Stalin period. The groups usually formed around a nucleus of one family, with a circle of friends, and expanded gradually. The first cities to have such groups were Moscow, Leningrad, Kiev, Lvov, Odessa, Vinnitsa, Tashkent and Bobruisk. Activity was limited at first to coming together on Jewish and Israeli holidays, mainly Israel Independence Day, and to research and discussion on the State of Israel and the history of the Jewish people. Information was given to the Israeli Embassy on the situation of Soviet Jews – where they lived, their attitude, both in general and to Israel. The meetings with Embassy personnel were few: diplomats were constantly watched and had instructions to avoid unnecessary contacts with the local Jews, both in order not to endanger them, and also because of the accepted Israeli policy of maintaining a 'low profile' in relations with the Soviet Union, which had only just renewed relations with Israel and had almost severed them again after the Sinai campaign. It is hard to estimate how many active Zionists took part in meetings of groups and circles, but there must have been hundreds, distributed among most of the centres of Jewish population in the Soviet Union. The first arrests, in 1955 and 1956, involved about a hundred people, most of whom were later freed or served as witnesses at trials of their comrades. The active workers were usually veteran Zionists with relations or former comrades in Israel, who could give Embassy members their addresses. There were also former Hebrew writers among them, Yiddish writers and artists and even people who had once been connected with the Evsektsia. The few young people who took part in Zionist activity at this stage were members of veteran Zionist families.[272]

1956 and 1957 marked a turning-point in the spread of Zionist revival to new circles, including young Jews previously unconcerned with Jewish and Zionist affairs. The 1956 Sinai campaign stimulated fund-raising for an 'Israel Defence Fund' and renewed interest in the possibilities of emigration to Israel. The catalyst for many Jews was the 'International Youth Festival' held in Moscow in August 1957:[273] the meeting with young Israelis, the information and the propaganda material distributed (Israeli badges, flags, postage stamps, etc.) and the joint appearances in public performances gave the Soviet Jews 'spiritual nourishment' which lasted for years. Zionist activists who emigrated to Israel argue that this new situation was not exploited by the State of Israel and the World Zionist Organization on behalf of Soviet Jewry, thus wasting a possible ten years of action. This may be true, but it is difficult to be sure that the situation from 1957 to 1960 was favourable for such a volte-face in Soviet policy towards the Jews, leading as it would to such mass emigration as occurred in 1971.

From the Youth Festival and to the Six-Day War, Zionist activity continued on an increased scale. The links with the Israeli Embassy multiplied and contacts became easier and less dangerous. Meetings took place with Jewish tourists from abroad, including delegations of rabbis and public workers. The 'iron curtain' began to lift sufficiently for people to exchange information with the outside world on events among the Jewish public in the Soviet Union. In addition to the Israeli Embassy staff and tourists, the main sources of information were newspapers and books that began to come in by devious routes (to public libraries, by despatches from abroad, from the Israeli Embassy and so on) and Western radio broadcasts. The organization of amateur Yiddish theatrical troupes and choirs brought Jews together and helped to spread Zionist ideas. Whereas Zionist groups in previous years had been composed of a family and close relatives, now the family aspect, though still present, was no longer dominant. This Zionist activity expanded from 1957 to 1967, but the main improvements in methods of work and propaganda took place in the three years from 1964 to 1967.

The importance of the Jewish *Samizdat* increased greatly. Amongst its publications were: articles from the Israeli and Western press, translated into Russian; works dealing with the State of Israel; translations of Hebrew and Yiddish classic literature into Russian; pamphlets on the subject of Soviet Jewry, like those of Y. Shapiro from Odessa on the pogroms in the Ukraine and on Jewish heroes of the Soviet Union; sections of history books, such as that of Sh. Dubnov, material translated from Yiddish into Russian; and even whole books, such as *Exodus* by Leon Uris, which was a great success and was published in different editions in different cities, and *Red Orchestra* by G. Perrault (translated from the French) about Trepper's exploits in the Second World War. Most of the material was prepared in Moscow (by Ezra Margolis, Shlomo Dolnik and others) and in Riga (by E. Rusinek, B. Slovin, D. Zilberman and others). In the 1960s, hundreds of copies of these *Samizdat* publications were prepared for first editions, and additional copies were made by photogravure, so that many thousands could be distributed. The circle of readers constantly expanded, the material being transferred in parcels and suitcases from Moscow and Riga to Leningrad, Kiev and other cities.

Second in importance to the *Samizdat* was participation in the various dramatic troupes that were appearing officially in this period. Their performances enabled Jews to meet in large numbers and to spread the word of Zionism in writing and conversation. There were even attempts, such as those of D. Garber in Riga, to include preeminently Jewish-national material in the repertoire, which had to receive official approval before it could be performed. We can also include here the Zionist activity facilitated by meetings at concerts given in the Soviet Union by Jewish and Israeli artists, such as Jan Pierce in 1961 and Geula Gil in 1966.

Third, from 1957 the synagogue again became important as a meeting place for young Jews with Zionist aspirations. The small number who came initially grew to hundreds and even thousands on certain High Holidays. At the centre of these events was the experience of singing together and dancing Israeli dances, giving a new, topical, national content to the Jewish Festivals.

Fourth, at the beginning of the 1960s the first actions were taken to perpetuate the memory of the Holocaust victims. The most effective were those of the Riga Jews in Rumbuli.[274] The Jewish–Zionist aspect was pre-eminently the act of commemoration itself, but included the action of many Jews in putting up the symbol of the Shield of David in public places.

and who was in the 'leadership'. Moreover, everything changed so fast among the dissident movements as a whole, and in particular among the national movements fighting for freedom to emigrate (Jews, Germans, Armenians, Meskhets, Koreans and Greeks), that one can only depict a given 'moment' and not the period as a whole. From the point of view of size, the number of *Samizdat* publications must be taken into account and also the people they refer to.[276] In his book, *Will the Soviet Union exist in 1984?*, Amalrik treated everyone 'who signed the petitions and whom we know something about' as a member of the dissident movements. This definition covered about 700 persons in the second half of the 1960s, two-thirds of whom (67%) were scientists and artists and only 6% workers.[277] B. Lewytskyj bases his figures on these data and adds new data to reach a total of 934 people, divided as follows – writers and artists 35%, newsmen 6%, students 5%, workers 25% and 'others' 11%.[278] As against this, C. Lubarsky bases his calculations on data concerning political prisoners: 400 tried on serious charges, 2,000 charged with defaming the Soviet Union (Clause 191), 500 held in psychiatric hospitals; in all, he puts the number of political prisoners at 8,000 to 9,000.[279] If we add the adherents to, and not only the activists in, the religious and nationalist movements, then according to Lubarsky we reach something like 300,000 persons.

Members of the Zionist movement can be divided into four categories: adherents who did not take any active part in Zionist work, apart from requesting 'application papers' from Israel and trying to get exit visas on the strength of these applications; members who signed at least one petition and thereby endangered themselves; activists initiating action on a large scale, who were recognized as such by others; and the leaders, including all those who were put on trial, as well as those who led Zionist activity in their towns for a relatively long time and were not tried. The following calculation estimates the number of open adherents of the Zionist movement: about 163,000 people emigrated to Israel from 1968 to 1982, to whom must be added about 10,000 whose requests for exit permits were refused, and another 20 to 30% from the 375,000 who received 'application papers' from Israel and did not emigrate, that is, to say 75,000 to 102,500 – in all 238,000 to 265,000 people.[280] This number approaches the total adherents of most of the religious and political dissident movements and some of the nationalist movements. As regards the second category of members (as defined above), 300 petitions were signed by 972 people between 1968 and 1970; 366 petitions were signed by 2,664 people in 1971; 353 petitions were signed by 1,336 people in 1972; 397 petitions were signed by 881 people in 1973; 314 petitions were signed by 623 people in 1974; 218 petitions were signed by 465 people in 1975; and 394 petitions were signed by 719 people from 1976 to 1978 (altogether, 5,454 people signed petitions in the years 1969–1978).[281] We see then that membership was specially high in the years 1968 to 1973, with a decline in the years 1974 to 1978. According to their regional and urban distribution, it emerges that Moscow has the most signatories. This is perhaps not surprising, since a quarter of a million Jews live in Moscow. The other cities with many Zionist members are Riga, Vilnius, Kiev (since 1974), Leningrad, Minsk, Kishinev and Odessa. As regards occupational distribution, data exist on 289 persons in the years 1968 to 1970: 35% were engineers, 13% workers, 12% doctors, 13.5% scientists and technicians and 5% students. Thus in comparison with the general political dissident movements, the majority in the Zionist movement are in the technical occupations.

It is more difficult to estimate the number of activists, our third category, in any given period. If we take as basic data a survey carried out in the Hebrew University of Jerusalem among 472 Zionist activists who reached Israel between 1965 and 1972, the number of activists in that period can be put at a thousand; the number dropped as a result of the large-scale emigration of activists, but there was also a wave of new adherents between 1974 and 1979.

To turn to the 'leadership', we take into account the number put on trial, which was eighty-seven in the years 1969 to 1983, in addition to some fifty in the earlier period. To them must be added outstanding activists who were not arrested or who were arrested for short periods, about 150 persons in the peak period from 1965 to 1975, with a substantial decline thereafter.

The foundations for Zionist work, including group organization, had been laid before the Six-Day War, which served rather as a catalyst, speeding up the process of Jewish national revival in the Soviet Union and spurring on the aspiration to realize Zionist objectives as soon as possible by immigration to Israel, than as an event which created the movement out of a vacuum. Widespread, organized and unified Zionist activity was later manifested during the period of the hardest struggle against the Soviet government, from 1968 to 1971.

Zionist activists can be divided ideologically into 'catastrophic' Zionists, who wanted to act with all available force for one purpose – immigration of Soviet Jews to Israel – without any concern for or interest in the survival of Jewish culture in the Soviet Union, and without any desire to collaborate with other dissident circles; and 'evolutionary' Zionists, who also wanted to fight for emigration, but wanted, too, to act together with other dissidents, at least in technical things such as transmitting information. As regards organizational structure, there were three main approaches: that of the Leningrad leadership (Mogilever, Butman, Chernoglaz and Vertlieb), also supported by the people in Kiev, based on the belief that open activity was pointless, since it could be ended at one stroke by the security services, and that a disciplined organization should be set up with a 'platform', a constitution, and small cells of members working clandestinely, without contact with or knowledge of the other cells (almost a Leninist idea: a revolutionary Party acting in conditions of illegality); the Moscow approach (supported mainly by Meir Gelfond), which supported concerted activity, but without any formal clandestine organization; and a third approach, which was a compromise in favour of dividing operations between legal and illegal activists. This last policy was supported by some of the Moscow and Riga people.

As regards coordination and cooperation between the Zionist groups in the different cities, the zenith was the establishment of the 'nation-wide co-ordinating committee' (VKK), which met a number of times in Moscow, Leningrad, Riga and Kiev. At these meetings, it was decided to publish a Zionist movement newspaper, to work out a 'division of labour' between the various cities, from the angle of responsibility for different fields of activity (money, printing, publication of the newspaper and its distribution), and for laying down policy for future Zionist activity.

As regards the character and forms of Zionist activity, a distinction can be drawn between the two sub-periods, 1968 to 1973 and from 1974 onwards. In the latter period, the emphasis was more on the long-term activity of entrenching and extending the study of the Jewish language, history and culture by publishing periodicals (*Jews in the Soviet Union* and *Culture*), arranging scientific symposia, and so on.

The main spheres of Zionist work in the Soviet Union from 1968 to the present day are indicated here. First, as we have seen, there has been a great deal of activity in organizing signed petitions and transmitting them to the West (2,366 petitions in ten years); second, many demonstrations have been held, with the participation of scores of people, in central sites, mainly in Moscow but in other cities as well, the greatest number taking place between 1971 and 1973, the main demand being for free emigration to Israel for all Jews wishing to emigrate; third, individuals and groups staged hunger-strikes throughout the 1970s; fourth, Hebrew-language education was considerably extended by study groups in private homes, following well-arranged courses, and meetings in secluded sites, such as the woods, for learning language and history; fifth, there was an expansion of *Samizdat* publications of both books and newspapers – the specifically Jewish *Samizdat* includes thirty-five volumes, not counting many literary works translated from other languages into Russian; sixth, a great deal of organizing work goes into arranging farewell parties for activists emigrating to Israel, with 200 to 250 people present on each occasion; seven, contacts with Western newsmen and with tourists from abroad have created links between Soviet Jews and the outside world; eight, the possibilities of telephone connections abroad have been exploited; nine, there has been more activity concerning Holocaust commemorations in the following places – Rumbuli, Babi Yar, Ponar, 'Fort 9'. Ceremonies are also held in memory of the Warsaw Ghetto rising. We should not forget the most daring and controversial action of all – the hi-jack plan, born in Leningrad but carried out mainly by Riga people with a number of others who had not been connected with Zionism before, like E. Kuznetsov and M. Dymshits – which ended with the arrest of all of them on 15 June 1970.

The Zionist movement can truly be said to be the only dissident movement in the Soviet Union to have achieved real success. The self-sacrificing and costly struggle brought a result that was impossible to imagine at the start of the 1970s: the emigration of more than 270,000 Jews within a relatively short period. As we have already noted, this success was only made possible by suitable conditions in the Soviet Union itself, together with convenient international developments, support for the Soviet Zionists from world opinion and from Israel, and the influence of the USA. The disappearance of this set of circumstances at the beginning of the 1980s brought emigration to a standstill and paralysed Zionist activity in the Soviet Union.

Connections with world Jewry and Israel

In the 'dark years', the Jews in the Soviet Union had been almost completely cut off from the rest of the Jews in the world. This was manifested by the ending of visits to the Soviet Union by delegations or individuals and by fears of writing to relations in other countries.

From 1953 onwards and particularly from 1956, Soviet Jews were once more able to make partial and supervised contacts with relations and acquaintances visiting the Soviet Union as tourists, to attend performances by visiting Jewish artists, and to take part in sports gatherings, festivals and exhibitions with Jews from Israel and other countries. At the same time unrestrained attacks were made in the Soviet media on Israeli Embassy personnel, Jewish delegations and tourists, in order to warn Soviet Jews and deter them from contact with foreign citizens; but it is apparent that these moves did not achieve their purpose until the beginning of the 1980s.

By its very nature the Soviet regime is bound to discourage contact between its citizens and people from outside its borders, including citizens of the socialist states. Opening the frontiers to tourists, newsmen and delegations of various kinds only occurred, on the whole, either when there was a government policy of *rapprochement* with the West or when circumstances dictated it.

Though some Zionist activists would not agree, it seems clear that contacts between Soviet Jews and Jews in Israel and the rest of the world were a factor in the Jewish nationalist revival and in large-scale Zionist organizing efforts in the Soviet Union. The question then is, what did the Jews of Israel and the rest of the world actually do on behalf of Soviet Jewry?

From 1948 to 1953, the period of the worst persecution of Soviet Jews, the big Jewish organizations like the World Jewish Congress, the 'Joint', and *B'nai Brith* did nothing at all for the Jews in the Soviet Union. Even graver was the position adopted by the State of Israel in those years, as a result of the failings of Israeli Embassy personnel, who did not always have an accurate perception of the Soviet regime, its functioning and policies, and of the prevailing objective conditions, which made it difficult to get reliable information on what was happening to Soviet Jews. Israeli governments took the line of not raising the question of Jews in the Soviet Union and did nothing to awaken world public opinion on the issue. It was not until the Slansky trial in Prague in November 1952 and the preparations for the

Doctors' Trial in January and February 1953 that the Israel government was inclined to take limited action – in the form of a protest in
the United Nations by Golda Meir – but this was not followed up,
either.

In 1955 the first moves were made to organize and coordinate
activities connected with Soviet Jewry. A body named BAR was set
up headed by Shaul Avigur, a close associate of David Ben-Gurion
and the man who had organized illegal Jewish immigration into
Palestine under the British Mandate. With the help of persons enlisted for this purpose in Israel and abroad, plans took shape for
transmitting information from Soviet Jewry to institutions, organizations and newspapers in the world, for sending material into the
Soviet Union and collecting material on Soviet Jewry itself. It is
interesting that Avigur's basic view on Soviet Jews and their national
identity was, on the whole, pessimistic, and he considered the activity
he directed as something in the nature of, 'Cast thy bread upon the
waters.'[282] There was also a division of opinion between Israel on the
one hand and the Jewish organizations on the other, and especially
with Naḥum Goldmann of the World Jewish Congress, as to the style
of policy to be adopted towards the Soviet Union, 'quiet diplomacy'
or making as much noise as possible. As a result it was not until 1960
that the first international conference of Jewish and non-Jewish personalities was convened in Paris under the auspices of the World
Jewish Congress on behalf of the Jews in the Soviet Union. The
conference set up a 'Committee for Soviet Jewry' headed by Daniel
Mayer.

If we ignore the sporadic independent activities of a number of
rabbis, headed by Rabbi Hollander, who visited the Soviet Union as
early as 1956, organized activity by the main Jewish organizations did
not begin until 1964.[283] The spurt of American action on behalf of
Soviet Jewry did not occur until after the Six-Day War. The climax of
Jewish and Israeli action on behalf of Soviet Jewry was the first Brussels Conference in 1971, which had tremendous repercussions in the
communications media and in the Soviet Union itself. The Israeli
organizations for Soviet Jewry – 'Magen' (established in the 1920s),
which began to act in the early 1950s; 'Maoz', established in 1959; the
'Executive Committee of Immigrants from the Soviet Union', set up in
1970; and the 'Public Council for Soviet Jewry' (also set up in 1970) –
did not receive mass support from any quarter and their activities were
relatively very limited. Much greater success was secured by the many

committees for Soviet Jewry set up in Western countries in the 1970s, which were marked by the voluntary work of their members and by their praiseworthy constancy; but they too seem to have wearied in recent years and less is heard of their activities.

A delay in Israeli radio broadcasting in Russian, whose importance as a source of information cannot be exaggerated, was another serious shortcoming; in fact, until 1960 there was only one fifteen-minute information bulletin *a week*, put out by volunteers. 1961 saw a marked change in the size and organization of the broadcasts, but the Russian section of the Voice of Israel was not created until 1968. The increase in broadcasts in Russian began with the large-scale immigration of 1971 to 1973. From surveys carried out in Israel among immigrants from the Soviet Union it is clear that these broadcasts were a source of information and real encouragement to Zionist activists and to thousands of other Jews in the Soviet Union.

The three major forces that rule the lives of Jews in the Soviet Union, and that will decide the solutions to be adopted in the future, interact constantly with each other. First, the Soviet government, itself affected, in making decisions, by many contradictory pressures within the Soviet Union itself. Second, the Soviet Jews, with backing from the State of Israel and world Jewry, can influence Soviet policy only if the Zionist movement has the strength to stand firm – but how much they can achieve, even in better days, depends on other more powerful factors. Third, there are the Western powers, and mainly the USA, which may or may not consider it in their interest to help the Soviet Jews and which will only be able to do so effectively in suitable international circumstances similar to those of the early 1970s.

As I write, on the eve of 1986, Soviet Jewry finds itself in a critical situation, and the immediate future is hard to prophesy. Will emigration start again, and if so will there be enough candidates for a mass movement, and will this emigration turn to Israel or, as in recent years, mainly to the Western countries, when the percentage of 'drop-out' rose from 18.8% in 1974 to 70.7% in 1982? After a transition period, will the new Soviet authorities adopt the famous formula of Pobedonostsev about the Jews: one third will assimilate, one third will die off (natural deaths, of course) and a third will be banished – the formula embraced in Poland in 1968? Or will there be a return to the *status quo ante* of the years 1953 to 1967, without Stalinist terror, without large-scale emigration, and without full equality of rights? If it should turn out to be the last of these, how will Soviet Jewry react?

Notes

INTRODUCTION

1 S. Dubnov, *Ob izuchenii istorii russkikh evreev i ob izuchenii russko-evreiskogo istoricheskogo obshchestva*, St Petersburg, A. E. Landau, 1891, p. 34.

2 I. Orshansky, *Evrei v Rossii*, St Petersburg, Baksin, 1872; *idem, Russkoe zakonodatelstvo o evreyakh*, St Petersburg, A. E. Landau, 1877.

3 On Orshansky, see I. Maor, 'Orshansky u-mkomo be-historiografia shel yehudei russia', *He-avar*, 1973, vol. 20, pp. 49–61.

4 Not everyone agrees with the view expressed by Dubnov (see *Evreiskaya starina*, 1912, vol. 5, p. 7) that Orshansky's research was mostly publicistic and one-sided. Ben-Zion Dinur thinks that, notwithstanding their publicistic tone, Orshansky's articles are among the best that have been written. See B-Z. Dinur, 'Shimon Dubnov', *Zion*, 1935, vol. 1, p. 113.

5 See P. Sofer, 'S. Bershadsky', *He-avar*, 1973, vol. 20, pp. 62–71.

6 A. Harkavy, *Skazaniya evreiskikh pisatelei o khazarakh i khazarskom tsarstve*, St Petersburg, Tipografiya Akademii Nauk, 1874.

7 A. Harkavy, *Ob yazyke evreev zhivshikh v drevneye vremya na Russi i o slavianskikh slovakh vstrechennykh u evreiskikh pisatelei*, St Petersburg, A. E. Landau, 1865.

8 Y. Gessen's first book, *Evrei v Rossii* (St Petersburg, A. Rozen, 1906), dealt with juridical, political and economic issues concerning the Jews. The first complete history of Russian Jews appeared in 1914, its title reflecting Gessen's thinking as it had developed up till then: *Istoriya evreev v Rossii*, St Petersburg, L. Ginzburg, 1914. The first volume of the expanded history of the Russian Jews appeared in 1916, under the new title of *Istoriya evreiskogo naroda*; the complete, up-to-date history appeared in the Soviet period: *Istoriya evreiskogo naroda v Rossii*, Leningrad (private publication), 1925–7, 2 vols.

9 Y. Slutski, 'Yuli gesen', *He-avar*, 1973, vol. 20, pp. 72–9.

10 See *Evreiskaya starina*, 1912, vol. 5, pp. 129–31, and 1918, vol. 10, pp. 303–11.

11 See E. Cherikover, 'Di yiddishe historishe visenshaft in mizrakh europe', *Yivo bleter*, 1931, vol. 1, pp. 97–113; I. Trunk, 'Historians and Russian Jewry', in *Russian Jewry, 1860–1917*, New York, Yoseloff, 1966, pp. 452–79; and Slutsky, 'Yuli gesen'.

12 See I. Elbogen, J. Meisl and M. Wischnitzer (eds.), *Festschrift zu Simon Dubnov's siebzigsten Geburtstag*, Berlin, Jüdischer Verlag, 1930; S. Ravidovich (ed.), *Sefer Shimon Dubnov*, London, Jerusalem and Waltham, Ararat Publishing Society, 1954; A. Steinberg (ed.), *Simon Dubnov. L'homme et son oeuvre*, Paris, Congrès Juif Mondial, 1963; *He-avar*, 1961, vol. 8 (special issue).

13 S. Dubnov, Istoriograf evreistva, *Voskhod*, 1892, nos. 2, 4, 5, 7, 8, 9.

14 It is interesting to note that Perez Smolenskin was far more outspoken on this topic than Dubnov. In 1876, he had already noted the Germano-centric orientation of Jewish historiography in Germany as the principal reason for its not considering itself bound to include Eastern European Jewry in a historical description of the nineteenth century. See R. Mahler, 'Shitat Dubnov', *Historionim ve-askolot historiot*, Jerusalem, The Historical Society of Israel, 1962, p. 94.

15 See S. Dubnov, *History of the Jews*, New York, Yoseloff, 1967, vol. 1, pp. 25–44.

16 N. Rotenstreich, in *Sefer Dubnov*, p. 141.

17 Their studies serve as source material for the present work and will be referred to below. See also the bibliography.

18 J. Meisl, *Geschichte der Juden in Polen und Russland*, Berlin, Schweischke und Sohn, 1921–5, vols. 1–3.

19 L. Greenberg, *The Jews in Russia*, New Haven, Yale University Press, 1944–51, 2 vols.

20 S. Baron, *The Russian Jew under Tsars and Soviets*, New York, Collier-Macmillan, 1964; 2nd edn 1976.

21 C. Shmeruk, 'Ha-kibuz ha-yehudi ve-ha-hitiashvut ha-haklait ha-yehudit be-belorusia ha-sovietit, 1918–1932', unpublished PhD dissertation, The Hebrew University, Jerusalem, 1961.

22 Z. Gitelman, *Jewish Nationality and Soviet Politics. The Jewish Section of the CPSU, 1917–1930*, New Jersey, Princeton University Press, 1972.

23 M. Altshuler, 'Maamada ha-politi ve ha-irguni shel ha-sektsia ha-yehudit be-miflagah ha-komunistit shel brit-ha-moazot, 1918–1930', unpublished PhD dissertation, The Hebrew University, Jerusalem, 1971.

24 B. Z. Dinur, *Be-mifne-ha-dorot*, Jerusalem, Mosad Bialik, 1972, p. 32. Dinur suggests taking 1700, the great Hasidic *aliyah*, as the date marking the beginning of the modern period in the history of the Jewish people. Graetz, however, prefers 1750, the rise of the *Haskalah*, and Dubnov puts it at 1789, the French Revolution (Ob izuchenii, p. 20).

25 Thus, except for Gessen, who does not lay down any clear period scheme, the historians divide Russian Jewish history as follows: (1) up to the first partition of Poland; (2) 1771 to 1825; (3) 1825 to 1855; (4) 1855 to 1881; (5) 1881 to 1894; (6) 1894 to 1917. Baron's three periods are: 1762 to 1825; 1825 to 1881; 1881 to 1917.

26 Dubnov, *Ob izuchenii*, p. 38.

27 Dubnov, *History of the Jews in Russia and Poland*, Philadelphia, Jewish Publication Society (JPS), 1916–20.

28 Gessen, *Istoriya evreiskogo naroda v Rossii*.

29 *Istoriya evreiskogo naroda v Rossii*, vol. 1.

30 Dinur, *Be-mifne ha-dorot*, p. 93.

I THE JEWS OF RUSSIA: HISTORICAL BACKGROUND

1 See, for example, the interesting lecture by O. Pritsak, 'The Origin of "Rus"', Cambridge, Mass., Harvard Ukrainian Research Institute, 1975.

2 I. Berlin notes that in the historiography of Russian Jewry the attitude towards sources was completely uncritical, giving repeated references to the same limited data: I. Berlin, *Istoricheskie sudby evreiskogo naroda na territorii russkogo gosudarstva*, Petrograd, 1919; p. 49. The various hypotheses and theories are subjected to sharp criticism by B. Weinryb in 'The Beginnings of East European Jewry in Legend and Historiography', *Studies and Essays in Honor of A. Neuman*, Leiden, Brill, 1962, pp. 445–502.

3 S. Veisenberg, 'Istoricheskie gnezda Kavkaza i Kryma', *Evreiskaya starina*, 1913, vol. 6, pp. 51–69, 'Evrei v Turkestane', *Evreiskaya starina*, 1912, vol. 5, pp. 390–405; R. Loewenthal, 'The Judeo-Tatars in the Caucasus', *Historia Judaica*, 1952, vol. 14, pp. 61–82.

4 According to Berlin, *Istoricheskie sudby*, p. 55, there is no scientific basis for this theory, which was developed by K. Gausner, *Vestnik russkikh evreev*, 1872, pp. 8–9.

5 This theory was developed by A. Harkavy, based on Armenian and Georgian sources and on items in the Talmud concerning 'Afriki', which he identified, following Schwartz and Cassel, as the Caucasus. See Berlin, *Istoricheskie sudby*, p. 56.

6 See S. Dubnov, *History of the Jews in Russia and Poland*, Philadelphia, 1916–20 (hereafter *History*), vol. 1, pp. 13–18; *idem,* 'Istoricheskie tainy Kryma', *Evreiskaya starina*, 1914, vol. 7, pp. 1–20.

7 The historian Meir Balaban has considered the possibility that Jews arrived in the Crimea from Western Europe as early as the fourth to ninth centuries. See M. Balaban, 'Kiedy i skąd przybyli Żydzi do Polski'. *Miesięcznik Żydowski*, 1930, no. 1, p. 6.

8 I. Malishevsky, 'Evrei v iuzhnoi Rusi i Kieve v X–XII vekakh', *Trudy Kievskoi Dukhovnoi Akademii*, 1878, no. 2, pp. 568–81.

9 See Berlin, *Istoricheskie sudby*, p. 54; I. Brutskus, 'Di geshichte fun di barg-idn oif kavkaz', *Historishe shriftn*, 1937, vol. 2, pp. 26–42; N. Babalikashvili, *Evreiskie nadpisi v Gruzii*, Tbilisi, Metsniereva, 1971, p. 4.

10 Several hundred items dealing with the Khazars appeared during the period 1930 to 1944 alone. See A. Zajączkovwski, *Ze studiów nad zagadnieniem chazarskim*, Kraków, Polska Akademia, Umiejętności, 1947, p. 2. And see M. Landau, in *Zion*, 1943, vol. 8, pp. 94–106. According to Zajączkowski, Khazar research twice became fashionable first from 1880–1930, then from 1930 until the outbreak of the Second World War. The first data on the Khazars actually appeared before 1880.

11 According to other researchers, it lasted until the twelfth to thirteenth centuries. See Zajączkowski, *Ze studiów*, p. 14; A. Polak, *Kazaria*, Jerusalem, Mosad Bialik, 1951, p. 9.

12 The following are the most important studies: P. Kokovtsev, *Evreisko-khazarskaya perepiska*, Leningrad, Akademia Nauk Soiuz Sotsialistiches-

kikh Sovetskikh Respublik, 1932; M. Artamonov, *Istoriya Khazar*, Leningrad, Ermitazh, 1962; D. Dunlop, *The History of the Jewish Khazars*, New Jersey, Princeton University Press, 1954; N. Golb and O. Pritsak, *Khazarian Hebrew Documents of the Tenth Century*, Ithaca–London, Cornell University Press, 1982.

13 On the question of the Khazars being Jewish, see, in addition to the works already cited, I. Brutskus, *Pismo khazarskogo evreya ot X veka*, Berlin, 1924.

14 The view that these sources are not genuine but were put together *post factum* is held not only by the researcher on the Karaites, Zajączkowski (*Ze studiów*, pp. 6–7), but also by the historian of Polish Jewry, B. D. Weinryb, *The Jews of Poland*, Philadelphia, Jewish Publication Society, 1972., p. 21.

15 For the Jews in the Principality of Kiev, see Dubnov, *History*, pp. 29–33; Malishevsky, in *Trudy Kievskoi Dukhovnoi Akademii*, 1878, no. 3, pp. 427–504; I. Darevsky, *K istorii evreev v Kieve*, Kiev, I. Rozet, 1907; Gessen, *Istoriya* (1916), pp. 1–5; M. Kulisher, 'Evrei v Kieve', *Evreiskaya starina*, 1924, vol. 11, pp. 93–109; S. Ettinger, 'Kievan Russia', *World History of the Jewish People – The Dark Ages*, Tel Aviv, Massada, 1966, pp. 319–34.

16 See Dubnov, *History*; pp. 33–6; *idem*, Istoricheskie tainy, pp. 7–16; R. Loewenthal, 'The Extinction of the Krimchaks in World War II', *American and East European Review*, 1951, no. 2, pp. 130–6.

17 There is much controversy regarding Khazari rule in the eastern Crimea. According to Brutskus, the name 'Khazkariya' or 'Gaskariya', which was current from the eleventh to sixteenth centuries, is a geographic descriptive term only and there was no such thing as Khazari – let alone Jewish – rule there. See I. Brutskus, 'Zekharia Kniaz Tamansky', *Evreiskaya starina*, 1918, vol. 10, p. 132.

18 J. Schiltberger, *The Bondage and Travels ... in Europe, Asia and Africa, 1396–1427*, London, 1879, pp. 49, 176, quoted in Baron, *The Russian Jew*, p. 353.

19 Brutskus, (Zekharia).

20 For the Krimchaks, see E. Peisakh, 'Krimtshakes', *Sovietish heimland*, 1974, nos. 7 and 9.

21 There are two conflicting trends in the historical writings on the period of the Principality of Moscow, and as regards Russian Jews in later periods. The first trend seeks to demonstrate that the Jews were treated with tolerance, and that they were not discriminated against in comparison with other foreigners, except perhaps during religio-political crises, or under the regimes of fanatical rulers. This thesis was most consistently argued by N. Gradovsky (see his *La situation légale des Israélites en Russie*, Paris, Cerf, 1890, vol. 1, pp. 2–52). It was supported, if less wholeheartedly, by Y. Gessen (see his *Istoriya evreev v Rossii*, pp. 1–22; and 'Evrei v Moskovskom gosudarstve XI–XVII v', *Evreiskaya starina*, 1915, vol. 8, pp. 1–19, 153–72. The second trend emphasizes that hostility towards the Jews was common, based on religious intolerance. Representatives of the second line of thought are: Orshansky, *Russkoe*

pp. 16–19; Demidoff-San-Donato, *La Question juive en Russie*, Brussels, Cerf, 1884, pp. 16–19; Dubnov, *History*, vol. 1, pp. 35–8, 242–61; S. Ettinger, 'Medinat moskvah be-yahas el ha-yehudim', *Zion*, 1953, vol. 18, pp. 136–68.

22 There is extensive literature on the subject. See especially *Registry i nadpisi. Svod materialov dlya istorii evreev v Rossii 80 g–1800 g.*, St Petersburg, Evreiskoe istorscheskoe etnografischeskoe obshchestvo, 2 vols., 1899–1913, vol. 1, nos. 201–2; G. Vernadsky, 'The Heresy of Judaizers and Ivan III', *Speculum*, 1933, vol. 8, pp. 448–52; S. Ettinger, 'Ha-hashpaa ha-yehudit al ha-tesisa ha-datit be-mizraha shel europa be-sof ha-meah ha-15', *Sefer yuval le-itzhak ber*, Jerusalem, Historical Society of Israel, 1960, pp. 228–47; J. Halperin, 'Judaizers and the Image of the Jew in Medieval Russia', *Canadian American Slavic Studies*, 1975, vol. 9, no. 2, pp. 141–55; Ya. Lurie, 'L'Heresie dites des Judaisants et ses sources historiques', *Revue des Etudes Slaves*, 1966, vol. 45, pp. 49–67.

23 Quoted in Ettinger, 'Medinat moskvah', p. 137.

24 Gradovsky, *La Situation légale*, p. 16.

25 See V. Stoklitskaya-Tereshkovich, 'Pervyi ritualnyi protses v Rossii', *Evreiskaya starina*, 1918, vol. 10, pp. 7–26.

26 See I. Gurland, in *Evreiskaya starina*, 1909, vol. 2, pp. 246–50.

27 Quoted in Ettinger, 'Medinat moskvah', p. 159.

28 Ibid.

29 The following Collections of laws and legal commentaries have been used as the basis for this chapter: V. Levanda, *Polnyi khronologichesky sbornik zakonov i polozhenii kasayushchikhsya evreev*, St Petersburg, K. Trubnikova, 1874; I. Gessen and V. Fridshtein, *Sbornik zakonov o evreyakh*, St Petersburg, N. Martynov, 1904; M. Mysh, *Rukovodstvo k russkim zakonam o evreyakh*, St Petersburg, M. Frolova, 1904; Y. Gimpelson and L. Bramson, *Zakony o evreyakh*, St Petersburg, Iurisprudentsiya, 1914–15, 2 vols.

30 See the interesting if controversial article by R. Pipes, 'Catherine II and the Jews', *Soviet Jewish Affairs*, 1975, no. 2, pp. 3–20. And see K. Klier, 'The Ambiguous Legal Status of Russian Jewry in the Reign of Catherine II', *The Slavic Review*, 1976, no. 3, pp. 504–17.

31 See S. Ettinger, 'Ha-yesodot ve-ha-magamot be-yizuv midiniuto shel ha-shilton ha-rusi klapei ha-yehudim im halukat polin', *He-avar*, 1972, vol. 19, p. 22.

32 *He-avar*, 1972, Vol. 19, p. 75.

33 Gradovsky, *La Situation légale*, p. 55.

34 Gradovsky, *La Situation légale*, p. 59; Pipes, 'Catherine II', p. 10.

35 Thus, for example, in 1781, of the 15,593 Jews in the Mohilev District, 10% were registered as traders, as against only 5.5% of the Christian population. In the Polotsk District, 6.5% of the population were Jewish merchants and 7.5% Christian merchants. See Gessen, *Istoriya evreiskogo naroda v Rossii*, vol. 1, p. 57.

36 Ibid., pp. 59–60.

37 See Dubnov, *History*, vol. 1, p. 316; Baron, *The Russian Jew*, p. 21; I. Bikerman, *Cherta evreiskoi osedlosti*, St Petersburg, Razum, 1911, p. 17.

38 Levanda, *Polnyi khronologichesky sbornik.*, pp. 42 *et seq.*

39 Ibid., pp. 43 *et seq.*
40 See *Proekt evreiskoi reformy*, in Gessen, *Evrei v Rossii*, pp. 449–52. Historians differ about the influences behind Friesel's proposed reform. According to Dubnov (*History*, vol. 1, pp. 326–7), Friesel based his ideas on the reforms presented to the Polish Sejm by Czacki and Buturomowicz, while according to Ettinger (see n. 31 above), 'The main lines of the reform were all taken from the *Haskalah* literature for *Tikun* (Reform) among the Jews in the West.' Friesel was probably aware both of the material from German–Jewish *Haskalah* circles and also of the debates in the 'Jewish Committee' of the Polish Sejm, and made use of both sources for his proposal.
41 See G. Derzhavin, *Sochineniya*, St Petersburg, Tipografiya Akademii Nauk, 1868–78, vol. 7, pp. 261–355.
42 Unlike most of the historians who pointed to the anti-Semitic line taken by Derzhavin in accordance with the well-established Polish tradition of hostility to the Jews, Arnold Springer thinks that an objective approach shows Derzhavin's views to have been far more complex and representative of his time. See A. Springer, 'Gabriel Derzhavin's Jewish Reform Project of 1800', *Canadian American Slavic Studies*, 1976, vol. 10, pp. 1–23.
43 Among the various influences were reports from the Governors and heads of the nobility, reform proposals made by Jewish *Maskilim* such as Note Notkin and V. Frank, and Prussian legislation on Jewish questions. Springer, however, finds no sign of any such influence and argues that Derzhavin adopted the accepted views of his time regarding Austrian Jews. A variety of Polish material must also have been taken into account.
44 See S. Bershadsky, 'Polozhenie o evreyakh 1804 g', *Voshkod*, 1895, no. 2, pp. 82–103, no. 3, pp. 69–96; no. 4, pp. 86–109; Gessen, *Evrei v Rossii*, pp. 74–139. Gessen thinks that Speransky, then a senior official in the Interior Ministry, played an important role on the committee that prepared the 1804 ordinances.
45 Levanda, *Polnyi khronologichesky sbornik*, pp. 59 *et seq.*
46 Gessen, *Istoriya evreiskogo naroda v Rossii*, vol. 1, p. 153. Dubnov, however, considers that half a million Jews were involved: *History*, p. 346.
47 See S. Ginzburg, *Otechestvennaya voina 1812 goda i russkie evrei*, St Petersburg, Razum, 1912.
48 This law is extremely detailed in comparison with the general law of conscription. See Levanda, *Polnyi khronologichesky sbornik*, pp. 154 *et seq.* It is perhaps worth recalling that as early as 1807 and 1823 proposals were discussed for conscripting 'harmful and criminal Jews'.
49 The reference is to the Order of 7 September 1794, according to which 500 roubles could be paid for every recruit.
50 See Kh. Korobkov, 'Evreiskaya rekrutchina v tsarstvovanie Nikolaya I', *Evreiskaya starina*, 1913, vol. 6, pp. 70–85, 244–83.
51 See, e.g., the memoirs of V. Nikitin, *Mnogostradalnye ocherki proshlogo*, St Petersburg, V. Komarov, 1895; S. Ginzburg, 'Mucheniki deti', *Evreiskaya starina*, 1930, vol. 13, pp. 50–79.
52 See Korobkov, 'Evreiskaya rekrutchina', pp. 70–85, 244–83.

53 Baron estimates that about 60,000 Jews were conscripted during the thirty years of recruitment: *The Russian Jews*, p. 37.
54 Levanda, *Polnyi khronologichesky sbornik*, p. 304 *et seq.*
55 As Orshansky rightly points out; Russian legislation in general was built up from numerous exceptions and unique instances: *Russkoe*, p. 3.
56 See Y. Gessen, 'Popytka emantsipatsii evreev v Rossii', *Perezhitoe*, 1908, vol. 1, pp. 144–63.
57 Gessen, *Istoriya evreiskogo naroda v Rossii*, p. 142.
58 See 'Zapiski ob emamtsipatsii evreev v Rossii (1859)', *Evreiskaya starina*, 1916, vol. 9, pp. 300 *et seq.*
59 See H. Sliozberg, 'Baron G. Ginzburg i pravovoe polozhenie evreev', *Perezhitoe*, 1909, vol. 2, pp. 94–115.
60 Levanda, *Polnyi khronologichesky sbornik*, pp. 892 *et seq.*
61 Ibid., pp. 955 *et seq.*
62 Greenberg, *The Jews in Russia*, vol. 1, p. 76.
63 See Gessen, *Istoriya evreiskogo naroda v Rossii*, vol. 2, p. 168.
64 See M. Usov, *Evrei v armii*, St Petersburg, Razum, 1911; Y. Slutski, 'Takanon hovat ha-zava ha-klalit ve-ha-yehudim', *He-avar*, 1975, vol. 21, pp. 3–19.
65 See H. Rogger, 'Tsarist Policy on Jewish Emigration', *Soviet Jewish Affairs*, 1973, no. 3, p. 29.
66 It is not certain that these were the exact words of Pobedonostsev, but they certainly express his outlook. See M. Davitt, *Within the Pale*, Philadelphia, J.P.S., 1903, pp. 49–50; Dubnov, *History*, vol. 3, p. 10; R. Byrnes, *Pobedonostsev: His Life and Thought*, Bloomington, Indiana University Press, 1968, p. 207; I. M. Aronson, 'The Attitudes of Russian Officials in the 1880s Toward Jewish Assimilation and Emigration', *Slavic Review*, 1975, vol. 34, no. 1, p. 1.
67 See I. Maor, *Sheelat ha-yehudim be-tenuah ha-liberalit ve-ha-mahapkhanit be-russia*, Jerusalem, Mosad Bialik, 1964, pp. 15–18.
68 B. Z. Dinur, 'Dmuta ha-historit shel ha-yahadut ha-rusit u-boayot ha-mehkar ba', *Zion*, 1957, vol. 22, pp. 93–118.
69 As quoted in B. Z. Dinur, 'Tokhniotav shel Ignatev', *He-avar*, 1963, vol. 10, pp. 42–3. See also *Trudy gubernskikh komissii po evreiskomu voprosu*, St Petersburg, 1884; I. M. Aronson, *Russian Bureaucratic Attitudes Toward Jews, 1881–1894*; PhD dissertation, Northwestern University, Evanston, 1974.
70 Dinur, 'Tokhniotav shel Ignatev …', p. 21; Gimpelson, and Bramson, *Zakony*, vol. 1, pp. 258–66.
71 Ibid., p. 2.
72 Ibid., pp. 189–90.
73 Gimpelson and Bramson, vol. 2, pp. 441–2.
74 See Slutski, 'Takanon'; Gimpelson and Bramson, vol. 2, pp. 471–97; Mysh, pp. 409–10.
75 Slutski, 'Takanon', p. 19.
76 Gimpelson and Bramson, vol. 2, pp. 535–55.
77 A. Feldman, 'Ha-manifest me-yom 17 be-oktober 1905; ha-rozen vite veha-sheelah ha-yehudit', in *Raphael Mahler Jubilee Volume*, Merhaviah, Sifriat poalim, 1974, p. 115.

78 See M. Anich, *Otmena cherty evreiskoi osedlosti*, Moscow, Evrei v Rossii, 1915; Y. Slutski, 'Diunei moezet ha-ministrim...', *He-avar*, 1966, vol. 13, pp. 41–58; *Arkhiv Russkoi revolutsii*, 1926, vol. 18, pp. 42–57; *Russkaya pechat' i obshhestvo ob otmene evreiskoi osedlosti*, Moscow, Evrei i Rossiya, 1915.

79 See S. Dubnov and G. Krasny-Admoni (eds.), *Materialy dlya istorii antievreiskykh pogromov v Rossii*, Petrograd, Gosizdat, 1919–23, 2 vols; *Die Judenpogrome in Russland*, Köln and Leipzig, Judischer Verlag, 1910, vols. 1–2; I. Slutski, 'Ha-geografia shel praot tarma', *He-avar*, 1962, vol. 9, pp. 16–25, and *He-avar*, 1963, vol. 10, pp. 144–9; Davitt, *Within the Pale*.

80 M. Vishniak 'Antisemitism in Tsarist Russia', in K. Pinson (ed.), *Essays on Antisemitism*, New York, Conference on Jewish Relations, 1946, p. 131.

81 See E. Cherikover, 'Naye materialn vegn di pogromen in russland', *Yivo historishe shriftn*, 1937, vol. 2, pp. 444–465; *Krasnyi arkhiv*, 1927, vol. 21, pp. 200–17; R. Kantor, 'Aleksandr III o evreiskikh pogromakh 1881–1883', *Evreiskaya letopis*, 1923, vol. 1, pp. 149–58.

82 Vishniak, 'Antisemitism', p. 136. On the Kishinev pogrom see *Ha-pogrom be-kishinev be-mleat 60 shanim*, Tel-Aviv, Haigud ha-olami shel yehudei besarabia, 1963.

83 As early as 1887, at the time of the pogroms in Odessa, Jewish students did try to organize themselves in self-defence, but it was only in Homel that the defenders succeeded in repulsing the rioters.

84 S. Dubnov, *Evrei v tsarstvovanii Nikolaya II*, St Petersburg, Kadima, 1921, p. 64.

85 Vishniak, 'Antisemitism' p. 138; *Encyclopaedia Judaica*, vol. 13, pp. 694–701.

86 Opinions are divided among historians over the personal responsibility of von Pleve for the Kishinev pogrom. Most of them judge him responsible for the pogrom, but Feldman writes: 'Pleve may have had some connection with the pogrom, but what kind of connection it was and how deeply he was involved we do not know.' See *He-avar*, 1970, vol. 17, p. 150.

87 See M. Samuel, *Blood Accusation. The Strange History of Beiliss Case*. Philadelphia, JPS, 1966; A. Tager, *Decay of Czarism, the Beiliss Case*, Philadelphia, JPS, 1935; H. Rogger, 'The Beiliss Case: Antisemitism and Politics in the Reign of Nicholas II', *Slavic Review*, 1966, vol. 25, no. 4, pp. 615–29.

88 See Dubnov, *History*, vol. 2, pp. 399–410; S. Vermel, *Moskovskoe izgnanie, 1891–1892*, Moscow, Emes, 1924; *He-avar*, 1971, vol. 18, pp. 3–62.

89 L. Aizenberg in *Evreiskaya starina*, 1930, vol. 13, p. 81. Other sources gave the number of 20,000 Aronson, p. 37; Rogger, 'Tsarist Policy', p. 30.

90 L. Garfunkel, '50 shanah le-gerush ha-yehudim me-palkhei kovna vekurland', *He-avar*, 1966, vol. 13, p. 6.

91 Baron, *The Russian Jew*, 2nd edn, (1976), p. 159.

92 See Rogger, 'Tsarist Policy', p. 27.

93 Dubnov, *History*, vol. 2, p. 285; Greenberg, *The Jews in Russia*, vol. 2, p. 62.

94 Maor, *Sheelat ha-yehudim*, p. 22.

95 N. Gelber, in *Yivo historishe shriftn*, 1937, vol. 2, p. 487.

96 Dubnov, *History*, pp. 306–7.

97 Rogger, 'Tsarist Policy', p. 28.

98 See A. Shoḥat, Mosad 'ha-rabanut me-taam' be-rusia, Haifa, Haifa University, 1975, pp. 109–0.

99 *Haluz u-maas, The Abraham Katsh Jubilee Volume*, Tel-Aviv, Avukah, 1975, pp. 55–64.

100 E. Schulman, *A History of Jewish Education in the Soviet Union*, New York, Ktav Publishing House, 1971, p. 3.

101 Ibid.

102 Thus, for example, figures for 1904 give 24,540 *heders* in Russia, with an average of fourteen pupils each, while ten years previously, as we saw, the number was only 13,689, and according to a different set of data the number did not exceed 9,255 in 1894. See S. Rabinovich in *Evreiskaya shkola*, 1904, no. 11, p. 10.

103 See M. Kreinin in *Shkolnoe delo v Rossii 1902–1903*, pp. 278–82.

104 E. Schulman, *Jewish Education*, p. 28.

105 Ibid., p. 23.

106 Ibid., p. 24 and see also *Evreiskaya entsyklopedia*, vol. 9, p. 58.

107 Z. Halevy, *Jewish University Students and Professionals in Tsarist and Soviet Russia*, Tel-Aviv, Diaspora Research Institute, 1976, p. 12.

108 Ibid., pp. 48, 52, 54.

109 S. Schwarz, *The Jews in the Soviet Union*, New York, Syracuse University Press, 1951, pp. 142–3.

110 See *Teater bukh*, Kiev, Kultur lige, 1927.

111 See Sh. Braiman, 'Ha-mifne be-mehshavah ha-ziburit ha-yehudit', *Shivat Zion*, 1953, nos. 2–3, pp. 83–227.

112 L. Pinsker, *Autoemanzipation, ein Mahnruf on Seine Stammesgenossen von einen russischen Juden*, Berlin, Commissions-Verlag von W. Issleib, 1882.

113 See J. Frankel, *Socialism and Jewish Nationalism in Russia, 1892–1907*, unpublished PhD dissertation, University of Cambridge, 1961; idem, J. Frankel, *Prophecy and Politics: Socialism, Nationalism and the Russian Jews 1862–1917*, Cambridge, Cambridge University Press, 1981.

114 See L. Schapiro, 'The Role of the Jews in the Russian Revolutionary Movement', *Slavonic and East European Review*, 1961, vol. 40, pp. 148–67.

115 See E. Mendelsohn, 'The Russian Roots of the American Jewish Labor Movement', *YIVO Annual of Jewish Social Science*, 1976, vol. 16, pp. 150–77; Kh. Turtel, 'Tnuat am-olam', *He-avar*, 1963, vol. 6, pp. 124–43.

116 See J. Tobias, *The Jewish Bund in Russia, From its Origins to 1905*, Stanford, Stanford University Press, 1972.

117 Ibid., pp. 98, 140, 239.

118 Vl. Kantorovich, 'Bund na kanune fevralskoi revolutsii', *Evreiskaya letopis*, 1923, vol. 2, pp. 37–54.

119 Gitelman, *Jewish Nationality*, p. 72.

120 See A. Patkin, *The Origins of the Russian Jewish Labour Movement*, Melbourne, F. W. Cheshive, 1947.
121 *Proekt programmy evreiskoi sotsialisticheskoi partii*, Kharkov, 1917.
122 *Volkspartei – evreiskaya narodnaya partiya*, St Petersburg, 1907.
123 See Ya Lifshits, *Zikhron Yaakov*, Kovna, Slobodka, 1930; E. Cherikover, *Yehudim be-eitot mahapekha*, Tel Aviv, Am oved, 1957, p. 359.
124 See Cherikover, ibid.; N. Bukhbinder, 'Iz istorii sektantskogo dvizheniya sredi russkikh evreev, *Evreiskaya starina*, 1924, vol. 11, pp. 238–65 and 1930, vol. 13, pp. 116–30; Y. Priluker, *Under the Czar and Queen Victoria*, London, James Nisbet, 1895.
125 *The City of London, Public Meeting Against the Persecution of the Jews in Russia*, London, 1882.
126 *Evreiskaya starina*, 1916, vol. 9, pp. 121–5.
127 I. Hailperin, 'Nisayon shel interventsia politit le-maan yehudei russiya', *Zion*, 1955, vol. 20, pp. 163–74; J. Raba, 'Reactions of the Jews of Vienna to the Russian Pogroms of 1905', *Michael*, 1973, vol. 2, pp. 135–44.

2 THE JEWS OF THE SOVIET UNION: THE YEARS OF CONSTRUCTION, 1917–39

1 Extreme anti-Jewish expressions are common in Marx's essay, 'On the Jewish Question', printed in 1844 and 'The Holy Family', written in 1845 in collaboration with Engels, as well as in a large number of his other writings. See E. Silberner, *Ha-sozialism ha-maaravi u-sheelat ha-yehudim*, Jerusalem, Mosad Bialik, 1955, p. 146.
2 V. Lenin, *Sobranie sochinenii*, Moscow, Politizdat, 1967–70, 55 vols. 5th edn., vol. 8, p. 27; vol. 10, p. 267.
3 Lenin, *Sobranie sochinenii*, vol. 8, p. 73.
4 Ibid.
5 Ibid, p. 75.
6 Ibid, p. 313.
7 I. Stalin, *Sochineniya*, Moscow, Politizdat, 1949–51, 13 vols., vol. 2, p. 334.
8 A. Chemerisky, *Di alfarband-komunistishe partei un di idishe masn*, Moscow, Shul un bukh, 1926, p. 72.
9 See pp. 71–6 and chapters 3 and 4.
10 Stalin, *Sochineniya*, vol. 2, p. 296.
11 *Desatyi s'ezd RKP (b)*, sten., otchet, Moscow, Gospoltizdat, 1963.
12 *KPSS v rezolutsiyakh*, Izdanie 7-e, Moscow, Gospolitizdat, 1954, pp. 709–18.
13 *A yor arbet fun der RKP (b)*, Moscow, Emes, 1924, p. 6.
14 *Di politik fun der KP(b)U in der natsionaler frage*, Kharkov, Literatur un kunst, 1931, p. 90.
15 *Di politik*, pp. 117–28.
16 Ibid., pp. 167–77.
17 *Istoriya sovetskoi konstitutsii, Sbornik dokumentov, 1917–1957*, Moscow, AN SSSR, 1957, p. 20.
18 Ibid., pp. 11, 117 Note that the three clauses are identical. The constitu-

From 1957 to 1960 the wave of arrests, interrogations and arrests affected both sets of Zionists: the younger people who had recently become energetically involved, such as Barukh Podolsky, Tina Borodetskaya, D. B. Shperling, Yosef Shneider, Anatoli Rubin, David Havkin, and veteran Zionists and religious Jews connected with the synagogues, such as Gedaliahu Pechersky, Nathan Tsirulnikov, A. Dynkin and B. Kaganov. They were tried on serious charges, such as collaboration with and passing information to a Foreign State through its Embassy, ideological sabotage, and defaming the Soviet Union. Except for the trial of Pechersky, Kaganov and Dynkin in Leningrad, these trials were held in secret, like their forerunners in 1956. The last big trial of this period was of Dolnik in 1966. These arrests weakened the Zionist movement, by eliminating the leading activists and intimidating others, but also helped to forge a new generation that would lead Zionism during its main period of activity, from 1968 to 1971.

1968 TO 1983

Political dissidents only began to act effectively in 1965 and 1966, when the trials of Sinyavsky and Daniel took place. The organized activity of the Ukrainian nationalist movement also started in the second half of the 1960s. The only active groups before the Zionists were the Crimean Tatars and the Germans. As early as 1957 the Tatars organized petitions, signed by between 6,000 and 25,000 people,[275] demanding full rehabilitation and the right to return to the Crimea. Between 1965 and 1967 the Germans organized three delegations to the heads of the Soviet government, which made similar demands and presented petitions signed by thousands of Germans. Though these groups obtained large numbers of signatures, they did not work as intensively or for as long a period as the Zionists. The Germans, like the Tatars demanded the correction of a historical wrong, but unlike the Zionists sought a solution within the Soviet State framework which would be more easily accepted by the leadership.

How large was the Zionist movement in the 1960s and 1970s? How wide was its action and what were its methods? To help answer these difficult questions, it is worth examining the scope of the other dissident movements in this period. They were illegal movements, persecuted by the authorities and acting clandestinely, and it is difficult to define who was a 'member' of which movement, who was an 'activist'

tions of the Republics of Belorussia and the Ukraine are practically word-for-word copies of the constitutions of the Russian Republic of 1918.

19 *Prakticheskoe razreshenie natsionalnogo voprosa v Belorusskoi sotsialisticheskoi sovetskoi respublike, chast I – Belorussizatsiya*, Minsk, Tsentralnyi Ispolnitelnyi Komitet Belorusskoi Sotsialisticheskoi Sovetskoi Respubliki, 1927, p. 122.

20 V. Durdenevsky, *Ravnopravie yazykov v sovetskom stroe*, Moscow, Institut sovetskogo prava, 1929, pp. 162–3.

21 As regards education, the resolution of 31 October 1918, requiring teaching by means of the mother-tongue in all elementary and secondary schools, should not be overlooked, see Durdenevsky, Ravnopravie, p. 53.

22 *Polozhenie o narodnom sude RSFSR 1917–1920*, Petrograd, 1921, p. 79; *Sobranie uzakonenii i rasporyazhenii rabochego i krestiyanskogo pravitelstva USSR*, Kiev, 1922.

23 Y. Kantor, *Ratenboyung tsvishn di yidishe masn*, Moscow, Emes, 1932.

24 Durdenevsky, *Ravnopravie*, pp. 147–54.

25 See *Prakticheskoe razreshenie*, vol. 1.

26 See ISK, pp. 252–3.

27 See G. Ginzburg, *Soviet Citizenship Law*, Leyden, Nijhoff, 1968; R. Beermann, 'Russian and Soviet Passport Laws', *Bulletin of Soviet Jewish Affairs*, 1968, no. 2, pp. VI/1–11.

28 For the *Narkomnats* and the Evsektsia, see in particular: M. Altshuler, *Ha-yevsektsia bi-vrit ha-moazot (1918–1930)*, Tel-Aviv, Sifriat poalim, 1980; Gitelman, *Jewish Nationality and Soviet Politics*, and for Soviet research: Ya. Sharapov, *Natsionalnye sektsii RKP(b)*, Kazan, Kazansky Universitet, 1967.

29 See Sh. Agursky, *Der yidisher arbeter in der komunistisher bavegung, 1917–21*, Minsk, Melukhe farlag, 1925, pp. 24–34; N. Nir-Rafalkes, *Pirkei ḥaim, be maagalei ha-dor veha-tnuah 1884–1918*, Tel-Aviv, Ha-Kibuẓ ha-meuḥad, 1958, p. 252.

30 'Novyi narkomnats', *Zhizn' natsionalnostei, 1922*, n. 16; 'Likvidatsiya Narkomnatsa', *Vlast sovetov*, 1924, n. 1, pp. 129–30; B. Kulbecherov, *Deyatelnost' soveta natsionalnostei i ego prezidyuma*, Moscow, TSIK SSSR, 1929.

31 In August 1920 there were the following National Sections: Jewish, German, Polish, Yugoslav, Lithuanian, Esthonian, Czech, Hungarian and Mari. See *Izvestiya Ts.K. R.K.P. 16*, 1921, no. 28, pp. 13–17.

32 *Sotsialnyi i natsionalnyi sostav VKP(b)*, Moscow, Gosizdat, 1928, p. 144.

33 Altshuler thinks there were only between 2,500 and 3,000 Evsektsia and even if we add the Komsomol members, the total is still about 4,000 to 4,500. M. Altshuler, *Ha-yevsektsia*, p. 188.

34 Stalin, *Sochineniya*, vol. 8, pp. 149–54.

35 *Partiinoe stroitelstvo*, 1930, no. 2(4), pp. 70–2; 1930, no. 6(8), pp. 22–6; G. Saks, *Rabota sredi natsionalnykh menshinsv, Opyt Leningradskoi oblasti*, Leningrad, OGIZ Priboi, 1931.

36 See M. Altshuler, 'Ha-vaad ha-ẓiburi ha-yehudi le-ezrat nifgaei ha-pogromim, 1920–1924', *Shvut*, 1982, no. 9, pp. 16–34; Y. Lvavi, 'Ozet-gezerd-ḥevra le-sidur haklai shel- yehudim amelim bi-vrit ha-moaẓot',

He-avar, 1961, vol. 16, pp. 118–30. Other public organizations that still existed in the 1930s were YEKOPO (the Jewish Relief Committee), ORT (The Society for Craft and Agricultural Labour among the Jews in Russia, founded in 1886) and OZET.

37 In his comprehensively researched article, Altshuler gives the figure of $2,800,000 for the years 1920 to 1922. According to Gitelman, *Jewish Nationality and Soviet Politics*, p. 238, aid from the 'Joint' to Soviet Jews in 1924 alone came to ten million dollars.

38 Y. Slutski, 'Tribuna'-ktav-et yehudi-rusi-sovieti, 1927–1937', *Behinot*, 1979, nos. 8–9, pp. 68–88.

39 B. Pinkus, 'Yiddish-Language Courts and Nationalities Policy in the Soviet Union', *Soviet Jewish Affairs*, 1971, no. 2, pp. 40–60.

40 The Soviet data on everything concerning national minorities and nationality law-courts are contradictory. We have attempted to give only data that seemed reliable and appeared in more than one source. See Y. Kantor, *Natsionalnoe stroitelstvo sredi evreev v SSSR*, Moscow, Vlast, sovetov, 1934, pp. 27–34; G. Zaitsev in *Vlast sovetov* 1926, no. 44–5, p. 14; G. Volkov in *Vlast sovetov*, 1927, no. 33–4, p. 9; I. Trainin in E. Pashukanis (ed.), *15 let sovetskogo stroitelstva*, Moscow, Ogiz, 1930, pp. 80–1; Schwarz, *The Jews*, pp. 150–6; A. Glensky, *Dergraikhungen un felern in der arbet tsvishn di natsionale minderkhaitn*, Kharkov, Tsentral farlag, 1931, pp. 25–46.

41 A. Bragin and M. Koltsov, *Sudba evreiskikh mass v Sovetskom Soyuze*, Moscow, Mospoligraf, 1924, pp. 17–26. For Jewish settlement in the Crimea in the 1920s see Y. Keren, *Ha-hitiashvut ha-haklait ha-yehudit be-ḥazi ha-i krim (1922–1947)*, Jerusalem, Zak, 1973; Y. Lvavi, 'Ha-mitiashvim ha-ḥaklaiim ha-yehudiim be-krim be-misparim', *Shvut*, 1984, no. 10, p. 55.

42 See Altshuler, *Ha-yevsektsia*, p. 191.

43 *Der emes*, 18 June 1924.

44 A. Chemerisky, *Di alfarband-komunistishe partei (bolshevikes) un di yidishe masn*, Moscow, Shul un bukh, 1926, p. 72.

45 Larin declared explicitly in 1926, 'Our line is to give a National Republic to every nationality living in our country', *Ershter alfarbandisher tsuzamenfar fun gezerd*, Moscow, Tsentralfarvaltung fun gezerd, 1927, pp. 93–4.

46 Quoted as in Altshuler, *Ha-yevsektsia*, p. 202.

47 Clause 9 of the Resolution of the Evsektsia Council of December 1926 stated *inter alia* 'Measures must be taken to allocate a bloc like this (for continuous Jewish settlement) in other more distant parts of the Soviet Union.' See *Alfarbandische baratung fun di yidishe sektsies fun der Al.K.P(b)*, Moscow, Shul un bukh, 1927, p. 238.

48 For the Birobidzhan project and its historical development, see Y. Lvavi, *Ha-hityashvut ha-yehudit be-birobidzhan*, Jerusalem, The Historical Society of Israel, 1965; H. Sloves, *Mamlakhtiyut yehudit bi-vrit ha-moazot, yovlah shel birobidzhan*, Tel-Aviv, Am oved, 1980; Kantor, *Natsionlnoe stroitelstvo*, pp. 110–35.

49 *Der emes*, 20 January 1928.

50 Shmeruk, *Ha-hityashvut ha-ḥaklait*, pp. 95–9.

51 In an article by Chemerisky cited in note 49, it is stated that 'the Birobidzhan project will objectively deal the heaviest blow to the Palestine-religious ideology and political Zionism.' For more details see I. Sudarsky, *Birobidzhan un palestine*, Kharkov, Tsentral farlag, 1929.

52 This document and others relating to Birobidzhan are given by Lvavi in *Ha-hitiyashvut*, pp. 350–61.

53 M. Kalinin, *Ob obrazovanii evreiskoi avtonomnoi oblasti*, Moscow, Emes, 1935, p. 22.

54 Kantor, *Natsionalnoe stroitelstvo*, pp. 118–19.

55 The data on internal migration in the years 1934 to 1937 are taken from Lvavi, *Ha-hityashvut*, pp. 90–100.

56 Lvavi, *Ha-hityashvut*, p. 115.

57 An example of attacks of this kind, which were also to be found in the Jewish press, appeared in *Tribuna*, the organ of OZET, on 15 September 1936. See also *Tribuna*, 1936, no. 17, pp. 1–2. Moshe Litvakov published an article vilifying Liberberg and his comrades: *Tribuna*, 1937, no. 9, and *Der Emes*, 18 April 1937.

58 Sharapov, *Natsionalnye sektsii*, pp. 239.

59 On Jews in the Russian revolutionary movement, see L. Schapiro, 'The Role of the Jews in the Russian Revolutionary Movement', *The Slavonic and East European Review*, 1961, vol. 40, no. 12; Gitelman, *Jewish Nationality*, pp. 105–19.

60 All the data on the composition of the top Communist Party institutions are based on a list of persons drawn from the party congresses. For lack of space we shall not detail all the bibliographical data on the subject.

61 *Meirevnik*, 1930, no. 6, pp. 28–30; *Sotsialnyi i natsionalnyi sostav*, p. 114.

62 T. M. Rigby, *Communist Party Membership in the USSR 1917–1967*, New Jersey, Princeton University Press, 1968, pp. 366–88.

63 Between 1925, when Jews constituted 4.8% of the Komsomol, and 1929 there was a decrease to 4%. This was apparently a reasonable figure, given the mass character of the organization (over two million members). See *Alfarbandische baratung*, p. 36.

64 *Sezdy sovetov v postanovleniyakh i rezolutsiyakh*, Moscow, Kommunisticheskaya Akademiya, 1935, p. 475.

65 *Sostav organov vlastii v Soyuze SSR*, Moscow-Leningrad, Ogiz, 1930, Table XIV.

66 Chemerisky, *Di alfarbandische*, p. 72.

67 *Vlast sovetov*, 1926, no. 19–20, p. 19.

68 Yu. Larin, *Antisemitizm v SSSR*, Moscow, Gosizdat, 1929, p. 115.

69 *Vlast Sovetov*, 1936, no. 9 (10).

70 Larin, *Antisemitizm*, p. 114.

71 Ibid., p. 115.

72 On Jews in the Army in the 1920s see Larin. *Ershter alfarbandischer tsuzamenfar* and M. Altshuler, 'Ha-ÿehudim be-ẓava ha-adom', *Shvut*, 1980, no. 7, pp. 36–40.

73 According to Leshchinsky, approximately 75,000 Jews were murdered from 1917 to 1921, about the same number wounded, and about 50,000 women widowed. To the war orphans were added about 100,000 or-

phans from the pogroms. Over 2,000 pogroms were recorded. About half a million Jews left their homes and fled to the cities: Y. Leshchinsky, *Ha-yehudim be-rusia-ha-sovietit*, Tel Aviv, Am oved, 1940, p. 53. According to Soviet publications, the number of those killed in the pogroms was around 180,000 to 200,000. See B. D. Weinryb, 'Antisemitism in Soviet Russia', in L. Kochan (ed.), *The Jews in Soviet Russia since 1917*, Oxford, Oxford University Press, 1978, p. 310; S. Gusev-Orenburgsky, *Bagrovaya kniga, Pogromy 1919–1920*, Kharbin, Dekopo, 1920.

74 See, for example, the numerous statements by Lenin in this period against anti-Semitism and pogroms: Lenin, *Sobranie sochinenii*, 5th edn., vol. 9, p. 333; vol. 10, pp. 83, 226–9, 373; vol. 12, pp. 38, 76–7; vol. 13, pp. 198–203, 209, 223, 280; vol. 14, pp. 3–5, 38; vol. 16, p. 17; vol. 20, p. 22, 326; vol. 21, pp. 17, 177–8, 278, 280; vol. 24, pp. 135, 183–5, 324; vol. 25, pp. 10, 14–18, 64–6, 85–6; vol. 30, p. 324; vol. 31, p. 12; vol. 34, p. 8.

75 The only discordant note in this approach to the phenomenon of anti-Semitism appears in the statement by Stalin in the published Report of the party congress of 1907, when he cited Aleksinsky's joke, in dubious taste, to the effect that one could have a pogrom in the Menshevik faction, with its majority of Jews, in order to seek a solution to the party's problems. See Stalin, *Sochineniya*, vol. 2, pp. 50–1.

76 *Izvestiya*, 27 July 1918.

77 Lenin, *Sobranie sochinenii*, vol. 38, pp. 242–3; it is interesting that this speech is among the few that were not included in the recording of all Lenin's speeches made in honour of the occasion of the hundredth anniversary of his birth, underlining the change that had taken place since Lenin's day.

78 In Russia alone in the first period, out of a total of 100 books published since the establishment of the regime, forty-six books and booklets were on the subject of anti-Semitism. See B. Pinkus, A. Grinbaum and M. Altshuler (eds.) *Pirsumim rusiim al yehudim ve-yahadut bi-vrit ha-moazot 1917–1967*, Jerusalem, The Historical Society of Israel, 1970, pp. 51–6.

79 For anti-Semitic expressions in this period and the campaign against them, see Schwarz, *The Jews*, pp. 241–308.

80 Trotsky's testimony on this point seems to carry great weight. In his biography of Stalin he affirms that Stalin and his aides were not fastidious in their choice of means. He and his henchmen even stooped to fish in the muddied waters of anti-Semitism. I recall particularly a cartoon in the 'Rabochaya gazeta' entitled 'Comrades Trotsky and Zinovyev'. There were any number of such caricatures of an anti-Semitic character in the party press. L. Trotsky, *Stalin, The Revolutionary in Power*, London Panther History, vol. 2, p. 224.

81 From 1927 to 1931, in Russia alone, thirty-two books and booklets devoted to anti-Semitism in the Soviet Union appeared. See note 78.

82 *KPSS v rezolutsiyakh*, Moscow, Gospolitizdat, 1953, vol. 2, p. 614.

83 Stalin, *Sochineniya*, vol. 13, p. 28.

84 Stalin's remarks were made public in a speech by Molotov on the New Soviet Constitution. See *Pravda*, 30 November 1936.

85 Ibid.
86 *Anti-Soviet 'Bloc of Rights and Trotskyites'*, Moscow, Peoples Commissariat of Justice of the USSR 1938, pp. 622–3.
87 See I. Deutscher, *The Prophet Outcast, Trotsky, 1929–1940*, London, Oxford University Press, 1970, pp. 368–9.
88 In 'Tabletalk', Hitler revealed that in 1939 Stalin told Ribbentrop that he was only waiting for a wide enough stratum of local intelligentsia to be formed before finishing off the Jews as a ruling élite. See *Hitlers Tischgespräche*, Bonn, Atheneum Verlag, 1951, p. 119.
89 On the population censuses in the Soviet Union, see L. Starodubsky, *Das Volkszählungswesen in der Union der sozialistischen Sowjetrepubliken*, Wien, Franz Deutecke Verlag, 1938; W. Poletika, *Annulierte Volkszählung von 1937 and Bevölkerungs-stand in der Sowjetunion*, Jena, Fischer Verlag, 1937.
90 For the 1926 and 1939 censuses' data, see F. Lorimer, *The Population of the Soviet Union*, 1941, Geneva, League of Nations, 1946.
91 A. Nove and J. A. Newth, in Kochan (ed.), *The Jews in Soviet Russia*, p. 139.
92 Larin, *Antisemitism*, p. 304.
93 Y. Leshchinsky, 'Yidn in sovietn-farband', *Yidisher Kemfer*, 1946, no. 669, p. 95.
94 Leshchinsky, *Ha-yehudim*, p. 94.
95 See Y. Korolnik, 'Pogrom materialn', *Bleter for yidishe demografie, statistik un ekonomik*, 1923, no. 1, pp. 24–7.
96 See E. H. Carr, *The Bolshevik Revolution, 1917–1923*, London, Penguin Books, 1952, vol. 2; S. Prokopovich, *Narodnoe khoziaistvo SSSR*, New York, Izd. Chekhova, 1952, vol. 1; Leshchinksy, *Ha-yehudim*, pp. 67–85; N. Gergel, *Di lage fun di yidn in rusland*, Warsaw, Brzoze, 1929, pp. 56–68.
97 Y. Levin, 'Di valn in di ratn in 1925–1926 yor', *Di roite velt*, 1927, p. 89.
98 Gitelman, *Jewish Nationality*, p. 358.
99 Zinger, *Dos banayte folk*, p. 46.
100 Zinger, ibid., p. 49.
101 Kantor, *Natsionalnoe stroitelstvo*, p. 145.
102 Zinger, *Das banayte folk*, p. 46; Gergel, *Di lage*, p. 90.
103 L. Zinger, *Natsionalnyi sostav proletariata v SSSR*, Moscow, 'Vlast Sovetov', 1934, p. 84.
104 On the Jewish Kolkhozes in Belorussia see *Ofn visenshaftlechn front*, 1935, no. 1–2, pp. 105–17; E. Gordon, *In di yidishe kolvirtn*, Moscow, Emes, 1940.
105 Zinger, *Dos banayte folk*, Moscow, 1941, p. 49.
106 Calculated according to Zinger, ibid., p. 90.
107 A. Margolis, *Viazoi lebn yidn in sovetland*, Moscow, Emes, 1940, p. 65, while according to Zinger, *Dos banayte folk*, p. 105, these data relate to 1939.
108 Zinger, *Dos banayte folk*, p. 106.
109 *Natsionalnaya politika VKP(b) V tsifrakh*, Moscow, Gospolitzdat, 1930, p. 288; K. E. Bailes, *Technology and Society Under Lenin and Stalin. Origins of*

Soviet Technical Intelligentsia 1917–1941, New Jersey, Princeton University Press, 1978, p. 204.

110 N. Hans and S. Hessen, *Educational Policy in Soviet Russia*, London, P. S. King, 1930, p. 184.

111 Halevy, *Jewish University Students*, pp. 102, 104.

112 For everything concerning legislation on religious affairs from 1917 to 1926, see P. Gidulyanov, *Otdelenie tserkvii ot gosudarstva v SSSR*, Moscow, Iuridicheskaya literatura, 1926; J. Rothenberg, 'The Legal Status of Religion in the Soviet Union', in R. Marshall, Jr. (ed.), *Aspects of Religion in the Soviet Union, 1917–1967*, Chicago, The University of Chicago Press, 1967, pp. 61–100; *Istoriya sovetskoi konstitutsii*, p. 145.

113 Compare with clause 124 of the Constitution of 1936 where the words 'religious propaganda' were concealed.

114 Gidulyanov, *Otdelenie*, pp. 622–9, 643–5.

115 *Sbornik uzakonenii i rosporiazhenii rabocho-krestianskogo pravitelstva RSFSR*, Moscow, 1929, no. 39.

116 *O religii i tserkvii. Sbornik dokumentov*, Moscow, Gosizdat, 1965.

117 For a variety of reasons, the fiercest campaign in this period was directed against the Catholic Church. See P. Mailleux, 'Catholics in the Soviet Union', in Marshall, *Aspects*, p. 363; W. Kolarz, *Religion in the Soviet Union*, London–New York, Macmillan, 1961, pp. 176–217.

118 *Izvestiya Ts. K RKP(b)*, 1921, nos. 31, 33.

119 Y. Kaplan, A. Leib and Y. Khinshin, *Der mishpet yibern khaider*, Vitebsk, Biuro fun di yidishe sektsie, 1922 and see A. Gershuni, *Yahadut be-rusia ha-sovietit*, Jerusalem, Mosad ha-rav kuk, 1961.

120 The calculations concerning anti-religious literature are based on Pinkus, Grinbaum and Altshuler (eds.), *Pirsumim rusiim*, pp. 21–36; Y. Y. Cohen, Y. Slutski and Ch. Shmeruk (eds.), *Pirsumim yehudiim bi-vrit ha-moazot, 1917–1960*, Jerusalem, The Historical Society of Israel, 1961, pp. 43–52.

121 *Voinstvuyushchie Bezbozhniki V SSSR za 15 let*, Moscow, Ogiz, Gaiz, 1932, p. 346.

122 *Natsionalnaya politika*, p. 325.

123 A. Yodfat, 'Jewish Religious Communities in the USSR', *Soviet Jewish Affairs*, 1971, no. 2, pp. 64–5.

124 *Antireligioznik*, 1938, no. 12, p. 56.

125 J. Rothenberg, *The Jewish Religion in the Soviet Union*, New York, Ktav Publishing House, 1971, pp. 42–3.

126 The Rabbi Medaliah was executed, see *Jews in Eastern Europe*, 1976, vol. 3, no. 5, p. 22.

127 Yodfat, 'Jewish Religious Communities', p. 63.

128 Cohen, *Pirsumim*, p. 36; the newspaper cited is *Komsomolskya Pravda*, 10 April 1928.

129 J. A. Gilboa, *Lashon omedet al nafsha, tarbut yivrit bi-vrit-ha-moazot*, Tel-Aviv, Sifriat poalim, 1977, p. 23.

130 E. Schulman, *A History of Jewish Education in the Soviet Union*, New York, Ktav Publishing House, 1971, p. 42.

131 Schulman, ibid., p. 57; Z. Halevy, *Jewish Schools Under Czarism and Communism*, New York, Shengold, 1976, pp. 16–17.

132 See Hans and Hessen, *Educational Policy in Soviet Russia.*

133 Schulman gives the datum for 1922 as only 128 schools; the datum of 300 schools in November 1921 is taken from a different Soviet source. See *Zhizn natsionalnostei*, 26 January 1922.

134 The data on the number of Yiddish schools and the number of pupils are taken from numerous and often contradictory Soviet sources: Kantor, *Natsionalnoe stroitelstvo*, pp. 170–5; *Narodnyi komissariat prosveshcheniya*, Moscow, 1925–1930; *Naye shule*, 1929, pp. 74–80; S. H. Klitenik, *Di kultur arbeit tsvishn di yidishe arbetndike inem ratn-farband*, Moscow, Tsentral felker farlag, 1931, pp. 9–13; Z. Lipset, 'Batei-ha-sefer ha-yehudiim bi-vrit ha-moazot ve-shkiatam', *Behinot*, 1970, no. 1, pp. 57–9.

135 *Bolshaya sovetskaya entsyklopediya*, 1948, vol. SSSR, p. 1821.

136 Lipset 'Batei-ha-sefer', p. 60, but he does not give the exact date of the issue in question.

137 S. Fuchs, 'Tkhanim leumiim be-veit ha-sefer ha-isodi be-yidish bi-vrit ha-moazot', *Behinot*, 1977–8, no. 8–9, pp. 89–112; Z. Silin-Vinograd, 'Kavim le-dmuto shel beit ha-sefer ha-yehudi bi-vrit ha-moazot', *Behinot*, 1974, no. 5, pp. 97–109.

138 *Of di veg tsu der neyer shul*, 1927, no. 6, p. 33.

139 The situation that prevailed in the Jewish schools at the end of the 1930s can be assessed from articles that appeared in the Jewish press in the Soviet Union. See *Ratnbildung*, 1937, no. 2, pp. 87–90.

140 *Der emes*, 24 June 1937; 26 August 1938; *Tribuna*, 1936, no. 11, 24–5; 1936, no. 17, p. 23; Y. A. Gilboa, 'Hebrew Literature in the USSR', in Kochan (ed.), *The Jews*, pp. 226–41; A. Greenbaum, 'Hebrew Literature in Soviet Russia', *Jewish Social Studies*, 1968, no. 3, pp. 135–48.

141 All these calculations are according to Slutski in Cohen *et al.*, *Pirsumim yehudiim*, pp. 19–34.

142 *Behinot*, 1977–8, no. 8–9, p. 162.

143 On the development of Yiddish literature in the Soviet Union, see N. Meisel, *Das yidishe shafn un der yidisher shrayber in sovietn farband*, New York, Yikuf farlag, 1959; Y. Yanasovich, *Mit yidishe shrayber in rusland*, Buenos Aires, Kiyum farlag, 1959; Ch. Shmeruk, 'Yiddish Literature in the USSR', in Kochan, *The Jews*, pp. 232–68.

144 The data are according to Shmeruk, in Cohen *et al.*, *Pirsumim yehudiim*, pp. 55–6.

145 M. Friedberg in Kochan, *The Jews*, pp. 197–225; Y. Klaiman, 'Evrei v noveishoi russkoi literature', *Evreisky vestnik*, 1928, pp. 155–8; J. Kunitz, *Russian Literature and the Jews*, New York, Columbia University Press, 1929.

146 See Shmeruk, *Pirsumim yehudiim*, pp. 125–31; G. Imart, 'Latinisation des alphabets en URSS', *Cahiers du monde russe et soviétique*, 1965, no. 2.

147 D. Shatslov and R. Rozilov, 'Gorskie evrei i latinsky alfabit', *Revolutsiya i gorets*, 1929, no. 5(7), pp. 60–2.

148 On *Habimah*, in the Soviet Union, see Gilboa, *Lashon omedet*, pp. 146–91 and the bibliographical list there.

149 On the Jewish theatre in Moscow and in the Soviet Union in general,

see Y. Lubomirsky, *Melukhishe yidisher teater in ukraine*, Kharkov, Literatur un kunst, 1931; *Teater bukh*; Kiev, Kultur lige, 1927; B. Picon-Vallin, *Le théâtre juif soviétique pendant les années vingt*, Lausanne, L'Age d'Homme, 1973; F. Burko, *The Soviet Yiddish Theatre in the Twenties*, unpublished PhD Dissertation, Southern Illinois University, 1978; M. Libermann, *Aus dem Ghetto in die Welt. Autobiographie*, Berlin (Ost), Verlag der Nation, 1977.

150 Litvakov in *Tribuna*, 1935, no. 3, pp. 12–13.

151 Lvavi, *Ha-hitiashvut*, p. 297.

152 Kantor, *Natsionalnoe stroitelstvo*, p. 180.

153 Sh. Shkarovsky, *Das ofgerikhte yidishe folk*, Kiev, Natsionale minderheitn, 1939, pp. 53–4.

154 Zinger, *Dos banayte folk*, p. 109.

155 B. Pestovski, 'Le théâtre des Juifs boukhariens', *Bulletin d'Information, Organ de la société pour les relations culturelles entre l'URSS et l'etranger*, 1928, nos. 7–8, p. 16.

156 E. Goldman, 'The Soviet Yiddish Film 1925–1933', *Soviet Jewish Affairs*, 1980, no. 3, pp. 13–28.

157 A. Greenbaum, *Jewish Scholarship and Scholarly Institutions in Soviet Russia 1918–1953*, Jerusalem, The Hebrew University, 1978.

158 M. Altshuler, 'Jewish Studies in the Ukraine in the Early Soviet Period', *Soviet Jewish Affairs*, 1977, no. 1, pp. 19–30.

159 *Yidn in F.S.S.R.*, Moscow, Emes, 1935, p. 126.

160 I. Pulner, 'Voprosy organisatsii evreiskikh etnograficheskikh muzeev', *Sovetskaya etnografiya*, 1931, nos. 3–4, pp. 156–63.

161 On the *Bund*, and the 'United' in their final period, see Altshuler, *Haevsektsia*, pp. 41–91; Gitelman, *Jewish Nationality*, pp. 151–230, A. Gelbard, *Der Judische Arbeiter Bund Russlands in Revolution 1917*, Wien, Europa Verlag, 1983.

162 Gitelman, *Jewish Nationality*, p. 218.

163 N. Nir-Rafalkes, *Pirkei haim, 1884–1918*, Tel-Aviv, Ha-kibbuz ha-meuḥad, 1958; Z. Blum, *Poalei Zion in ratnfarband*, Tel-Aviv, Perets farlag, 1978; Z. Abramovich, *Be-sherut ha-tnuah*, Tel-Aviv, Perets farlag, 1965.

164 See Y. Erez (ed.), *Sefer Z.S.Le-korot ha-miflagah ha-zionit-sozialistit u-brit noar Z.S. be-rusia*, Tel-Aviv, Ayanot, 1963; I. Maor, *Ha-tnuah ha-zionit be-rusia*, Jerusalem, Ha-sifriya ha-zionit, 1973, pp. 510–37.

165 On the '*He-haluz*', in Russia, see D. Pines, *He-haluz be-khur ha-mahapekha*, Tel-Aviv, Davar, 1938; *He-haluz be-rusia, le-toldot he-haluz ha-bilti legali*, Tel-Aviv, Mishlaḥat ha-huz shel he-haluz ha-bilti legali, 1932; I. Openheim, *Tnuat he-haluz be-polin, 1917–1929*, Jerusalem, Magnes Press, 1982.

166 Pines, *He-haluz*, p. 234.

167 *He-haluz be-rusia*, p. 227.

168 See S. R. Marguliers, *The Pilgrimage to Russia, The Soviet Union and the Treatment of Foreigners, 1924–1937*, Madison, The Union of Wisconsin Press, 1968; D. Caute, *The Fellow Travelers. A Post-script to Enlightenment*, New York, Macmillan, 1973.

169 Y. Bauer, *My Brother's Keeper. A History of the American Jewish Joint Distribution Committee 1929–1939*, Philadelphia, JPS, 1974; L. Gourvitsch,

O.S.E. (1912–1937), Paris, Edition de L'Union d'OSE, 1937; E. Morrissey, *Jewish Workers and Farmers in the Crimea and Ukraine*, New York (privately printed), 1937; J. N. Rosenberg, *On the Steppes A. Russian Diary*, New York, A. Knopf, 1927; Z. Szajkowski, *Jews, Wars and Communism*, New York, Ktav Publishing House, 1972–7, 2 vols.

170 D. Ben-Gurion, *Zikhronot*, Tel Aviv, Am Oved, 1973, vol. 1, pp. 220–64.
171 I. Maor, *Ha-tenuah ha-zionit*, p. 532.
172 N. Goldmann, *Mein Leben als deutscher Jude*, München, Langen-Muller, 1980, pp. 292, 314–15.
173 See B. Pinkus, 'The Emigration of National Minorities from the USSR in the Post-Stalin Era', *Soviet Jewish Affairs*, 1983, no. 1, pp. 3–36.
174 Maor, *Ha-tenuah ha-zionit*, p. 538.
175 *Natsionalnaya politika*, p. 41.
176 Z. Gitelman, 'The Jews', *Problems of Communism*, 1967, no. 5, p. 99.

3 THE YEARS OF DESTRUCTION, 1939–1953

1 While anti-Semitism assumed its most serious form when charges of collaboration with the Nazis in the occupied territories destroyed Jewish people, less extreme anti-Semitism in the Red Army was expressed mainly in the charge that Jews were work-shy, black marketeers and, above all, cowards. The last accusation was made by the Nazis and readily accepted throughout the Soviet Union.
2 Throughout the war only one pamphlet was published dealing with Nazi anti-Semitism, and even this appeared at the beginning of the war: V. V. Struve, *Fashystsky antisemitizm*, Moscow-Leningrad, Akademia nauk SSR, 1941. Even articles on the subject were minimal in number, see Schwarz, *The Jews*, pp. 168–87.
3 See his speech on 8 November 1941, at the Moscow Soviet: Stalin, *Sochineniya*, Stanford, Hoover Institution, 1967, vol. 2(15), p. 22.
4 There is evidence of the anti-Jewish feelings of a number of senior members of the Soviet Government, e.g. Shcherbakov, member of the Politburo, head of the Sovinformburo and of the Political Administration of the army; General Shtemenko, who held senior posts in the army; Ponomarenko, one of the heads of the Belorussian Republic and Soviet Ambassador to Poland in the 1950s; and Ignatyev, who was responsible for the security services at the time of the Doctors' Plot. See H. Salisbury, *Russia on the Way*, New York, Macmillan, 1946, pp. 290–3; P. F. de Villemarest, *La marche au pouvoir en URSS*, Paris, Fayard, 1969, pp. 60–2; Schwarz, *The Jews*, pp. 196–7; G. D. Embree, *The Soviet Union Between the 19th and 20th Party Congress, 1952–1956*, The Hague, Nijhoff, 1959, pp. 14–17.
5 According to Stanislaw Kot, Stalin even repeated this insulting phrase twice – 'bad and miserable soldiers'. See S. Kot, *Listy z Rosji do Generala Sikorskiego*, London, 1956, p. 204; *Conversations with the Kremlin and Dispatches from Russia*, Oxford University Press, 1963, p. 153. For General Anders' version, see W. Anders, *Bez ostatniego rozdzialu, wspomnenia z lat 1939–1946*, 3rd edn., London, Gryf Publishers, 1959, p. 99.

6 See the evidence of Stettinius, the American Foreign Minister at that time, who wrote: 'Stalin observed that the Jewish problem was extremely difficult. The Soviet Union had tried to establish a national home for the Jews but they stayed only two or three years before returning to the cities. The Jews were natural traders, he added, but much had been accomplished by putting small groups of them in agricultural areas.' E. R. Stettinius, Jr., *Roosevelt and the Russians. The Yalta Conference*, New York, Doubleday and Co., 1949, p. 278.

7 See E. Evtushenko, *Avtobiografiya*, London, Flegon Press, 1964, pp. 89–94; S. Allilueva, *Dvatsat pisem k drugu*, New York, Harper and Row, 1968, pp. 150–83. Also important are the testimonies of V. Grossman and A. Kuznetsov; see V. Grossman, *Vse techet*, Frankfurt a/M, Posev, 1980; A. Anatoli (Kuznetsov), *Babi Yar*, New York, Pocket Books, 1971. To these one can add numerous accounts by new immigrants to Israel from the Soviet Union.

8 S. R. Loewenstein, *Psychanalyse de l'antisémitisme*, Paris, PUF, 1952, p. 7.

9 M. Litvinov, *Notes for a Journal*, New York, Williams, Morrow and Co., Inc., 1955, p. 55.

10 B. Wolfe, *Three Who Made a Revolution*, London, Penguin Books, 1966, pp. 461–5; I. Deutscher, *Stalin*, London, Pelican Books, 1966, pp. 21–45; B. Souvarine, *Staline*, Paris, Plon, 1935, pp. 7–21.

11 Zeev Ben-Shlomo's claim that Mikoyan exhibited an anti-Semitic attitude when he was sent to Czechoslovakia in 1951 to prepare Slansky's trial is unconvincing, since in this case he was acting on Stalin's orders. Z. Ben-Shlomo, 'The Krushchev Apocrypha', *Soviet Jewish Affairs*, 1971, no. 1, pp. 63–4; J. Pelikan (ed.), *The Czechoslovak Political Trials, 1950–1954*, London, MacDonald, 1970, p. 106.

12 For example, Kamenev and Galperin; see Leo Trotsky, *Stalin*, London, Panther Books, 1969, vol. 1, pp. 72, 80.

13 Stalin, *Sochineniya*, vol. 2, pp. 50–1.

14 See R. V. Daniels, *The Conscience of the Revolution*, Cambridge, Mass., Harvard University Press, 1960, pp. 104–7; L. Shapiro, *The Origin of the Communist Autocracy*, London, Bell and Sons, 1956, pp. 245–52.

15 S. Allilueva, *Dvatsat pisem*, pp. 150–83; *idem, Tolko odin god*, New York, Harper and Row, 1970, pp. 133–5, 352–5; M. Djilas, 'Antisemitazm', *Borba*, 14 December 1952.

16 For example, Stalin's personal grudge against Molotov's wife, Polina Zhemchuzhina, because of her 'fatal influence' over his own wife which allegedly led to her suicide in 1932, or his bitter opposition to the marriages of his children to Jews. S. Allilueva, *Twenty Letters to a Friend*, New York, Harper and Row, 1967, pp. 109–11.

17 *Khrushchev Remembers*, Boston, Little, Brown and Company, 1970, pp. 259–69.

18 See for example Djilas, 'Antisemitazm'.

19 His exiling of different peoples during the war, even when victory over Germany was assured, is well-known. Reports of a plan for the mass exile of the Jews began to reach the West after Stalin's death; see Embree, *The Soviet Union*, p. 285; Schechtman, *Zionism*, pp. 42–3; B. Z.

Goldberg, *The Jewish Problem in the Soviet Union*, New York, Crown Publishers, 1961, pp. 148–9.

20 *O partiinoi i sovetskoi pechati. Sbornik dokumentov*, Moscow, Izdatelstvo Pravda, 1954, pp. 528–9.

21 *KPSS v rezolyutsiyakh i resheniyakh syezdov, konferentsii i plenumov Ts.K.*, 8th edn. Moscow, Politizdat, 1971, vol. 6, pp. 130–4.

22 See M. Morozov, 'Ob istorii Kazakhskoi SSR', *Bolshevik*, 1945, no. 6, pp. 74–8.

23 F. Barghoorn, 'Stalinism and the Russian Cultural Heritage', *Review of Politics*, 1952, (vol. 14), no. 2, pp. 178–203.

24 See *Pravda Ukrainy*, 30 June 1947; K. Litvin, 'Ob istoril ukrainskogo naroda', *Bolshevik*, 1947, no. 7, pp. 41–56; 'Rezolyutsiya Prezidium pravlenia soyuza sovetskikh pisatelei', *Oktyabr*, 1946, no. 9, p. 185.

25 It included the Armenians, Uzbeks, Kirgiz, Buryat-Mongols, Moldavians, and Azerbaidzhans. See Lowell Tillet, *The Great Friendship*, Chapel Hill, The University of North Carolina Press, 1969, pp. 84–109; F. Barghoorn, *Soviet Russian Nationalism*, New York, Oxford University Press, 1956, pp. 61–6.

26 'A shlakht program farn ideologishn front', *Eynikayt*, 24 September 1946.

27 S. Rabinovich, 'In krumen shpigl', *Eynikayt*, 10 October 1946.

28 I. Dobrushin, 'Vos darfn mir bahandlen', *Eynikayt*, 12 October 1946.

29 'Dekn dem khoyv farn land un folk', *Eynikayt*, 14 October 1946.

30 'Far a hoykhn kinslerishn ideish angezetiktn estrade repertuar', *Eynikayt*, 5 April 1947; M. Bloshteyn, 'Di yidishe estrade-kunst in chernovits', *Eynikayt*, 5 April 1947; M. Notovich und Sh. Roytman, 'Oktyabr un di yidishe sovetishe literatur', *Heymland*, 1947, no. 1, p. 141.

31 The story by Kipnis was published immediately after the war, in *Eynikayt* on 26 July 1945, with the 'nationalistic' sections omitted. The unabridged version appeared in the Lodz Yiddish newspaper *Dos naye lebn*, the organ of the Central Committee of Polish Jews, on 19 May 1947.

32 'Natsionalizm untern shleyer fun felker frayntshaft', *Eynikayt*, 3 July 1947.

33 Kvitko also arraigned the literary critics Dobrushin and Nusinov, who he said had brought about the disorientation of Yiddish literature. See L. Kvitko, 'Tsu nayes ideish kinslerishe hoykhn', *Eynikayt*, 5 July 1947.

34 Ibid., and see also the strong criticism of Kipnis by the writer Itsik Fefer, 'Mitn kop arop', *Eynikayt*, 9 August 1947.

35 *Literaturna gazeta*, 25 September 1947.

36 G. Polyanker and M. Talalaevsky, 'Pro odne shkidlyve opovidannya', *Literaturna gazeta*, 18 September 1947, as quoted in B. J. Choseed, *Reflections on the Soviet Nationalities Policy in Literature: The Jews, 1938–1948*, unpublished PhD dissertation, Columbia University, New York, 1968; pp. 332–3.

37 Ibid., p. 333.

38 'Za ideinu chistotu ukrainskoi radyanskoi literatury', *Literaturna gazeta*, 23 October 1947. The meeting, as is stated in the conference Resolution, did not accept Itsik Kipnis's self-criticism.

39 M. Notovich, 'Di sovetishe yidishe literatur ofn nayem etap', *Eynikayt*, 28 October 1947.

40 H. Loytsker, 'Far ideyisher reynkayt fun undzer literatur', *Der Shtern*, 1948, no. 2, pp. 105–12.

41 In addition to the articles previously referred to, one may mention the following: A. Miral, in *Eynikayt*, 17 February 1948; D. Bendas, in *Eynikayt*, 20 March 1948.

42 Loytsker continually counts the number of times Osherovich or Grubian use the word 'Jew'. In one of the stories, Loytsker exclaims, this word appears thirteen times.

43 For example, *sekilah, mestame, metaher, eglah arufah, gezar zavaah*: ibid.

44 For example, the vision of the dry bones, Naomi and Ruth, the burning bush, Noah's Ark, etc.: Loytsker, 'Far ideyisher reynkayt'.

45 How is it possible, thunders Loytsker, for Kipnis to want the symbol of the fight against the Nazis and the symbol of militant Zionism to be worn side by side on the breast of the Soviet soldier? Ibid.

46 The liquidation of Jewish culture and its principal bearers is described in this chapter.

47 'Vysoko nesti prapor radyanskogo patriotyzma', *Vitchyzna*, 1949, no. 3, p. 16, as quoted in B. Choseed, 'Jews in Soviet Literature', in E. Simons (ed.), *Through the Glass of Soviet Literature*, New York, Columbia University Press, 1953, p. 148.

48 'Vyshe znamya sovetskogo patriotizma', *Literaturnaya gazeta*, 12 March 1949. V. Seduro, *The Byelorussian Theatre and Drama*, New York, Research Programme on the USSR, 1955, p. 225.

49 *Pravda Ukrainy*, 8 February 1949.

50 L. Dmiterko in *Literaturnaya gazeta*, 9 March 1949.

51 *Pravda Ukrany*, 19 March 1949.

52 M. Lukonin in *Zvezda*, 1949, no. 3, p. 195.

53 S. Ivanov in *Vechernyaya Moskva*, 21 March 1949.

54 E. Kovalchyk in *Literaturnaya gazeta*, 12 February 1949.

55 This tendency reached its peak in Stalin's speech to Red Army officers; see *Pravda*, 25 May 1945.

56 N. Baltiisky in *Novoe vremya*, 1945, no. 1(11), p. 6.

57 *Pravda*, 10 February 1946.

58 'Doklad t. Zhdanova o zhurnalakh 'Zvezda' i 'Leningrad', *Zvezda*, 1946, nos. 7–8, pp. 7–22.

59 See *Decisions of the Central Committee, CPSU (Bolsheviks) on Literature and Art (1946–1948)*, Moscow, Foreign Languages Publishing House, 1951.

60 'Vospitanie sovetskogo patriotizma – vazhneishaya zadacha ideologicheskoi raboty', *Bolshevik*, 1947, no. 14, p. 5.

61 *Bolshevik*, 1947, no. 16, pp. 7–23.

62 *Oktyabr*, 1947, no. 7, pp. 148–63. The only person who dared to criticize Fadeev, particularly for his stand on Veselovsky's theory of literature, was V. Shishmarev. See his article in *Oktyabr*, 1947, no. 12.

63 Fadeev, ibid., p. 154.

64 Fadeev, ibid., p. 155.

65 R. Hankin, 'Post-War Soviet Ideology and Literary Scholarship', in

Simons (ed.), *Throught the Glass of Soviet Literature*, p. 265. Sharp attacks on Nusinov in particular appeared in 1948 until his arrest; see *Literaturnaya gazeta*, 24 January 1948; Kirpotin in *Oktyabr*, 1948, no. 1; A. Tarasenkov in *Novy mir*, 1948, no. 8; *Voprosy filosofii*, 1948, no. 1; V. Ermilov in *Literaturnaya gazeta*, 29 August 1948.

66 P. Vyshinsky in *Bolshevik*, 1947, no. 18, p. 33.

67 A. Zhdanov, 'O mezdunarodnom polozhenii', *Bolshevik*, 1947, no. 20, pp. 10–39.

68 *Bolshevik*, 1947, no. 21, p. 16.

69 See, for example, L. Plotkin, in *Zvezda*, 1946, no. 7–8, pp. 212–17; A. Isbakh, in *Novy mir*, 1947, no. 4, pp. 162–80; A. Shtein in *Novy mir*, 1947, pp. 190–208.

70 I. Erenburg, 'Zashchitniki kultury', *Novoe vremya*, 1947, no. 46, pp. 5–10.

71 See, for example, the attack on the historian Solomon Ya. Lurye, in *Vestnik drevnei istorii*, 1948, no. 1.

72 *Novy mir*, 1948, no. 2.

73 Z. Paperny, in *Literaturnaya gazeta*, 5 June 1948.

74 R. Miller-Budnitskaya, in *Novy mir*, 1948, no. 6.

75 See *Sovremenaya Rossia, Ocherki nashei gosudarstvennoi obshchestvennoi zhizni*, St Petersburg, Tipografiya Suvorina, 1889, p. 323.

76 As, for example: spy, traitor, enemy of the people, etc. See the article of Georgii Aleksandrov, who had himself been attacked earlier by Zhdanov, in *Voprosy filosofii*, 1948, no. 3.

77 *Literaturnaya gazeta*, 21 July 1948.

78 Among those attacked were a good many Jews. 'The Biology Discussion: A Commentary', *Soviet Studies*, 1949, vol. 1, no. 2, pp. 106–18; Zh. Medvedev, *The Rise and Fall of F. D. Lysenko*, New York–London, Columbia University Press, 1969.

79 A detailed but 'processed' report appeared in the journal *Oktyabr* 1949, no. 2.

80 Stalin's personal interest in the anti-cosmopolitan campaign and his demand that it be intensified were reported by the writers K. Simonov and A. Fadeev, who was Chairman of the Writers' Union and one of the perpetrators of this policy. See I. Erenburg, *Sobranie sochinenii*, Moscow, Khudozhestvennaya literatura, 1967, vol. 9, p. 574.

81 *Kultura i zhizn*, 30 January 1949.

82 The reader will find this material in the collection of Russian language documents which I edited: *Evrei i evreisky narod 1948–1953*, Jerusalem, Centre for Documentation of East European Jewry, 1973 (7 volumes).

83 *The New York Times* journalist in Moscow at this period reported that a special meeting of Soviet newspaper editors took place, at which they were told by representatives of the Central Committee to restrain the campaign. H. Salisbury, *Moscow Journal. The End of Stalin*, Chicago, The University of Chicago Press, 1961, p. 29. And see the evidence of Ilya Erenburg, *Sobranie sochinenii, loc. cit.*

84 Erenburg, for example, relates in his memoirs that he wrote a letter to

Stalin, complaining that for two months his articles had ceased to be published. See Erenburg, *Sobranie sochinenii*, Vol. 9, p. 573. On the interruption of the publication of the book by the economist E. Varga, as early as 1948, see *Planovoe khozyaistvo*, 1948, no. 5, pp. 82–9.

85 A partial scrutiny of the literary journals of these years shows that a number of the writers and literary critics were unable to publish their works for a short period only, between 1949 and 1950.

86 It is interesting that among the first to disclose pseudonyms was the theoretical organ of the Central Committee *Bolshevik*; see the article of Golovchenko, *Bolshevik*, 1949, no. 3.

87 Melnikov (Melman); see: 'Peredovaya sovetskaya literatura na novom podyeme', *Bolshevik*, 1951, no. 14.

88 See for example the coverages of the plenum of the Ukrainian Writers' Union, *Pravda Ukrainy*, 6 March 1949.

89 See for example H. Swayze, *Political Control of Literature in the USSR 1946–1959*, Cambridge, Mass.: Harvard University Press, 1962, p. 63; A. Yarmolinsky *Literature Under Communism*, Bloomington, Indiana University Press, 1960, p. 81.

90 G. Struve, *Soviet Russian Literature 1917–1950*, Norman, University of Oklahoma Press, 1951, p. 344. W. Vickery, 'Zhdanovism: 1946–1953', in *Conference on Soviet Literature 1917–1962*, Oxford, Oxford University Press, 1962, pp. 17–18.

91 The Soviet 'theory of the dialectical amalgam' was, it seems, so successful that it deceived Western scholars, who believed every word written in the Soviet Union, without checking the real intentions of the government in any particular publication.

92 Mirzo Fursan-Zade, in *Literaturnaya gazeta*, 19 February 1949; Kh. Rasulev, in *Pravda Vostoka*, 14 August 1952.

93 Among those who attacked cosmopolitanism in the Ukraine were the poets Rylsky and Tychina, who were known to be personal friends of many Yiddish writers and sympathetic to the Jewish people.

94 Two doctoral dissertations have been written on the subject of Soviet–Israel relations between 1947 and 1957: M. W. Allen, *The Policy of the USSR towards the State of Israel*, unpublished PhD dissertation, University of London, 1961; Y. Ro'i, *Yahasei brit ha-moazot yisrael 1947–1954*, PhD dissertation, The Hebrew University, Jerusalem, 1972. And see also: W. Laqueur, *The Struggle for the Middle East*, London, Routledge, 1969, pp. 43–63; A. Dagan, *Moscow and Jerusalem*, New York, Abelard-Schuman, 1970; M. Namir, *Shlihut be-moskvah*, Tel Aviv, Am Oved, 1971; A. Krammer, *The Forgotten Friendship: Israel and the Soviet Block 1947–1953*, Urbana, University of Illinois Press, 1974.

95 In 1939 and 1940, about 23 million people of various nationalities, among them about two million Jews, were added to the Soviet Union. According to one estimate, 1,692,000 persons out of a total of 12.5 million – i.e. over 13% – were exiled from regions formerly belonging to Poland. The rate of exile among Jews being similar to that among the population as a whole, some 163,000 Jews from Poland (about 13% of 1,250,000) were exiled to forced labour camps and particularly difficult

areas, along with an apparent 70,000 from the other territories – a total of approximately 233,000. Among the exiled Jews, in addition to Zionists, there were also Bundists, members of the 'bourgeoisie' and the intelligentsia, who were not always members of parties. See P. Barton, *L'Institution concentrationnaire en Russie 1930–1957*, Paris, Plon, 1959, pp. 108–9. According to Schechtman's estimate, about 400,000 Jews were exiled in the years 1939 to 1941. See Schectman, *Zionism*, p. 113.

96 Reports on the various meetings are to be found in the following Israeli archives: The Central Zionist Archives in Jerusalem, The Weizmann Archives in Jerusalem – Reḥovot, the *Ha-shomer ha-zair* Movement Archive in Merḥaviah, the *Avodah* Archive in Tel Aviv, the *Iḥud ha-kvuzot ve-ha-kibbuzim* Archive; and in private collections of people who participated at these meetings. See also '*Yediyot, alon liga "V"'*, *Sbornik*, Jerusalem, 1943; A. Kohen, *Im ambulansim le-teheran*, Merḥaviah, Ha-kibbuz ha-arzi ha-shomer ha-zair, 1943.

97 See Roi, *Yahasei*, p. 43.

98 According to what Roosevelt told Stephen Wise in March 1945 (Weizmann Archives, 18 March 1945): 'The Big Three agreed on handing over Palestine to the Jews. As far as the immediate future is concerned, Jewish immigration will be continued.'

99 *Jewish Chronicle*, 23 February 1956, as quoted in Roi, *Yahasei*, p. 46. On a meeting of members of the *Histadrut* delegation with the Soviet delegation member, M. Tarasov, see *Palkor*, 1945, no. 51, pp. 2–3.

100 Although the consent of the Soviet authorities was apparently necessary, one cannot ignore the influence which the governments of Poland, Czechoslovakia and Romania still had in this period in everything concerning their internal affairs.

101 K. Serezhin, 'Problemy arabskogo Vostoka', *Novoe vremya*, 1946, no. 3, p. 15.

102 In another article written two months later, he again stresses that the solution is not to be found in immigration into Palestine but in restoring the uprooted Jews to normal lives. See K. Serezhin in *Novoe vremya*, 1946, no. 11, pp. 14–17.

103 K. Serezhin, 'Sovremennaya Palestina', *Novoe vremya*, 1946, no. 15, p. 21.

104 V. Lutsky, *Palestinskaya problema*, Moscow, Pravda, 1946.

105 Ibid., p. 29.

106 Roi, *Yahasei*, p. 86.

107 General Assembly, Official Records, 1st and 2nd Sessions, vol. 1, p. 132.

108 These apprehensions increased after Harry Truman's speech of 11 March 1947.

109 Such as the vote in favour of partition on 29 November 1947, the opposition to the trusteeship plan which the United States proposed in March 1948, the *de jure* recognition of Israel immediately it was established, the opposition to the Bernadotte programme, the opposition to the Arab States' annexation of territories of Palestine, etc.

110 The terms employed by the Soviet representatives at the UN and by the Soviet press were: 'the legitimate aspiration of the Jewish people to

establish an independent state in Palestine, to which it has been tied since ancient times' (Gromyko's speech in the Political Committee of the General Assembly: *Izvestiya*, 23 April 1948), 'the legitimate right of the Jewish and Arab populations to establish their own States' (*Pravda*, 29 May 1948), the 'right of all nations to self-determination', and the like.

111 V. Lutsky, *Angliisky i amerikansky imperializm na Blizhnem Vostoke*, Moscow, Pravda, 1948, pp. 24, 26.

112 A. Kanunnikov, 'Kto vinovat v palestinskoi tragedii', *Novoe vremya*, 1948, no. 37, pp. 29–31. It is interesting to note that four months previously the same commentator had written in a quite different vein. See *Novoe vremya*, 1948, no. 22, pp. 8–10.

113 See the pamphlet by I. Genin, *Palestinskaya problema*, Moscow, Pravda, 1948. And see too other attacks on Zionism at the end of 1948: *New Times*, 1948, no. 51, p. 16; P. Osipova in *Voprosy istorii*, 1948, no. 12.

114 See *Eynikayt*, 20 May 1948.

115 See *Eynikayt*, 19 June 1947; 26 February, 19 June and 16 November, 1948.

116 See *Eynikayt*, 11 December 1947.

117 See *Eynikayt*, 1 November 1947; 30 March, 1948.

118 See *Eynikayt*, 18 November 1948.

119 'The current reactionary position of the "Joint"', wrote Fefer, 'is no novelty for us.' See *Eynikayt*, 26 February 1948.

120 See G. Mindlin's article, referred to in note 118, and that by the editor of *Eynikayt*, G. Zhits: *Eynikayt*, 19 October 1948.

121 For a detailed description of these demonstrations, see Namir, *Shlihut bemoskvah* and *Jewish Chronicle*, 8 and 27 October 1948.

122 See his speech at the symposium held in Moscow at the Institute for Economics and Pacific Ocean Studies on the subject of the struggle for national liberation in the colonies and semi-colonies. *Voprosy ekonomiki*, 1949, no. 10, pp. 83–7. Two of the sharpest articles were unquestionably those by a member of the Academy of Science, Mark Mitin, a Jew (see 'Sionistskaya agentura amerikanskogo imperializma'), *Za prochny mir, za narodnuyu demokratiyu*, 20 February 1953) and by V. Minaev, 'Sionistskaya agentura amerikanskoi razvedki', *Novoe vremya*, 1953, no. 4, pp. 13–16. Articles harshly attacking the 'Joint' are to be found in *Pravda Ukrainy*, 11 February 1953; *Trud*, 15 February 1953; *Literaturnaya gazeta*, 24 February 1953; *Meditsinsky rabotnik*, 3 March 1953.

123 'Panislamskie plany vsemirnogo khalifata', *Novoe vremya*, 1949, no. 44, pp. 30–2.

124 'Ocherednie zadachi istorikov vostokovedov', *Voprosy istorii*, 1950, no. 12, p. 5. On the Comintern's Resolutions on this matter, see Jane Degras (ed.), *The Communist International, 1919–1943*, London, Oxford University Press, 1956, vol. 1, pp. 143–4, 365, 366, 385; vol. 2, p. 183; vol. 3, pp. 76–84.

125 On the 'chauvinistic ideology of Zionism', see Mitin, 'Sionistskaya agentura'.

126 On the declaration of the legate Kubovi as *persona non grata* in Czechoslovakia and Poland, see *Pravda*, 9 December 1952.

127	See especially Anna Lungu, 'V Izraile', *Literaturnaya gazeta*, 22 July 1951; P. Khazov, 'Poezdka v Izrail', *Novoe vremya*, 1951, no. 35, pp. 22–5; A. Leonidov, 'Anglo-amerikanskaya duel v Izraile', *Novoe vremya*, 1951, no. 47, pp. 22–7.

128	On the tragic episode of Erlich and Alter, who were to have headed the new Jewish Anti-Fascist Committee the Soviet authorities wanted to establish, see *The Case of Henryk Erlich and Victor Alter*, New York, American Representation of the General Jewish Workers Union in Poland, 1943; *Henryk Erlikh un Victor Alter*, New York, Undzer tsayt, 1951.

129	No serious research has yet been done on this period in general and on the wave of arrests in particular, principally because of the few sources at the researcher's disposal. On the rumours about the arrests and the exile of Jews to Siberia, see *Jewish Telegraphic Agency Bulletin* (hereafter *JTA*), 4 January 1945, p. 4; 26 April 1946, p. 2.

130	Except for incidents of smuggling, which indeed occurred, and which for the Soviet authorities constitute a grave offence against State security and are punished accordingly.

131	See Erenburg's article in *Pravda*, 21 September 1948. This was the first sign that the Soviet authorities had decided to sever the contacts between Soviet Jewry and Zionism and Israel.

132	In information received in 1949 by the Israel Legation in Moscow from a Soviet Jew it was stated: 'The law courts pervert judgment and maliciously stiffen penalties on Jews. This year many have been thrown into prison and sent to camps for sympathizing with Israel or showing a desire to emigrate to Israel or for taking part in street demonstrations last year in honor of our Legation.' Among those imprisoned he named Mordechai Dubin, one of the leaders of *Agudat yisrael* in Latvia: Namir, *Shlihut be-moskvah*, pp. 307–8. Among the immigrants who have arrived in Israel in recent years are many who had been imprisoned for Zionism during this period, including Meir Gelfond, Vitaly Svechinsky and Mikhail Margolis.

133	An important document in this connection refers to the case of a Jew sentenced at the beginning of 1953 to twenty-five years' imprisonment in labour camps by the Military Collegium of the Supreme Court of the Soviet Union and whose sentence was mitigated on appeal to ten years. Namir, *Shlihut be-moskvah*, p. 331.

134	The death penalty, which had been abolished in 1947, was reintroduced in January 1950. The almost standard term of imprisonment handed down by the Special Boards of the MGB in this period was ten years' forced labour under harsh conditions with the possibility of a further five-year extension.

135	See, for example, the case of the Jewish workers in the 'Serp i Molot' factory in the city of Kharkov, twelve of whom were dismissed from their jobs in February 1953, and were tried immediately afterwards and exiled to Siberia.

136	This report appeared in the Yiddish newspaper, *Morning Journal*, 17 July 1949, as quoted in *American Jewish Yearbook*, 1951, p. 533.

137	Most of the writers and cultural functionaries (such as Zhitz, editor of the journal *Eynikayt*, and Y. Strongin, director of the publishing house 'Der Emes') were arrested in December 1948 and January 1949, namely: Leyb Kvitko, David Bergelson, Der Nister, Itsik Fefer, Perets Markish, Itsik Kipnis, Haim Loytsker, and many others. See A. Pomerants, *Di sovietishe harugey-malkhes*, Buenos Aires, Yiddish Scientific Institute in Argentina, 1962.

138 From the material which began to be published in 1956, and especially at the beginning of the sixties, the following picture emerges: among the first to be arrested were the poet David Hofshteyn and the literary critics Yitzhak Nusinov and Yehezkel Dobrushin. In this period – apparently the beginning of December (see L. Leneman, *La Tragédie des Juifs en URSS*, Paris, Desclée de Brouwer, 1959, pp. 68–72) – a meeting of the Yiddish writers in Moscow was especially convened by the Soviet Writers' Union, in order to condemn the nationalist writers.

139 S. M. Broderzon, *Mayn laydn-veg mit Moyshe Broderzon*, Buenos Aires, Union Central Israelita Polaca en la Argentina, 1960, pp. 55, 65.

140 Among those arrested were Itsik Fefer's wife (in 1949) and sister, and the wives of Leyb Kvitko, Binyamin Zuskin, David Bergelson, Perets Markish, and Aharon Kushnirov (he himself was not arrested because of his illness). The arrests and exiles occurred at the end of 1952 and the beginning of 1953, that is to say, after the trial and execution of their husbands. See Pomerants, *Di sovietishe harugey malkhes*; Esther Markish, *Le Long Retour*, Paris, Laffont, 1974, pp. 209–18.

141 See Leneman, *La Tragédie*, p. 67; *Folks mishpt*, New York, Jewish Labor Committee, 1956, pp. 54–62; Y. A. Gilboa, *The Black Years of Soviet Jewry, 1939–1953*, Boston, Little, Brown and Co. 1971.

142 J. Cang, *The Silent Millions: A History of the Jews in the Soviet Union*, London, Rapp-Whiting, 1969, pp. 225–8.

143 Ibid., p. 103.

144 For example, among those arrested in the 1930s were: Abchuk, Bukhbinder, Kiper, Kirzhnits, Levin, Merezhin, Sudarsky and Viner. Among those apparently not arrested but who appear in the list are: Baumvol, Borokhovich, Holdes, Pervomaisky (it is not clear why Pervomaisky is listed among the Yiddish-language writers), Volkshteyn and Telesin.

145 We have no proof that such a trial was indeed about to take place, but it is a reasonable presumption.

146 In many official Soviet publications, 12 August 1952, is given as the day of execution.

147 S. Broderzon writes that twenty-four people were tried: *Mayn laydn-veg*, p. 165. This is also the number specified by Dr Haim Shoshkes after his return from the Soviet Union. See Leneman, *La Tragédie*, p. 89.

148 Much has been written about the 'Crimea Affair' which served as grounds for this accusation, but there is still no clear picture of the origin and evolution of the episode. See, e.g. H. Vaynroykh, *Blut oyf der zun*, New York, Mensh un Yid, 1950, pp. 10–11; E. Emiot, *Der birobidzhaner inyen*, New York, Bogorad, 1960, p. 8; Y. Yanasovich, *Mit yidishe shrayber in rusland*, Buenos Aires, Kiyum farlag, 1959, pp. 255–8; Leneman, *La*

Tragédie, pp. 88–9. According to Esther Markish, her husband opposed
the Crimea plan and supported the establishment of a Jewish republic
in the Volga region in place of the Germans who had been expelled
from there. She also states, apparently incorrectly, that the Crimea
Affair occurred in 1947, and that the proposal came from Kaganovich
and Molotov, who suggested to the heads of the Jewish Anti-Fascist
Committee that they apply to Stalin on the matter. See Markish, *Le Long
Retour*, p. 178.

149 According to other information, Yitzḥak Nusinov was also sentenced to
twenty-five years' imprisonment. The poet David Hofshteyn was apparently not executed but died in a mental hospital.

150 See: *Pravda Ukrainy*, 11.1.48, 21.10.48, 19.11.48, 3.12.48, 3.2.49; *Pravda
vostoka*, 10.7.48, 1.9.48, 15.9.48, *Vechernyaya Moskva*, 5.9.49, 7.6.50; *Izvestiya*, 24.6.51.

151 See *Vechernyaya Moskva*, 24.12.52; *Pravda Ukrainy*, 28.12.52; *Izvestiya*,
30.1.53; *Pravda*, 1.2.53, 6.2.53.

152 Reports reached the Israel Embassy that, at the beginning of 1952, Jews
accused of economic crimes had been exiled from Ukrainian cities (Poltava, Kharkov, Lvov and Dneproderzhinsk) to labour camps in Birobidzhan.

153 Within the competency of the military courts was the trying of offences
involving military personnel (espionage, sabotage, treason, acts of terror, disclosure of state secrets, theft, sale and purchase of arms). See D.
Karev, *Organisisatsiya suda i prokuratury v SSSR*, Moscow, Gosyurizdat,
1954, pp. 146–7.

154 See, for example, the testimony of the Israeli witness Mordechai Oren at
the Slansky Trial. The Czechoslovak interrogator told Oren: 'We have
all the proof that you, as a central envoy of international Zionism,
responsible for the organization of Zionist activity in the Socialist countries, are among the chief organizers of the Zionist-nationalist underground operating in the Soviet Union... Your vital interest demands
that you reveal to us the full truth of this matter. Otherwise we will be
compelled to transport you to another place – very far from here – and
you will be interrogated by someone else. There the truth will certainly
be obtained from you.' See M. Oren, *Reshimot asir prag*, Merḥaviah, Ḥa-
kibuẓ ha-arẓi, ha-shosmer ha-ẓair, 1958, p. 287. Defendants such as
Oren, being Israeli citizens, were particularly suitable as witnesses in a
trial involving the charge of Zionism and the link between Jewish institutions and the Western espionage services.

155 For example, in the 'Leningrad Case', the 'Mingrelian Affair' and the
campaign against nationalism in the Ukrainian and other Republics;
and, in the Jewish sphere the Writers' Trial, the economic trials and the
acrimonious anti-Zionist campaign. On Stalin's general policy in this
period, see R. Conquest, *Power and Policy in the USSR*, New York, St
Martin Press, 1961, pp. 95–153.

156 F. Kozlov, 'Politicheskaya bditelnost-obyazannost chlena parti', *Kommunist*, 1953, no. 1, pp. 46–55.

157 'Arrest gruppy vrachei-vreditelei', *Pravda*, 13 January 1953.

158 Clearly there was no need to wait for Krushchev's revelations at the twentieth party congress in February 1956 to be aware that this was Stalin's programme. 'The security services', stated *Pravda*, 'failed to expose in good time the terrorist sabotage organization which operated among the doctors', *Pravda*, 13 January 1953.

159 Such as the necessity of carefully preparing all the details of a show trial, mainly the preparation of those defendants who would be willing to play the roles allotted them properly, with the attendant risk (as in the case of Traichko Kostov in Bulgaria in 1949) that some of them might refuse to do so.

160 While Khrushchev did note in his secret speech that Dr Lidya Timashuk – whose letter to Stalin was the direct cause of the doctors' arrest – worked in the security services, he did not explain on whose orders she was acting when she sent the letter.

161 The writer Boris Pilnyak published a story in the periodical *Novy Mir* about the death of Frunze, who was one of the heads of the Red Army and who had died following an unnecessary operation in 1925 ('Povest nepogashennoi luny', *Novy mir*, 1926, no. 5). Pilnyak was compelled to deny that there was any connection between his story and the rumours about Frunze's death. See G. Katkov, *The Trial of Bukharin*, London, Batsford, 1969, p. 171. Before his suicide, Ioffe, one of the leading diplomats of the 1920s and a close associate of Trotsky's, wrote, in a letter to Trotsky, that he had no faith in Professors Davidenko and Levin (the same Dr Levin who was charged in the Bukharin Trial of 1938 with having participated in the murder of the communist leaders). See Katkov, *ibid.*

162 Like the doctors Levin, Pletnev and Kazakov. See *Anti-Soviet Bloc of Rights and Trotskyites*, Moscow, People's Commissariat of Justice, 1938, pp. 530–614.

163 At his trial Slansky confessed to having delegated Dr Haskovec, who belonged to the Freemasons, as Gottwald's personal physician in order to cut short the life of the President of the Czechoslovak Republic. See *Procès des dirigents du centre de conspiration contre l'Etat dirigé par Rudolf Slansky*, Prague, Ministère de la Justice, 1953, p. 102.

164 How far this consideration was correct can be seen from the publication of the declaration of French doctors (among them four Jews) on 23 January 1953, which expressed full support for the Soviet authorities in their war against the criminal acts of the accused doctors. See *Humanité*, 27 January 1953, as quoted in *Commission pour la verité sur les crimes de Staline*, 1963, no. 2, p. 10.

165 Erenburg, *Sobranie sochinenii*, vol. 9, p. 729.

166 Vinogradov was the medical expert at the trial on 21 March 1938, which confirmed the charges against the doctors Levin, Pletnev and Kazakov, while Vovsi and Kogan took part in the condemnation of the 'sadistic doctor' and 'enemy of the people', Pletnev, in June 1937. (In the campaign conducted against him in this period, Pletnev was among other things accused of having bitten a woman's breasts so hard as to draw blood and of having thus made her seriously ill.) See *Pravda*, 8–11 June 1937.

167 Particularly prominent in these denunciations were the satirical journal *Krokodil*, the organ of the Trades Union, *Trud*, and the organ of the Communist Youth Organization, *Komsomolskaya pravda*.

168 Erenburg relates in his memoirs that shortly before he was to receive a prize on 27 January, he was called in by Grigoryan, who told him: 'It will be a good thing if, during the ceremony, you mention the criminal doctors'. I. Erenburg, *Sobranie sochinenii*, vol. 9, p. 729.

169 See Erenburg's novella, *The Thaw*; A. Terts (Siniavsky), *The Trial Begins*, London, Collins and Harvill Press, 1960, and E. Feldman, *Kele le-lo sugar*, Tel Aviv, Am ha-sefer, 1964, pp. 150–1.

170 V. Grossman, *Forever Flowing*, New York, Harper and Row, 1972, pp. 21–2.

171 See pp. 76ff.

172 In this connection, the annexation of the Western Ukraine to the Soviet Union in 1939 presents a special problem from the point of view of statistical data.

173 This estimate of half a million Jews in the Red Army is cited by the Soviet Jewish demographer, Y. Kantor. See his article, 'Yidn oyf dem grestn un vikhtiks tn front', *Folks-shtime*, 18 April 1963, pp. 8, 11.

174 With the annexation of the territories from Poland, Romania and the Baltic States, the Soviet Union's population stood at 193 million (not taking into account the natural increase of 1939–40). If we accept the estimate of five million Jews in the USSR prior to the outbreak of the Soviet–German war in June 1941, then the Jews constituted 2.5% of the entire population. See *Bolshaya Sovetskaya Entsiklopediya*, first edition, volume devoted wholly to the entry 'The Soviet Union', Moscow, 1948, p. 50.

175 According to Severyn Bialer, there were fifteen Jewish members and candidates on the Central Committee, and not fourteen as we have determined; but as Bialer does not provide a nominal list of the Central Committee members, it is not clear who, according to him, was the fifteenth member of Jewish origin. See S. Bialer, 'How Russians Rule Russia', *Problems of Communism*, 1964, no. 5, p. 46.

176 See *Rezolutsies fun der XVIII alfarbandisher konferents fun der ALKP (B)*, Moscow, Emes, 1941, pp. 27–8.

177 See *Dokumenty obvinyayut, Sbornik dokumentov*, Moscow, 1943, vol. 1. The second volume of the document collection appeared in 1945, and contained a number of documents dealing with the Nazi extermination of the Jews. See *Dokumenty obvinyayut*, Moscow, Gospolitizdat, 1945, vol. 2, pp. 17, 23, 140–3, 151.

178 *Pravda*, 19 December 1942.

179 There were also exceptions to this policy, particularly at the end of 1944, when the Commission reported on Nazi atrocities against the Jews in the Lvov and Latvia regions. See S. Schwarz, *Evrei v sovetskom soyuze*, New York, AERL, 1966, p. 148.

180 Ibid., p. 146.

181 Of seventy-nine books that appeared between 1941 and 1945, twenty-one were about Jews in the war. See Ch. Shmeruk, in *Sifrut yehudei brit-*

ha-moazot be-yemei ha-shoah ve-akhareha, Jerusalem, 1960, p. 28. Particularly important were two collections of documents edited by Ilya Erenburg, in which material appeared on the slaughter perpetrated by the Nazis in the occupied areas of the Soviet Union. See I. Erenburg, *Merder fun felker*, Moscow, Emes, 1944–5, vols. 1–2.

182 *Information Bulletin*, Embassy of the USSR, Washington, D.C., 2 June 1942.

183 On the establishment and activity of the Commission, see the testimony of a Yiddish poet living in Israel, A. Sutskever: A. Sutskever, 'Ilya Erenburg a kapitl zikhroynes fun di yorn 1944–46', *Di goldene keyt*, 1967, no. 61, pp. 34–5. On *The Black Book* in general, se D. Litani, 'Sefer shaḥor al shoat yehudey brit-ha-moazot', *Yediot yad va-shem*, 1960, no. 23–4, pp. 24–6; M. Altshuler in *Pirsumim Russim...*, pp. LXV–LXVI; Y. A. Gilboa, *The Black Years of Soviet Jewry, 1939–1953*, Boston, Little Brown, 1971, pp. 72–7.

184 *Eynikayt*, 21 May 1946. Parts of this collection were published in the two pamphlets edited by Erenburg (see note 181).

185 Erenburg writes in his memoirs: 'They told us the book would appear at the end of 1948... At the end of 1948 they disbanded the Jewish Anti-Fascist Committee, [closed] the newspaper *Emes* [this should of course read *Eynikayt*], dissolved *The Black Book*'. It is interesting that in the reprint of Erenburg's memoirs in his *Collected Works*, the passage on *The Black Book* was omitted (cf. *Novy mir*, 1965, no. 2, pp. 54–5, and Erenburg, *Sobranie sochinenii*, vol. 9, pp. 571–2).

186 *The Black Book – The Nazi Crime Against the Jewish People*, New York, Jewish Black Book Committee, 1946.

187 Ilya Erenburg, Vasily Grossman, Lev Ozerov and Vladimir Lidin, *Cartea Neagra*, Bucharest, Editura Institutlui Roman du Documentare, 1947.

188 *Morgen frayhayt*, 3 December 1947.

189 See Erenburg, *Sobranie sochineii*, vol. 9, pp. 376–7. Erenburg adds that following these remarks by Kondakov he appealed to the latter's superior, Shcherbakov, who told him that his deputy had admittedly shown exaggerated diligence, but that the text must be changed. Referring to Erenburg's articles, Shcherbakov added, *inter alia*: 'The soldiers want to hear about Suvorov, and you quote Heine.' ibid., p. 377.

190 According to the editor of the Hebrew edition of this book, Binyamin Vest, it is not known whether the manuscript was printed and published. See B. Vest, 'Le-korot ha-shoah ve-ha-partizaniyut ha-yehudit bi-vrit-ha-moazot', *Gesher*, 1966, no. 2–3, p. 242. It appears, however, that the book was printed but not circulated.

191 A poem by A. Surkov, written in 1942, mentions the Maccabees. See A. Surkov, 'Like Birds about their Ravaged Nest', in *The Road to the West*, quoted by Choseed, *The Jews*, p. 327.

192 Maksim Tank, writing of the ruins of the Minsk ghetto, says:

even the lament of *Jeremiah*
Hath not the strength to resurrect the dust grown cold

M. Tank, *Stikhotvorenia*, Moscow, 1948, pp. 28–9, quoted by Choseed, *The Jews*, p. 246.

193 In this poem 'To the Jewish People' (1942), M. Rylsky wrote:

> Upon us will beam great *Marx* and *Heine*...
> boldy we march
> With a sage sneer, like that of old *Mokher Seforim*
> Like your Shvartsman with a sword.

See M. Rylsky, *Stikhotvoreniya i poemy*, Moscow, 1945, p. 260, quoted by Choseed, *The Jews*, p. 252.

194 On Tychyna's poem, see Choseed, *The Jews*.

195 The authoress V. Panova uses the story of David and Goliath and mentions the kings of Israel – especially King David's words: 'the truth shall be your weapon'. See V. Panova, Sputniki (Travelling Companions), Moscow, 1946, as quoted in Choseed, *The Jews*, p. 345.

196 L. Leonov, *Russky les*, Moscow, 1967; see also M. Hayward, 'Some Observations on Jews in Post-Stalin Soviet Literature', *Bulletin on Soviet and East European Jewish Affairs*, 1969, no. 4, pp. 16–19.

197 V. Kochetov, 'Zhurbiny', *Zvezda*, 1952, no. 2.

198 It may be assumed that among them were M. Kalinin (who died in 1946), one of the initiators of the programme, and L. Kaganovich, who in the thirties was a kind of guardian of the Jewish Autonomous Region. Even though Stalin admitted, during his discussion with Roosevelt at Yalta on 10 February 1945, the failure of the Birobidzhan project, he certainly had no objections to the renewal of attempts to settle the region with Jewish immigrants after the Second World War. See Roi, *Yahasei*, p. 321.

199 As was said on Radio Moscow: there is no basis for the claims that the Jewish people in the Soviet Union is doomed to extinction, for the name of the Jewish Autonomous Region is engraved in letters of gold in the Stalin Constitution. See I. Fefer's remarks *Summary of World Broadcast, Part I*, 24 June 1947.

200 This notion that the Soviet government, under the influence of the Jewish Anti-Fascist Committee, made an unsuccessful attempt in 1945 to influence the Polish Committee for National Liberation (i.e. the Provisional Polish government, under the protection of the USSR) to consent to the former Jewish citizens of Poland being directed to Birobidzhan, is cited in Leneman, *La Tragédie des Juifs*, pp. 30–1.

201 According to the reports in the newspaper *Eynikayt*, the registration began in the Ukrainian city of Vinnitsa. See *Eynikayt*, 19 October 1946.

202 Lvavi, *Ha-hityashvut*, pp. 103–5.

203 I. Fefer, 'Fact and Fancy on Birobidzhan', *Jewish Life*, January 1949, pp. 9–10. The overall number of Jews in the Region was estimated at between 30,000 and 35,000.

204 L. Zinger, 'Post-War Reconstruction', *Jewish Life*, March 1949, pp. 24–5.

205 Among the prominent personages arrested were: Mikhail Levitin, former Chairman of the Regional Executive Committee, and the authors Israel Emiot, Dov-Ber Slutsky, Buzi Miler, Hershl Rabinkov, Leva Vaserman, Khaim Maltinsky, and others. See Kh. Maltinsky, *Der moskver mishpet iber di birobidzhaner*, Tel Aviv, Naye lebn, 1981.

206 See, for example, *Jewish Chronicle*, 12 January and 2 February 1951. The extent to which information on what was happening in Birobidzhan was lacking, even for the Israel legation in Moscow, may be seen in Namir, *Shliḥut be-moskvah*, pp. 310–12.
207 *Bolshaya Sovetskaya Entsiklopedia*, vol. SSR, 1948, p. 1821. In the same period there were no less than thirteen Uzbek schools in the Ukraine, even though that region had a very small Uzbek population.
208 Schulman, *Jewish Education*, p. 163.
209 *Jewish Chronicle*, 15 December 1939, as quoted in Sh. Redlich, *The Jews Under Soviet Rule During World War II*, unpublished PhD dissertation, Columbia University, New York, 1968, p. 32.
210 Redlich, *The Jews under Soviet Rule*, p. 35.
211 Schulman, *Jewish Education*, p. 163; Lvavi, *Ha-hityashvut*, pp. 264–73; J. Emiot, *Der Birobidzhaner inyen*, pp. 9–10; *Eynikayt*, 20 March 1948.
212 Lvavi, *Ha-hityashvut*, pp. 270, 272, 277.
213 *Eynikayt*, 24 April 1945.
214 H. Osherovich in *Eynikayt*, 18 March 1948.
215 The last report on the opening of a new academic year at this school appeared in *Eynikayt*, 7 September 1948. According to information received from a former principal of this school who emigrated to Israel, the school still existed in 1950.
216 *Eynikayt*, 31 January 1948.
217 On the Jewish Anti-Fascist Committee, See Sh. Redlich, 'The Jewish Anti-Fascist Committee in the Soviet Union', *Jewish Social Studies*, 1969, no. 1, pp. 25–36; Y. Litvak, 'Ha-vaad ha-yehudi ha-antifashisti', *Gesher*, 1966, nos. 2–3, pp. 218–32; Gilboa, *The Black Years of Soviet Jewry*, pp. 42–86.
218 See E. Pavlovski, *Pan-Slavism During World War II*, unpublished PhD dissertation, Georgetown University, 1968.
219 Shmeruk, *Sifrut yehudei*, p. 97.
220 Ibid., p. 99.
221 Several books of *belles-lettres* were published in editions of 10,000 to 25,000 copies.
222 About 64% of all the books in these years were *belles-lettres*.
223 The total circulation of these three periodicals was 12,000–15,000: Shmeruk, *Sifrut yehudei*, p. 123; M. Altshuler, 'Introduction', in Pinkus, Greenbaum and Altshuler *Russian Publications*, pp. 73–4.
224 Erenburg, *Sobranie sochinenii*, vol. 3, p. 435.
225 I. Erenburg, *Voina*, vol. 1–3, Moscow, 1942–4; 'Konets getto', *Novy mir*, 1944, no. 3.
226 A. Bezymensky in *Tzum zig*, Moscow, Der emes, 1944, pp. 62–9.
227 In the poems 'I Saw It' (1942), 'Kerch' and 'Kandava'. See *Znamya*, 1945, nos. 1–2; *Sbornik stikhov*, Moscow, 1947, p. 7.
228 In the poems 'Babi Yar', 'Maidanek'; see L. Pervomaisky, *Sochinenia*, Kiev, vol. 1, pp. 480–1.
229 In his poem 'No Eternal Memory', published in 1946, the poet notes his connection with thousands of years of the history of the Jewish people and uses the words *Shema Yisrael* (*Znamya*, 1946, no. 7, pp. 64–5).

230 In his autobiographical poem 'Your Victory' (*Znamya*, 1945, no. 9, pp. 1–28), Aliger gives expression to the crisis experienced by a generation of Jews in the USSR who believed that assimilation was the answer to the nationality problem: but the war put this faith to the test. Margarita Aliger is proud of being a descendant of the brave Maccabees, though she admits that it was only the Germans who reminded her of her links to her people.

231 Ozerov (Goldberg) wrote the poem 'Babi Yar' in 1944–5 (though it was published only in 1946; see *Oktyabr*, 1946, nos. 2–3, pp. 160–3) This is one of the most stirring works written in the USSR on the subject of the Jewish Holocaust. The poet identifies with all those who were put to death and buried at Babi Yar for him.

232 Before the war ended, Khelemsky wrote two poems devoted to the liberation of Riga (*Znamya*, 1945, no. 4, pp. 51–2), in which he expresses the feeling of a Jewish fighter who arrives at the liberated city and finds nothing but a desolate ghetto without a living being.

233 S. Ivanov in *Vechernyaya Moskva*, 21 March 1949.

234 Zinger, *Dos banayte folk*, p. 109. According to Mikhoels, there were twenty such theatres; see *Yidishe kultur*, 1943, nos. 6–7, p. 66.

235 *Antireligioznik*, November 1938, p. 58, quoted in R. Conquest (ed.), *Religion in the USSR*, London, The Bodley Head, 1963, pp. 112–13.

236 See, for example, the appeal of the synagogue committee of the city of Sverdlovsk to English Jewry in 1943: *The Russian Jews in the War*, London, 1943, pp. 60–1.

237 *Naye prese*, 28 January 1953.

4 THE POST-STALIN PERIOD, 1953–1983

1 See *Kommunist*, 1954, no. 18, pp. 14–20; *Voprosy filosofii*, 1954, no. 6, pp. 3–16.

2 *Sotsialisticheskie natsii SSSR*, Moscow, Gospolitizdat, 1955, pp. 17, 51.

3 From 1957 to 1967 about 300 publications appeared in the Soviet Union dealing with the national question; see N. Matiushkin, 'XXII sezd KPSS i zadachi sovetskikh istorikov', *Voprosy istorii*, 1961, no. 12, pp. 3–13.

4 See the Soviet scientific review: *Sovetskaya etnografiya*.

5 See S. Tsvigun, 'Borotsya s ideologicheskimi diversiyami vragov sotsializma', *Kommunist*, 1969, no. 11, pp. 102–12; *Ogoniok*, 1969, no. 30, pp. 26–9.

6 L. Brezhnev, *Izbrannye proizvedeniya*, Moscow, Politizdat, 1981, vol. 2, p. 77; *Materialy XXIV kongressa KPSS*, Moscow, Politizdat, 1971, p. 203.

7 S. Tokarev, 'Problemy tipov etnicheskikh obshchnostei', *Voprosy filosofii*, 1964, no. 11, p. 51.

8 I. Tsameryan, 'Aktualnye voprosy marksistko-leninskoi teorii natsii', *Voprosy istorii*, 1967, no. 6, p. 109.

9 Tokarev's approach was criticized by the ethnographer, Kozlov. See V. Kozlov, 'Etnos i ekonomika. Etnicheskaya i ekonomicheskaya obshchnost', *Sovetskaya etnografiya*, 1970, no. 2, p. 48; *idem*, 'O poniatii etnicheskoi obshchnosti', *Sovetskaya etnografiya*, 1967, no. 2, pp. 110–11.

10 V. Kozlov, 'Sovremennye etnicheskie protsessy V SSSR', *Sovetskaya etnografiya*, 1969, no. 2, p. 72.

11 M. Dzhunusov, 'Natsiya kak sotsialno-etnicheskaya obshchnost liudei', *Voprosy istorii*, 1966, no. 4, p. 28.

12 I. Tsameryan, *Natsii i natsionalnye otnosheniya v razvitom sotsialisticheskom obshchestve*, Moscow, Nauka, 1979, pp. 54–7.

13 Yu. Bromley, 'Opyt tipologizatsii etnicheskikh obshchnostei', *Sovetskaya etnografiya*, 1972, no. 5, pp. 61–80.

14 L. Vostokov, 'Antinarodnaya deyatelnost sionistov v Rossii', *Voprosy istorii*, 1973, no. 3, p. 28.

15 E. Evseev, *Fashizm pod goluboi zvezdoi*, Moscow, Molodaya gvardya, 1971, pp. 27–35.

16 V. Begun, *Polzuchaya kontrevolutsiya*, Minsk, Belorus, 1974, p. 105.

17 This exceptional display of erudition is cited by another anti-Zionist 'expert' of Jewish origin in the city of Kishinev. See M. Goldenberg, *Sotsialno-politicheskaya doktrina sionizma*, Kishinev, Shtiintsa, 1973, pp. 36–7.

18 *Politichesky dnevnik 1964–1970*, Amsterdam, Fond imeni Gertsena, 1970, pp. 90–1.

19 R. Medvedev, 'Blizhnevostochny konflikt i eyreisky vopros v SSSR', *Evreisky samizdat*, Jerusalem, The Hebrew University, 1976, vol. 10, pp. 22–49.

20 *Volnoe slovo*, 1972, vol. 5, pp. 55–117.

21 *Programma demokraticheskogo divizheniya*, Amsterdam, Fond imeni Gertsena, 1970; *Memorandum akademika Sakharova*, Frankfurt, Posev, 1970.

22 *Programma*, pp. 21–2.

23 D. Pospelovsky, 'The Resurgence of Russian Nationalism in Samizdat', *Survey*, 1973, vol. 19, no. 1, pp. 51–74; *Volnoe slovo*, 1975, no. 17–18, pp. 24–41.

24 I. Dzyuba, *Internationalism or Russification?* London, Weidenfeld and Nicolson, 1968.

25 Khrushchev's contention that Kaganovich's attitude was clearly anti-Semitic is unacceptable and must be regarded rather as a settling of accounts with a political rival: *Khrushchev Remembers*, London, 1971, p. 243.

26 If the testimony reaching us is accurate, it appears that Molotov and Voroshilov, together with Kaganovich and Mikoyan, opposed Stalin's plant to exile the Jews, which was debated in the Politburo at the end of February 1953. See J. B. Schechtman, *Star in Eclipse: Russian Jewry Revisited*, New York, Yoseloff, 1961, pp. 42–3; Goldberg, *The Jewish Problem in the Soviet Union*, pp. 148–9; *Jewish Chronicle*, 14 June 1957; K. Voroshilov, 'Rasskazy o zhizni', *Oktyabr*, 1967, no. 9, p. 37, 46; no. 10, pp. 148–90.

27 Franz Borkenau was one of the first to stress Zhdanov's favourable attitude to the Jewish question as contrasted with that of Malenkov. See F. Borkenau, 'Was Malenkov Behind the Anti-Semitic Plot', *Commentary*, 1953, vol. 15, pp. 438–46.

28 W. Hahn, *Postwar Soviet Politics. The Fall of Zhdanov and the Defeat of Moderation*, Ithaca and London, Cornel University Press, 1982.

29 M. Ebon, *Malenkov: Stalin's Successor*, New York, McGraw Hill Book Company, 1953, pp. 10–12, 100.

30 H. Salisbury, *To Moscow and Beyond*, New York, Harper and Brothers, 1960, pp. 70–1.

31 M. Wyziemblo, 'Odwrotna strona slowianofilstwa', *Kultura* (Paris), 1970, no. 9, p. 3.

32 *Pravda*, 16 March 1944.

33 Leneman, *La Tragédie des Juifs*, p. 17.

34 Ibid., p. 178.

35 A. Sutskever, 'Ilia Erenburg', *Di goldene keit*, 1967, no. 61, p. 30.

36 *The Anti-Stalin Campaign and International Communism*, New York, Columbia University, 1956, pp. 63–4.

37 Schechtman, *Star in Eclipse*, p. 81; *Jewish Chronicle*, 17 May 1957 and 10 January 1958; Anon., 'USSR and the Politics of Polish Anti-Semitism, 1956–1968', *Soviet Jewish Affairs*, 1971, no. 1, p. 20.

38 Leneman, *La Tragédie des Juifs*, p. 167.

39 *Les Réalités*, 1957, no. 136, pp. 64–7, 101–4; *Jewish Life*, February 1957, pp. 23–4, 42–3; *Le Figaro*, 9 April 1958.

40 *Pravda*, 19 November 1957.

41 *Pravda*, 10 March 1963.

42 B. Pinkus, *The Soviet Government and the Jews 1948–1967. A Documented Study*, Cambridge, 1984, pp. 127–33.

43 P. Gavrutto, *Tuchi nad gorodom*, Moscow, Moskovsky rabochii, 1965.

44 *Literaturnaya gazeta*, 9 August 1966.

45 Pinkus, *The Soviet Government and the Jews*, pp. 114–26, 435–38.

46 A. Werth, *Russia: Hopes and Fears*, London, Penguin Books, 1969, p. 210.

47 In 1965 Kosygin declared that anti-Semitism was 'a vestige of a past alien to us, which contradicts our world-outlook', *Pravda*, 19 July 1965. He repeated this in 1967: *The New York Times*, 26 June 1967.

48 *Pravda*, 24 March 1981.

49 A striking example of this class of *feuilletons* is the article by Lanskoi: M. Lanskoi, 'Potomki Ostapa Bendera', *Literaturnaya gazeta*, 7 October 1958.

50 See R. Nudelman in *Anti-Semitism in the Soviet Union, Its Roots and Consequences*, Jerusalem, The Hebrew University. 1979, vol. 1, pp. 35–7.

51 Y. Nir, *The Israeli–Arab Conflict in Soviet Caricatures, 1967–1973*, Tel-Aviv, Cherikover Publishers, 1976, p. 10.

52 Vogt in *Anti-Semitism in the Soviet Union*, vol. 3, pp. 159–94.

53 H. Swayze, *Political Control of Literature in the USSR, 1946–1959*, Cambridge, Mass., Harvard University Press, 1962; G. Gibian, *Interval of Freedom. Soviet Literature during the Thaw, 1954–1957*, Minneapolis, The University of Minnesota, 1960.

54 N. Chukovsky, 'Brodiaga', in *Literaturnaya Moskva*, 1956, pp. 418–35, 'Variya', in *Izbrannoe*, Moscow, 1963, pp. 215–91.

55 N. Ilyina, 'Vozvrashchenie', *Znamya*, 1957, nos. 1–4.

56 V. Tevekelyan, 'Granit ne plavitsya', *Moskva*, 1962, no. 3.

57 A. Dimarov, 'Shlyakhamy zhyttya', *Dnipro*, 1963, nos. 9–10.

58 G. Makhorkin, *I snova zhizn*, Moscow, 1964.

59 V. Tevekelyan, 'Za Mostovoyu-rekoyu', *Moskva*, 1966, no. 9.
60 I. Shevtsov, *Liubov i nenavist*, Moscow, 1978; *Nabat*, Moscow, 1978.
61 V. Kochetov, 'Ugol padeniya', *Oktyabr*, 1967, no. 10; V. Zakrutkin, 'Sotvorenie mira', *Oktyabr*, 1967, no. 6.
62 A. Ivanov, 'Vechnyi zov', *Roman gazeta*, 1978, no. 2; M. Kolesnikov, *S Otkrytym zabralom*, Moscow, 1977.
63 V. Pikul, 'U poslednei cherty', *Nash sovremennik*, 1979, nos. 4–6.
64 Based on the compilation from the Soviet press, *Evrei i evreisky narod*, Jerusalem, Hebrew University, covering some 200 newspapers but not the local press, where there are many reports of trials. For further details on economic trials see Pinkus, *The Soviet Government and the Jews*, *pp. 201–7*; G. Kline, 'Economic Crimes and Punishment', *Survey*, 1965, no. 57, pp. 67–72; 'Economic Crimes in the Soviet Union' *Journal of the International Commission of Jurists*, 1964, vol 5, no. 1.
65 See Khrushchev's remarks in a talk with French Socialist leaders: *Les réalités*, 1957, no. 136; and Minister of Culture, Furtseva, in an interview with US newspaper, *National Guardian*, 25 June 1956. Myshin was far more categorical on the subject: V. Myshin, *Obshchestvennyi progress*, Gorky, Volgo-Vyatskoe Izdatelstvo, 1970.
66 Thus not a single jew was accepted from among the 300 candidates for admission to the Faculty of Mathematics in Leningrad (where there is a population of *c.* 170,000 Jews). See S. A. Rozenblum, *Etre Juif en URSS*, Paris, Collection de la Revue Politique et Parlementaire, 1982, p. 57.
67 See *Réalités*, 1957, no. 136.
68 When Professor L. Feuer proposed a meeting with the heads of the Philosophical Institute of the Academy of Sciences to conduct research of this kind, he was met with a blank refusal. See: L. Feuer, 'Meeting the Philosophers', *Survey*, 1964, no. 51, pp. 21–2.
69 In a Harvard University project of 1950–1 the 329 Soviet immigrants interviewed were also asked a number of questions on their attitude to Jews; but they constituted a special population group not representing the whole Soviet population, and referred to a special period, that of the war and after it. See W. Korey, 'Origins and Development of Soviet Anti-Semitism', *Slavic Review*, 1972, no. 1, pp. 111–13.
70 An example of this type of answer, expressing popular anti-Semitism, is to be found in the touching story by A. Valtseva, 'Kvartira No. 13', *Moskva*, 1957, no. 1, and also in the testimony of André Blumel, a supporter of the Soviet Union, *Undzer vort*, 24 October 1960.
71 Vassili Grossman again offers important testimony to this in his story, 'Good Luck to You', *Soviet Literature*, 1969, no. 6. So does the manifesto posted in the town of Malakhovka, not far from Moscow. *Jews in Eastern Europe*, 1959, pp. 9–10; 1960; pp. 15–16.
72 *Undzer vort*, 7 October 1959; 2 October 1960; E. Markish, *Le Long Retour*, Paris, Laffont, 1974, p. 284.
73 *Kommunist* (Buinaksk), 9 August 1960, 11 August 1960; *Jews in Eastern Europe*, 1963 (May), pp. 34–6; *Soviet Weekly*, 7 February 1963.
74 E. Evtushenko, 'Stantsiya zima', *Oktyabr*, 1956, no. 10.
75 Y. Bondarev, 'Tishina', *Novyi mir*, 1962, nos. 3–5, 'Dvoe', *Novyi mir*,

1964, nos. 4–5; G. Nikolaeva, *Bitva v puti*, Moscow, Sovetsky pisatel, 1959.

76 See pp. 278–9, 318.

77 *Literaturnaya gazeta*, 10 October 1959.

78 *Literaturnaya gazeta*, 19 September 1961; Pinkus, The *Soviet Government and the Jews*, pp. 114–16. Evtushenko read his poem to an audience numbering thousands.

79 D. Starikov, 'Ob odnom stikhotvorenii', *Literatura i zhizn*, 27 September 1961.

80 A. Ladygina, 'Slushaya trinadtsatuyu simfoniyu', *Sovetskaya Belorussiya*, 2 April 1963; S. Volkov (ed.), *Testimony, the Memoirs of Dmitrii Shostakovich*, New York, Harper and Row, 1979, pp. 156–9, 185.

81 E. Solmar, 'Protokoly antisionistkikh mudretsov', *Evreisky samizdat*, vol. 16, p. 136.

82 T. Rigby, *Communist Party Membership*, pp. 366–88; J. Newth and Z. Katz, 'Proportion of Jews in the Communist Party of the Soviet Union', *Bulletin on Soviet and East European Jewish Affairs*, 1969, no. 4, pp. 37–8.

83 'KPSS v tsifrakh', *Partiinaya zhizn*, 1976, no. 10, p. 16.

84 E. Jacobs, 'A note on Jewish Membership of the Belorussian Communist Party', *Soviet Jewish Affairs*, 1980, no. 2, p. 53.

85 Pinkus, *The Soviet Government and the Jews*, pp. 341–5; M. Altshuler, *Hakibuz ha-yehudi bi-vrit ha-moazot be-yameinu, nituah sozio-demografi*, Jerusalem, Magnes Press, 1979, pp. 238–43.

86 *Izvestiya*, 18 March 1954; 19 March 1958; *Deputaty Verkhovnogo Soveta SSSR*, Moscow, 1962, 1966, 1970, 1974; *Pervaya sessiya Verkhovnogo Soveta SSSR*, Moscow, 1979.

87 *Deputaty Verkhovnogo Soveta Moldavskoi SSR*, Kishinev, 1976, p. 70.

88 *Sostav deputatov Verkhovnykh Sovetov soyuznykh, respublik i mestnykh sovetov*, Moscow, 1959; *Itogi vyborov i sostav deputatov verkhovnykh respublik i Avtonomnykh respublik*, Moscow, 1971, 1973, 1975.

89 See note 88.

90 A. Rukhadze, *Jews in the USSR, Figures, Facts, Comment*, Moscow, Novosti, 1978, p. 17.

91 *The New York Times*, 21 June 1954, 22 June 1954, H. E. Salisbury, *American in Russia*, New York, Harper and Brothers, 1955, pp. 281–4.

92 *Jewish Chronicle*, 3 September 1954.

93 News published mainly in the Warsaw Yiddish newspaper, *Folkshtimme*, and the Paris Yiddish newspaper *Naye presse*; see *Jewish Chronicle*, 22 November 1955, 25 November 1955, 9 December 1955.

94 *Naye prese*, 24 April 1958.

95 *Sovetskaya Rossiya*, 6 August 1958.

96 *Evreiskaya avtonomnaya oblast*, Khabarovsk, Khabarovskoe knizhnoe izdatelstvo, 1959.

97 S. Groussard, 'Le Monde. Propos libres avec N. Khrouchtchev', *Le figaro*, 9 April 1958.

98 Y. Lvavi, 'He-arot al birobidzhan', *Shvut*, 1982, no. 9, p. 123.

99 Y. Lvavi, *Ha-hityashvut*, pp. 244–6.

100 A. Vinokur, 'Ugasanie drevnei very', *Nauka i religiya*, 1967, no. 1, pp. 41–3.
101 *Dalnii Vostok*, 1978, no. 6.
102 See Mikoyan's statement in the United States: *The New York Times*, 16 January 1959.
103 Negotiations began in Bulgaria between the Israeli Ambassador in that country Dr Ben-Zion Razin, and the Soviet Ambassador, Mikhail Bodrov. See *Ma-ariv*, 10 March 1972.
104 A. Palmor, 'Yahasei yisrael brit-hamoazot', *Behinot*, 1970, no. 1, p. 98.
105 It is interesting that news appeared in the Western Press, including the *New York Times*, in 1955, that the Soviet Union would demand a ransom of $3,000 for every immigrant, as had been done in the 1930s, but the Soviet government issued a denial. *Ha-arez*, 2 March 1955.
106 *Izvestiya*, 24 January 1954.
107 *Pravda*, 2 October 1955.
108 *Pravda*, 30 December 1955.
109 Articles dealing with Israel did not generally mention Zionism, see e.g. *Novoe vremiya*, 1954, no. 23, pp. 27–9; 1956, no. 30, pp. 24–6; but there were exceptions, articles which attacked 'reactionary Zionism' and the connection between Zionism and US imperialism. *Novoe vremiya*, 1956, no. 5, pp. 30–2.
110 We are preparing research on the Zionist Movement in the Soviet Union from 1948 to 1985, which will deal in full with Zionist activity and the fight waged against it.
111 *Pravda*, 6 November 1956.
112 *Pravda*, 8 November 1956.
113 *Pravda*, 11 November 1956.
114 *Pravda*, 6 November 1956; *Izvestiya*, 28–29 November 1956, 14 December 1956.
115 *Pravda*, 4 March 1957.
116 *Jewish Chronicle*, 5 April 1957, 19 April 1957.
117 *Pegishot be-moskvah 1957*, Merhaviah, Sifriat poalim, 1957; *Jewish Chronicle*, 2 August 1957, 16 August 1957, 13 September 1957.
118 *Jewish Chronicle*, 20 September 1957, 27 September 1957.
119 *Pravda*, 22 September 1957.
120 *Mezhadunarodnaya zhizn*, 1957, no. 12, pp. 52–62.
121 *Le Figaro*, 9 April 1958; Pinkus, *The Soviet Government and the Jews*, p. 67–9, 71.
122 *Pravda*, 2 March 1959.
123 K. Ivanov and Z. Sheinis, *Gosudarstvo Izrail i ego polozhenie i politika*, Moscow, Gospolitizdat, 1959.
124 Ibid. p. 21; *Sovremennyi Vostok*, 1957, no. 5, pp. 17–19.
125 *Le Figaro*, 9 April 1958.
126 See A. Gorev, 'Mif o izrailskom sotsializme', *Sovremennyi Vostok*, 1959, no. 8, pp. 11–14; B. Prakhie, *Pravda o zemle obetovannoi*, Odessa, Odesskoe knizhnoe izdatelstvo, 1961, p. 6.
127 K. Ivanov and Z. Sheinis, *Gosudarstvo Izrail*, p. 134; G. Zyskin, *Iudaizm i*

sionizm; komu i kak oni sluzhat, Kuibyshev, Kuibyshovskoe knizhnoe izdatelstvo, 1963, pp. 44–5.

128 Zyskin, *Iudaizm i sionizm*, p. 43.

129 F. Mayatsky, *Sovremennyi iudaizm i sionizm*, Kishinev, Karta Moldovien-
aske, 1964, pp. 53–4.

130 *Trud*, 16 March 1961, 11 March, 1963, 9 June 1963, 30 August 1964;
Znamya kommunizma, 15 April 1960, 14 April 1963, 7 July 1964; *Vechernii
Rostov*, 19 June 1964; *Sovetskaya Latviya*, 24 March 1961.

131 Pinkus, *The Soviet Government and the Jews*, pp. 54–8, 61–3, 67–71; *Jewish
Chronicle*, 9 December 1966.

132 On Jewish emigration from the Soviet Union see B. Pinkus, 'The Emigration of National Minorities from the USSR in the Post-Stalin Era',
Soviet Jewish Affairs, 1983, no. 1, pp. 3–36.

133 K. Kaz, *Budapest, varshah, moskvah, Shagrir el medinot mitnakrot*, Tel-Aviv,
Sifriat poalim, 1976, p. 116.

134 Even an article headed 'A Conference of Bankrupts', dealing with the
twenty-sixth Zionist Congress, did not offer slanders against Zionism
such as we have seen in the Khrushchev period: *Literaturnaya gazeta*, 25
February 1965.

135 KGB circles were apparently dissatisfied with this new policy and often
tried to stage some act of provocation, as in Odessa in April 1965. See
Jews in Eastern Europe, 1965, vol. 3, no. 3, pp. 67–71.

136 *Izvestiya*, 5 December 1966.

137 *New York Times*, 2 January 1967; J. Frankel, The Soviet Regime and
Anti-Zionism: An Analysis, Research paper no. 55, Jerusalem, The
Hebrew University, 1984, pp. 34–9.

138 *Pravda*, 22 December 1973; Y. Roi (ed.), *The Limits of Power. Soviet Policy
in the Middle East*, New York, St Martins Press, 1979.

139 See A. Yodfat, 'Brit ha-moazot ve-ha-sikhsukh ha-yisraeli-mizri', *Shvut*,
1980, no. 7, pp. 62–3.

140 See Gromyko's statement, *Pravda*, 26 March 1979.

141 The list of books is based on B. Pinkus, 'Reshimah bibliografit', *Behinot*,
1970, no. 1, pp. 202–6; no. 2–3, pp. 187–92; D. Zeichner, 'Pirsumim al
yahadut brit-ha-moazot', *Behinot*, 1974, no. 5, pp. 174–200; N. Bibi-
chkova, 'A Short list of Anti-Semitic and Anti-Israel Publications', *Anti-
Semitism in the Soviet Union*, vol. 1, pp. 345–52; vol. 3, pp. 369–74.

142 Based on Frankel, *The Soviet Regime*, p. 65.

143 *Pravda*, 1 January 1983; *Research Report of the Institute of Jewish Affairs*,
London, 1983, no. 6; *Soviet Jewish Affairs*, 1983, no. 3, pp. 55–68.

144 *Pravda*, 28 July 1983; *Komsomolskaya pravda*, 2 September 1983; *Vechernyaya Moskva*, 24 August 1983.

145 For the anti-Zionist trials, see A. Rozhansky (ed.), *Antievreiskie protessy v
Sovetskom Soyuze, 1969–1975*, Jerusalem, The Hebrew University,
1979–1984, 3 vols., T. Taylor, *Court of Terror, Soviet Criminal Justice and
the Jewish Emigration*, New York, 1976; *Ha-inteligenzia ha-yehudit bi-vrit-ha-
moazot*, 1980, no. 4, pp. 98–100; no. 6, p. 143.

146 On the German national movement in the Soviet Union see my book:
Die Deutschen in der Sowjetunion, Geschichte einer Nationalen Minder-

eit in *20 Jahrhundert*, Baden-Baden, 'Nomos', 1987. With I. Fleischhauer.
147 Y. Tenenbaum, *Malkhut ha-geza ve-ha-resha*, Jerusalem, 1961, p. 365.
148 *Folks-shtime*, 18 April 1963; A. Greenbaum in Ch. Berlin (ed.), *Studies in Jewish Bibliography, History and Literature in Honor of I. E. Kiev*, New York, Ktav Publishing House, 1971, p. 147.
149 D. Valentei, 'Naselenie i voina', *Nedelya*, 1965, no. 19, p. 17.
150 For data see Pinkus, *The Soviet Government and the Jews*, pp. 24–6; M. Altshuler, *Ha-kibuz*, pp. 80–109; *Naselenie SSSR*, Moscow, Politizdat, 1980, pp. 24–30.
151 *Naselenie zemnogo shara*, Moscow, Statistika, 1965, p. 33.
152 H. Carrère d'Encausse, *L'empire éclaté*, Paris, Flammarion, 1978, pp. 34–68; Altshuler, *Ha-kibuz*, pp. 110–18.
153 L. Katz (ed.), *Handbook of Major Soviet Nationalities*, New York, The Free Press, 1975.
154 Altshuler, *Ha kibuz*, p. 253.
155 Z. Nezer in *Ha-inteligenzia ha-yehudit bi-vrit ha-moazot*, 1982, no. 6, p. 87.
156 Altshuler, *Ha-kibuz*, pp. 125–64.
157 Altshuler, ibid., pp. 158–63; Pinkus, *Soviet Government and the Jews*, pp. 29–33; Halevy, *Jewish University Students and Professionals*, pp. 195–243; *Moskva v tsifrakh 1979 goda*, Moscow, Statistika, 1979.
158 Alshuler, ibid., pp. 147–8.
159 *Sovetskaya Moldaviya*, 16 May 1964; *Soviet Weekly*, 4 June 1966; *Moscow News*, 24 November 1962; A. Rukhadze, *Jews in the USSR*, p. 17.
160 Alshuler, ibid., p. 166.
161 See Pinkus, *The Soviet Government and the Jews*, pp. 54–61, 289–90.
162 A. Katsh, 'The Soviet Anomaly', *Jewish Spectator*, March 1972.
163 *Freundschaft*, 23 March 1976, B. Khasanov, *Yazyki narodov Kazakhstana*, Alma-Ata, Nauka, 1976; L. Hirszowicz, 'Jewish Cultural Life in the USSR', *Soviet Jewish Affairs*, 1977, no. 2, p. 16.
164 W. Korey, 'International Law and the Right to Study Hebrew in the USSR', *Soviet Jewish Affairs*, 1981, no. 1, pp. 3–18.
165 *Evreisky samizdat*, vols. 17, 20, 22, 23; J. E. Singer, *The Case of Yosif Begun*, Jerusalem, 1979.
166 *Literaturnaya gazeta*, 29 December 1955.
167 *Literaturnaya gazeta*, 24 January 1956, 29 March 1956, 15 May 1956, 30 October, 1956.
168 *Folks-shtime*, 2 August 1957.
169 *Morgn freyhayt*, 20 July 1957.
170 *Politichesky dnevnik*, Amsterdam, Fond imeni Gertsena, 1972, pp. 102–5.
171 *Pechat v SSSR, 1959–1981*, Moscow, Statistika, 1959–82.
172 Rukhadze, *Jews in the USSR*, p. 23.
173 Ch. Shmeruk, 'Yiddish Literature in the USSR', L. Kochan (ed.), *The Jews in Soviet Russia*, 3rd edn., p. 277.
174 *Pechat v SSSR*, Moscow, 1960, pp. 46–53.
175 Ya. Taits, *Neugasimyi svet*, Moscow, 1961.
176 A. Brunshtein, *Viesna*, Moscow, 1961.
177 S. Marshak, 'V nachale zhizni', *Novyi mir*, 1960, no. 2.

178 I. Erenburg, *Men, Years, Life*, London, Macgibbon and Kee, 1962–6.

179 D. Halkin, 'Tsimbalisty', *Oktyabr*, 1967, no. 12.

180 A. Rybakov, 'Tyazhelyi pesok', *Oktyabr*, 1978, nos. 7–9.

181 I. Selvinsky, *Lirika*, Moscow, 1964, pp. 427–30.

182 *Novyi mir*, 1959, no. 6, pp. 114; B. Slutsky, *Rabota*, Moscow, 1964, pp. 93–4.

183 Naum Korzhavin in *Soviet Poetry*, Moscow, 1965, pp. 304–05.

184 L. Pervomaisky, 'Dikii med', *Oktyabr*, 1963, nos. 2–3.

185 L. Sheinin, 'Volki v gorode', *Oktyabr*, 1965, no. 1.

186 I. Brodsky in *Grani*, 1965, no. 58, pp. 167–70; A. Galich, *Pesni*, Frankfurt, 1969.

187 J. Stora, 'Pasternak et le Judaisme', *Cahiers du monde russe et soviétique*, 1968, no. 3–4, pp. 353–64.

188 N. Arzhak (Y. Daniel), *Govorit Moskva*, Washington, 1962.

189 B. Yakobishvili in *Jewish Culture in the Soviet Union*, Jerusalem, The Cultural Department of the World Jewish Congress, 1973, p. 129.

190 *Birobidzhaner shtern*, 14 October 1981; *Sputnik*, 1981, no. 9, pp. 83–9.

191 Hirszowicz, 'Jewish Cultural Life', p. 16.

192 *Folks-shtime*, 5 November 1961, 19 March 1966, 29 March 1966.

193 M. Kalik in *Jewish Culture*, p. 15.

194 *Folks-shtime*, 19 July 1958, 20 February 1960, 26 April 1961, 24 January 1963, 8 August 1970.

195 See G. Sharbatov (ed.), *Semitskie yazyki*, Moscow, Akademiya Nauk, 1965.

196 For books before 1967, see Pinkus, Greenbaum and Altshuler (eds.), *Russian Publications*, pp. 21–36 and see note 141.

197 *Nyurnbergsky protsess*, Moscow, Gosyurizdat, 1965.

198 *Dnevnik Anny Frank*, Moscow, Internatsionalnaya literatura, 1960.

199 M. Rolnikaite, *Tariu popsakati*, Vilnius, 1963; *Ia dolzhna raskazat*, Moscow, Politizdat, 1965.

200 See Pinkus, *Soviet Government and the Jews*, pp. 421–38.

201 D. Fish, 'The Jews in Syllabuses of World and Russian History', *Soviet Jewish Affairs*, 1978, no. 1, pp. 3–25; R. Okuneva in *Anti-Semitism in the Soviet Union*, vol. 3, pp. 51–92; W. Korey, *The Soviet Cage Anti-Semitism in Russia*, New York, Viking Press, 1973, pp. 83–97.

202 *Voprosy ideologicheskoi raboty*, Moscow, Gospolitizdat, 1961, pp. 61–5.

203 *Pravda*, 11 November 1954.

204 *Nauka i religiya*, Moscow, Gospolitizdat, 1957.

205 *Naye prese*, 30 June 1954, 2 September 1954.

206 *Jewish Chronicle*, 6 July 1956.

207 *Jewish Observer and Middle East Review*, 1 June 1956, p. 1.

208 Ibid., p. 3.

209 *Jewish Chronicle*, 24 August 1956.

210 *Jewish Chronicle*, 12 October 1956, 2 November 1956.

211 *Jewish Chronicle*, 9 March 1956, 8 June 1956; *Naye prese*, 19 August 1955.

212 *Jews in Eastern Europe*, 1959, no. 2, pp. 33–4.

213 *Jewish Chronicle*, 14 June 1957.

214 *Izvestiya*, 18 March 1955, 28 November 1956, 29 November 1956, 14 December 1956.

215 B. Bociurkiv, 'Church–State Relations in the USSR', in *Religion and the Soviet State*, pp. 96–7.
216 *Evrei i evreisky narod*, London, Contemporary Library, 1960–4.
217 D. Powell, *Antireligious Propaganda in the Soviet Union 1959–1963* PhD Thesis, Yale University, 1967, p. 105.
218 *Agitator*, 1960, no. 8, p. 63.
219 *Pravda*, 4 April 1964.
220 *Zhovten*, 1952, nos. 7–9; *Literaturnaya gazeta*, 10 February 1953.
221 Iu. Aleksandrov, 'Mestnye sovety i zakonodatelstvo o kultakh, *Agitator*, 1966, no. 13, pp. 57–9; Iu. Rozenbaum, 'Otdelenie tserkvii ot gosudarstva v SSSR', *Sovetskoe gosudarstvo i pravo*, 1972, no. 3, pp. 56–64.
222 J. Rothenberg, *Jewish Religion in the Soviet Union*, pp. 180–1; Rozenblum, *Etre Juif en URSS*, p. 82.
223 A. Yodfat, 'Jewish Religious Communities in the USSR', *Soviet Jewish Affairs*, 1971, no. 2, p. 66.
224 *American Jewish Yearbook*, 1961, p. 287.
225 *American Jewish Yearbook*, 1964, p. 269.
226 R. Conquest (ed.), *Religion in the USSR*, London, Bodley Head, 1968, p. 116.
227 Rothenberg, *Jewish Religion*, p. 180; Yodfat, 'Jewish Religious Communities', p. 66.
228 *The New York Times*, 19 June 1959, 13 July 1959; *Izvestiya*, 24 July 1959.
229 *Jews in Eastern Europe*, 1963, vol. 2, no. 2, p. 61.
230 G. Simon, 'Der Kampf für die Glaubenstoleranz', in H. Brahm (ed.), *Opposition in der Sowjetunion*, Düsseldorf, Droste Verlag, 1972, p. 142.
231 *New York Times*, 17 March 1964.
232 *Jews in Eastern Europe*, 1963, vol. 2, no. 3, p. 26.
233 *Izvestiya*, 21 March 1964; *Pravda Vostoka*, 17 March 1969; *Sovetskaya Moldaviya*, 26 March 1964.
234 'Pussover and Mazoth: A Case History of Soviet Policy', *Congress Bi-Weekly*, 1966, vol. 33, no. 16, pp. 13–19.
235 *Jewish Chronicle*, 13 November 1959; *Jews in Eastern Europe*, 1963, vol. 2, no. 3.
236 Rothenberg, *Jewish Religion*, p. 74.
237 *Daily Mail*, 9 November 1961.
238 J. Rothenberg, ibid., p. 80.
239 *Jews in Eastern Europe*, 1966, vol. 3, no. 4, pp. 29–30.
240 *New York Herald Tribune*, 27 July 1965.
241 Conquest (ed.), *Religion in the USSR*, p. 117.
242 *My ne mozhem molchat*, Moscow, Novosti, 1961.
243 *Pravda*, 24 March 1971.
244 I. Shapiro, 'Jewish Believers in the USSR', *Moscow News*, 7 February 1976.
245 G. Bakanursky, *Iudaizm i sovremennost*, Moscow, Znanie, 1978, p. 60.
246 *Nauka i religiya*, 1980, no. 9, pp. 38–9.
247 *Sputnik*, 1981, no. 12, pp. 68–73.
248 *American Jewish Yearbook*, 1984, vol. 84, p. 218.
249 *Nauka i religiya*, 1980, no. 9, pp. 38–9.

250 V. Kuroedov, *Religiya i tserkov v Sovetskom, gosudarstve*, Moscow, Gospoli-tizdat, 1981; *Izvestiya*, 28 January 1978.

251 Carrère d'Encausse, *L'empire éclaté*, p. 229.

252 I. A. Hebby, *Protestants in Russia*, Belfast, Christian Journals, LTO 1976, p. 109.

253 A. Babii, M. Goldenberg and D. Tabankaru, *Preodolenie religii i utver-zhdenie ateizma v moldavskoi SSR*, Kishinev, Shtiintsa, 1983, pp. 63, 67.

254 L. Hirszowicz, 'Jewish Cultural Life', p. 11; I. Shapiro in *Sputnik*, 1981, no. 2; G. Bakanursky, *Iudaizm*, p. 61.

255 B. Fein, 'Ha-zehut ha-yehudit shel yehudei brit-ha-moazot', *Ha-inteli-genzia ha-yehudit bi-vrit ha-moazot*, 1981, no. 5, p. 88. Published in English as *Jewishness in the Soviet Union. Report of an Empirical Survey*, Jerusalem, Center for Public Affairs, 1984.

256 D. N. Jacobs (ed.), *Studies of the Third Wave*, Colorado, Westview Press, 1981, p. 23.

257 Babii, Goldenberg and Tabenkaru, *Preodolenie*, p. 153; *Moscow News*, 7 February 1976.

258 Y. Roi, 'Jewish Religious Life in USSR', *Soviet Jewish Affairs*, 1980, no. 2, pp. 41–3.

259 S. Rozenblum, *Etre Juif en URSS*, p. 104; *Moscow News*, 7 February 1976.

260 See note 150.

261 Altshuler, *Ha-kibuz*, p. 60.

262 A. Kholmogorov, *Internatsionalnye cherty sovetskoi natsii*, Moscow, Mysl, 1979, p. 89.

263 L. Hirszowicz, 'Uni-National and Mixed Marriages in the USSR', *Research Report of the Institute of Jewish Affairs*, 1983, no. 9, p. 4.

264 Altshuler, *Ha-kibuz*, p. 44.

265 Fein, '*Ha-zehut*', p. 89.

266 T. Friedgut, 'Soviet Jewry: The Silent Majority', *Soviet Jewish Affairs*, 1980, no. 2, pp. 3–19.

267 Moscow Broadcast: 'Ehrenburg on the Writers' Mission', *Moscow Home Service*, GMT, 26 January, 1961.

268 L. Kopelev, *The Education of a True Believer*, London, Wilwood House, 1981, p. 112.

269 *Evreisky samizdat*, vol. 4, p. 42.

270 A. Itai and M. Neishtat, *Korot shel tnuat nezah be-latvia*, Tel-Aviv, Am oved, 1972; B. Gurevich, 'Al mahteret ha-briha be-lita u-be-latvia, bi-shnat 1946', *Shvut*, 1984, no. 10, pp. 101–12.

271 M. Gelfond, 'Tyuremnye vstrechi', *Sion*, 1972, no. 1, pp. 111–12.

272 Interviews with the Israeli Embassy staff in the Soviet Union.

273 N. Shaham, *Pegishot be-moskvah, 1957*, Merhaviah, Sifriat poalim, 1957.

274 M. Perah, 'Ha-mitingim be-rumbuli', *Yalkut moreshet*, 1973, no. 13, pp. 5–16.

275 A. W. Fisher, *Crimean Tatars*, Stanford, Hoover Institution Press, 1978, p. 176.

276 See S. P. de Boer, E. Y. Drissen and H. L. Verhaar (eds.), *Biographical Dictionary of Dissidents in the Soviet Union, 1956–1975*, The Hague, Nijhoff, 1982.

277 A. Amalrik, *Prosushchestvuet li sovetsky soyuz do 1984 goda?*, Amsterdam, Fond imeni Gertsena, 1969, p. 12.
278 B. Lewytskyj, *Politische Oppostion in der Sowjetunion 1960–1972*, München, DTV, 1972, p. 41.
279 C. Lubarsky, *Soziale Basis und Umfang des swojetischen Dissidentums*, Köln, BIOS, 1979, p. 8.
280 B. Pinkus, 'National Identity and Emigration Patterns Among Soviet Jewry', *Soviet Jewish Affairs*, 1985, no. 3, pp. 3–28.
281 *Petitsii, pisma i obrashcheniya evreev SSSR*, Jerusalem, The Hebrew University, 1973–1980. 10 vols.
282 Interview with Mr Shaul Avigur, Kineret, 28 June 1976.
283 W. Orbach, *The American Movement to Aid Soviet Jews*, Amherst, University of Massachusetts, 1979.

Select bibliography

PUBLICATIONS IN RUSSIAN, ENGLISH, GERMAN AND FRENCH

Abosch, H. *Antisemitismus in Russland: Eine Analyse und Dokumentation zum sowietischen Antisemitismus*, Darmstadt, 1972.

Adler, C. and Margalit, A. *With Firmness in the Right*, New York, 1946.

Admiration is not Enough: The Russian Jews in the War, London, n.d.

Agar, H. *The Saving Remnant: An Account of Jewish Survival*, New York, 1960.

Ainsztein, R. *Jewish Resistance in Nazi-Occupied Eastern Europe*, New York, 1974.

Allen, M. W. 'The Policy of the USSR Towards the State of Israel', unpublished PhD dissertation, University of London, 1961.

Allilueva, S. *Twenty Letters to a Friend*, New York, 1967.

Only One Year, New York, 1969.

The Anti-Stalin Campaign and International Communism, New York, 1956.

Altshuler, M. 'Some Statistical Data on the Jews among the Scientific Elite of the Soviet Union', *Jewish Journal of Sociology*, 1973, vol. 1, pp. 45–55.

Anatoli, A. (Kuznetsov), *Babi Yar*, New York, 1971.

Anich, M. *Otmena cherty evreiskoi osedlosti*, Moscow, 1915.

Anti-Semitism in the Soviet Union: Its Roots and Consequences, Jerusalem, 1979–84, 3 vols.

Antonov, B. *Masked as Fighters for Human Rights*, Kiev, 1981.

Aranyossy, G. (ed.). *La presse antisémite en URSS*, Paris, 1978.

Aronson, G. (ed.). *Russian Jewry, 1917–1967*, New York, 1969.

Aronson, I. M. 'Russian Bureaucratic Attitudes Towards Jews', 1881–1894, unpublished PhD dissertation, Northwestern University, Evanston, 1973.

Axelbank, A. *Soviet Dissent; Intellectuals, Jews and Détente*, New York, 1975.

Azbel, M. Y. *Refusenik, Trapped in the Soviet Union*, Boston, 1981.

Bakanov, B. *Zionist Falsehoods*, Mowcow, 1974.

Barany, G. 'Jewish Prisoners of War in the Soviet Union During World War II', *Jahrbücher für Geschichte Ost Europas*, 1983, vol. 31, no. 2, pp. 162–209.

Barghorn, F. *Détente and the Democratic Movement in the USSR*, New York, 1976.

Baron, S. *The Russian Jew under Tsars and Soviets*, New York, 1964; 2nd edn. 1976.

Bauer, Y. *My Brother's Keeper. A History of the American Jewish Joint Distribution Committee, 1929–1939*, Philadelphia, 1974.
Ben-Arie, A. and Redlich, S. (eds.). *Evrei i evreisky narod. Petitsii, pisma i obrashcheniya evreev SSSR*. Jerusalem, 1973–1982, 10 vols.
Benyaminov, M. R. *Bukharskie evrei*, New York, 1983.
Bikerman, I. *Cherta evreiskoi osedlosti*, St Petersburg, 1911.
The Black Book: The Nazi Crime Against the Jewish People, New York, 1946.
Blatberg, W. *The Story of the Hebrew and Yiddish Writers in the Soviet Union*, New York, 1953.
Boim, L. 'The Passport System in the USSR and its Effect upon the Status of Jews', *Israel Yearbook on Human Rights*, 1975, vol. 5, pp. 141–168.
Brafman, M. and Schimel, D. *Trade for Freedom: Détente, Trade and Soviet Jews*, New York, 1975.
Braham, R. L. *Jews in the Communist World*, New York, 1961.
Bramson, L. *K istorii nachalnogo obrazovaniya evreev v Rossii*, St Petersburg, 1896.
Brod, P. *Die Antizionismus-und Israelpolitik der UdSSR: Voraussetzung und Entwicklung bis 1956*, Baden-Baden, 1980.
Brumberg, J. and Brumberg, A. *Sovyetish Heymland: an Analysis*, New York, 1966.
Brutskus, B. *Professionalnyi sostav evreiskogo naseleniya Rossii*, St Petersburg, 1908.
Bugaenko, E. *People I Know in Birobidzhan*, Moscow, 1975.
Burg, S. L. 'Russians, Natives and Jews in the Soviet Scientific Elite', *Cahiers du monde russe et soviétique*, 1979, no. 1, pp. 43–59.
Burko, F. 'The Soviet Yiddish Theatre in the Twenties', unpublished PhD dissertation, University of Southern Illinois, Carbondale, 1978.
Cang, J. *The Soviet Millions, A History of the Jews in the Soviet Union*, London, 1969.
Carrère d'Encausse, H. *L'Empire éclaté*, Paris, 1978; trans. as *Decline of an Empire: Soviet Socialist Republics in Revolt*, London, 1980.
Cherikover, I. *Istoriya obshchestva dla rasprostraneniya prosveshcheniya v Rossii*, St Petersburg, 1913.
Choseed, B. 'Categorizing Soviet Yiddish Writers', *Slavic Review*, 1965, no. 1, pp. 102–8.
  'Reflections of the Soviet Nationalities Policy in Literature: The Jews 1938–1948', unpublished PhD dissertation, Columbia University, New York, 1968.
Cohen, E. *The New Red Anti-Semitism. A. Symposium*, Boston, n.d.
Cohen, R. (ed.). *Let My People Go*, New York, 1971.
Conférence internationale sur la situation des Juifs en Union Soviétique, Paris, 1960.
Dagan, A. *Moscow and Jerusalem*, New York, 1970.
Davitt, M. *Within the Pale*, Philadelphia, 1903.
A Decade of Destruction: Jewish Culture 1948–1958, New York, 1958.
Demidoff-San-Donato, *La question juive en Russie*, Brussels, 1884.
Dennen, L. *Where the Ghetto Ends: Jews in Soviet Russia*, New York, 1934.
Deutsch, L. *Rol evreev v russkoi resvolutsii*, Berlin, 1923.
Dinshtein, Y. 'Freedom of Emigration and Soviet Jewry', *Soviet Jewish Affairs*, 1974, no. 2, pp. 17–23.

Discours prononcés à la Douma et au Conseil de l'Empire sur la situation du Peuple Juif en Russie, Lausanne, 1915.

Djilas, M. *Conversations with Stalin*, New York, 1962.

Domalsky, I. *Russkie evrei vchera i segodnya*, Jerusalem, 1975.

Dubnov, S. *Dve kontseptsii evreigskogo natsionalnogo vozrozhdeniya*, Jerusalem, 1981.

History of the Jews in Russia and Poland, Philadelphia, 1916–20.

Evrei v tsarstvovanii Nikolaya II, St Petersburg, 1921.

Evrei v Rossii i zapadnoi Evrope v epokhu antisemitskoi reaktsii, Moscow, 1923.

Kniga zhizni, Riga–New York, 1934–57, 3 vols.

Dubnov, S. and Krasnyi-Admoni, G. (eds.). *Materialy dlya istorii antievreiskikh pogromov v Rossii*, Petrograd, 1919–23, 2 vols.

Eckman, L. S. *Soviet Policy Towards Jews and Israel 1917–1974*, New York, 1974.

The Jewish Resistance: the History of the Jewish Partisans in Lithuania and White Russia during the Nazi Occupation 1940–1945, New York, 1977.

'Economic Crimes in the Soviet Union', *Journal of the International Commission of Jurists*, 1964, vol. 5, no. 1.

Elbogen, I., Meisl, J. and Wischnitzer, M. (eds.). *Festschrift zu Simon Dubnovs siebzigsten Geburstag*, Berlin, 1930.

Emiot, E. *Der birobidzhaner inyen*, New York, 1960; transl. as *The Birobidzhan Affair. A Yiddish Writer in Siberia*, Philadelphia, 1981.

E(h)renburg, I. *Men, Years, Life*, London, 1962–66, 6 vols.

E(h)renburg, I. and Grossman, V. (eds.). *The Black Book*, New York, 1981.

Evrei i evreisky narod, London and Jerusalem, 1960–1982, 102 vols.

Evreiskaya avtonomnaya oblast, Khabarovsk, 1959.

Evreisky samizdat, Jerusalem, 1974–82, 25 vols.

Fluk, L. R. *Jews in the Soviet Union* [Bibliography], New York, 1975.

Frankel, J. 'The Anti-Zionist Press Campaigns in the USSR 1969–1971. An Internal Dialogue?', *Soviet Jewish Affairs*, 1972, no. 3, pp. 3–26.

Prophecy and Politics: Socialism, Nationalism and the Russian Jews 1862–1917, Cambridge, 1981; 2nd edn 1984.

Frey, S. *The Truth About Jews in the Soviet Union*, New York, 1960.

Friedberg, M. *Why They Left*, New York, 1972.

The Jew in Post-Stalin Soviet Literature, New York, 1978.

Frumkin, A. B., Aronson, G. and Goldenweiser, A. (eds.). *Russian Jewry 1860–1917*, New York, 1966.

Genin, I. *Palestinskaya problema*, Moscow, 1948.

Gessen, I. and Fridshtein, V. *Sbornik zakonov i polozhenii*, St Petersburg, 1904.

Gessen, Y. *Istoriya evreiskogo naroda v Rossii*, Leningrad, 1916; 2nd edn 1925–7, 2 vols.

Gilison, J. (ed.). *The Soviet Jewish Emigré*, Baltimore, 1977.

Gimpelson, Y. and Bramson, L. *Zakony o evreakh*, St Petersburg, 1914–15, 2 vols.

Gitelman, Z. *Assimilation, Acculturation and National Consciousssmess Among Soviet Jews*, Ann Arbor, Michigan (mimeo), 1972.

Jewish Nationality and Soviet Politics. The Jewish Section of the CPSU 1917–1930, New Jersey, 1972.

'Soviet Political Culture Insights from Jewish Emigrés', *Soviet Studies*, 1977, no. 4, pp. 543–64.

'Moscow and the Soviet Jews: A Parting of the Ways', *Problems of Communism*, 1980, no. 1–2, pp. 18–34.

Becoming Israelis: Political Resocialization of Soviet and American Immigrants, New York, 1982.

Glazer, N. (ed.), *Perspectives on Soviet Jewry*, New York, 1971.

Golb, N. and Pritsak, O. *Khazarian Hebrew Documents of the Tenth Century*, Ithaca–London, 1982.

Goldberg, B. Z. *The Jewish Problem in the Soviet Union*, New York, 1961.

Goldberg, D. *Sussman Sees It Through. A. Reappraisal of the Jewish Position Under the Soviets*, New York, 1935.

Goldhagen, E. (ed.). *Ethnic Minorities in the Soviet Union*, New York, 1968.

Goldman, G. *Zionism Under Soviet Rule (1917–1928)*, New York, 1960.

Goldman (Gorev), B. *Evrei v proizvedeniyakh russkikh pisatelei*, Petrograd, 1917.

Goldstein, A. *The Soviet Attitudes Towards Territorial Minorities and the Jews*, New York, 1953.

Golitsyn, N. *Istoriya russkogo zakonodatelstva o evreyakh*, St Petersburg, 1886.

Gordon, D. *The British Reaction to the Persecution of Russian Jewry, 1881–1882*, Baltimore, 1974.

Govrin, Y. 'Israel–Soviet Relations 1964–1966' (Research Paper), Jerusalem, 1978.

Gradovsky, N. *La Situation légale des Israélites en Russie*, Paris, 1890.

Greenbaum, A. A. *Jewish Scholarship and Scholarly Institutions in Soviet Russia 1918–1953*, Jerusalem, 1978.

Greenberg, L. *The Jews in Russia*, New Haven, 1944–51, 2 vols.

Gurland, A. R. *Glimpses of Soviet Jewry*, New York, 1948.

Gurevitz, B. *The Bolshevik Revolution and the Foundation of the Jewish Communist Movement in Russia*, Tel Aviv, 1976.

Halevy, Z. *Jewish Schools Under Czarism and Communism. A Struggle for Cultural Identity*, New York, 1976.

Jewish University Students and Professionals in Tsarist and Soviet Russia, Tel Aviv, 1976.

Halperin, J. 'Judaizers and the Image of the Jew in Medieval Russia', *Canadian American Slavic Studies*, 1975, vol. 9, no. 2, pp. 141–55.

Harcave, S. 'Jewish Political Parties and Groups and the Russian State Duma from 1905 to 1907', unpublished PhD dissertation, University of Chicago, 1943.

Heller, A. *Die Lage der Juden in Russland von der Marz-Revolution 1917 bis zur Gegenwart*, Breslau, 1935.

Hen-Tov, J. *Communism and Zionism in Palestine. The Comintern and the Political Unrest in the 1920s*, Cambridge, Mass, 1974.

'Contacts Between Soviet Ambassador Maisky and Zionist Leaders During World War II', *Soviet Jewish Affairs*, 1978, no. 2, pp. 46–55.

Hirszowicz, L. 'Birobidzan after Forty Years', *Soviet Jewish Affairs*, 1974, no. 2, pp. 38–47.

'Jewish Cultural Life in the USSR', *Soviet Jewish Affairs*, 1977, no. 2, pp. 3–21.

Israel, G. *The Jews in Russia*, New York, 1975.
Ivanov, K. and Sheinis, Z. *Gosudarstvo Izrailti ego polozhenie i politika*, Moscow, 1959.
Ivanov, Y. *Ostorozhno sionizm*, Mowcow, 1969.
Jacobs, D. N. *Studies of the Third Wave. Recent Migration of Soviet Jews to the United States*, Boulder, Colorado, 1981.
Jacobs, E. M. 'Jewish Representation in Local Soviets, 1950–1973', *Soviet Jewish Affairs*, 1976, no. 1, pp. 18–26.
'Further Considerations on Jewish Representation in Local Soviets and in the CPSU', *Soviet Jewish Affairs*, 1978, no. 1, pp. 26–34.
Jelen, Ch. Unger, L. *Le Grand Retour*, Paris, 1977.
Die Judenpogrome in Russland, Köln-Leipzig, 1910.
Jewish Culture in the Soviet Union, Jerusalem, 1973.
Kaminska, I. *My Life, My Theatre*, New York, 1973.
Kaminska-Turkov, R. *I Don't Want to be Brave Anymore*, Washington, 1978.
Kantor, L. M. *Tuzemnye evrei v Uzbekistane*, Samarkand, 1923.
Kantor, Y. *Natsionalnoe stroitelstvo sredi evreev v SSSR*, Moscow, 1934.
Katz, Z. (ed.). *Handbook of Major Soviet Nationalities*, New York, 1975.
Khrushchev Remembers, Boston, 1970.
Khrushchev Remembers, The Last Testament, Boston, 1974.
Khvolson, D. *O nekotorykh srednevekovykh obvineniyakh protiv evreev*, St Petersburg, 1880.
Kleimman, M. *Evreiskaya obshchina, ee sushchnost i kharakter*, Moscow, 1917.
Klier, J. 'Alexander I. Soldiers Cloth and the Jews', *Canadian American Slavic Studies*, 1975, no. 4, pp. 463–71.
'The Ambiguous Legal Status of Russian Jewry in the Reign of Catherine II', *The Slavic Review*, 1976, no. 3, pp. 504–17.
Klinchin, P. *Evreiskoe naselenie Rossii*, Petrograd, 1917.
Kochan, L. (ed.). *The Jews in Soviet Russia since 1917*, London, 1978. 3rd edn.
Kopelev, L. *Khranit' vechno*, Ann Arbor, Michigan, 1975.
The Education of a True Believer, London, 1981.
Korey, W. *The Soviet Cage: Anti-semitism in Russia*, New York, 1973.
Krammer, A. *The Forgotten Friendship. Israel and the Soviet Bloc, 1947–1953*, Illinois, 1974.
Kucherov, S. *Courts, Lawyers and Trials Under the Last Three Tsars*, New York, 1953.
Kunitz, J. *Russian Literature and the Jews*, New York, 1929.
Lambroza, A. 'Plehve, Kishinev and the Jewish Question. A Reappraisal', *Nationalities Papers*, 1984, no. 1, pp. 117–21.
'The Pogrom Movement in Tsarist Russia, 1903–1906', unpublished PhD dissertation, Rutgers University, 1981.
Larin, Y. *Evrei i antisemitizm v SSSR*, Moscow, 1929.
Lawrance, G. *Three Millions More*, New York, 1970.
Lazaris, B. *Dissidenty i evrei*, Tel Aviv, 1981.
Leftwich, I. *Abraham Sutskever: Partisan, Poet*, New York, 1971.
Leneman, L. *La Tragédie des Juifs en URSS*, Paris, 1959.
Levanda, V. *Polnyi khronologichesky sbornik zakonov i polozhenii kasayushchikhsya evreev*, St Petersburg, 1874.

Levitas, I. *The Jewish Community in Russia, 1772–1844*, New York, 1943.
The Jewish Community in Russia, 1844–1917, Jerusalem, 1981.
Levy, H. *Jews and the National Question*, London, 1958.
Linfield, H. *The Communal Organization of the Jews in Soviet Russia*, New York, 1925.
Loewenthal, R. 'The Extinction of the Krimchaks in World War II', *American and East European Review*, 1951, no. 2, pp. 130–6.
'The Judeo-Tatars in the Caucasus', *Historica Judaica*, 1952, vol. 14, pp. 61–82.
'The Jews of Bukhara', *Revue des Etudes Juives*, 1961, no. 120, pp. 345–51.
Lowe, H. D. *Antisemitismus und reaktionäre Utopie. Russische Konservatismus im Kampf gegen den Wandel von Staat und Gesellschaft, 1880–1917*, Hamburg, 1978.
Lozovsky (Lozinsky), S. (ed.). *Kazennye evreiskie uchilishcha*, St Petersburg, 1920.
Ludwig, D. *Struktur und-Gesellschaft des Chazaren Reiches im Licht der schriftlichen Quellen*, unpublished PhD dissertation, Münster University, 1982.
Lurie, Ya. 'L'Hérésie dites Judaisants et ses sources historiques', *Revue des Etudes Slaves*, 1966, vol. 45, pp. 49–67.
Lvov-Rogachevsky, V. *Goniteli evreiskogo naroda v Rossii*, Moscow, 1917.
Magid, D. *Evrei na Kavkaze*, Petrograd, 1918.
Manaokh, B. *Plenniki Salmansara. Iz istorii evreev Vostochnogo Kavkaza*, Jerusalem, 1984.
Marek, P. *Ocherki po istorii prosveshcheniya evreev v Rossii*, Moscow, 1909.
Markish, E. *Le Long Retour*, Paris, Laffont, 1974; transl. as *The Long Return*, New York, 1978.
Maurach, R. *Russische Judenpolitik*, Berlin, Leipzig, 1939.
Mayatsky, F. *Sovremennyi iudaizm i sionizm*, Kishinev, 1964.
Meisl, J. *Haskolah. Geschichte der Aufklärungbewegung inter den Juden in Russland*, Berlin, 1919.
Geschichte der Juden in Polen und Russland, Berlin, 1921–5, 3 vols.
Mendelsohn, E. *Class Struggle in the Pale. The Formative Years of the Jewish Worker Movement in Tsarist Russia*, Cambridge, 1970.
Mikhelson, F. *I Survived Rumbuli*, New York, 1979.
Mikhoels, S. *Stati, besedy, rechi. Stati i vospominaniya o Mikhoelse*, Moscow, 1981.
Miller, J. (ed.). *Jews in Soviet Culture*, New Brunswick, 1984.
Mirski, B. *Les Juifs et la révolution*, Paris, 1921.
Morand, B. *L'U.R.S.S des profondeurs*, Brussels, 1978.
Das Moskauer Jüdische Akademische Theater, Berlin, 1928.
Mysh, M. *Rukovodstvo k russkim zakonam o evreyakh*, St Petersburg, 1904.
Nekrich, A. *The Punished Peoples*, New York, 1978.
Otreknis ot strakha. Vospominaniya istorika, London, 1979.
Netchvoladov, A. *L'empereur Nicolas II et les Juifs*, Paris, 1924.
Nikitin, V. *Evrei zemledeltsy, 1807–1877*, St Petersburg, 1877.
Mnogostradalnye ocherki proshlogo, St Petersburg, 1895.
Nikitina, G. *The State of Israel. A Historical, Economic and Political Study*, Moscow, 1973.
Nir, Y. *The Israeli–Arab Conflict in Soviet Caricatures 1967–1973*, Tel Aviv, 1976.

Nove, A. 'Jews in the Soviet Union', *Jewish Journal of Sociology*, 1961, vol. 3, pp. 108–19.

Orbach, Wila 'The Destruction of the Jew in the Nazi-Occupied Territories of the USSR', *Soviet Jewish Affairs*, 1976, no. 2, pp. 14–51.

Orbach, William W. *The American Movement to Aid Soviet Jews*, Amherst, 1979.

Orenstein, S. *Source Book on Soviet Jewry. An Annotated bibliography*, New York, 1981.

Orshansky, I. *Evrei v Rossii*, St Petersburg, 1872.

Russkoe zakonodatelsvo o evreyakh, St Petersburg, 1877.

Paikin, S. *Evkombed Gruzii*, Tiflis, 1933.

Paretzki, E. *Die Entstehung der Jüdischen Arbeiterbewegung in Russland*, Riga, 1932.

Patkin, A. *The Origins of the Russian-Jewish Labour Movement*, Melbourne and London, 1947.

Pereferkovich, K. *Religioznye voprosy u sovremennykh evreev*, St Petersburg, 1911.

Pervaya Duma o evreakh. Rechi deputatov, St Petersburg, 1908.

Picon-Vallin, B. *Le théâtre juif soviétique pendant les années vingt*, Lausanne, 1973.

Pinchuk, B. Z. 'Soviet Media and the Fate of Jews in Nazi-Occupied Territory, 1939–1941', *Yad Va-Shem Studies*, 1976, vol. 11, pp. 221–33.

Pinkus, B. 'Yiddish-language Courts and Nationalities Policy in the Soviet Union', *Soviet Jewish Affairs*, 1971, no. 2, pp. 40–60.

'The Emigration of National Minorities from the USSR in the Post-Stalin Era', *Soviet Jewish Affairs*, 1983, no. 1, pp. 3–36.

The Soviet Government and the Jews 1948–1967. A Documented Study, Cambridge, 1984.

'National Identity and Emigration Patterns Among Soviet Jewry', *Soviet Jewish Affairs*, 1985, no. 3, pp. 3–28.

Pinkus, B. (ed.) *Evrei i evreisky narod, 1948–1953*, Jerusalem, 1973, 7 vols.

Pinkus, B., Greenbaum, A. and Altshuler, M. (eds.). *Russian Publications on Jews and Judaism in the Soviet Union, 1917–1967*, Jerusalem, 1970.

Pinson, K. (ed.). *Essays on Antisemitism*, New York, 1946.

Pipes, R. 'Catherine II and the Jews', *Soviet Jewish Affairs*, 1975, no. 2, pp. 3–20.

Plisetsky, M. *Religiya i byt gruzinskykh evreev*, Moscow, 1931.

Pommer, H. I. *Antisemitismus in der UdSSR und in den Sateliten Staten*, Bern, 1963.

Powell, D. *Anti-religious Propaganda in the Soviet Union. A Study of Mass Persuasion*, Cambridge, Mass., 1975.

Porath, J. D. *Jews in Russia: the Last Four Centuries*, New York, 1974.

Porter, J. N. (ed.). *Jewish Partisans: A Documentary of Jewish Resistance in the Soviet Union During World War II*, Washington, 1982.

Pozner, S. V. *Evrei v obshei shkole*, St Petersburg, 1914.

Prital, D. (ed.). *In Search of Self. The Soviet Jewish Intelligentsia and the Exodus*, Jerusalem, 1982.

Raba, J. 'Reaction of the Jews of Vienna to the Russian Pogroms of 1905', *Michael*, 1973, vol. 2, pp. 135–44.

Rabinovich, S. *Jews in the Soviet Union*, Moscow, 1967.

Rabinovich, V. *Lithuanian Hassidism*. New York, 1971.

Rass, R. and Brafman, M. *From Moscow to Jerusalem*, New York, 1976.
Redlich, Sh. 'The Jews under Soviet Rule During World War II', unpublished PhD dissertation, New York University, 1968.
Propaganda and Nationalism in Wartime Russia. The Jewish Anti-fascist Committee in the USSR. 1941–1948. Boulder, Colorado, 1982.
Remenik, G. *Ocherki i portrety. Statii o evreiskikh pisatelyakh*, Moscow, 1975.
Rest, M. *Die russische Judengesetsgebung von der ersten polnischen Teilung bis zum 'Polozhenie dlya evreev' (1804)*, Wiesbaden, 1975.
Rogger, H. 'The Beiliss Case: Antisemitism and Politics in the Reign of Nicholas II', *Slavic Review*, 1966, no. 4, pp. 615–29.
'Tsarist Policy on Jewish Emigration', *Soviet Jewish Affairs*, 1973, no. 3, pp. 26–36.
'Russian Ministers and the Jewish Question', *California Slavic Studies*, 1975, vol. 8, pp. 15–16.
'Government, Jews, Peasants and Land in Post-Emancipation Russia', *Cahiers du monde russe et soviétique*, 1976, vol. 27, pp. 5–25.
Ro'i, Y. *Soviet Decision-making in Practice. The USSR and Israel, 1947–1954*, New Brunswick, 1980.
Rosenberg, L. R. *Jews in the Soviet Union. An Annotated bibliography 1967–1971*, New York, 1971.
Rosenberg, S. A. *Rabbi Reports on Russia*, Toronto, 1961.
Rosenthal, A. M. *L'antisémitisme en Russie. Des origines à nos jours*, Paris, 1982.
Rossiya i evrei, Paris, 1972.
Rothenberg, J. *An Annotated bibliography of Writing on Judaism in the Soviet Union, 1960–1965*, Waltham, Mass., 1969.
Jewish Religion in the Soviet Union, New York, 1971.
Rozenblum, S. A. *Etre Juif en URSS*, Paris, 1982.
Rozhansky, A. (ed.). *Antievreiskie protsessy v Sovetskom Soyuze 1969–1975*, Jerusalem, 1979–84, 3 vols.
Rubin, R. (ed.). *The Under-deemed: Anti-Semitism in the Soviet Union*, Chicago, 1968.
Rubinshtein, J. *Soviet Dissidents. Their Struggle for Human Rights*, Boston, 1980.
Rudy, H. *Die Juden in der Sowjetunion: Schicksal und Nationalitätenpolitik*, Vienna, 1966.
Rukhadze, A. *Jews in the USSR. Figures Facts, Comment*, Moscow, 1978.
Rusinek, A. *Like a Song, Like a Dream. A Soviet Girl's Quest for Freedom*, New York, 1973.
The Russian Jews in the War, London, 1943.
Salisbury, H. *Russia on the Way*, New York, 1946.
To Moscow and Beyond, New York, 1960.
Moscow Journal. The End of Stalin, Chicago, 1961.
Samuel, M. *Blood Accusation. The Strange History of Beiliss Case*, Philadelphia, 1966.
Sanford, M. *Soviet Jews. Hostages for Trade*, Miami, 1979.
Sawyer, T. *The Jewish Minority in the Soviet Union*, Boulder, Colorado, 1979.
Sbornik, materialov ob ekonomicheskom polozhenii evreev v Rossii, St Petersburg, 1904.
Schapiro, L. 'The Role of the Jews in the Russian Revolutionary Movement', *The Slavonic and East European Review*, 1961, vol. 40, pp. 148–67.

'Anti-Semitism in the Communist Word', *Soviet Jewish Affairs*, 1979, no. 1, pp. 42–52.
Schechtman, J. B. *Star in Eclipse. Russian Jewry Revisited*, New York, 1961.
Zionism and Zionists in Russia. Greatness and Drama, New York, 1966.
Schloss, R. *Lass Mein Volk ziehen. Eine Dokumentation*, Munich, 1971.
Schroeter, L. *The Last Exodus*, New York, 1974.
Schulman, E. *A History of Jewish Education in the Soviet Union*, New York,1971.
Schwarz, S. *The Jews in the Soviet Union*, New York, 1951.
Evrei v Sovetskom Soyuze (1939–1965), New York, 1966.
The Second Soviet Jewish Anti-Fascist Meeting, Moscow, 1942.
Shafer, H. *The Soviet Treatment of Jews*, New York, 1974.
Sharapov, Ya. *Natsionalnye sektsii RKP (b)*, Kazan, 1967.
Shindler, C. *Exit Visa, Détente, Human Rights and the Jewish Emigration Movement in the USSR*, London, 1978.
Shneiderman, S. L. *Ilya Erenburg*, New York, 1968.
Silberfarb, M. *Die Verwaltung der jüdischen Gemeinden in Russland*, Pressburg, 1911.
Sistematichesky ukazatel literatury o evreakh na russkom yazyke so vremenii vvedeniya grazhdanskogo shrifta 1708–1889, St Petersburg, 1892.
Skoizylas, E. *The Realities of Soviet Antisemitism*, Philadelphia, 1964.
Sloves, H. *La culture juive en URSS*, Paris, 1959.
L'Etat Juif de l'Union Soviétique, Paris, 1982.
Smolar, B. *Soviet Jewry: Today and Tomorrow*, New York, 1971.
Soifer, P. E. *Soviet Jewish Folkloristics and Ethnography; An Institutional History 1918–1948*, New York, 1978.
Sotsialnyi i natsionalnyi sostav VKP (b), Moscow–Leningrad, 1928.
Soveshchanie evreiskikh obshchestvennykh deyatelei v g Kovne 1909 goda, St Petersburg, 1910.
Die Sozialen Verhaltnisse der Juden in Russland, Berlin, 1906.
Springer, A. 'Gabriel Derzhavin's Jewish Reform Project of 1800', *Canadian American Slavic Studies*, 1976, vol. 10, pp. 1–23.
Stanislawski, M. *Tsar Nicolas I and the Jews. The Transformation of Jewish Society in Russia, 1825–1855*, Philadelphia, 1983.
Steinberg, A. (ed.). *Simon Dubnov. L'homme et son oeuvre*, Paris, 1963.
Stora-Sandor, J. *Isaac Babel. L'homme et l'oeuvre*, Paris, 1968.
Svirsky, G. *Hostages; The Personal Testimony of a Soviet Jew*, New York, 1976.
Szajkowski, Z. *Jews, Wars and Communism*, New York, 1972–74, 2 vols.
The Mirage of American Jewish Aid in Soviet Russia, 1917–1939, New York, 1977.
Tager, A. *Decay of Czarism, the Beiliss Case*, Philadelphia, 1935.
Taylor, T. *Court of Terror, Soviet Criminal Justice and the Jewish Emigration*, New York, 1976.
Teller, J. L. *The Kremlin, the Jews and the Middle East*, New York, 1957.
Tobias, J. *The Jewish Bund in Russia. From its Origin to 1905*, Stanford, 1972.
Tökès, R. (ed.). *Dissent in the USSR. Politics, Ideology and People*, Baltimore, 1975.
Trudy gubernskikh komissii po evreiskomu voprosu, St Petersburg, 1884.
Tsinberg, I. *Istoriya evreiskoi pechati v Rossii*, St Petersburg, 1915.
Ukrainians and Jews: A Symposium, New York, 1966.

Usov, M. *Evrei v armii*, St Petersburg, 1911.
Evreistvo i krestyanstvo, Petrograd, 1917.
Vago, B. (ed.). *Jewish Assimilation in Modern Times*, Boulder, Colorado, 1981.
Vago, B. and Mosse, G. (eds.). *Jews and Non-Jews in Eastern Europe, 1918–1945*, New York, 1974.
Vergelis, A. *On the Jewish Street. Travel Notes*, Moscow, 1971.
Vernadsky, G. 'The Heresy of Judaizers and Ivan III', *Speculum*, 1933, vol. 8, pp. 448–52.
Voronel, A. and Yakhot, V. (eds.). *Jewishness Rediscovered; Jewish Identity in the Soviet Union*, New York, 1974.
Weinryb, S. B. *Neuste Wirtschaftsgeschichte der Juden in Russland und Polen*, Breslau, 1934.
West, B. *Struggle of a Generation. The Jews Under Soviet Rule*, Tel Aviv, 1959.
The White Book: Evidence, Facts, Documents, Moscow, 1981.
Wiesel, E. *The Jews of Silence*, Philadelphia, 1967.
Wilkinson, S. *In the Land of the North. The Evangelization of the Jews in Russia*, London, 1905.
Wischnitzer, M. *To Dwell in Safety. The Story of Jewish Migration Since 1800*, Philadelphia, 1948.
Wolf, L. (ed.). *The Legal Sufferings of the Jews in Russia*, London, 1912.
Yarmolinsky, A. *The Jews and Other Minor Nationalities Under the Soviets*, New York, 1928.
Yodfat, A. 'Jewish Religious Communities in the USSR', *Soviet Jewish Affairs*, 1971, no. 2, pp. 61–7.
'Rabbis and Jewish Clergy in the USSR, 1917–1924', *Judaism*, 1972, vol. 21, no. 2, pp. 184–94.
Zand, M. 'Bukharan Jewish Culture under Soviet Rule', *Soviet Jewish Affairs*, 1979, no. 2, pp. 15–23.
Zaslavsky, V. and Brym, R. *Soviet Jewish Emigration and Soviet Nationality Policy*, London, 1984.
Zivs, S. L. *Anatomiya Izhi*, Moscow, 1982.

PUBLICATIONS IN YIDDISH AND HEBREW

Altshuler, M. *Ha-kibuz ha-yehudi bi-vrit ha-moazot be-yameinu, nituaḥ sozio-demografi*, Jerusalem, 1979.
Ha-yevsektsia bi-vrit ha-moazot (1918–1930), Tel-Aviv, 1980.
Baazov, F. *Ha-mezoraim*, Herẓliya, 1978.
Bartal, I. *Ha-yehudim ve-hevratam ba-sifrut ivrit ve-yidish be-mizraḥ eiropa bein ha-shanim 1855–1914*, unpublished PhD dissertation, Jerusalem, 1980.
Ben-Horin Ma *kore sham: sipuro shel yehudi mi-vrit ha-moazot*, Tel-Aviv, 1971.
Blum, Z. *Poalei-zion in ratnfarband*, Tel-Aviv, 1978.
Broderzon, S. M. *Mayn laydn-veg mit Moyshe Broderzon*, Buenos Aires, 1960.
Brutskus, B. *Di yidishe landvirtshaft in mizrakh eirope*, Berlin, 1926.
Cherikover, E. 'Fun di rusishe arkhivn', *Historishe shriftn*, 1929, vol. 1, pp. 779–92.
'Der arkhiv fun Shimon Dubnov', *Historishe shriftn*, 1937, vol. 2, pp. 591–600.

Yehudim be-eitot mahapekha, Tel-Aviv, 1957.
Cohen, Y. Y., Slutski, I. and Shmeruk, Ch. (eds.), *Pirsumim yehudiim bi-vrit-ha-moazot, 1917–1960*, Jerusalem, 1961.
Dinur, B. Z. *Be-olam she-shaka*, Jerusalem, 1958.
Be-imei milhamah u-mahapekha, Jerusalem, 1960.
Be-mifne ha-dorot, Jerusalem, 1972.
Dorot u-reshumot, Jerusalem, 1978.
Dombrovska, D. and Pinkus, B. (eds.). *Yahadut brit-ha-moazot be-aspaklariah shel ha-periodika ha-maaravit*, Jerusalem, 1972.
Dubnov, S. *Toldot ha-hasidut*, Tel-Aviv, 1930–2, 3 vols.
Eliashiv, S. *Rishmei masa*, Tel-Aviv, 1951.
Eliashvili, N. *Ha-yehudim be-gruziah u-be-erez yisrael*, Tel-Aviv, 1975.
Etkes, R. R. Yisrael Salanter ve-reshitah shel tenuat ha-musar, Jerusalem, 1984.
Ettinger, S. 'Medinat moskvah be-yahas el ha-yehudim', *Zion*, 1953, vol. 18, pp. 136–68.
'Takanot 1804', *He-avar*, 1975, vol. 22, pp. 87–110.
Ha-antishemiut be-eit ha-hadasha, Tel-Aviv, 1978.
Even-Shushan, S. *Sipuro shel masa, Esrim yom bi-vrit-ha-moazot*, Tel-Aviv, 1964.
Feldman, E. *Kele le-lo-sugar*, Tel-Aviv, 1964.
Gergel, N. *Di lage fun di yidn in rusland*, Warsaw, 1929.
Gershuni, A. *Yahadut be-rusia ha-sovietit*, Jerusalem, 1961.
Ginzburg, S. *Mishumadim in tsarishn rusland*, New York, 1946.
Hailperin, I. 'Nisayon shel interventsiya politit le-maan yehudei rusia', *Zion*, 1955, vol. 20, pp. 163–74.
Yehudim be-mizrah eiropa, Jerusalem, 1968.
Horodetsky, S. *Ha-hasidut ve-ha-hasidim*, Berlin–Jerusalem, 1923.
Itai, A. *Korot ha-shomer ha-zair be sssr*, Jerusalem, 1981.
Katz, B. Z. *Rabanut, hasidut, haskalah*, Tel-Aviv, 1952, 2 vols.
Katz, K. *Budapest, varshah, moskvah, Shagrir el midinot mitnakrot*, Tel-Aviv, 1976.
Kelner, I. *Filantropiah ve-tikhnun hevrati be-hevrah ha-yehudit 1842–1882*, unpublished PhD dissertation The Hebrew University, Jerusalem, 1973.
Keren, I. *Ha-hityashvut ha-haklait ha-yehudit be-hazi ha-i krim (1922–1947)*, Jerusalem, 1973.
Klauzner, M. *Duah al yahadut rusia*, Tel-Aviv, 1966.
Leshchinsky, Y. *Ha-yehudim be-rusia ha-sovietit*, Tel-Aviv, 1940.
Levin, A. *Kantonistn*, Warsaw, 1934.
Levin, D. *Lohamim ve-omdim al nafsham. Milhemet yehudei lita ba-nazism, 1941–1945*, Jerusalem, 1974.
Lifshitz, I. and Altshuler, M. (eds.). *Briv fun yidishe sovietishe shraibers*, Jerusalem, 1979.
Livne, Z. *Ikarim yehudim be-rusia*, Tel-Aviv, 1967.
Lvavi, J. *Ha-hityashvut ha-yehudit be-birobidzhan*, Jerusalem, 1965.
Mahler, R. *Divrei yimei yisrael. Dorot ahronim*, Merhaviah, 1962, 4 vols.
Maltinsky, Kh. *Der moskver mishpet iber di birobidzhaner*, Tel-Aviv, 1981.
Maor, I. *Sheelat ha-yehudim be-tenuah ha-liberalit ve-ha-mahapkhanit be-rusia*, Jerusalem, 1964.
Ha-tenuah ha-zionit be-rusia, Jerusalem, 1973.

Margolis, O. *Geshikhte fun yidn in rusland*, Moscow, 1930.

Mints, M. *Ber Borohov, Ha-maagal ha-rishon*, 1900–1906, Tel-Aviv, 1976.

Mintz, M. *Hogrim u-mifathim. Le-toldot shel havurat 'dror' be-rusia*, Tel-Aviv, 1983.

Mishkinsky, M. *Reishit tenuat ha-poalim ha-yehudit be-rusia*, Tel-Aviv, 1981.

Namir, M. *Shlihut be-moskvah*, Tel-Aviv, 1971.

Neishtat, M. *Yehudei Gruzia. Maavak al ha-shivah le-zion*, Tel-Aviv, 1970.

Oren, M. *Reshimot asir prag*, Merhaviah, 1958.

Pinchuk, B. Z. *Yehudei brit-ha-moazot mul pnei ha-shoah*, Tel-Aviv, 1978.

Pinkus, B. 'Hitpathut ha-teoria be-baaia ha-leumit bi-vrit ha-moazot be-tekufah shel le-ahar Stalin', *Behinot*, 1970, no. 1, pp. 35–55.

Yahadut brit-ha-moazot, 1917–1973, Jerusalem, 1974.

Pomerants, A. *Di sovietishe harugey malkhes*, Buenos Aires, 1962.

Preigerzon, Z. *Yoman ha-zikhronot*, Tel-Aviv, 1976.

Rafaeli (Zenziper), A. *Eser shnot redifot*, Tel-Aviv, 1930.

Rosental, I. *Toldot hevrat marbei ha-haskalah*, St Petersburg, 1885.

Rosental, N. *Yidish lebn in ratnfarband*, Tel-Aviv, 1971.

Rosental-Shneiderman, E. *Naftulei drakhim*, Tel-Aviv, 1970–2, 2 vols.

Sasar, M. *Yisraeli be-moskvah, Rishmei siyur bi-vrit ha-moazot*, Jerusalem, 1961.

Schulman, E. *Sovietish-yidishe literatur, etyudn*, New York, 1971.

Shaham, N. *Pegishot be-moskvah, 1957*, Merhavia, 1957.

Shein, J. *Arum moskver yidishn teater*, Paris, 1964.

Shmeruk, Ch. *Ha-kibuz ha-yehudi ve-hahityashvut ha-yehudit ha-haklait be-belorusia. 1918–1932*, unpublished PhD dissertation, The Hebrew University, Jerusalem, 1961.

'Ha-tarbut ha-yehudit bi-vrit ha-moazot', *Gesher*, 1966, nos. 2–3, pp. 58–64.

Shohat, A. *Mosad 'ha-rabanut me-taam' be-rusia*, Haifa, 1975.

Shurer, H. *Arbaim yom bi-vrit ha-moazot*, Tel-Aviv, 1961.

Slutski, I. *Ha-itonut ha-yehudit-rusit be-meah ha-19*, Jerusalem, 1970.

Ha-itonut ha-yehudit-rusit be-reshit ha-meah ha-20, Tel-Aviv, 1978.

Smolar, H. *Tohelet ve-shivra*, Tel-Aviv, 1978.

Oif der letster pozitsye, mit der letster hofnung, Tel-Aviv, 1982.

Yehudim sovietiim me-ahorei gderot ha-geto, Tel-Aviv, 1984.

Tsinberg, I. *Toldot sifrut yisrael*, Tel-Aviv, 1960, vols. 6–7.

Vaynroykh, H. *Blut oyf der zun*, New York, 1950.

Vovsi-Mikhoels, N. *Avi Shlomo Mikhoels*, Tel-Aviv, 1982.

Yahadut brit-ha-moazot, maamarim u-reshimot, Tel-Aviv, 1967.

Yanasovich, Y. *Mit yidishe shrayber in rusland*, Buenos Aires, 1959.

Yehudi sovieti almoni, El ahai bi-midinat yisrael, Jerusalem, 1956.

Yidn in p.s.s.r. Moscow, 1935.

Zerubabel, Y. *Bikur bi-vrit ha-moazot reshamim u-pegishot*, Tel-Aviv, 1964.

Zinger, L. *Dos banayte folk*, Moscow, 1941.

Dos ofgerikhte folk, Moscow, 1948.

Zohari, M., Tartakover, A. and Zand, M. (eds.). *Hagut yivrit bi-vrit-ha-moazot*, Jerusalem, 1976.

Index

Abelman, M., 244
Abkhaz Autonomous Republic, 71
Abramov, A., 248
Abramov, P., 117
Abramovich, R., 129
Academy of Sciences, 9, 111, 123–5; 157, 176, 195, 203–4, 234, 281–2, 284, 359 n. 68
acculturation *see* assimilation
Adelgeim, E., 157
Adigeans, 241
Afghanistan, 255–6, 308
Africa, 249
Agibalova, A., 283
Agmon, A., 250
AGRO, 65
Agro-Joint, 133
Agudat Yisrael, 46, 129, 284
Aḥad Ha'am (Asher Ginzberg), 37, 40–1, 44
Aḥdut Avodah, 131
Aḥiasaf, 37
Akhmatova, A., 151
Akhron, Y., 123
Al Azhar, 171
Aleksandria, 29
Aleksandrov, G., 152
Aleksandrovka, 27
Aleksei Mikhailovich, 8
Aleksinsky, G., 144, 335 n. 75
Alexander I, 15, 17, 20, 22
Alexander II, 20–2, 31
Alexander III, 22–3, 27, 30–2
Aliger, M., 197, 199, 276, 356 n. 230
Allilueva, S., 144
All-Soviet Writers' Union, 147–8, 152, 154, 158, 233, 273

Alter, V., 173, 195
Altman, I., 154, 158–9
Altman, N., 123
Altshuler, M., xiii
Altshuler, Moshe, 281
Am olam, 42
Amalrik, A., 315
America, 75, 163–4, 172, 176, 178–180, 203, 205, 220–1, 239, 250
Aminov, M., 117
Amusin, Y., 281
Anders, W., 140
Andropov, Yu., 209, 211, 222, 226, 293
Ansky *see* Rappoport-Ansky
anti-Semitism, 23, 50, 170, 188, 216–34, 250, 340 n. 1; in Russia, 4–5, 7–11, 15, 22–4 27–34, 44, 84, 199, 283, 327 n. 42; in the Soviet Union, 65, 73, 75, 84–8, 101, 128, 138–45, 159–60, 175, 188, 190–1, 207, 216–34, 240, 256, 287, 300, 302, 307–8, 335 n. 80, 359 nn. 68–70
Anti-Zionist Committee, 257, 276
Antokolsky, P., 150, 158, 197, 199, 276, 335 n. 229–30
Antselovich, B., 83, 183, 185
Arab League, 166
Arabs, 3, 118, 163, 165–8, 170–1, 215, 224, 245–9, 252–55
Arbatov, G., 236
Argentine, 32, 65, 75
Armenia, 212, 225, 237, 259, 268, 277, 315, 324 n. 5
army, 85, 140, 163, 179, 198, 219; Jews in, 18, 20–1, 25–6, 83–4, 139, 182, 188–9, 195, 199, 205, 219, 240, 261, 263, 310, 352 n. 173

Holy Synod, xiv
Homel, 29, 329 n. 83
Honikman, Y., 205
Horenshtein, D., 134
Huberman, I., 201
Hungary (Hungarians in the Soviet Union), 171, 213, 233, 238, 272, 275, 311

Iashvili, H., 278
ICA (Jewish Settlement Association), 32, 95
Idegei, 146
Igantyev, N., 23–4, 28, 32
Ignatyev, S., 340 n. 4
Igtaic, (dialect), 6
IKOR, 65
Ilyichev, L., 271
Ilyina, N., 225
Imber, V., 277
intelligentsia, 29, 39, 71, 85, 97–8, 149, 161, 221, 232–4, 247
Institute for Proletarian Jewish Culture, 125, 203
Iofe, A., 86, 351 n. 161
Isbakh, A., 150, 199–200
Israel, xiv, 1–2, 15, 35, 40–1, 65, 71, 73–5, 109, 114, 119, 123, 127, 131, 134–6, 139, 161–70, 172–3, 188, 192, 197, 199, 203, 207, 213, 216–17, 224, 231, 241, 244–60, 270, 277, 281–2, 284, 286, 290, 292–3, 298, 302–5, 307–12, 315, 317–21, 346 n. 98, 346 n. 102, 346 n. 109, 348 n. 132
Israel Defence Fund, 312
Israel the Eternal, 129
Istomin, 31
Italy, 172
Itkind, Y., 280
Ivan III, 6–7
Ivan IV (the Terrible), 7–8
Ivanov, A., 227
Ivanov, K., 282
IVOSM, 131

Jabotinsky, Z., 172
Jacob, M., 123
Japan, 29, 74, 84
Jerusalem, xiv, 282, 316
Jerusalem (Religious organization), 46
Jewish Anti-Fascist Committee, 138, 141, 147, 163–4, 168–9, 174–5, 177, 187–8,

191–2, 194–5, 197, 203, 206, 218, 276, 285, 350 n. 148, 353 n. 185, 354 n. 200
Jewish Chronicle, 145
Jewish Committee, 20, 24 *see also* District Commissions on the Jewish Question
Jewish Museum in Vilnius, 205
Jewish Musical Chamber Theatre, 243, 278–9
Jewish People's Theatre, 278
Jewish Proletarian Workers' Union, 113
Jewish Research Institute, 124
Jewish Socialist Workers Party, 44, 77
Jews and The Jewish People, 256
Jews in the Soviet Union, 317
Joint (Joint Distribution Committee), 63, 133, 168, 171–2, 176, 179, 319
Just, I. M., xi
JTA (Jewish Telegraphic Agency), 87
Judaism, 2–3, 103–4, 150, 284, 287, 293–4, 304
Judaizes (sect), 4, 7
Judas Iscariot, 221, 227
Judea, 282 *see also* Israel
Judophobia *see* anti-Semitism

Kaganov, B., 314
Kaganovich, L., 62, 74, 78, 80, 82–3, 121, 183–4, 217, 221–2, 236, 239, 350 n. 148, 354 n. 198
Kaganovich, M., 80, 82, 222
Kaganovich Yiddish Theatre, 193, 200, 202
Kahanshtam, A., 36
Kahat, M., 246
Kakhovsky, M., 11
Kalik, M., 280
Kalinin, M., 52, 61, 72, 74–75, 85, 354 n. 198
Kalinindorf, 67, 122
Kalmanovich, A., 83
Kalmanzon, Y., 285
Kamenets-Podolsky, 29
Kamenev, L., 63, 78, 80, 82, 85, 119, 143
Kanovich, H., 279
Kantor, I. L., 37
Kantor, Y., 261
Kanunnikov, A., 168
Kaplan, E., 296
Kaplan, F., 223
Kaplan, T., 280
Karaev, I., 117
Karaites, 6, 25
Karakalpak Republic, 297

388   *Index*

42486097R00255

Made in the USA
Lexington, KY
17 June 2019